Intermediary Cities and Climate Change

AN OPPORTUNITY FOR SUSTAINABLE DEVELOPMENT

Please cite this publication as:
OECD/UN-Habitat (2022), *Intermediary Cities and Climate Change: An Opportunity for Sustainable Development*, OECD Publishing, Paris, https://doi.org/10.1787/23508323-en.

ISBN 978-92-64-63820-4 (print)
ISBN 978-92-64-61271-6 (pdf)
ISBN 978-92-64-55947-9 (HTML)
ISBN 978-92-64-50418-9 (epub)

Photo credits: © Cover design by Mélodie Ly Descours (OECD Development Centre) on the basis of images from Doggygraph, Rendyfrmn/Shutterstock.com.

Corrigenda to publications may be found on line at: www.oecd.org/about/publishing/corrigenda.htm.

Foreword

The OECD Development Centre and UN-Habitat formed a strategic alliance in 2018 to investigate the role of intermediary cities in development. The first step was an expert meeting held in Paris comprising a diverse set of stakeholders including international organisations, local and national governments, and academics from around the world to discuss the main challenges and opportunities facing these cities. The meeting resulted in a set of strategic insights including the untapped transformational potential of these urban centres. Also identified were three interrelated gaps that systematically affect intermediary cities in developing countries: gaps in knowledge, policy and financing. It was agreed that these gaps are interrelated and should be addressed simultaneously. To do so, local governments, national authorities and development partners need to work together to develop coherent development strategies.

Cities Connect was created to respond to this call. The OECD Development Centre and UN-Habitat contribute to this initiative, which was funded thanks to the financial support of the Swedish International Development Agency (SIDA). This collaboration aims to advance a policy dialogue on intermediary cities and their transformative potential in the international arena.

To achieve this, the initiative supports both local and national authorities in sub-Saharan Africa, Southeast Asia and Latin America in addressing the main constraints faced by intermediary cities and provides guidance on how to leverage their potential for local and national development. Cities Connect elevates the profile of intermediary cities by providing a space for international policy dialogue, carrying out empirical analysis and drafting policy-oriented reports.

This is Cities Connect's first report, developed by the OECD Development Centre and UN-Habitat. Building on the expertise and comparative advantages of both institutions, this report is the first attempt at an international level to analyse climate change and intermediary cities together.

Climate change and rapid urbanisation are increasingly recognised as two of the most daunting challenges faced by our generation. What is less known is that intermediary cities are at the forefront of both processes. These cities play a critical role in urbanisation dynamics as they are central to the flow of population, goods and services between urban and rural areas. As such they are pivotal to guiding the rural-urban continuum towards an innovative development model that is more inclusive, sustainable and resilient. In most developing countries, however, intermediary cities face systematic constraints that limit their climate adaptation and mitigation capacity. These constraints include lack of data, a persistent financing gap, weak governance and limited capacity. These constraints are exacerbated by the fact that intermediary cities are often overlooked in national and urban development strategies, as well as in international co-operation programmes.

This report provides evidence and policy guidance to help local and national authorities, as well as development partners, in designing more effective climate strategies. To this end, the report builds on innovative datasets and original empirical policy analysis to identify key areas for reform. It presents evidence on the different channels through which climate change affects intermediary cities in developing countries and on how these cities contribute to greenhouse gas emissions. It also describes how intermediary cities in Asia, Africa and Latin America are currently coping with climate change, and provides guidance on how such cities can reduce the financing gap hindering climate action.

Intermediary cities present an unprecedented opportunity for improving climate resilience and reducing emissions across developing countries. These cities can be climate-proofed as they develop and avoid a "grow now, clean later" path, which ultimately costs more financially, socially and politically. However, since many intermediary cities are urbanising very quickly, the window of opportunity is narrow.

Acknowledgements

Climate Change and Intermediary Cities: An opportunity for Sustainable Development was jointly prepared by the OECD Development Centre and UN-Habitat, under the overall leadership of Director Ragnheiður Elín Árnadóttir. Federico Bonaglia (OECD), Deputy Director, and Annalisa Primi (OECD), Head of Economic Transformation and Development Division, supervised the project. Vicente Ruiz (OECD) and Melissa Permezel (UN-Habitat) coordinated the report. Support from Semhar Haile (OECD) and Hazel Kuria (UN-Habitat) has been invaluable for the preparatory activities and research for the report. Marco Kamiya (UN-Habitat) coordinated the report in an early stage.

Vicente Ruiz and Semhar Haile authored chapters one to three. David Satterthwaite and Jorgelina Hardoy, from the International Institute for Environment (IIED), drafted a paper that served as the basis for Chapter 4; while Michael Lindfield, Climate Finance Expert, authored Chapter 5 under the supervision of Melissa Permezel. Farah Kammourieh assisted with the initial research for the project, while Rebeca Perez Lopes provided support with quantitative and statistical analysis. Eugenia Klimenka and Myriam Andrieux provided support in co-ordinating administrative tasks. The report was edited by Meg Bortin. Delphine Grandrieux and Elizabeth Nash turned the draft into a publication. Melodie Descours designed the cover.

We are extremely grateful to OECD and UN-Habitat colleagues, as well to external experts, for their technical inputs, insights, and comments. The contributions from colleagues in the OECD Development Centre are gratefully acknowledged, they include Daniel Gay, Manuel Toselli, Vasiliki Mavroeidi, Elisabeth Lambrecht, Yumika Yamada, Antonio Vicencio, Thang Nguyen, Antoine Bonnet, Alexander Pick, and Henry-Bernard Solignac-Lecomte. Aimee Aguilar and Mariana Mirabile from the OECD Environment Directorate provided extensive comments and invaluable insights that help shaping the report. We are also grateful to David Burgalassi, Tadashi Matzumoto, and Isabelle Chartry from the OECD Centre for Entrepreneurship, SMEs, Regions, and Cities for their useful comments and feedback. From UN-Habitat, Melissa Permezel and Hazel Kuria in the Innovation Section provided extensive inputs and comments to all chapters in the report. Remy Sietchiping and Maria Tellez Soler from the Policy, Legislation and Governance Section contributed with helpful comments; Bernhard Barth from the Climate Change and Urban Environment (Regional Office for Asia and the Pacific) provided extensive feedback and insights. The report also benefited from comments and feedback from external partners including Prof. Angela Penagos (Universidad de Los Andes), Karim Hussein (Senior International Development Expert and Strategic Advisor to IFAD), Jeremy Gorelick, Strategic Advisor (Green Finance Institute), Marco Kamiya, Chief of Division of Innovation Strategies and Digitalization (UNIDO).

The study's draft results were presented and discussed with different stakeholders and experts in multiple international fora. The interactions with several participants in the various online and physical events organised along this project help to develop and refine the policy insights presented in this report. These events include an expert meeting organised by the OECD and UN-Habitat that took place between the 17th and 19th of November 2020; two sessions in the UCLG Second World Forum on Intermediary Cities, October 2021; a panel of experts during the Innovate4Cities Conference organised by the Global Covenant of Mayors for Climate and Energy (GCOM) and UN-Habitat, October 2021; a session during the 9th Edition of Africities Summit, in Kisumu (Kenya), May 2022; and through a network event during the World Urban Forum in Katowice, Poland, June 2022. We wish to thank all who participated in these events.

This document has been financed by the Swedish International Development Cooperation Agency, Sida. Sida does not necessarily share the views expressed in this material. Responsibility for its contents rests entirely with the author.

Editorial

Rising global temperatures, more frequent extreme events, and erratic climate patterns are reshaping cities and livelihoods around the world and increasingly exposing large shares of the global population to unprecedented risks. The Sixth Assessment of the Intergovernmental Panel on Climate Change (IPCC) warns that global warming is expected to reach or exceed 1.5°C on average over the next 20 years, and possibly by the early 2030s, ten years ahead of previous projections. Many ecosystems will shortly reach tipping points resulting in irreversible damage and increasing socio-economic costs.

In that upsetting context, human settlements around the world are rapidly transforming. In the next three decades, the urban population in many countries in sub-Saharan Africa and Asia will double. Between 2018 and 2050, countries like China, India and Nigeria are expected to grow respectively by 255 million, 416 million and 189 million urban dwellers; together, they will account for almost 35% of global urban population growth over that period.

Most of the big cities where people live, are already built, too often in ways that aggravate climate change and its impacts. Even in Latin America, where the pace of urbanisation has been slowing compared to other developing regions, most cities are struggling to cope with increasing levels of congestion and inequality.

Where can we still find scope to shape the urbanisation process in developing countries, in ways that are less damaging for climate and more protective of people? This report argues that intermediary cities, defined as urban centres with fewer than 1 million inhabitants, can provide an opportunity towards more climate-friendly urbanisation patterns.

In 2020, intermediary cities accounted for 58% of the urban population in less developed regions. By 2035, they will still account for close to 53%. As actors of both adaptation and mitigation, intermediary cities naturally have a number of specific assets. First, their size offers opportunities for more effective governance and management, greater social cohesion through a greater sense of identity and belonging, and a more balanced relationship with the surrounding natural environment. Second, many of these cities are not yet caught in an unsustainable development path that defines some of their larger peers. There is thus significant scope for shaping them for greater resilience, leveraging off their strengths, and avoiding carbon lock-in.

Unleashing the potential of intermediary cities in the fight against climate change, requires innovative development strategies involving local governments, national authorities and international partners, as well as the private and non-government sectors. Based on comprehensive diagnosis, this report supports such strategies by pointing to actions leading to better data and knowledge creation, multi-level actions and policy complementarities that simultaneously address both development and climate objectives, as well as financial mechanisms for climate actions that are tailored to intermediary cities.

Now is the time to scale up efforts in support of intermediary cities to proactively address climate change and promote sustainable urbanisation processes. The OECD Development Centre and UN-Habitat stand ready to support intermediary cities and their national governments through this process. This report is only the first step.

Ms. Maimunah Mohd Sharif

Executive Director, UN-HABITAT

Ragnheiður Elín Árnadóttir

Director of the OECD Development Centre

Table of contents

FIGURES

TABLES

Executive summary

Intermediary cities provide an unprecedented opportunity for advancing with climate mitigation and adaptation efforts. Increasing evidence, including the latest assessment of the International Panel on Climate Change, reaffirms that global anthropogenic greenhouse gas (GHG) emissions are not decreasing at the expected pace. The world is thus reaching a tipping point that could lead to irreversible damage to ecosystems and our societies. In parallel, intermediary cities in developing countries are transforming. Many are rapidly expanding, sometimes outpacing the capacity of governments to reduce vulnerability to climate shocks, invest in low-carbon infrastructure and establish plans, mechanisms and institutions that limit climate-risks and GHG emissions. If adequate actions take place now, many of these small and medium-sized cities can experience a green transition by design, i.e. they can be planned and organised to grow in a sustainable way that avoids the "grow now, clean later" strategy followed by many larger cities.

Yet intermediary cities – defined in this report as those with 50 000 to 1 million inhabitants – are often overlooked in national, regional and urban development policies. Given the urgency of the climate challenge, they deserve increased attention. First, these cites encompass a large share of the urban population most at risk from a changing climate. Cities with fewer than 1 million inhabitants accounted for 58% of the urban population in less developed regions in 2020, and will still account for 53% by 2035. Second, these cities generally play an intermediation role linking rural and metropolitan areas, which allows them to contribute to development efforts at the regional and national levels, including efforts to build climate resilience. Third, rapid urbanisation is hindering the capacity of authorities in intermediary cities to provide public services and an environment safe from increasingly frequent extreme climate events.

This report studies the complex relationship between intermediary cities and climate change. It uses multiple datasets to better understand how climate change affects intermediary cities, and how these cities are contributing to GHG emissions (Chapter 2). The report also explores how climate shocks that affect rural areas can indirectly affect intermediary cities due to the disruption of food systems and rural-to-urban migration (Chapter 3). Understanding these interactions is fundamental for more effective policies. Yet little is known about the strategies of intermediary cities in developing countries for coping with climate change. The report aims to address this gap by analysing climate strategies across intermediary cities in Africa, Asia and Latin America, and by identifying factors that led to the implementation of these polices as well as major challenges (Chapter 4). The report recognises that without adequate financing mechanisms, the policies necessary for addressing climate change across intermediary cities can end up being a set of green good intentions. For this reason, it analyses the mechanisms that can help to boost the financial resources for climate action across intermediary cities, as well as showcasing key areas for reform (Chapter 5).

Overall, this study shows that there is no single narrative regarding the way in which climate change affects intermediary cities in developing countries. Certain climate shocks have a greater effect on intermediary cities than on larger cities, and vice versa. For instance, based on the sample of cities analysed, 63% of the built-up area in intermediary cities with a population of 50 000 to 100 000 inhabitants in 2015 was potentially exposed to riverine flooding. In contrast, in cities with more than 1 million inhabitants, the share was lower, at 38%. In the case of heat waves, a different pattern emerges. Overall, heat waves have a negative effect on gross domestic product (GDP) in the sample of cities studied. However, these effects increase with city size, i.e. extreme heat events have a greater effect on the GDP of larger cities. This is particularly the case of cities in cooler climates.

As the urbanisation of intermediary cities continues, and their economies transform accordingly, their emission levels will increase, too. Not surprisingly, big cities produce most of the urban CO_2 emissions in developing countries. In 2015, cities of more than 1 million inhabitants produced almost five times more CO_2 than the average amount produced by cities with 500 000 to 1 million inhabitants, 37 times more than cities of 100 000 to 500 000 people and 132 times more than cities of 50 000 to 100 000 people. However, this is not a static process. As intermediary cities grow, their contribution to GHG will increase, too.

The report analyses existing climate policy strategies for intermediary cities in Africa Asia, and Latin America. In many of the cities studied, entry points for climate action have included disaster risk management, the upgrading of informal settlements and territorial development. However, it is not an easy task to consolidate multiple development agendas and anchor climate policy in local strategies. For climate policy to survive political cycles, local champions who can develop local capacity and promote participatory processes are often required. Yet, as noted in this study, local authorities cannot address the complex challenges brought by climate change alone. National governments are key for developing coherent climate strategies and scaling up effective policies, while international organisations can help by piloting innovative climate actions and supporting peer learning processes.

Financing is a critical aspect of the climate agenda, yet the lower overall fiscal capacity of intermediary cities can limit their access to adequate finance. They may have limited ability to raise the fees and taxes required to provide needed revenue streams and debt service capacity. Improving the financial capacity of intermediary cities to implement climate policies requires addressing constraints on both the demand and the supply sides of finance markets. Another issue is neglect of intermediary cities in broader development policies, which can leave them with poor infrastructure and weak urban governance.

The report highlights key areas for advancing the climate agenda in intermediary cities:

- *Climate mitigation policy* is still pending in many intermediary cities. Reducing GHG emissions can be perceived as an additional cost, both financially and politically. Yet the climate agenda overlaps with many critical development goals. Robust analytical tools, like systems thinking, can help to identify actions with strong mitigation potential that can also address other development priorities.
- *Spatial planning* is a critical aspect for building climate resilience and avoiding carbon lock-in. This includes integrating infrastructure, housing and transport policies into spatial planning, while accounting for the needs of vulnerable populations in informal settlements. Timing is critical, however, since these interventions will be more effective at an early stage of development.
- *The underlying socio-economic conditions of urban populations* must be addressed when considering the vulnerabilities of intermediary cities to climate change. This includes taking account of the linkages of intermediary cities with neighbouring towns and rural areas.
- *National authorities and development partners* have a key role to play. This not only requires setting up multilevel governance co-ordination mechanisms within countries, but also establishing platforms that bring intermediary cities onto the international development agenda.
- *Accessing the climate finance market* presents major difficulties for intermediary cities. To overcome these constraints, it is important that the supply and demand sides of the climate finance market be strengthened together, as strengthening financial institutions will be of limited use if cities do not have the fiscal space or capacity to utilise the available finance.

Intermediary cities have the potential to contribute to the reduction of global GHG emissions and to act as a laboratory for innovative solutions if they are endowed with adequate resources and targeted policies. However, the report argues, this calls for a shift in policy approaches.

1 Overview: An opportunity for sustainable development

This chapter presents an overview of the challenges and opportunities facing intermediary cities in the developing world due to rapid urbanisation coupled with climate change. It assesses how climate change is impacting intermediary cities, which play a key role in linking urban and rural areas, and how these cities can help in the effort to reduce global greenhouse gas emissions. The chapter then reviews the climate policies and strategies already adopted by intermediary cities in Africa, Asia, and Latin America in order to identify enabling factors and key actors that contribute to success. It considers a major obstacle faced by these cities: access to the finance required to invest in climate adaptation and mitigation. It concludes with a summary of key factors that can help intermediary cities tap into their potential to address the many challenges presented by climate change.

A fast-changing climate in a quickly urbanising world

Climate change and fast urbanisation are among the biggest challenges facing developing countries today. Rising global temperatures are reshaping livelihoods and increasingly exposing large shares of the population to unprecedented risks. The Sixth Assessment of the Intergovernmental Panel on Climate Change (IPCC) warns that global warming is expected to reach or exceed 1.5°C on average over the next 20 years, and possibly by the early 2030s, ten years ahead of previous projections (IPCC, 2021[1]). As such, many ecosystems will shortly reach tipping points that lead to irreversible damage, while socio-economic costs will continue to increase.

Along with the looming climate crisis and ecological breakdown that we are witnessing today, human settlements in developing countries are rapidly transforming. The urban population in many countries in sub-Saharan Africa and Asia will double in the next three decades (UNDESA, 2018[2]), while certain Latin American cities will struggle to cope with high levels of congestion and increasing inequality. Urbanisation can be a critical factor in enhancing economic growth and well-being. However, when it takes place too fast, it is not necessarily conducive to development. Rapid urbanisation can make it harder for governments to deliver basic services, update institutional frameworks and provide the infrastructure necessary for the private sector to thrive. Contrary to public perception, some of the most important changes in urban areas will not take place in large urban agglomerations, but rather in intermediary cities.

Intermediary cities are small and medium-sized cities that play an intermediation role by connecting urban and rural areas. In less developed regions, these are dynamic cities that support the flow of population, goods and services between rural areas and larger urban centres. To analyse their dynamics and linkages to climate change, this report builds on a series of data sources, in particular the Global Human Settlement Urban Centre database (GHS-UCDB) developed by the European Commission. This dataset gives access to information on more than 10 000 cities across different periods in less developed regions and is the main source for the analysis presented in the report. For practicality, and due to the lack of an internationally agreed definition, this report will classify intermediary cities as those urban centres with a population of 50 000 to 1 million.

Intermediary cities will play a critical role in the urbanisation process of developing countries. First, they will continue to account for a large share of the urban population in the coming decades. In 2020, intermediary cities (those with fewer than 1 million inhabitants) accounted for 58% of the urban population in less developed regions. Although this share is expected to decrease, by 2035 these cities will still account for close to 53% of the urban population in developing countries (UNDESA, 2018[3]). Second, the built-up area of many intermediary cities is expanding very quickly. Intermediary cities tend to have the highest built-up growth rates in developing regions. In certain cases, this fast expansion of built-up land has led to a decline in population density. Figure 1.1 shows the percentage of cities in developing countries that lost population density during the period 2000-15. This drop in density was most acute in intermediary cities. For instance, around 63% of cities with 50 000 to 100 000 inhabitants lost density over the period, compared to only 31% of cities with more than 1 million inhabitants.

Figure 1.1. Percentage of cities where density decreased over 2000-15

By city size

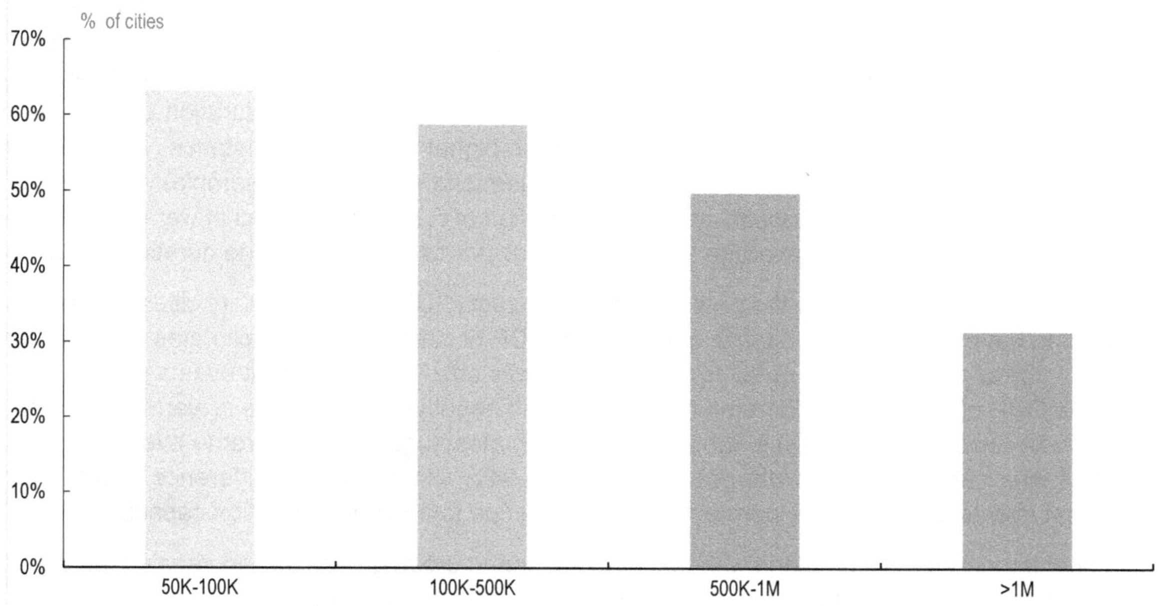

Note: The sample does not include cities in high-income countries.
Source: Authors' computation using GHS Urban Centre Database (2019[4]).

The way cities develop has a major effect on their climate resilience and greenhouse gas (GHG) emissions. This is particularly true of urban sprawl, which can contribute to both higher GHG emissions and increased vulnerability to climate shocks. Urban sprawl transforms land use and shapes urban dwellers' commuting patterns and needs. The expansion of built-up areas implies a reduction in the amount of land covered by vegetation, and thus reduced absorption of CO_2 into the soil (UN-Habitat, 2011[5]). This not only leads to higher GHG emissions but also imposes higher economic costs, as it leads to a higher spatial dispersion of population and economic activities, which reduces accessibility (Litman, 2014[6]). Moreover, unplanned urban expansion and informal settlements increase the vulnerability of urban dwellers to climate shocks such as flooding, landslides and heat waves. This is because informal urban populations, in addition to residing in high-risk zones, have comparatively limited access to basic services (like water and electricity) and adequate infrastructure (like sewerage and water draining systems).

Assessing the effects of climate change on intermediary cities

Climate change acts as a threat multiplier for intermediary cities in developing economies. Climate change does not discriminate across cities. Climate shocks and their magnitude depend on geography and local weather patterns. The extent to which they affect urban areas also depends on cities' characteristics. Fast urban expansion, paired with lack of infrastructure, weak governance and limited capacity, can hinder the capacity of cities to adapt to and mitigate the effects of climate change. Unfortunately, many of these features characterise intermediary cities in developing countries.

Climate change has a direct impact on intermediary cities

Climate change directly affects intermediary cities in multiple ways. Some of the most important include heatwaves, water stress, riverine floods, storm surges and rising sea levels.

Since the mid-20th century cities have experienced a higher frequency of **heat waves** than rural areas, and this is expected to increase in the coming decades. The built-up growth of cities plays a key role in this process since buildings absorb heat, which intensifies both the duration and intensity of heat waves. This is particularly relevant for cities in warmer climates where the frequency and duration of extreme heat events (temperatures above 46° C) are increasing at higher rates. For instance, in 2016, cities characterised by low temperatures (those below the median temperature in the sample) went through an average of five extreme heat events with an average duration of 5.3 days, whereas in warmer cities (those above the median) there were on average 12 extreme heat events with an average duration of 8.8 days.

Extreme heat events can influence the gross domestic product (GDP) of intermediary cities. Overall, these events tend to have a larger and negative effect on the GDP of cities with cooler climates (independent of city size). In cooler climates, these effects increase with city size – extreme heat events have a stronger effect on the GDP of larger cities. Extreme heat events also negatively affect cities in warmer climates, but only those with fewer than 500 000 inhabitants. Our estimates suggest that extreme events can reduce the GDP of intermediary cities in warmer climates by 0.04% to 0.07%. The difference in the effect of extreme heat events on cooler and warmer cities could be due to a better adaptation capacity of the latter.

Rising global temperatures, combined with fast and unplanned urban growth, risk increasing the exposure of cities to **water stress and droughts**. Growth in urban population implies increasing demand for water and very often the depletion of natural resources, which places increasing strains on local (often declining) freshwater resources. In turn, this often results in limited access to water or in polluted water sources (Gebre and Gebremedhin, 2019[7]). For instance, water stress is already occurring in fast-growing small and medium-sized cities in Nepal and India. In Nepal, fast population growth, coupled with the increasing effects of climate change and urban sprawl, has led to the depletion of groundwater resources in the cities of Dharan and Dhulikhel (Straits Times, 2019[8]). Similarly, in 2019, the city of Chennai in India experienced a drought with severe water shortages, leading it to import 2.5 million litres of water (Straits Times, 2019[8]).

A large share of the population of intermediary cities is exposed to **flooding**. Figure 1.2 shows the share of cities that are exposed to riverine floods and storm surges (left), as well as the share of built-up areas exposed to riverine floods and of population exposed to storm surges (right), all by city size in 2015. It can be seen that, as cities become larger, the risk of disaster events increases but the percentage of the population and built-up area at risk decreases. For example, only 4% of the cities with a population of 50 000 to 100 000 are exposed to storm surges, but within these cities almost 90% of the population is exposed to this type of climate shock. In contrast, in the group accounting for the largest cities, 17% are exposed to storm surges, which affect 41% of their population. A similar pattern is observed in the case of riverine flooding: 26% of cities with 50 000 to 100 000 inhabitants are exposed to floods, while 60% of their built-up area is exposed to this phenomenon. In contrast, almost half of the cities with more than 1 million inhabitants were exposed to riverine floods, whereas only 38% of their built-up area was exposed.

Figure 1.2. Exposure to riverine floods and storm surges in 2015

Share of cities potentially exposed to storm surges and floods (left) and share of population and built-up areas potentially exposed (right)

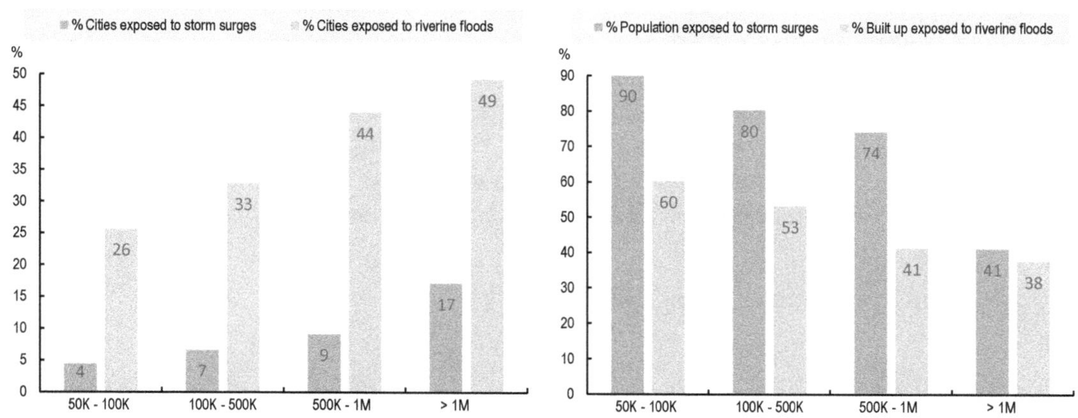

Note: The figure on the right side only considers cities with built-up areas and population potentially exposed to riverine flooding and storm surges. The sample does not include cities in high-income countries.
Source: Authors' own calculations using GHS Urban Centre Database (2019[4]).

Rising global sea levels threaten the populations of large cities in low-lying coastal areas and on small islands. Low coastal areas in developing countries are particularly vulnerable due to the acceleration of anthropogenic land subsidence caused by fast population growth and the expansion of built-up areas. A large share of the developing world's urban population lives in close proximity to coastal areas. In 2015, around 22% of the population of cities in the developing world, or more than 635 million people, lived in areas below 50 metres of altitude and within 5 kilometres of the coast. These areas are particularly exposed to sea-level rise and urban flooding. The percentage of the developing world's urban population living near coastal areas differs according to city size. In the sample of cities studied, cities of more than 1 million inhabitants accounted for 36% of the population, or 450 million people, that reside in low-lying areas. The percentage is lower for smaller cities in coastal areas, but a sizeable share of the population is still at risk. Among cities of 100 000 to 500 000 inhabitants, for instance, 11% of the population, or 107 million people, reside in low-lying coastal areas.

Climate change also impacts intermediary cities indirectly

Given the intermediation role of intermediary cities, climate change also affects their development indirectly by disrupting the linkages connecting rural and urban areas. These disruptions materialise through different channels, two of the most important being food systems and internal migration.

Climate change affects **food systems** by reducing crop productivity, damaging infrastructure, disrupting storage facilities and transportation services, and hindering rural livelihoods. Intermediary cities are particularly affected by these disruptions due to their strong reliance on local food markets. These effects of climate change can translate into food insecurity and fewer opportunities for income diversification, for both urban and rural populations. Vulnerable populations such as women, youth and rural migrants are particularly affected, and such disruptions further widen social inequalities.

Loss of livelihood, whether partial or complete, can increase **internal migration** as people leave rural areas for intermediary cities. Estimates suggest that climate change could lead to 216 million additional internal migrants across the world by 2050 (Clement et al., 2021[9]). As temperatures increase and precipitation patterns shift, many livelihoods will be affected. This will be particularly the case for households that rely strongly on the primary sector, as in many developing countries, particularly for people living in rural areas and intermediary cities. A large portion of these displacements are expected to take place across a short distance, i.e. many migrants in small towns and rural areas are expected to move to neighbouring intermediary cities. The analysis in this report captures part of this process and suggests that increasing temperatures are associated with changing population levels in cities across developing countries. However, this relationship follows a U-shape, suggesting that the influence of temperature on city population depends on baseline climatic conditions – where temperatures are historically higher (warmer places), this relationship is positive. Moreover, this relationship is stronger for cities with fewer than 1 million inhabitants. City population levels are also associated with increasing precipitation. For our sample, this relationship is positive overall but only significant for cities with fewer than 500 000 inhabitants.

Figure 1.3. The rural-urban interface and climate change

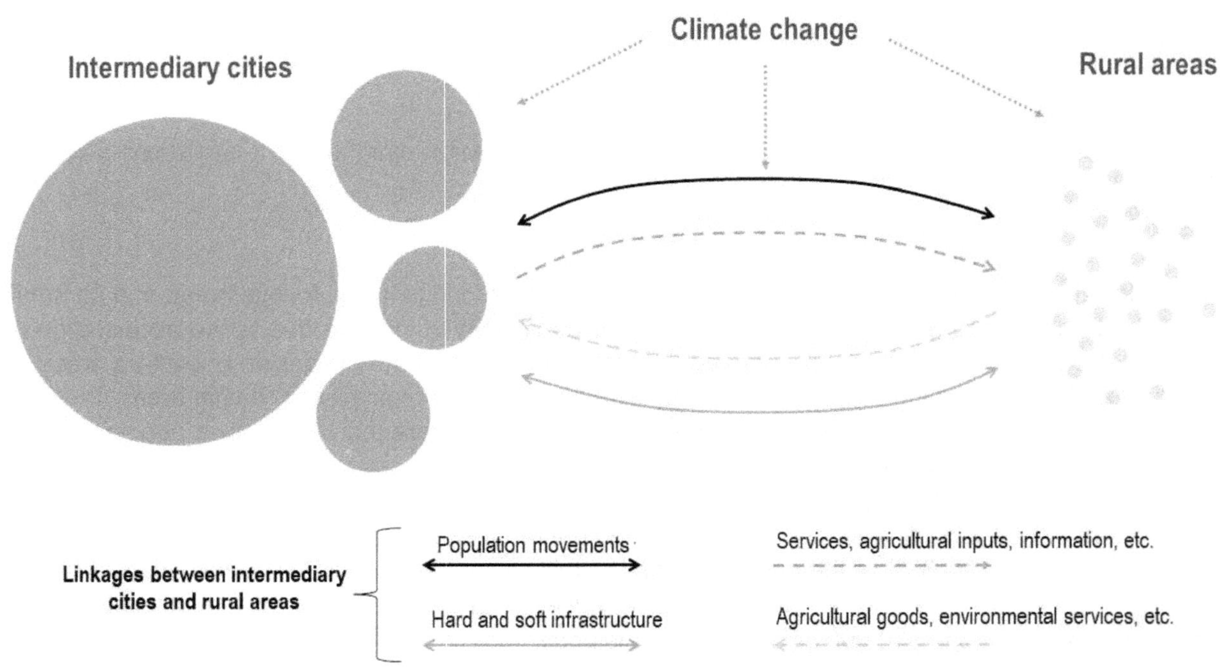

Note: The arrows in the figure connecting intermediary cities and rural areas refer to flows of people, goods, and services, as well as infrastructure linking both places. The green arrows coming out from climate change refer to climate shocks and changes in climatic patterns that affect intermediary cities, rural areas, and their linkages.
Source: Author's elaboration.

Intermediary cities can play a critical role in reducing GHG emissions

Cities are key in national and international climate-change mitigation efforts. Although urban areas account for merely 2% of the Earth's surface, they account for 60% of global GHG emissions (UN-Climate Action, 2018[10]), and 70% of total CO_2 emissions (IEA, 2021[11]).

In developing countries, most urban CO_2 emissions are produced by big cities. In 2015, cities of more than 1 million inhabitants produced around 13 million tons of CO_2 on average. This is almost five times more than the average amount of CO_2 produced by cities with 500 000 to 1 million inhabitants, 37 times higher than for cities of 100 000 to 500 000 people and 132 times higher than for cities of 50 000 to 100 000 people. Overall, cities of more than 1 million inhabitants accounted for 57% of all CO_2 emissions in 2015 (Figure 1.4). The contribution to CO_2 emissions by city size further depends on the sector of activity. As shown in Figure 1.4, large cities produce around two-thirds of CO_2 emissions in the transport and industry sectors, and more than half of the emissions in the residential sector. In contrast, intermediary cities account for the largest share of emissions in the energy and agriculture sectors.

Figure 1.4. Contribution of cities of different sizes to CO_2 emissions

Estimates by sector, 2015

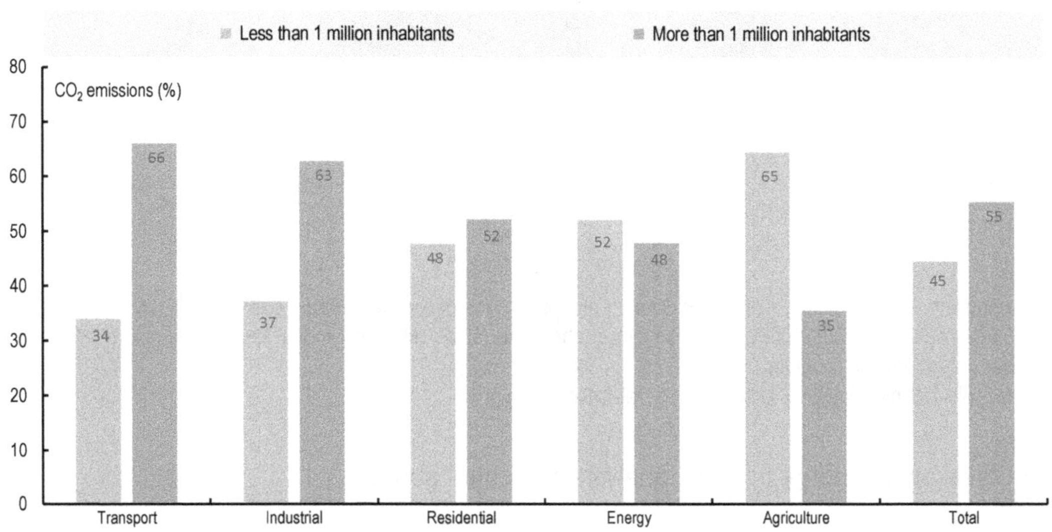

Note: The sample does not consider cities in high-income countries.
Source: Author's own calculations using GHS Urban Centre Database (2019[4]).

CO_2 emission levels are strongly associated with a city's degree of urbanisation and wealth. Figure 1.5 shows the relationship between CO_2 emissions and GDP for cities in developing countries in 2015. An increase of 1% in GDP among cities of more than 1 million inhabitants is associated with a 0.38% increase in CO_2 emissions on average, whereas for cities of 50 000 to 100 000 inhabitants, a similar rise in GDP leads to an increase of only 0.13% in CO_2 emissions. As for population, there is no significant difference between intermediary and large cities. An increase in built-up areas is only significantly correlated with rising CO_2 emissions in cities that have fewer than 500 000 inhabitants, where a 1% increase in built-up expansion is related to an increase in total CO_2 emissions of 0.15% to 0.18%.

Figure 1.5. CO_2 emissions and GDP across cities of different sizes

Data for cities in developing countries in 2015

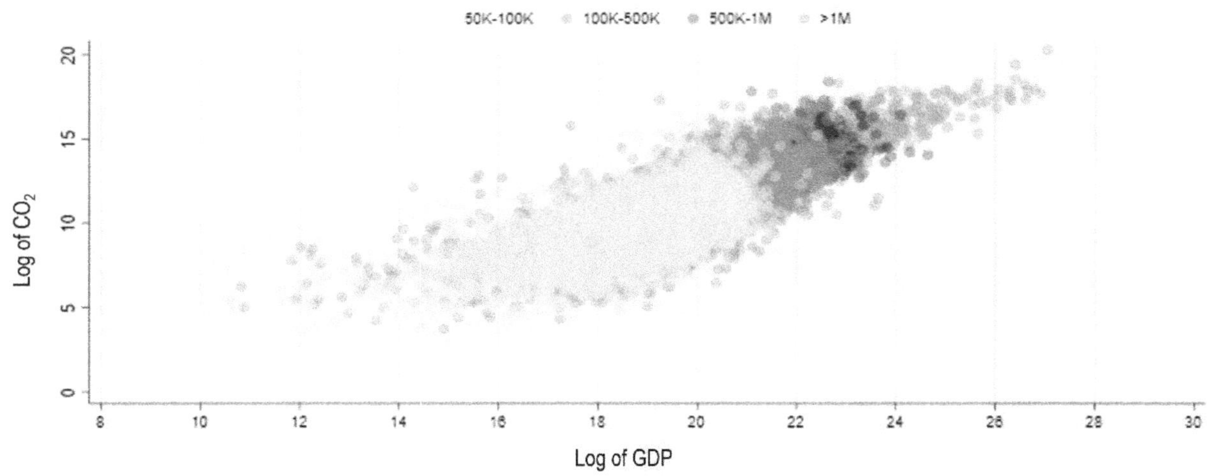

Note: Each circle represents a city. Colours account for different groups of cities depending on their size: 50 000-100 000 inhabitants (50K-100K), 100 000-500 000 inhabitants (100K-500K), 500 000-1 million inhabitants (500K-1M), and 1 million inhabitants or more (>1M). The sample does not include cities in high-income countries.
Source: Author's own calculations using GHS Urban Centre Database (2019[4]).

Two important messages emerge from the analysis presented above:

- The effects of climate change are not evenly distributed across cities of different sizes. This distribution is not static, however, since many intermediary cities are growing very quickly in terms of both population and built-up expansion. They will shortly become large cities and face challenges similar to those faced today by larger urban centres.
- There is an unprecedented opportunity to guide the design of intermediary cities from a very early stage for improved climate resilience and reduced emissions. This can be achieved by building them as climate-proof cities instead of climate-proofing them later. In this sense, intermediary cities differ from large cities and national capitals. They can avoid the "grow now, clean later" path, which costs more both financially and politically. However, since many intermediary cities are urbanising quickly, there is only a small window of opportunity.

To build on these messages, it is necessary to understand the strategies, actors and enabling environment that have driven the development of climate policies across intermediary cities in the last decades.

Strategies and policies adopted by intermediary cities to address climate change

Cities are increasingly recognised as key agents for economic development in terms of both the Sustainable Development Goals (SDGs) and the Paris Agreement. Indeed, no global meeting is complete without a mayor or two. There is, however, a large information gap regarding strategies for addressing climate change in intermediary cities. Most surveys, as well as national and international initiatives on urban climate change, tend to focus on high-income regions and large cities, particularly those conducted in developing countries. To address this gap, this report analyses existing climate policy strategies for intermediary cities in Africa, Asia, and Latin America in order to identify enabling factors, key actors and the main policy instruments put in place.

Climate policy is often built on previous development strategies

Disaster risk management (DRM) and the upgrading of Informal settlements have often served as **entry points** for climate actions. This is because there are strong overlaps in strategies that aim to target climate vulnerabilities and those addressing wider socio-economic goals (health, infrastructure, etc.). Both strategies aim to improve conditions for vulnerable urban dwellers by addressing their need for risk-reducing infrastructure. Vulnerable urban populations need (sufficient and affordable) access to piped and safe water, good-quality sanitation and electricity, all-weather access roads, storm and surface drainage, and street lighting. Beyond infrastructure, they need risk-reducing services including hospitals/health care, emergency services, road-traffic management and the rule of law (Revi et al, 2014[12]). The upgrading of informal settlements in particular has been an entry point for climate policies across intermediary cities in Asia and Africa, often taking place in collaboration with international partners. In Latin America, DRM has often been integrated into local urban planning in intermediary cities. Territorial development strategies, as well as urban and environmental planning, have also been entry points for building climate policies in Latin America and in some cities across Asia.

Enabling factors and key actors help to anchor climate policies

Across the cities reviewed, a series of underlying conditions acted as **enabling factors** that facilitated successful climate actions. Governance mechanisms that promote participatory planning, accountability and transparency are critical enablers, since well-governed cities are better able to plan and implement climate policies while also being accountable to those they serve. Decentralisation is another institutional factor that can promote climate action by providing local governments with adequate autonomy, resources and mandates while strengthening democracy and ensuring that local needs are met with greater transparency and accountability. This requires building effective multilevel governance systems that facilitate consultation with, and the participation of, other relevant stakeholders. Strong local capacity and resources (human, financial, technical, political and data resources) are the foundation for successful climate actions (Carmin et al., 2011[13]). Natural disasters can act as triggers that lead cities to transition from emergency responses to an integrated strategy (such as DRM plans). Local actors can be incentivised to plan with “a risk lens” when pushed to understand, and take responsibility for, the risks of city expansion into highly vulnerable areas, including difficulties in water management and basic service provision.

Key actors contribute to the success of climate action across intermediary cities. Local champions, national governments and international organisations are critical enablers. *Local champions*, such as mayors, can engage key stakeholders and ensure the durability of programmes, and can systematically integrate climate change and environmental issues as cross-cutting themes in the local agenda. *National governments*, with their larger capacity and greater legislative power, are critical for establishing and implementing policies that go beyond city boundaries, scaling up successful local actions and mainstreaming climate standards across sectoral policies. As such, national governments can help to build coherent policies and strategies across different levels of government and different sectors. *International organisations* can also play important roles in supporting local policies. They can help to pilot climate actions in cities (SEI, 2020[14]; Bulkeley and Castán Broto, 2013[15]); support cities in accessing networks of experts or other cities; and create platforms for peer learning and profile building (SEI, 2020[14]). International organisations also have better financial capacities and are free from many of the political barriers that may constrain city actors, lending them a great capacity to invest in a wider scope of projects. Meanwhile, the active engagement of civil society, academia and grassroots organisations has played a key role in many cases where Latin American cities have successfully implemented sustainability policies. They help cities to acquire the technical know-how needed to launch these policies and to sustain climate initiatives over the long term despite shifts in local administrations.

Intermediary cities need robust financing mechanisms to advance climate action

A critical and sometimes overlooked aspect of the development of climate policies across intermediary cities is the financial feasibility and sustainability of these policies. Boosting cities' access to climate finance is therefore essential in climate mitigation and adaptation efforts. Limiting the global temperature increase to below 2°C by 2100 will require an annual investment in global infrastructure of USD 6.9 trillion between 2016 and 2030; approximately two-thirds of this, or about USD 4 trillion per year over the same period, is needed for developing countries (OECD, 2017[16]). The magnitude of investment necessary to meet the Paris targets requires that climate finance be reframed as a mainstream form of financing that supports investments to reduce GHG emissions. As such, and to incentivise environmentally sound investment in urban infrastructure and services, all urban investment financing should promote climate objectives.

Intermediary cities face challenges in securing financial resources

Intermediary cities often struggle to access fiscal resources due to a series of constraints. Their overall lower income per capita and generally limited capacity to mobilise local resources are among the main factors preventing access to climate finance. Intermediary cities may be limited in their ability to take on debt due to the limited size of their urban economy and revenues. They may also have limited ability to raise the fees and taxes required to provide needed revenue streams and debt-service capacity. In addition, in comparison to large cities, intermediary cities generally have lower land values and can provide less leverage. This limits their ability to react to and influence the commercial conditions that provide the context for private investment through instruments such as land-use controls.

Intermediary cities are further constrained by structural shortfalls in existing financing mechanisms that prevent effective engagement. Climate finance, whether through existing financing and funding streams or through specialist climate funds, needs to address these shortfalls. They include: a lack of climate budgeting that recognises the many linkages between national climate goals and the resources of local governments; an absence of climate issues in urban planning; a lack of the technical capacity and resources needed to access climate finance; a lack of capacity to manage the technical aspects of a climate project; and a lack of funding and partnerships.

In many cases, action on climate change falls beyond the policy scope of intermediary cities. For instance, local governments can be limited in their capacity to address the larger-scale impact of emissions produced by enterprises based in the city. Spatial constraints relating to distance and remoteness compound the problems for some intermediary cities, particularly in small island developing states. As such, industries in intermediary cities (including in industrial clusters) often struggle to achieve scale and are more likely to face higher transaction costs for financing, which undermines their competitiveness and efficiency in supporting urban populations.

Barriers to mobilising climate finance exist for cities and institutions alike

Intermediary cities face constraints on both the demand side and the supply side of urban climate finance markets. The demand side refers to the agencies that make investment decisions in cities, while the supply side refers to the institutions that supply the finance for these investments.

Bottlenecks on the **demand side** of climate finance in intermediary cities are diverse and vary on a city-by-city basis. A common challenge in access to finance is the inflexible structure of intergovernmental transfers. Intermediary cities tend to be highly reliant on transfers from central governments (Farvacque-Vitkovic and Kopanyi, 2014[17]), which tend to be formula-based (e.g. based on population size) or tied to specific uses. Inflexible systems limit cities' autonomy to utilise more innovative financing. Moreover, intermediary cities are limited in their capacity to take on debt due to their limited creditworthiness. Local governments' creditworthiness is often determined by their ability to use central transfers effectively and the extent to which local revenue is maximised. As noted above, intermediary cities struggle this.

On the **supply side**, intermediary cities face barriers to mobilising large-scale private institutional and commercial finance. Institutional investors can face challenges in finding investment opportunities that are low risk, reliable and with stable return, particularly around infrastructure and general climate projects, which must meet climate objectives in addition to the general requirements of technical, financial and regulatory standards. Furthermore, the generally low credit rating of intermediary cities creates an obstacle in the investment decisions of financing institutions. In addition, the focus among investing institutions on short-term investments with quick returns works against long-term investments, such as in infrastructure. Other challenges include lack of experience in urban investment and regulatory constraints that limit the ability to invest in urban climate and infrastructure projects. Factors such as a lack of appropriate financing vehicles for smaller projects, as well as wider macroeconomic conditions that affect inflation and foreign exchange (which shape aggregate demand), can also deter financing institutions.

On both the demand and supply sides, actions to alleviate these constraints need to focus on producing transparent processes for defining clear city climate objectives and for detailing the programme of investments that will meet those objectives. For the required investments to be financed efficiently, they need to be structured as financing mechanisms that are appropriate to intermediary cities. Competent and effectively mandated implementing agencies need to be assigned clear responsibility for investments in green infrastructure; enterprise capital for renewable energy and energy efficiency; cluster support systems; and human capital development. These can initially be linked to COVID-19 recovery, but as recovery from the pandemic proceeds, they will need increasing emphasis on the implementation of nationally determined contributions, which represent national government promises of aggregate cuts in emissions and increased climate resilience.

It is important that the demand and supply sides of the climate finance market be strengthened in tandem. Strengthening financial institutions will be of limited use if cities do not have the fiscal space or capacity to utilise the available finance on both sides of the market and at national and subnational/local levels. As such, interventions need to address structural issues. However, the effectiveness of these interventions critically depends on the strength of enabling frameworks and other capacity support structures.

Untapping the potential of intermediary cities to address climate change

Intermediary cities have great untapped potential to help address climate change. To utilise this potential, local and national authorities, and their development partners, must consider a series of key issues.

Climate mitigation policy is still pending in many intermediary cities

Most intermediary cities in developing countries are trying to cope with the consequences of climate change, but few are implementing consistent mitigation policies. For many local authorities, reducing emission levels is perceived as an additional cost, both financially and politically. This creates a sense of trade-off between environmental sustainability and wider development objectives, exacerbated by the continuous financing gap that many of these cities face. Yet this is a false perception: various policy actions can help reduce (potential) emissions while also addressing other development objectives. However, these actions require robust analytical frameworks that allow for the identification of policy complementarities and policies that address the real underlying phenomena that lock cities into carbon-intensive paths. For instance, adopting a **system thinking** approach to climate mitigation can help cities shift from an economic growth-oriented model towards a more holistic wellbeing-oriented model. Systems thinking enables the design of policies that aim to reduce GHG emissions, while simultaneously enhancing the well-being of populations, by conferring the ability to understand and capture the interlinkages across sectors, thereby allowing policy makers to minimise trade-offs (OECD, 2019[18]).

Early spatial planning is critical to building climate resilience and avoiding carbon lock-in

Establishing spatial planning frameworks that aim to reduce urban sprawl and promote compact and accessible urban forms can reduce future GHG emissions while also enhancing the well-being of urban dwellers. Moreover, early planning can avoid the high costs associated with changing already-built urban infrastructure and established urban forms (IPCC, 2014[19]). Spatial planning must consider factors that are key to limiting future GHG emissions and strengthening resilience. This can be achieved by:

- *integrating infrastructure, housing and mobility policies into spatial planning* in order to enable intermediary cities adequately to meet the demands of a growing population while reducing the risk of carbon lock-in and reducing the scope for urban sprawl.
- *accounting for food systems and internal migration*. As these are key channels that connect intermediary cities to rural areas, it is critical to build coherent and sustainable frameworks that stretch across sectors and strengthen rural and urban linkages.
- *addressing the needs of vulnerable populations in informal settlements* and integrating them into spatial plans.

Please note that none of these actions will be effective without the data, statistics and indicators needed to build a comprehensive understanding of local vulnerabilities and assets.

Climate-change resilience requires developing both cities and their rural surroundings

Fostering local economic development and better access to services for both rural and urban dwellers is critical for climate-change resilience. For instance, tapping into fast-transforming food systems and the growth of post-farm-gate activities can provide large opportunities for local development in intermediary cities and their surrounding rural areas. Moreover, effective local development requires improving access to basic services for surrounding rural populations by fostering closer ties with intermediary cities. This allows better use of rural resources by the cities while simultaneously improving the quality of these resources. Better access to urban markets is equally important. It enables rural producers to increase their earnings; further invest in more diversified economic activities (Hussein and Suttie, 2016[20]); access agricultural inputs and technology; achieve stronger integration into food supply chains; and reduce their climate vulnerabilities (FAO, 2008[21]). This is a perfect example of the potential synergy between sustainability and wider developmental goals.

Intermediary cities need national support in addressing climate change

National governments have a critical role to play in supporting local governments in implementing climate actions and building local resilience. Their involvement is key to supporting and scaling up smaller, more local, climate actions. The wider scope and greater policy-making capacity of national authorities enable them to promote place-based policies that take account of different levels of government and encompass both rural and urban territories. Their larger political, administrative and financial capacities give them access to resources and the ability to improve co-ordination between regions and policies. Moreover, this scope allows them to adopt a systemic approach by envisioning intermediary cities as part of a wider urban system and fostering stronger partnerships, connectivity and collaboration across cities.

Effective climate financing in intermediary city requires action on all fronts

Redressing the financing gap faced by intermediary cities requires addressing demand-side and supply-side constraints simultaneously.

On the demand side, this implies boosting actions by national and subnational governments, as well as other urban investment agents, with the aim of strengthening their capacity to finance climate projects. Some of these actions include:

- *building local capacity to integrate climate objectives into local plans*, for example by localising nationally determined contributions towards cuts in emissions and increased climate resilience
- *leveraging internal and external development assistance* for the development of bankable projects with high climate performance that can attract international and private financing.
- *improving fiscal management systems* to maximise their own sources of revenue in order to provide intermediary cities with better access to climate finance.

On the supply side, actions should aim to strengthen the enabling framework for subnational climate financing and the capacity of financial institutions and their regulators to finance climate projects developed or proposed by urban investment agents. These actions include:

- *increasing financing flexibility*. National governments and partner institutions can enhance the ability of capital market institutions to accommodate the higher risk profiles of intermediary cities and their enterprises through more flexible financing systems.
- *establishing regulatory frameworks* for greening the financial system, building capacity and establishing mechanisms for aggregating small-scale projects in order to maximise intermediary cities' access to climate finance.

References

Bulkeley, H. and V. Castán Broto (2013), "Government by experiment? Global cities and the governing of climate change", *Transactions of the Institute of British Geographers*, Vol. 38/3, https://doi.org/10.1111/j.1475-5661.2012.00535.x. [15]

Carmin, J. et al. (2011), *Planning climate resilient cities: early lessons from early adapters*, https://www.researchgate.net/publication/273764560. [13]

Clement, V. et al. (2021), *Groundswell: Acting on Internal Climate Migration - Part 2*, World Bank, Washington DC, http://www.worldbank.org. [9]

FAO (2008), *Climate Change and Food Security: A Framework Document*, Food and Agriculture Organization of the United Nations, Rome, http://www.fao.org/3/au035e/au035e.pdf (accessed on 17 February 2021). [21]

Farvacque-Vitkovic, C. and M. Kopanyi (2014), *Municipal Finances: A Handbook for Local Governments*, World Bank, Washington DC, https://openknowledge.worldbank.org/handle/10986/18725 (accessed on 18 October 2021). [17]

Florczyk, A. (2019), *GHS Urban Centre Database 2015, multitemporal and multidimensional attributes*, http://data.europa.eu/89h/53473144-b88c-44bc-b4a3-4583ed1f547e (accessed on 13 July 2021). [4]

Gebre, T. and B. Gebremedhin (2019), "The mutual benefits of promoting rural-urban interdependence through linked ecosystem services", *Global Ecology and Conservation*, Vol. 20, https://doi.org/10.1016/j.gecco.2019.e00707. [7]

Hussein, K. and D. Suttie (2016), *Rural-urban linkages and food systems in sub-Saharan Africa*, International Fund for Agricultural Development, Rome, http://www.ifad.orgwww.ruralpovertyportal.orgwww.facebook.com/ifadinstagram.com/ifadnewswww.twitter.com/ifadnewswww.youtube.com/user/ifadTV. [20]

IEA (2021), *Empowering Cities for a Net Zero Future: unlocking resilient, smart, sustainable urban energy systems*, International Energy Agency, Paris, https://iea.blob.core.windows.net/assets/4d5c939d-9c37-490b-bb53-2c0d23f2cf3d/G20EmpoweringCitiesforaNetZeroFuture.pdf (accessed on 23 December 2021). [11]

IPCC (2021), "Summary for Policy Makers", in IPCC (ed.), *Climate Change 2021: The Physical Science Basis*, Cambridge University Press, Cambridge, https://www.ipcc.ch/report/ar6/wg1/downloads/report/IPCC_AR6_WGI_SPM.pdf (accessed on 25 October 2021). [1]

IPCC (2014), *Chapter Climate Change 2014 Synthesis Report Summary for Policymakers Summary for Policymakers*, IPCC, Geneva, https://www.ipcc.ch/site/assets/uploads/2018/02/AR5_SYR_FINAL_SPM.pdf. [19]

Litman, T. (2014), *Analysis of Public Policies That unintentionally encourage and subsidize urban sprawl*, http://www.lsecities.net. [6]

OECD (2019), *Accelerating Climate Action: Refocusing Policies through a Well-being Lens*, OECD Publishing, Paris, https://doi.org/10.1787/2f4c8c9a-en. [18]

OECD (2017), *Technical note on estimates of infrastructure investment needs: Background note to the report Investing in Climate, Investing in Growth*, OECD, Paris, https://www.oecd.org/env/cc/g20-climate/Technical-note-estimates-of-infrastructure-investment-needs.pdf (accessed on 18 October 2021). [16]

Revi et al (2014), *Urban Areas in Climate Change 2014: Impacts, Adaptation, and Vulnerability*, IPCC, Cambridge, https://www.ipcc.ch/report/ar5/wg2/. [12]

SEI (2020), *Governing sustainability in secondary cities of the Global South*, Stockholm Environment Institute, Stockholm, http://www.sei.org. [14]

Straits Times, T. (2019), *Water express delivers emergency supplies to drought-hit Indian city*, The Straitstimes, Asia, https://www.straitstimes.com/asia/south-asia/water-express-delivers-emergency-supplies-to-drought-hit-indian-city (accessed on 25 October 2021). [8]

UN-Climate Action (2018), *Cities and Pollution contribute to climate change: Cities and local action*, https://www.un.org/en/climatechange/cities-pollution.shtml (accessed on 22 June 2020). [10]

UNDESA (2018), *World Urbanization Prospects 2018 Highlights*, UNDESA, New York, https://population.un.org/wup/Publications/. [2]

UNDESA (2018), *World Urbanization Prospects: The 2018 Revision*, Online edition, https://population.un.org/wup/ (accessed on 23 April 2020). [3]

UN-Habitat (2011), *Cities and Climate Change - Global Report on Human Settlements 2011*, Un-Habitat, London - Washington DC, https://unhabitat.org/cities-and-climate-change-global-report-on-human-settlements-2011. [5]

2 The linkages between climate change and intermediary cities

The objective of this chapter is to reduce the knowledge gap on the linkages between climate change and intermediary cities. Although knowledge about climate change has seen constant increase over the last two decades, little is known about how it is affecting small and medium-sized agglomerations in developing countries. Such cities are playing a key role in urbanisation in regions like Southeast Asia and Sub-Saharan Africa. However, due to socio-economic, institutional, and geographical issues, these intermediary cities are disproportionally exposed to climate change.

Climate change and fast urbanisation are arguably among the biggest challenges facing the world today. Climate change is reshaping our livelihoods and increasingly exposing large shares of the population to unprecedented risks. The Sixth Assessment of the Intergovernmental Panel on Climate Change (IPCC) warns that global warming is expected to reach or exceed 1.5°C on average over the next 20 years, and possibly by the early 2030s, ten years ahead of previous projections (IPCC, 2021[1]).[1] As such, many ecosystems will shortly reach tipping points that lead to irreversible damage, while socio-economic costs will continue to increase. Along with the looming climate crisis and ecological breakdown that we are witnessing today, human settlements in developing countries are also rapidly transforming. The urban population in many countries in Sub-Saharan Africa and Asia will double in the next three decades (UNDESA, 2018[2]), while in Latin America several cities will struggle to cope with high levels of congestion and increasing inequality. While urbanisation can present large benefits for socio-economic gains and rural-urban transformation (i.e. economic transformation in rural areas triggered by urbanisation, such as poverty reduction, changes in food consumption and production, etc.), it can also present systemic challenges that can further expose urban dwellers to climate shocks and promote carbon lock-in. As such, managing the adverse effects of climate change on urban areas, while promoting low-carbon standards, is an urgent issue for local, national and international agendas.

Although intermediary cities are key for addressing climate change, they are often overlooked in both the international development agenda and the climate debate. This report considers "intermediary cities" by the key intermediation role they play in connecting metropolitan centres with rural areas, and for practicality they can be defined to be urban centres with a population of 50 000 to 1 million. In developing countries, these are dynamic agglomerations that connect rural and urban areas, as well as cities of different sizes within urban systems. They are usually small and medium-sized urban areas, i.e., not capitals or large cities that are strongly linked to rural economies. In many cases, intermediary cities have the potential to foster well-being, promote job creation and contribute to poverty reduction. They can also act as powerful laboratories for piloting new solutions and fostering social and economic innovation. However, many of these agglomerations are also characterised by limited capacity, poor governance frameworks and weak urban planning. These issues, paired with rapid urbanisation, hinder the capacity of authorities to provide public services and an environment safe from increasingly frequent extreme climatic events. Moreover, as these cities grow and become wealthier, they tend to move towards carbon-intensive energy sources, further contributing to greenhouse gas (GHG) emissions and climate change. For these reasons it is urgent to include the effects of climate change on intermediary cities in the development agenda.

There is a significant knowledge gap surrounding the nexus between intermediary cities and climate change. In studies of climate change and cities, large or capital cities have received more attention. Overall, for each publication about intermediary cities or small and medium-sized cities, there were close to 142 publications studying big cities (including scientific articles, peer-reviewed articles and reports from development institutions). In the case of climate change the gap narrows, but there are still ten publications about climate change and big cities per each publication about climate change and intermediary cities.[2]

To address this gap, this chapter uses novel datasets in order to better understand the relationship between climate change and cities of different sizes. In particular, it uses the Urban Centres Dataset developed by the European Commission and the OECD. As such, the chapter analyses the urban dynamics characterising intermediary cities and their multidimensional vulnerabilities to climate change, as well as their contribution to greenhouse gases.

The chapter highlights that there is no simple narrative linking intermediary cities and climate change. It shows that the effects of climate change, and the contribution to greenhouse gases, are not homogenous across the urban system. This is not linked to city size itself. Instead, it depends on geographic factors, such as distance to low-lying coastal zones, location in relation to the equator, etc.; the capacity of authorities to limit climate vulnerabilities and emissions; and governance mechanisms that ensure a sustainable path. Many of these features are not present – yet – in intermediary cities. By defragmenting knowledge and presenting new evidence, the chapter aims to promote future discussion of the management of urban systems in developing countries. It also aims to convey an optimistic message: the small(er) size of many intermediary cities could actually be a lever for achieving a sustainable transformation that avoids locking these agglomerations onto an unsustainable path, as has been the case for many larger agglomerations in developing and developed countries.

Why do intermediary cities in developing countries matter for climate change?

Climate action needs to take place now, and urban areas can play a critical role in both adaptation and mitigation efforts. Increasing evidence, including the latest assessment of the IPCC, reaffirms that global anthropogenic greenhouse gas emissions are not decreasing at the expected pace. Thus, the world is reaching a tipping point that could lead to irreversible damage to ecosystems and our societies.

As urban areas continue to grow, cities in developing countries are increasingly exposed to climate change. Urban areas in developing countries not only host a high share of the population but are also centres of economic activity, as well as nodes in complex networks of infrastructure including transportation, communication and information. Cities are also critical hubs for the provision of basic public services (health, education, etc.) that benefit not only urban dwellers but also the population of neighbouring rural areas. Events associated with climate change – such as floods, changes in precipitation, rising sea levels, etc. – threaten the intricate functioning of urban areas.

Until recently, limited attention has been paid to the role of intermediary cities in the international debate concerning climate change. There are different reasons for this, including a strong bias towards capital cities, limited available data on smaller agglomerations and an overall development narrative that has placed significant weight on the potential of large urban areas for national economic growth. However, national governments and international development partners are increasingly recognising the potential of intermediary cities for improving local well-being in developing countries. Due to their intermediation role, these cities act as hubs for the provision of goods and services, facilitate rural-urban migration and provide a conducive environment for income diversification and poverty alleviation.

Intermediary cities can also play an important role in building resilience to and mitigating the effects of climate change:

- **Intermediary cities have a major role in the urbanisation of developing countries**. Intermediary cities will continue to host more than half the urban population of developing countries in the coming decades (UNDESA, 2018[3]). Moreover, intermediary cities in developing countries are continuing to expand, and in some cases very quickly. This has made these cities prone to losing density compared to metropolitan areas and capital cities. Urban processes underpinned by low density and fast expansion risk exposing vulnerable urban dwellers to the effects of climate change, while leading urban areas to emit higher levels of GHGs. This results from longer commuting times, increased use of motor vehicles, higher congestion, and reduced provision of services.
- **The intermediation role of these cities links their economies and societies to rural areas**. By definition, intermediary cities have closer socio-economic and geographic linkages with rural areas. Intermediary cities act as nodes that connect people and socio-economic activities across rural and urban territories. As such, changes in climatic patterns that reduce agricultural productivity, increase the pressure on natural resources and limit rural livelihoods indirectly affect intermediary cities. These effects spread through different channels, two of the most important being food systems and internal migration. In other words, intermediary cities face the compounded effects of climate change: a direct effect resulting from more frequent extreme climatic events, and an indirect effect resulting from disruptions in food systems and historic migration patterns. Similarly, climate effects on intermediary cities largely affect rural areas and the well-being of their populations. It is therefore important to understand their intricate relations and the effects of climate change on their mutual linkages.

Due to the complexity of the indirect effects of climate change on intermediary cities, this topic is the main focus of Chapter 3, while being briefly explained in this section. Box 2.1 outlines the definition of intermediary cities for this report and highlights the three constraints they face: knowledge gaps, policy gaps and financing gaps.

Box 2.1. What constitutes an intermediary city?

Intermediary cities are urban agglomerations that play an intermediation role that allows them to connect metropolitan and rural areas as well as different groups of cities within urban systems. There is, however, no universal definition for intermediary cities. Although intermediary cities are characterised by their intermediation role, there is no consensus on how to identify this role based on their main features. Moreover, there is limited data on the economic activities, employment share and economic specialisation occurring among these cities in developing countries.

For this reason, in this report, **intermediary cities are considered to be those urban centres with a population ranging between 50 000 and 1 million inhabitants**.

The main benefit of this approach is its simplicity. This is a clear rule that can be easily applied to existing information. Moreover, across developing countries, it does a good job separating small and medium-sized cities, which usually play an intermediation role, from large and capital cities.

There are, however, a number of caveats, the most important being that this approach does not rely on the function(s) of a given city within the urban system. In addition, it does not take into account the fact that highly populated countries tend have highly populated cities, meaning that in some countries this threshold may be too low. This is probably the case for countries like China and India.

A methodology for identifying intermediary cities in developing countries is envisaged as one potential output of the Development Centre during the next programme of work.

Intermediary cities play a critical role in the urbanisation of less developed regions

Urbanisation is a global phenomenon. In 2020, 55% of the total global population resided in urban areas (UNDESA, 2018[2]). However, urbanisation rates differ across regions. For instance, North America is the most urbanised region in the developed world, with 82% of its population residing in urban areas, followed by Europe (74%) and Oceania (68%). Latin America and the Caribbean (LAC) is the most urbanised region in the developing world, with 81% of its population residing in urban areas, followed by Asia and Africa, with 50% and 43% respectively (UNDESA, 2018[2]).

Urban populations are expected to grow very rapidly in emerging regions. Countries in Africa and Asia are urbanising most quickly. For instance, between 2018 and 2050, countries like China, India and Nigeria are expected to grow, respectively, by 255 million, 416 million and 189 million urban dwellers; these three countries together will account for almost 35% of total urban population growth around the world (UNDESA, 2018[2]). Figure 2.1 shows the urbanisation dynamics for developing countries in Asia, Africa, LAC and Oceania. The figure shows that, although China and India are – and will remain – the countries hosting the largest urban populations in the next three decades, they are not the ones expected to grow most quickly. Indeed, the fastest growing urban populations are based in Africa. The urban population of countries like Niger, Burundi, Uganda and Malawi will grow on average at annual rates above 4.5%. This implies that by 2050, these countries will be significantly more urbanised, and some of them may double their respective shares of urban population compared to their levels in 2018.

Figure 2.1. Urbanisation rates across developing countries

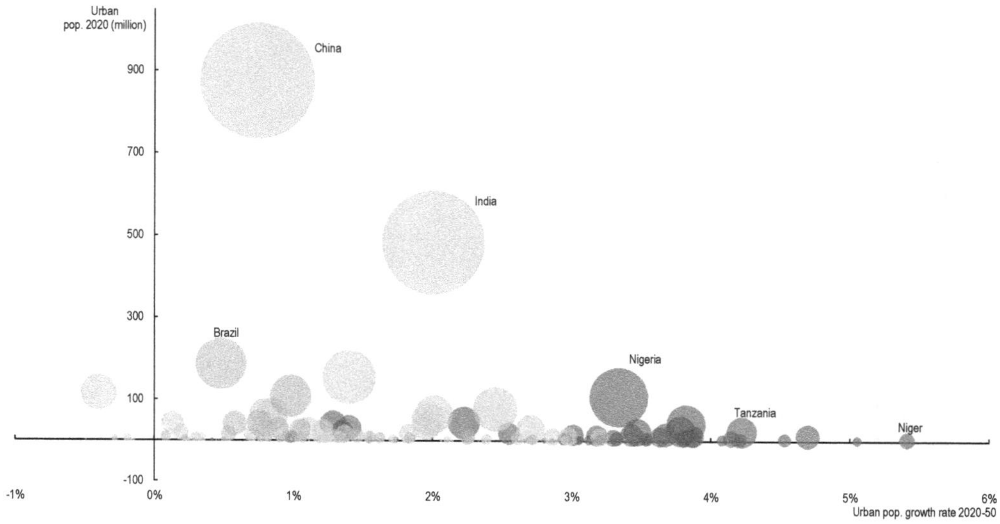

Note: The vertical axis shows the total population in urban areas in 2020, while the horizontal axis shows the expected annual growth rate of urban population between 2020 and 2050. The size of the circles represents the expected urban population in 2050. Countries in LAC are represented in orange; Africa in navy blue; and Asia in light blue. The sample does not include cities in high-income countries.
Source: UNDESA (2018[3]).

Intermediary cities account for a large share of the urban population in developing countries

Most urban dwellers in less developed regions will reside in small and medium-sized cities by 2035. Big cities are constantly in the spotlight due to their strong potential for generating economic growth, their function as hubs for knowledge and culture, and because they host large shares of national populations. Alongside large cities, urban areas with fewer than 1 million inhabitants are expected to continue hosting an important share of the world's urban population in the next decades. Figure 2.2 shows the distribution of urban population across cities of different sizes in less developed regions. It shows that, in 2020, cities with fewer than 1 million inhabitants accounted for 58% of the urban population in less developed regions. Although this portion is expected to decrease in the next couple of decades, by 2035 these cities will still account for close to 53% of urban population in developing countries. The fact that small and medium-sized cities will host a significant share of the urban population in developing countries makes them key actors for climate adaptation and mitigation. Growth dynamics also imply that many large cities of the future are currently intermediary cities. This calls for urgent action now in order to ensure a sustainable growth pattern.

Figure 2.2. Share of urban population by city size, 1990-2035

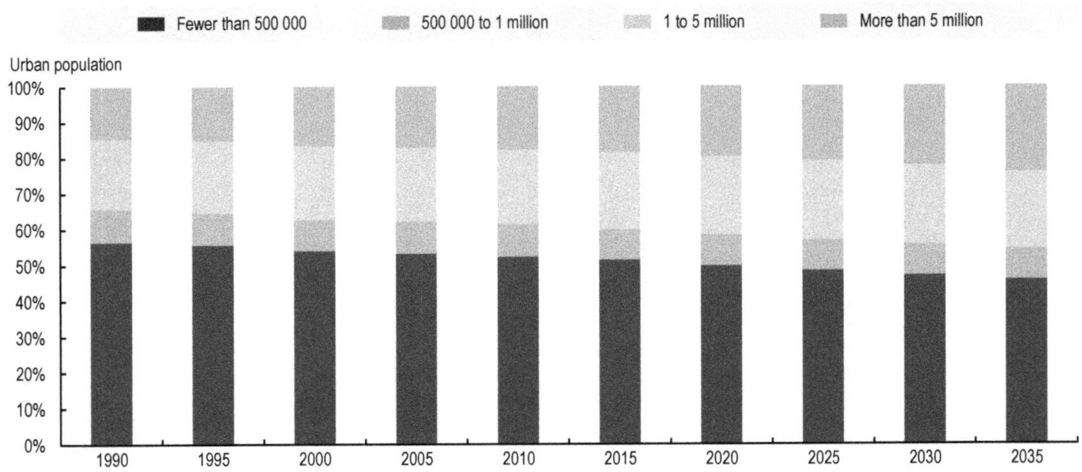

Note: The sample does not consider cities in high-income countries.
Source: UNDESA (2018[3]).

How have intermediary cities grown in the last decades?[3] Figure 2.3 shows average yearly growth rates of both population and built-up land across cities of different sizes between 2000 and 2015. Two important things to note:

- **The population of intermediary cities has not increased fastest across the board**. Cities with a population of less than a million have experienced the highest population growth rates in Western Asia, Northern Africa and Latin America and the Caribbean (left-hand side of Figure 2.3). In contrast, cities with more than 1 million inhabitants grew fastest in Sub-Saharan Africa, South Central Asia and Southeast Asia. However, this does not imply that attention should be limited to larger agglomerations in the latter regions, since intermediary cities have also grown very fast in some of them. In Sub-Saharan Africa, agglomerations with a population of 500 000 to 1 million experienced an average growth rate of 3% over the period. At this growth rate, the population of these cities will double in 25 years. For local authorities this implies a massive mobilisation of resources in other to provide services and infrastructure to twice as many citizens.
- **But intermediary cities are growing fastest in terms of the expansion of built-up areas**. Indeed, except for Western Asia and LAC, cities with fewer than 500 000 inhabitants experienced higher growth rates of built-up land than bigger cities across all regions (right-hand side of Figure 2.3). This is particularly the case for cities with 50 000 to 100 000 inhabitants in Sub-Saharan Africa, where average annual growth during the period reached 1%.

Across the world, urban expansion has become a growing concern. The IPCC (2014[4]) estimates that during the first 30 years of the 21st century, urban land cover will grow faster than what we have witnessed so far, approximately twice as fast as urban population growth. Asia is expected to account for almost half of the growth in global land cover. China and India are expected to account for 55% of the total regional land-cover increase, with China alone accounting for 18% of the total global increase in land cover (IPCC, 2014[4]). Urban expansion is expected to be most rapid in Africa, with almost 600% more urban land cover in 2030 compared to 2000 levels (Seto et al., 2012[5]). As will be highlighted in later sections, uncontrolled urban expansion can have major negative implications in terms of both climate mitigation and climate adaptation, and it particularly poses large risks for rapidly growing small and medium-sized cities.

Figure 2.3. Average growth rate of urban population and built-up land by world region, 2000-15

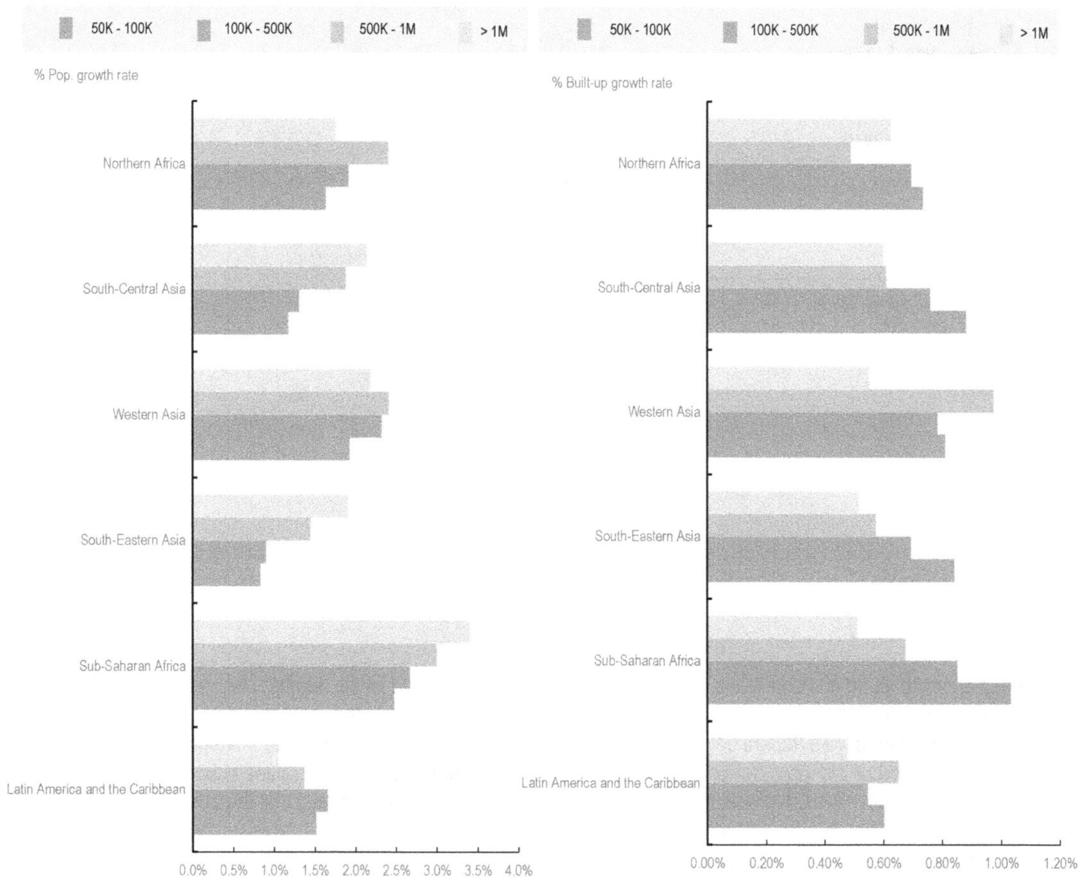

Note: The left-hand graphic shows the yearly average growth rate of city population between 2000 and 2015; the right-hand graphic shows the yearly average growth rate of built-up land. The sample does not include cities in high-income countries.
Source: Authors' computation using GHS Urban Centre Database (2019[6]).

While the previous figures highlight trends across major developing regions, they mask important differences. Figure 1.1 compares the growth rates of population and built-up areas of intermediary and non-intermediary cities in developing countries for the period 2000-15. To account for national differences, both growth rates are expressed as standard deviation from the national mean. In other words, observations close to zero – on either axis – represent cities with growth rates close to the national mean; in contrast, observations with values closer to 3 (or -3) represent cities with growth rates significantly higher (or lower) than the national average. The figure shows high levels of dispersion for growth rates of both population and built-up land. However, in the case of built-up areas, cities with more than 1 million inhabitants show a strong tendency to concentrate below their country average, while cities with fewer than 1 million tend to be more dispersed, surpassing 2 standard deviations. As such, cities with fewer than 1 million inhabitants tend to have high built-up growth rates that are at times paired with high population growth rates and at others with low population growth, in which case cities tend to lose population density.

Figure 2.4. Dispersion of population and built-up growth rates from 2000 to 2015

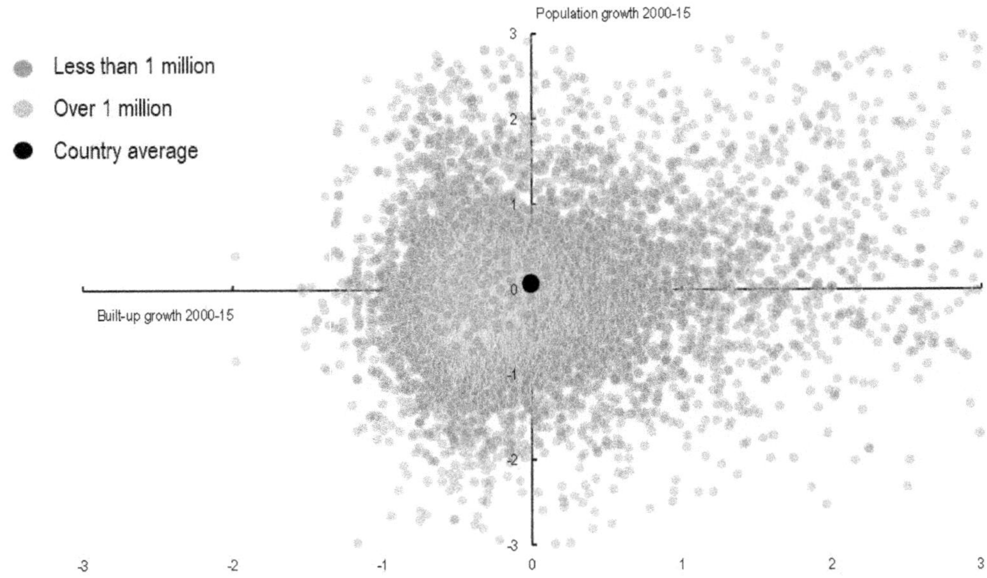

Note: Dispersion of annual built-up and population growth rates (2000-2015), measured as the number of standard deviations away from the national average. Blue dots represent small and medium-sized cities (50K-1M inhabitants) and orange dots represent big cities with more than 1 million inhabitants. The figure shows the annual growth rates for both population (vertical axis) and built-up areas (horizontal axis) for the period 2000-15. Rates are expressed as standard deviations from the country average. As such, lower values indicate that observations are closer to the country mean (the value 0 in both axes, represented by a black dot), while higher values suggest that the observations tend to be more dispersed. The sample does not include cities in high-income countries.
Source: Authors' computation using GHS Urban Centre Database (2019[6]).

Intermediary cities lose density when built-up expansion outpaces population growth

Many small and medium-sizes cities have lost density since 1990 because the rapid expansion of built-up areas has outpaced population growth. Figure 2.5 shows the percentage of cities in developing countries that lost population density during the period 2000-15. This drop in density was most acute in intermediary cities. For instance, around 63% of cities with 50 000 to 100 000 inhabitants lost density over the period, compared to only 31% of cities with more than 1 million inhabitants.

Despite the high heterogeneity of growth patterns in intermediary cities, and once we control for cities and countries' characteristics, small(er) size is associated with decreasing population density, according to results from econometric analysis for the 2000-15 period. Indeed, the odds of density decreasing in cities of 50 000 to 100 000 inhabitants are around 5.4 times higher than in cities with more than 1 million inhabitants (holding all variables constant); almost 3.5 times higher for cities with population of 100 000 to 500 000 inhabitants; and 2.3 higher for cities with population of 500 000 to 1 million inhabitants (Figure 2.6). In contrast, being a coastal city decreases the odds by 40-50%, holding all variables constant.

Figure 2.5. Percentage of cities where density decreased over 2000-15

By city size

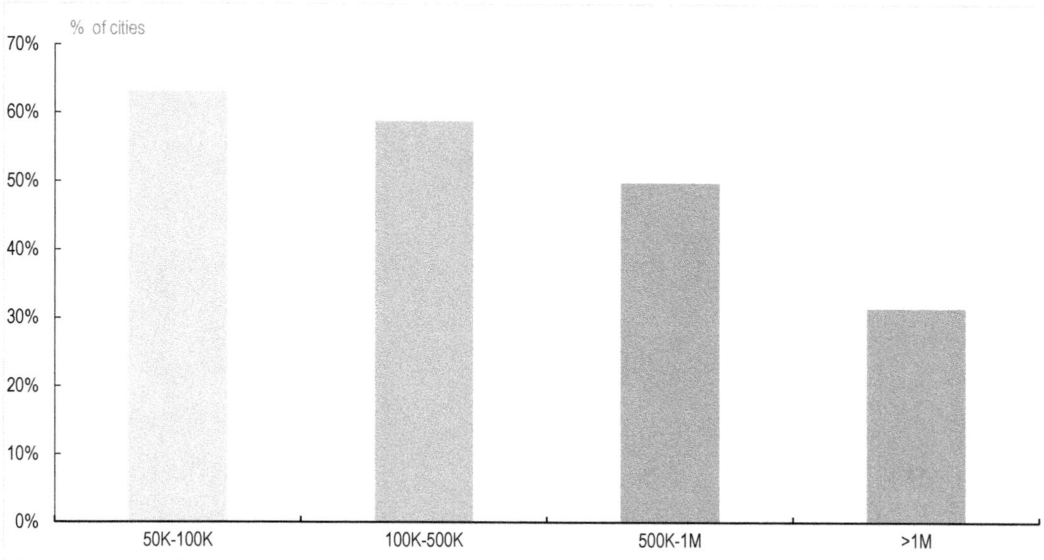

Note: The sample does not include cities in high-income countries.
Source: Authors' computation using GHS Urban Centre Database (2019[6]).

Figure 2.6. Results from logistic regression analysing density decrease

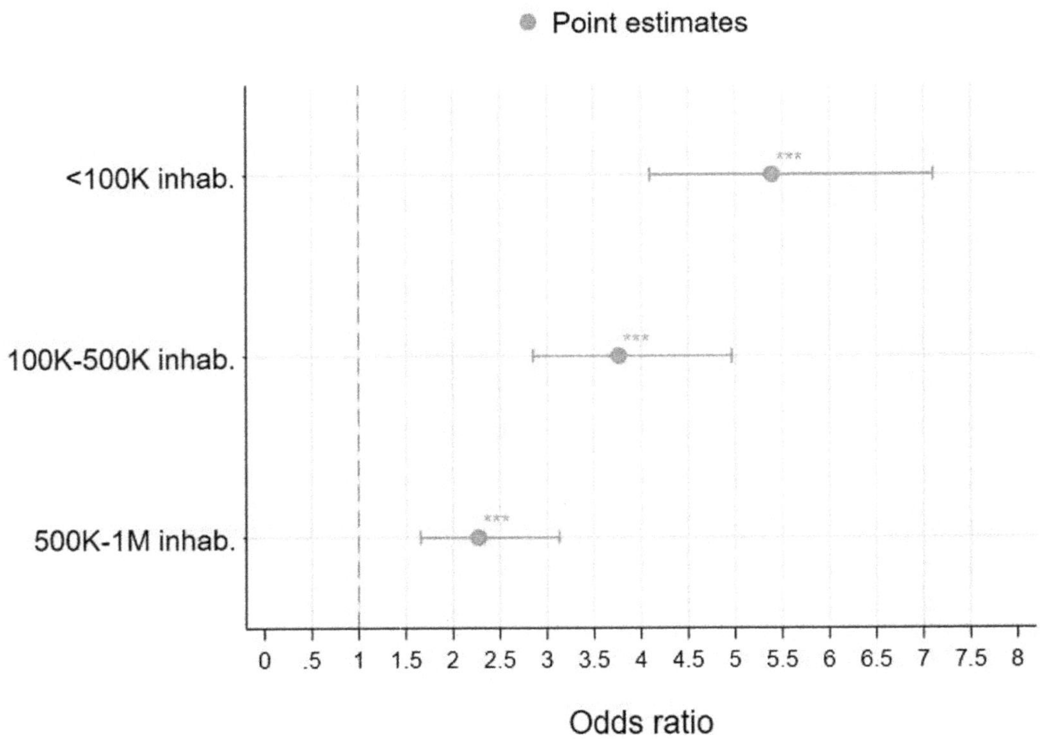

Note: The values in this figure, expressed as odds ratios, represent the odds of a city decreasing in density (versus not decreasing). As such, values higher than one indicate a greater chance of density decreasing, while values lower than one indicate the opposite. The base size for comparison is an urban population of over 1 million. A detailed description of these results is presented in Annex 2.A1, Table 2.A.1. The sample does not include cities in high-income countries.
Source: Estimates using data from the GHS Urban Centre Database (2019[6]).

How cities develop has a major effect on their climate resilience and GHG emissions

Declining population density is strongly associated with urban sprawl. Yet urban sprawl is a complex phenomenon: the term is used inconsistently, which can lead to confusion (Bae and Richardson, 2004[7]; Rubiera-Morollón and Garrido-Yserte, 2020[8]). For a working definition of urban sprawl, this section uses Bae and Richardson (2004[7]). The authors define urban sprawl as "a pattern of land-use in an urban area that exhibits low levels of some combination of eight distinct dimensions: density, continuity, concentration, clustering, centrality, nuclearity, mixed used and proximity". They also link the concept to the notion of automobile dependency.

Sprawling and car-dependent cities can be referred to as high-demand systems with limited scope for a climate-sensitive development model. These systems are difficult to decarbonise and tend to perform poorly in terms of well-being outcomes like health, access to opportunity or safety. They can also lead to high GHG emissions and limit the potential of public policies and investment (e.g., in public transport) to improve such outcomes. Sprawling urban areas are often characterised by single-family dwellings -- the most common type of construction in suburban areas. Single-family dwellings are high-demand in terms of space, consumption of materials and heating, and are often less efficient than the multistorey buildings found in compact areas.

Urban sprawl, with associated declining population density, leads to higher GHG emissions as it tends to transform land use and shape commuting patterns. The expansion of built-up areas implies that there is less land covered by vegetation, and thus less absorption of CO_2 into the soil (UN-HABITAT, 2011[9]). Moreover, land clearing and deforestation for urban expansion lead to CO_2 emissions (Seto et al., 2012[5]). Another study, by Burgalassi and Luzzati (2015[10]), found that urban sprawl in Italy is associated with higher PM2.5 emissions from residential heating and CO_2 emissions from the transport sector. Furthermore, and despite limited evidence, there appears to be a correlation between the form of cities and energy consumption. Residential energy consumption tends to be higher in low-density urban areas, as suburban homes tend to be large and detached, requiring higher energy for heating than urban apartments (Litman, 2014[11]). Similarly, land consumption per capita is higher in low-density urban areas – and by reducing the amount of land available for agriculture, increased land development reduces overall agricultural production (Litman, 2014[11]).

Sprawling cities, along with scattered and single-use development, also mean that people need to travel long distances to meet almost every need (work, school, the grocery store, etc.). In this context, people tend to depend on cars (or other motorised private vehicles) to access places and opportunities, since active and shared modes of transport are no longer a convenient option for them (if an option at all) (OECD, 2021[12]). A sprawled urban system thus encourages, and many times imposes, car-centred mobility, which is a high-demand type of mobility in terms of space, fuel consumption, material demand, emissions and cost, both for individual users and governments. In other words, sprawling low-density cities lead to higher GHG emissions, higher commuting time and energy use, lower public transportation services (OECD, 2018[13]) and higher traffic congestion and air pollution (NCE, 2018[14]).

Sprawling cities with low density also impose higher economic and social costs. They lead to a dispersion of economic activities, which in turn leads to lower accessibility, especially for the poorest and most vulnerable urban dwellers, as space for walking and cycling as well as public transit is reduced (Litman, 2014[11]). Additionally, sprawl increases the cost of public service delivery for local authorities (NCE, 2018[14]), which in practice leads to lower service provision and higher dependency on private transport (OECD, 2018[13]). In fact, urban sprawl is conservatively estimated to account for a loss of 7% in the annual GDP of the United States (NCE, 2018[14]), reflecting a yearly cost of USD 400 billion in reduced public health and fitness and of USD 625 billion in costs borne by commuters (Litman, 2014[11]).[4]

In terms of well-being, evidence suggests a negative correlation between urban sprawl and environmental, economic and social outcomes, including health, housing affordability, access to opportunities, cost-effective public services, resilience and environmental sustainability (OECD, 2021[12]). Sprawling, car-dependent territories significantly constrain the scope of policies for improving well-being, with policy makers sometimes forced to make politically unpalatable trade-offs. For example, in sprawling urban areas where distances to places that people need to reach are long and alternatives to the car are not available or convenient, reducing emissions via policies that discourage car use (e.g., carbon prices) can result in lower quality of life, and thus be politically unattractive, if at all feasible. Box 2.2 describes the underlying factors that led cities in OECD countries to develop in an expansionary manner and the implications of this development on well-being.

Box 2.2. How policy choices fuelled urban sprawl in OECD countries

The drivers underlying urban sprawl have been widely analysed in the literature. They include land value (Pendall, 1999[15]), demographics (e.g. young couples with children seeking affordable housing) , land financialisation (Savini and Aalbers, 2016[16]), rising incomes that allow people to live in bigger homes in low-density areas (Carruthers and Ulfarsson, 2002[17]), decreasing commuting costs (OECD, 2021[12]; Brueckner, 2000[18]) and racial strife (Daniels, 1999). Many these drivers may be perceived as independent, individual preferences. For example, it is often perceived that people choose to live in bigger houses with gardens and to buy a car as soon as their income allows them to.

However, a systemic analysis of urban areas indicates that such choices are not solely the result of personal preferences but are instead largely determined by policy choices, and to a large extent by transport and urban planning policy choices, which are intrinsically linked. For instance, OECD (2021[12]) finds that decades of transport policies focused on mobility and privileging road construction have led to the dynamics of induced demand, urban sprawl and the erosion of sustainable transport modes. Induced demand is the phenomenon by which investments in road expansion to reduce congestion end up increasing congestion because the more roads there are, the more the use of cars becomes attractive, leading more people to choose to drive. The dynamic of urban sprawl in OECD (2021[12]) refers to the phenomenon by which people move further away from cities as road infrastructure allows them to reach places of interest (often concentrated in city centres) within a reasonable time, e.g. 30 minutes by car. The more roads expand, the more this is possible, illustrating how transport policies focused on road construction can incentivise choices leading to scattered and low-density development. In turn, induced demand and urban sprawl lead to the erosion of sustainable modes. As distances increase, active modes such as walking, cycling or micromobility are no longer an option. Moreover, as density decreases and single-use development expands, public transport is also less of an option, as it is difficult to get good service. These modes are, as a result, not competitive vis-à-vis the car.

Combined, these dynamics are at the source of car-dependent and expanded territories. They also determine the reach and effectiveness of public policies, and thus the capacity of authorities to improve people's daily lives sustainably and cost effectively (e.g. the road infrastructure costs of car-dependent and scattered territories can be significantly higher than in more compact areas).

While the policy focus of the last decades has locked numerous countries into high-demand systems with poor well-being outcomes, the analysis above implies that urban development can take a different path and that climate policies can be aligned with other agendas. Understanding the dynamics underlying car dependency and expansionary development is fundamental to identifying which policies foster such vicious cycles and which could instead reverse them and lead to more virtuous cycles.

Developing countries have an enormous opportunity to avoid reproducing the patterns of urban development in Western countries. In this sense, the notion of leapfrogging, which is often limited to refer only to technology transfers from developed to developing countries, can be expanded and applied more holistically.

Low economic development increases the climate vulnerability of intermediary cities

What do we mean by climate vulnerability? Gasper et al. (2011[19]) highlight the nuances between climate vulnerabilities and climate risks. Climate vulnerabilities refer to the aspects or characteristics that render certain groups, individuals or cities vulnerable to climate-induced risks. These often include the socio-economic dynamics of the city, as well as the level of development and infrastructure. Climate risks refer to the likelihood of hazards affecting certain cities or areas due to their geographical location or to overall changes in climate (Gasper et al, 2011[19]).

The main underlying factors contributing to the vulnerability of urban dwellers in less developed regions are linked to the socio-economic dynamics of their cities. Population size and composition, geography, spatial development patterns, economic structure, inequality levels and the extent of informality are determinants of the resilience of urban dwellers to climate risks. In particular, what leads to losses in the economy, lives and livelihoods – and limits the ability of poor households and local communities to respond to and recover from disasters – are low income per capita, weak institutions and low adaptive capacities at household level and across different levels of government (Filho et al., 2019[20]). Most importantly, the availability and quality of early warning systems and effective post-disaster relief are essential for reducing the impact of climate hazards on the most vulnerable groups (Revi et al, 2014[21]). Reduction of climate risks largely depends on local governance capacity, i.e. the level of available human and material resources and technical know-how as well as the planning capability of local governments (see Chapter 4). This differs highly across countries. For instance, countries like Thailand and Bhutan have multilevel governance that makes them more resilient to climate risks than Myanmar, parts of Pakistan and Bangladesh, which are more vulnerable due to limited governance capacity (Busby et al., 2018[22]).

Climate change acts as a "threat multiplier". It increases cities' socio-economic vulnerabilities, such as income inequality, resource depletion and poverty. Other environmental problems, such as air and water pollution, poor waste management and limited sanitation services, are exacerbated by climate change. This is particularly pertinent to cities in developing countries, where a large number of inhabitants live in poor-quality housing and informal settlements, heightening the vulnerability of the urban poor.

Climate change also presents health-related risks that are specific to the urban fabric. A rise in the global mean temperature of more than 1.5°C will intensify the effects of urban heat islands (UHI) as well as urban pollution levels (Mika et al., 2018[23]). It will also cause more frequent and intense heat waves in cities. A global mean temperature increase of 1.5°C will double the number of large cities experiencing heat stress by 2050, exposing approximately 350 million additional people to heat waves (Hoegh-Guldberg et al., 2018[24]; Ebi et al., 2018[25]). Inevitably, at 2°C warming there will be a stronger rise in heat-wave frequency and intensity (Mika et al., 2018[23]). By 2050, such a rise in global temperatures would leave more than 1.6 billion urban dwellers living in 970 cities – 45% of the global urban population – exposed to heat waves (UCCRN, 2018[26]). [5]

Infrastructure and service provision will be affected by climate change. As centres of economic activity, cities are highly dependent on complex networks of transportation, communication and information. Moreover, cities are hubs for the provision of social infrastructure such as health, education and administrative services to urban and surrounding rural dwellers. Public services and economic activities are interdependent and linked through various and complex networks, which makes them particularly vulnerable to climate-induced disruptions. Weather shocks can cause serious physical damage that disrupts both urban and rural economies (OECD, 2010[27]). For instance, floods can cause shortages in energy supply and damage to roads, transportation systems and water treatment centres. These disruptions affect not only the population but also key industries. In 2004, damage resulting from the flooding that hit Dhaka, the capital of Bangladesh, affected more than 681 garment factories and caused losses estimated at USD 9.1 billion. Similarly, floods in Dhaka in 1998 caused USD 30 million USD in losses for large firms and USD 36 million for small and medium-sized firms (Gasper et al, 2011[19]). Damage from weather shocks also affects rural areas surrounding cities since these climate events disrupt agricultural value chains and interrupt the provision basic services, which in turn reduces agricultural productivity and can lead to food insecurity and a decrease in rural income (Revi et al, 2014[21]).

Cities in Asia and Africa will be particularly affected by climate change

Cities in Asia and Africa are among the most vulnerable to climate change. According to the Maplecroft Climate Change Vulnerability Index, 95% of the total 234 cities identified in 2018 as facing extreme climate risks were located in Asia and Africa. In Africa, these cities included capitals such as Kampala (Uganda) and Addis Ababa (Ethiopia), as well as cities that serve as commercial hubs like Lagos (Nigeria) (Marplecroft, 2018[28]). Cities across Asia face different types of risks, depending on their geography and the capacity of national and local institutions. Cities located in low-elevation areas such as Myanmar, Bangladesh and northwest and southeast India are particularly exposed to cyclones and flooding, while cities in other parts of Asia – like northern Pakistan, Thailand, Sri Lanka and Cambodia – face water shortages and irregular precipitation (Busby et al., 2018[22]).

Similarly, climate risks differ in Africa according to the geographic location of cities. For example, precipitation is projected to increase in cities in eastern and western Africa, while cities located in coastal areas or along rivers will face increased flooding. This was the case for Maputo[6] (Mozambique), where floods in 2019 caused 45 deaths (Cambaza et al., 2019[29]), or Bamenda (Cameroon) where 25% of the city's 250 000 residents live in flood-prone areas (Tume et al., 2019[30]). Cities in western, eastern and northern Africa also face a high risk of more frequent and more intense heat waves. A study by Rohat et al. (2019[31]), assessing more than 150 large cities across 43 African countries, projects that by the end of the 21st century (2090) the number of people facing dangerous heat conditions will increase 20 to 50 fold compared to 2019 levels (Rohat et al., 2019[31]). North African cities will face increasing desertification and a rise in average temperatures of 1.5°C to 3°C by 2060 (Rohat et al., 2019[31]). Rising sea levels will affect other cities, such as Mombasa (Kenya), which is projected to lose 17% of its land area due to a sea-level rise of 0.3 metre (Okaka and Odhiambo, 2019[32]).

Inadequate infrastructure and low governance capacity increase climate vulnerability

The socio-economic and physical dynamics that shape intermediary cities render them disproportionally vulnerable to climate change. One factor affecting intermediary cities in emerging regions is the rapid expansion of both population and built-up land. In terms of the vulnerability of cities to climate change, Birkmann (2016[33]) notes that the rate of population growth matters more than the size of cities. Fast urban growth tends to outpace the capacity of local authorities to provide public goods and services to city dwellers (Birkmann, 2016[33]). Inadequate urban planning and land management in rapidly expanding intermediary cities also contributes to their vulnerability. Rapid expansion without proper planning leads to sprawl and peri-urbanisation characterised by high levels of inequality and spatial segregation, a prevalence of informal settlements with low or no access to basic services, and environmental degradation (Roberts et al., 2016[34]). This disproportionally exposes intermediary cities to the higher mortality rates associated with weather shocks and to loss of income and livelihoods, while weakening the ability of local authorities to recover from climate disasters.

The frequently weak institutional capacity of intermediary cities further contributes to their vulnerability to climate change. Inadequate decentralisation is one of the main constraints affecting local governments' institutional capacities. Paterson et al. (2017[35]) argue that the large shift of responsibilities from central governments towards local authorities that is entailed in decentralisation has often not been complemented with adequate financial and human capacity, so that relevant decision-making power remains highly centralised at the national level. Local governments are left with insufficient political power, as well as limited financial and human capacities to manage growing urban demands (Paterson et al., 2017[35]). This is the case among most small and intermediary cities across emerging regions, where local governments have a very limited base for revenue collection and central governments tend to be reluctant to fund urban development effectively, often for political motives (Satterthwaite, 2016[36]). For instance, in Portland, Jamaica, despite decentralised institutional architecture, the power, expertise and resources for Disaster Risk Management (DRM) still remain concentrated at the national level (Blackburn, 2014[37]). Similarly, in Karonga, Malawi, despite a constitutional requirement for decentralised governance, the absence of local governance since 2005 has caused weak urban planning and adaptation mechanisms for managing climate risks (Manda and Wanda, 2017[38]). In contrast, Argentina, which is one of the most decentralised countries in Latin America (OECD/UCLG, 2016[39]), has had some of the most successful climate actions at city level (see the case of Rosario and Santa Fe, in Chapter 4). However, it is important to highlight that decentralisation in Argentina has been a long and complex process (Chapter 4).

Weak institutional capacities also affect the capacity of intermediary cities to manage and implement climate adaptation and mitigation plans. This creates a risk of trade-offs, with other services that are under the responsibility of local authorities, such as education, health and infrastructure, competing with climate adaptation and mitigation costs for financing and attention.

Low economic development characterising many intermediary cities in developing countries translates into low resilience to climate change. Limited diversification and low income per capita not only increase the vulnerability of urban areas to climate threats but are also key factors for the adaptation and response capacity of cities (Garschagen and Romero-Lankao, 2013[40]). Intermediary cities usually lack the economic and political capital of large cities. Many intermediary cities have lower market access, less economic diversification, less ability to attract private investment and lower employment opportunities than larger cities. Most of the economic activities in intermediary cities, especially in low-income countries, depend on primary sectors, such as agriculture, mining and, to some extent, tourism and light manufacturing (Roberts et al., 2016[34]). These factors affect the resilience of intermediary cities and impact local governments' ability to mobilise resources to cope with and respond to damage resulting from climate-induced disasters (Birkmann, 2016[33]). Additionally, a large share of urban dwellers in intermediary cities are employed in the low-end informal economy, such as construction, street vending, waste management/pickers (Satterthwaite et al., 2020[41]). In this context, climate-induced risks such as flooding, and heat waves can lead to disproportionate loss of livelihood as well as reducing productivity and income.

Unplanned urban expansion with extensive informal settlements increases the vulnerability of inhabitants of intermediary cities to climate risks. High population density and economic activities drive urban land costs upwards, pushing poor urban dwellers to settle on illegal and/or unregulated land. Such settlements have limited safety controls and do not comply with land-use regulations and building standards that can help reduce climate shocks (Satterthwaite et al., 2007[42]). In 2020, approximately 1 billion urban dwellers were living in informal settlements, most of them located in developing countries (Satterthwaite et al., 2020[41]). In other words, these settlements account for one-third of the global urban population (Abunyewah, Gajendran and Maund, 2018[43]).

Urban dwellers in informal settlements are exposed to climate risks due to a series of factors. First, many informal settlements in cities (including in small and medium-sized cities) tend to be located in low-lying and/or river-bank areas that are prone to flooding (Abunyewah, Gajendran and Maund, 2018[43]; John, 2020[44]). Second, most informal settlements lack adequate infrastructure and services, and their poor-quality housing cannot withstand floods, storms and heat waves (Satterthwaite et al., 2020[41]). Third, informal settlements tend to be densely populated with households that are vulnerable due to low economic capabilities (Abunyewah, Gajendran and Maund, 2018[43]). The combination of these factors leaves informal-settlement dwellers ill prepared to cope with the risks brought by climate change. Furthermore, across high-density informal settlements, the line between industrial and residential land use is often blurry. This can cause major safety hazards, for instance through exposure to polluted water and air. This is exacerbated by the fact that these areas often lack space for emergency evacuation, while overcrowded housing complexes can intensify the spread of diseases (Satterthwaite et al., 2007[42]).

High levels of informality and urban inequality also create dual energy-use systems. Urban dwellers in informal settlements, with poor access to infrastructure, energy and electricity, rely on traditional wood-based biomass, which can have negative health impacts in addition to leading to higher particulate matter emissions. This further exacerbates social inequalities (IPCC, 2014[4]) and can put additional strain on climate mitigation efforts.

Climate shocks in rural areas create a ripple effect on intermediary cities

Intermediary cities' role as a link between rural and urban areas exposes them to the compounded effects of climate change. This section provides a brief explanation of how the intermediation role characterising these agglomerations increases the risk of climate shocks. (Due to the complexity of these processes, interested readers are invited to turn to Chapter 3, which expands this topic and provides a detailed analysis of the channels connecting climate change, rural areas and intermediary cities.)

Intermediary cities are key actors in the rural-urban interface, especially in developing countries. The rural-urban interface encompasses rural areas, small towns and intermediary cities of various sizes, and is an important area that accounts for a large share of both the global population (Berdegué et al, 2014[45]) and smallholder farmers (FAO, 2017[46]). Intermediary cities act as nodes that connect rural, urban and metropolitan areas. They play a large role in helping to reduce rural and urban poverty by acting as hubs for the provision of goods and services and for access to local and international markets, and by facilitating circular migration and enabling the diversification of rural and urban income and livelihoods (Berdegué et al, 2014[45])

Intermediary cities are highly reliant on surrounding rural areas. They rely on the supply of agricultural goods, rural labour and rural consumers for their economic development and the adequate functioning of food systems (Hussein and Suttie, 2016[47]). Similarly, rural areas are highly dependent on intermediary cities for accessing basic public goods and services, circular migration and livelihood diversification (Christiaensen and Todo, 2013[48]; Turok, 2018[49]). For instance, Tacoli and Vorley (2016[50]) highlight the importance of urban areas for rural development across mountain areas of Tanzania, where an increasing number of farmers are switching the production of cash crops to perishable agricultural goods for surrounding urban markets. This study also shows that rural farmers rely on urban areas for diversifying their incomes through activities such as wage earning and contract farming (Tacoli and Vorley, 2016[50]). As such, negative shocks associated with climate change have major implications for the social and economic networks that link urban and rural territories.

Rural livelihoods tend to be particularly threatened by climate variations. Climate change directly affects the incomes and assets of rural households, especially smallholder producers and farmers, who depend on rain for agricultural production and have lower adaptive capacities. Climate change also depletes the assets of rural households and their ability to invest and build adaptive capacities (Dasgupta et al., 2014[51]; FAO, 2016[52]). Moreover, reduced access to urban services in nearby towns and intermediary cities disrupts the economic systems that connect rural and urban areas.

The effects of global warming risk disrupting the channels linking intermediary cities and surrounding rural areas, and in particular **food systems** and **internal migration**. Climate change is increasingly disrupting agricultural supply chains, harming infrastructure, livelihoods, remittances and demand for rural products. In parallel, climate change can lead to changes in the pattern and scale of rural-to-urban migration. The following sections give a brief overview of the intricate ways in which climate change can negatively affect food systems, change the scale of migration and create a ripple effect on intermediary cities.

Climate change poses multiple risks to food systems across the rural-urban interface

Food systems are highly vulnerable to disruptions caused by climate change. A food system is the set of activities, actors and interactions that take place along food value chains, from supply of production inputs, agricultural crops and livestock to all post-production activities including processing, transportation, wholesaling and preparation for consumption and disposal. Food systems also include policy and regulatory frameworks around the food economy (IFPRI, 2020[53]). Climate change will affect value chains across food systems, including multiple elements of food production (FAO, 2016[52]).

Climate shocks affecting agricultural production are particularly disruptive for food systems. Evidence increasingly shows that agricultural productivity is reduced by the negative impact of climate change on water resources, soil quality and rural infrastructure (Nyahunda, Tirivangasi and Tirivangasi, 2019[54]), with changes in precipitation and temperature patterns expected to reduce crop yields. Water stress will be the main challenge, with lower soil fertility increasing the impact. Indeed, soil degradation is one of the main channels through which climate change will affect agricultural production. Variations in temperature and moisture, as well as increasing CO_2 levels, are affecting soil and its fertility (Pareek, 2017[55]). Higher temperatures in arid and semi-arid regions will lead to soil salinisation due to a loss in underground water resources (Maharjan and Joshi, 2012[56]). Other regions will be confronted with soil erosion resulting from excessive precipitation and floods, with reduced soil quality and fertility leading to decreasing crop yields (OECD, 2014[57]). Estimates show that global yields of wheat and maize fell by 5.5% and 3.8%, respectively, between 1980 and 2008, compared to a stable climate scenario (Lobell et al., 2011[58]).

Climate change will also affect non-food crops and can lead to significant economic losses in rural and urban areas. Cash crops such as tea, coffee, and cocoa account for a significant share of agricultural production. They are the main source of income for millions of small producers across Africa, Asia and Latin America who are already experiencing yield losses and are forced to carry out agricultural diversification (Dasgupta et al., 2014[51]). In Uganda, for example, climate change is threatening coffee production with extinction within the next 30 to 70 years (Parker et al., 2019[59]). Similarly, in Nicaragua, one of the poorest countries in Central America, cash crops including coffee, maize and beans are particularly vulnerable to climate change (Parker et al., 2019[59]). Rising temperatures will have varying implications on Nicaragua's agricultural production. For example, 68% of the total land area used for bean production is vulnerable to temperatures rising above 25°C by 2030. Further, rising temperatures may force farmers to switch production to new types of crops that may be vulnerable to changing precipitation and the spread of diseases (World Bank, CIAT and CGIAR, 2015[60]).

Climate shocks are causing damage and losses across food post-production networks while depleting the livelihoods and assets of rural and urban dwellers engaged in the sector. Post-production activities, including storage, processing, transportation and retailing of agricultural goods, are vulnerable to changes in climate. Extreme events can disrupt electricity supply and damage air-conditioning systems, reducing the life span of perishable goods. Similarly, networks of transportation and roads that are essential for the distribution of rural and agricultural goods can be interrupted and damaged by extreme weather events (Vermeulen, Campbell and Ingram, 2012[61]). Disruptions across food systems and networks can cause food insecurity, especially among the most vulnerable urban and rural populations.

Intermediary cities are at the core of the complex networks of food systems and risk bearing the effects of climate-induced disruptions in food supply chains across the rural-urban interface. Their close linkages with and reliance on rural areas imply that negative climate shocks affecting rural livelihoods will affect intermediary cities, too. First, intermediary cities in developing countries tend to rely on primary sectors (Berdegué et al, 2014[45]), with climate effects on rural economies potentially leading to significant economic losses in intermediary cities. Second, losses in rural production can increase the risk of food insecurity across these cities (Reardon and Zilberman, 2018[62]). Third, climate-induced disruptions in the rural-urban interface can limit the capacity of urban dwellers to diversify their livelihoods and incomes across rural and urban areas. Indeed, as will be highlighted in Chapter 3, a large share of the inhabitants of small and medium-sized cities conduct part of their livelihood in rural areas as a means of diversifying their income. Climate-induced disruptions and limitations on rural-urban mobility can put these urban dwellers under strain.

Climate change is also disrupting internal migration

The impact of climate change on rural livelihoods is shifting internal migration patterns between rural and urban areas. As will be discussed in Chapter 3, internal migration remains an important driver of urbanisation for many developing regions, and it is a key factor in income diversification strategies, technology diffusion and rural development (Tacoli, C. et al., 2014[63]; Hussein and Suttie, 2016[47]). As certain climate shocks intensify, migration patterns within the rural-urban interface will be disrupted. The latest (conservative) estimates by the World Bank indicate that by 2050 there will be 216 million climate-induced internal migrants across Sub-Saharan Africa, North Africa, South Asia, East Asia and the Pacific, Eastern Europe and Central Asia, and Latin America (Clement et al., 2021[64]). And many developing countries are already being challenged by climate-induced displacement. For instance, tropical cyclone Idai, which hit Mozambique in 2019, caused the displacement of approximately 146 000 people (Podesta, 2019[65]).

Climate change will particularly affect internal migration in regions with high socio-economic vulnerabilities. In Brazil, for instance, internal migration rates are expected to rise by 9.7% between 2041 and 2070 under a low-emission scenario (Oliveira and Pereda, 2020[66]), while in Bangladesh, climate change will increase the number of internal migrants by 3-10 million by 2050 (Hassani-Mahmooei and Parris, 2012[67]). Moreover, climate-induced migration can increase socio-economic and spatial inequalities. For instance, Brazil's Northeast region may lose up to 2.5% of its population;[7] a significant share of this migration flow will move towards the richer southeast regions of the country (Oliveira and Pereda, 2020[66]).

However, the link between climate change and internal migration is a complex and widely debated issue. Although climate-induced migration has received increasing attention from governments and academics, large knowledge gaps remain, primarily due to: high uncertainty about the effects of climate change in these territories; limited empirical evidence on migration rates and patterns (e.g. rural-to-urban and seasonal); and the role of non-climatic or environmental socio-economic factors in shaping migratory decisions (Tacoli, 2011[68]).

Patterns and causes of rural-to-urban migration are highly complex and context specific. Areas that experience sudden climate shocks, such as floods or hurricanes, can experience high out-migration rates as people are forced evacuate and eventually leave. However, in the case of slow climatic changes, it is harder to establish a direct link to the decision to migrate or not. In Ghana, for example, land degradation and declining crop yields have been key determinants for internal migration, yet poverty and low income are also push factors for internal migration (Van der Geest, 2011[69]). Other socio-economic dynamics in developing countries – such as the urbanisation rate, the country's economic base (whether it is industrialised or agriculture-based) and its economic growth rate – have a major role in determining migrants' destinations. For instance, highly urbanised countries in Latin America and the Caribbean, and regions with high economic growth and industrial expansion, tend to have larger rural-to-urban migration flows, while low-income agricultural countries are often characterised by rural-to-rural migration (Tacoli, 2011[68]). In the case of Africa, Henderson et al. (2017[70]) find that climate-driven urbanisation primarily takes place towards towns and cities with an industrial base that can absorb rural labour.

Intermediary cities play an important role in the coping strategies and livelihood diversification plans of rural dwellers. As the effects of climate change intensify many intermediary cities could be confronted with higher migration flows, even though they have limited resources and capacity to meet the needs of their current inhabitants. Rural migrants make up a disproportionate share of the urban poor and tend to live in vulnerable conditions, including working in informal settings, with low income and limited access to public services (Tacoli, C. et al., 2015[71]). As such, they could be further exposed to the climate threats that affect intermediary cities. There are different ways in which local authorities can reduce the vulnerability of rural migrants, such as effective urban planning and increased financing and investment in infrastructure and local government capacity (Tacoli, C. et al., 2015[71]).

How does climate change affect intermediary cities?

The increasing concentration of GHG has a direct effect on global temperatures. Temperatures have been rising each decade since the 1980s (IPCC, 2014[72]). Figure 2.7 shows global temperature anomalies between 1880 and 2019. Each anomaly represents the difference between the temperature registered in a given month and the average monthly temperatures between 1901 and 2000. Since 1980, practically all anomalies have been positive, i.e. global temperatures have been higher than the 20th century average. Moreover, anomalies after the 1970s show a positive trend, reaching an increase of up to 1.1°C by 2019. In fact, 2019 was the second warmest year ever recorded, after 2016.

Figure 2.7. Global land and ocean temperature anomalies

Monthly deviations from the 1901-2000 average

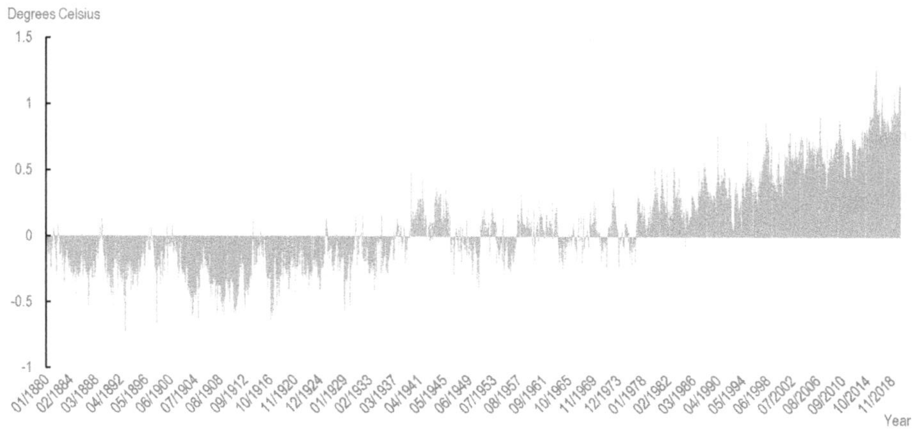

Source: NOAA National Center for Environmental information, Climate at a Glance: Global Time Series (2020[73]).

Rising global temperatures will have a series of detrimental effects on global ecosystems. In 2018, the IPCC's Special Report on Global Warming warned that exceeding 1.5°C above pre-industrial levels by 2100 would lead to high uncertainty on possible climate scenarios and large risks to humanity. Box 2.3 and Box 2.4 highlight some of the most critical effects of climate change on livelihoods and human well-being.

Despite increasing awareness about climate change, current efforts do not seem enough to limit the rise in global temperatures to 1.5°C before the end of the century. Five years after the Paris Agreement, global GHG emissions continue to increase. The IPCC's Sixth Assessment brings forward the notion of "code red for humanity" as the planet reaches the brink of a tipping point that will lead to irreversible changes (IPCC, 2021[1]). The report highlights that unless deep measures to reduce CO_2 and other GHG emissions are taken now, the global temperature is projected to exceed the 1.5°C threshold by the early 2040s, i.e. ten years ahead of the projections of the IPCC special report published in 2018. The report notes that the atmospheric concentration of CO_2 is higher than it has been in at least 2 million years; that the global warming experienced between 1970 and 2020 is the fastest in the last 2000 years; and that sea-level rise has been faster since 1900 than in any period in the last 3000 years.

It is highly likely that human activities are the main contributors to global warming. Human activities account for approximately 1.0°C of the increase in temperatures since 1850-1900. The rise in temperatures has contributed to: *a)* more frequent and extreme land heat waves; *b)* doubling the number of marine heat waves; *c)* heavy precipitation; *d)* ecological and agricultural droughts; and *e)* increased sea-level rise, among other changes (IPCC, 2021[1]).

Global temperatures are expected to continue rising during the 21st century. The IPCC projects global warming based on five emissions scenarios for three periods of the 21st century: near-term (2021-40), mid-term (2040-60), and long term (2081-2100). Average surface temperatures from 1850-1900 are used for comparison for each of these periods. Table 2.1 shows projected global temperatures based on the five scenarios. Across all the scenarios, global surface temperatures are projected to rise, at least until the mid-21st century. Moreover, in most of the scenarios, global temperatures are expected to exceed the 1.5°C threshold in the medium and long term. These estimates project higher long-term temperatures than the previous assessment, carried out in 2014 (IPCC, 2021[1]).

Table 2.1. Emissions scenarios of the Sixth IPCC Assessment

Emissions scenarios	Global temperature in the near term (2021-2040)	Mid term (2041-2060)	Long term (2081-2100)
	Best estimates	Best estimates	Best estimates
Very low emission pathways (SSP1-1.9)	1.5 ° C	1.6 ° C	1.4° C
Very high emissions pathway (SSP5-8.5)	1.6 ° C	2.4 ° C	4.4° C
Lower (relatively) emissions (SSP3-7.0)	1.5 ° C	2.1 ° C	3.6° C
Emissions with strong climate mitigation (SSP2-4.5)	1.5 ° C	2.0 ° C	2.7° C
Emission with limiting warming below 2° C (SSP1-2.6)	1.5 ° C	1.7 ° C	1.8° C

Note: SSP1-1.9: very low emissions pathways with warming below 1.5°C in 2100 and limited temperature rise during 21st century. SSP5-8.5: very high emissions pathways with very high warming; SSP3-7.10: lower emissions than SSP5-8.5 with CO_2 emissions doubling by 2100 compared to current levels; SSP2-4.5 and SSP1-2.6: emissions with stronger climate mitigation and lower GHG emissions; SSP1-2.6 scenario to limit warming to below 2°C.
Source: IPCC (2021[1]).

Compared to previous estimates, these new scenarios suggest a higher risk of disruptive climate events as well as a higher likelihood of irreversible changes across different ecosystems. The risks include:

- **increased and greater regional variability in global precipitation and associated flooding.** Global extreme daily precipitation is projected to intensify by 7% for each increase of 1°C, with increased intensity of tropical cyclones. Precipitation will increase particularly in high-latitude areas, whereas regions located in the subtropics will experience declining precipitation. For instance, heavy precipitation and flooding are projected to further intensify in the equatorial Pacific islands, parts of the monsoon regions, as well as in high latitude regions such as in regions of North America and Europe.
- **increased global mean sea levels throughout the 21st century.** Rising sea levels are projected to affect approximately two-thirds of the global coastline, while the global mean rise will reach two meters by 2100 and five meters by 2150 (under the very high GHG emissions scenario). Sea-level rise will lead to a higher frequency and intensity of flooding, especially in low-lying areas. Extreme climate shocks driven by sea-level rise (i.e. flooding) will occur at least annually in more than half of all tide-gauge locations by 2100 (IPCC, 2021). A rise in ocean temperatures is one of the main factors contributing to sea-level rise. At least 83% of the ocean surface will experience temperature rise throughout the 21st century across all five scenarios, with a projected increase of 2.89°C under high emissions scenarios.
- **less efficient CO_2 absorption by ocean and land carbon sinks.** As emissions increase, land and ocean carbon sinks are projected to absorb an increasing amount of CO_2 emissions. Over time, under the high GHG emissions scenario, there will be a decrease in their efficiency, which will lead to a higher proportion of CO_2 in the atmosphere. Under an intermediate emissions scenario, ocean and land carbon sinks will also gradually decrease their storing capacity by the mid-21st century. Under a very low emission scenario, ocean and land carbon sinks will absorb less carbon but this will be due to the declining presence of CO_2 in the atmosphere.

Box 2.3. How climate change is affecting livelihoods and human well-being

Extreme events are disrupting our livelihoods and negatively impacting economic development. Over the next decades, heat waves are expected to increase in terms of both intensity and frequency, while there will be less occurrence of extreme cold weather (IPCC, 2014[72]). These extreme weather events cause large human and economic losses. Between 2015 and 2019, heat waves were the most frequent and deadliest hazards (WMO, 2019[74]). Similarly, cyclones, storms and floods have caused significant economic losses during the last years. For instance, Hurricane Harvey, which struck Texas and Louisiana in 2017, led to an economic loss of more than USD 125 billion (WMO, 2019[74]).

Climate change is projected to cause large economic losses

The world will face significant economic losses unless substantial mitigation actions are taken to meet the 2050 net-zero emissions target set by Paris Agreement. Recent estimates by the Swiss Re Institute (2021[75]) project that under current global temperature trajectories and stated mitigation pledges,[8] global temperatures would reach 2.0-2.6°C by 2050, and global GDP will decline by 11%-14%, compared to a scenario of no climate change. Even meeting the Paris Target by mid-century would lead to GDP loss of 4.2%. Under a more severe temperature increase scenario of 3.2°C by 2050, global GDP is set to decline by 18% (Swiss Re Institute, 2021[75]). The economic losses will affect all regions but will be most severe in developing countries in Latin America, Asia and Africa. For instance, a 2°C increase in temperatures by 2050 would lead to a loss in GDP of 11% in Latin America, 14% in the Middle East and Africa, and 15% in Asia, compared to a GDP loss of 7.6% in OECD countries (Swiss Re Institute, 2021[75]). The IPCC's special report on 1.5°C also warned of global economic losses, although with lower estimates. According to the IPCC, a global temperature rise to 3.6°C by 2100 under a no-mitigation scenario will lead to a total global GDP loss of 2.6%, compared with a GDP loss of 0.3% at 1.5°C and 0.5% at 2°C (Hoegh-Guldberg et al., 2018[24]).

Countries and regions with higher levels of social vulnerability are predisposed to higher losses. Baarsch et al. (2020[76]) estimate that African countries have already sustained economic losses of 10%-15% of GDP due to climate change between 1986 and 2015. Countries in East and West Africa suffered the highest impact due to their high reliance on the agriculture sector and limited adaptation systems, the study reports. The countries least affected were those with more diversified economies, a higher natural resource endowment or a larger share of the service sector. Indeed, climate shocks seem to have deeper effects on countries highly reliant on agriculture following a productivity loss. Declining yields have a major impact on food prices, affecting the well-being of rural and urban households as well as the terms of trade at country and global level (Lobell et al., 2011[58]; Knox et al., 2012[77]; Sultan and Gaetani, 2016[78]; Hertel et al., 2010[79]). Countries that are net food exporters will benefit from higher commodity prices, while the terms of trade of net importer countries will deteriorate. Similarly, households that are net agricultural producers would tend to benefit from higher prices, while poverty among net consumer households will worsen (Hertel et al., 2010[79]).

Climate change imposes large economic costs in various ways. It causes physical damage to infrastructure and transportation services and increases the demand for public health services (IPCC, 2014[72]). Climate change also disrupts production factors, such as capital stock (e.g. factories and production centres) and productivity, including the capacity of factories to operate, as well as the use of roads and other infrastructure networks. Climate shocks directly affect certain sectors, such as agriculture, and indirectly affect less climate-sensitive sectors such as manufacturing (Lecocq and Zmarak, 2007[80]). For instance, damage caused by sea-level rise is expected to reduce Viet Nam's economic growth prospects by 2050, mainly due to the degradation of infrastructure and agricultural yields (Arndt et al, 2015[81]).

Climate change will also lead to losses in labour productivity and working hours. Heat stress reduces labour productivity, as it negatively affects workers' physical and cognitive capacity. According to the ILO (2019[82]), provided that global temperatures do not rise by more than 1.5°C by 2100, there will be a 2.2% loss in total working hours by 2030. This corresponds to a total global loss of 80 million full-time jobs and estimated economic losses of USD 2 400 billion by 2030. The subregions of Western Africa and Southern Asia will be particularly impacted by heat-stress-induced economic losses, with 43 million and 9 million full-time job losses, respectively, by 2030 (ILO, 2019[82]). A rise in temperatures will especially affect outdoor and physically difficult labour. Knittel et al. (2020[83]) find that within Europe, countries in the Mediterranean region, such as Italy, Malta and Spain, will be the most impacted by a reduction in work ability or labour productivity. Other regions, such as Southeast Asia, India and oil exporting countries, will also experience a severe reduction in labour productivity (Knittel et al., 2020[83]).

Box 2.4. Climate change will cause severe health risks and increase in mortality

Climate change presents a series of health risks, especially to vulnerable populations in low-income countries. Extreme weather events such as heat waves, droughts, increased air and water pollution, and changes in precipitation pose direct and indirect health risks (Berry et al., 2018[84]). Watts et al. (2018[85]) find that intense heat waves affected 125 million adults between 2000 and 2016. Indirect effects take place through changes in ecosystems caused by climate change (Watts et al., 2015[86]). These include increased air and water pollution, which can lead to an increase in the spread of vector-borne diseases, such as dengue. Since 1950, the spread of vector-borne diseases has increased by 9.4% (Watts et al., 2018[85]). In 2019 the number of reported cases of dengue in Central and Latin America alone reached 2.8 million, with 1 250 deaths in the region. Between August and October 2019, countries including Brazil, Mexico, Colombia, Nicaragua, Philippines, Thailand and Malaysia accounted for 85% of the total 1.05 million dengue cases reported (WMO, 2019[74]). Other indirect effects include health risks caused by changes in crop nutrient values, food security and respiratory diseases. Health risks caused by water scarcity are on the rise, despite not being accounted for in current estimates. Moreover, health risks caused by climate change vary based on socio-economic conditions, social factors and social norms such as gender, etc. (Watts et al., 2015[86]).

Extreme events are increasing mortality rates around the world. Between 1995 and 2015, extreme temperatures were the cause of 27% of total weather-related deaths; 90% of them were caused by heat waves, while almost 92% of heat-related deaths took place in high-income countries, especially in Europe (UNISDR, 2016[87]). According to WHO estimations (2014[88])[9], under a base-case scenario climate change is expected to cause 250 000 additional deaths per year between 2030 and 2050. The study finds that the highest mortality rates by 2030 will be in Sub-Saharan Africa, while by 2050 South Asia will be the most affected region (WHO, 2014[88]). However, estimates on climate-induced mortality might be underestimating death rates, especially when other indirect causes, such as poverty, hunger, malnutrition and climate-induced conflicts are taken into account (Parncutt, 2019[89]).

Although climate change is a global phenomenon, emerging and developing countries are disproportionally vulnerable to climate risks. For instance, Revi et al. (2014[21]) note that low- and middle-income countries accounted for 95% of deaths recorded from floods and storms between 2000 and 2013 (Revi et al, 2014[21]). Asia is one the regions most affected by weather-related disasters. Between 1995 and 2015, Asia accounted for 2 495 of the total 6 457 weather-related disasters recorded globally, which affected 3.7 billion people and killed 332 000 persons (UNISDR, 2016[87]). Additionally,

Southeast, Southern and Eastern Asia accounted for 89% of the total 2.74 billion people killed and affected worldwide due to climate-related disasters between 2000 and 2012 (Busby et al., 2018[22])

The effects of climate change on health will put significant pressure on public health sectors, which are already under strain, especially in developing countries. The health implications of climate change come with large financing costs. WHO estimates that annual health care costs associated with climate change will be USD 2-4 billion between 2030 and 2050, and that developing countries with poor health infrastructure will face larger challenges in coping with rising costs (WHO, 2018[90]). Health-care cost estimations vary highly by region as well as the type of climate variabilities and health risks taken into account. The OECD (2016[91]) estimates that the rise in the global health-care cost of outdoor air pollution will range from USD 21 billion to USD 176 billion between 2015 and 2060, while the adaptation cost for malaria and diarrhoea will reach USD 2 billion between 2010 and 2050. A large share of the latter costs will be primarily borne by countries in sub-Saharan Africa (Pandey, 2010[92]).

Heat, drought, floods and rising seas will directly affect cities

The following sections highlight some of the most critical effects of climate change on urban areas. They analyse potential differences among cities of different sizes when it comes to climate shocks and outline key socio-economic characteristics of intermediary cities that shape their vulnerability to climate change.

Cities will be exposed to rising temperatures and more and hotter heat waves

Cities have experienced a higher frequency of heat waves since the mid-20th century, and this trend is expected to increase in the next decades. The built-up land of cities plays a key role in this process, since it absorbs heat, which intensifies both the duration and intensity of heat waves (KFW, 2015[93]). In London, for example, annual number of nocturnal heat waves have increased by four days since the 1950s, with an average increase of heat intensity of 0.1°C (Revi et al, 2014[21]). By 2050, London's nocturnal heat-wave intensity in August is expected to increase by 0.5°C, with a 40% rise in the frequency of heat-wave episodes (Revi et al, 2014[21]; OECD, 2010[27]). Overall, by 2050, heat waves will affect around 970 cities, with a disproportionate number of cities exposed in Asia, Africa and North America (UCCRN, 2018[26]). By 2090, the number of people exposed to heat waves in Eastern African cities, including Kampala (Uganda), Lusaka (Zambia), Blantyre-Limbe (Malawi) and Likasi, Kolwazi and Lubumbashi (DRC) will increase two thousand fold (Rohat et al., 2019[31]).

Extreme heat waves can cause mortality due to heat-related deaths, famine and the spread of infectious and non-infectious diseases. For example, the heat wave in Europe in 2003 claimed 70 000 victims, of whom a significant proportion came from urban areas (OECD, 2010[27]).

Urban heat islands (UHI) make cities particularly vulnerable to increasing temperatures (Rosenzweig et al., 2015[94]). The replacement of natural land cover with pavement and buildings makes cities particularly vulnerable to increasing temperatures. As cities grow, and population and infrastructure density increase, the surrounding environment is altered. This directly affects the capacity of a city to react to the consequences of climate change (Revi et al, 2014[21]). Growing urban areas tend to experience higher temperatures than surrounding places with a lower density (rural areas) and other agglomerations that are less congested (Chapman et al., 2017[95]). The effect of UHI is compounded by cities' economic and industrial activities, as well as by the use of motor vehicles, which produce heat and increase urban temperatures (Ningrum, 2017[96]; World Bank, 2010[97]). The fact that urban centres are made of heat-absorbing materials, such as concrete, with less vegetation and green areas than rural areas, reduces their capacity for natural water retention and their infiltration potential (KFW, 2015[93]).

The combination of UHI and climate change also contributes to air pollution and GHG emissions. Air pollution is one of the most prominent issues facing urban areas across the world. UHI and warmer temperatures increase the concentration of air pollutants, including ozone, acid aerosol and small particulates (OECD, 2010[27]). The fact that emissions in cities have higher concentrations of pollutant particles leads to higher urban pollution intensity (Li et al., 2018[98]). Interactions between UHI and urban air pollution can increase the effects of both on urban areas. Warmer temperatures caused by UHI can disperse and increase the mixing of air pollutants and lead to higher concentrations of pollutants (like PM 10), eventually leading to an increase in longwave radiation (Li et al., 2018[99]). At the same time, an increase in aerosol pollution enhances urban heat islands (Cao et al., 2016[100]).

It is important to note that not just large cities are affected by UHI. As discussed in Box 2.5, intermediary cities in Brazil are already experiencing the effects of UHI despite having limited industrial activity.

Box 2.5. Urban heat islands in medium-sized and small cities in Brazil

While research on UHI is predominantly focused on large cities, the growth of small and medium-sized cities implies that they will also be impacted. Assessing UHI in these urban centres is important due to their rapid population growth and the expansion of built-up land, which implies a reduction in vegetation and absorption of heat into the ground. UHI can present a larger challenge to small and medium-sized cities as they tend to be poorly planned.

A study of three such cities in Brazil – Paranavaí (Paraná), Rancharia (São Paulo) and Presidente Prudente (São Paulo) – highlights changes in nocturnal heat islands. UHI have been detected in the three cities despite their low population density (Paranavaí, 87 316; Rancharia, 25 828; Presidente Prudente, 223 749) and limited industrial activities. The cities, which have different urban forms, are characterised by high temperatures during spring and summer, and milder winds and lower temperatures in winter. UHI were detected to cause increases in temperatures of 2.3°C to 5°C in Paranavaí and 3.5°C to 6°C in Presidente Prudente. UHI in these cities were mainly underpinned by changes in urban land cover and morphology. Areas with higher population density were also associated with a higher intensity of UHI.

Source: Cardoso et al (2017[101]).

Episodes of excessive heat in cities are becoming more common in developing countries. The heat index developed by the US National Weather Service measures the perception of heat when temperature and humidity are combined. When there is a heat index of at least 40.6º C (105º F), people face a danger of heat exhaustion and heat strokes with prolonged exposure and physical activity. Throughout this section, such events are referred as "extreme heat events".

On average, extreme heat events are more frequent in developing countries than in richer economies. In 2016, cities in high-income countries went through an average of four events of excessive heat, while cities in poorer countries had an average of ten events. In developing countries, cities that are characterised by high temperatures[10] are experiencing longer and more frequent extreme heat events. In 2016, cities characterised by low temperatures went through an average of five extreme heat events with an average duration of 5.3 days, while in warmer cities there were on average 12 extreme heat events that lasted 8.8 days. Moreover, the frequency of such events is increasing faster in warmer cities (Figure 2.8). From 1987 to 2016, the frequency of these events grew annually by 0.3% in low-temperature cities and the duration by 0.5%; in high-temperature cities, the frequency grew by 0.7% and the duration by 0.6%.

Figure 2.8. Average frequency and duration of extreme heat events (1987-2016)

Cities in areas historically characterised by high and low temperatures.

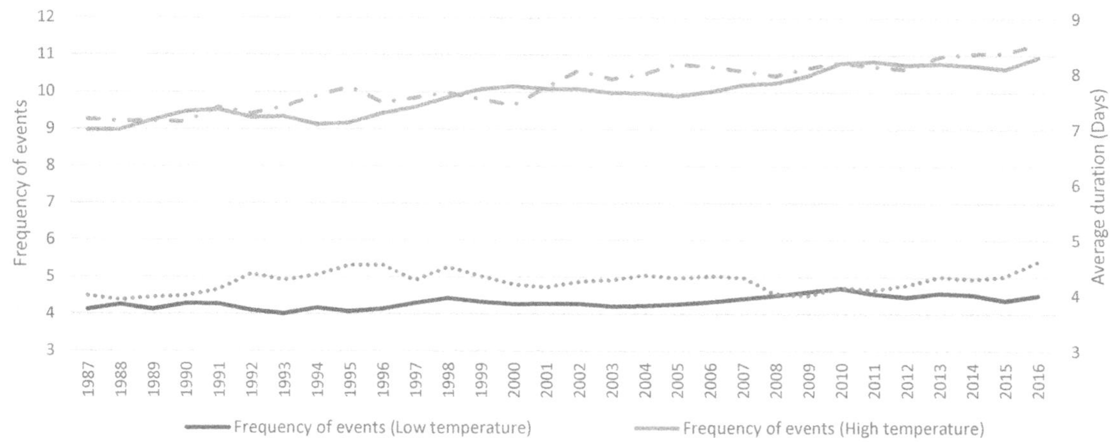

Note: Data expressed as a moving average of the last five years. Frequency and length of events for which the heat index was above 40.6°C. The sample does not include cities in high-income countries.
Source: Author's own calculations using GHS Urban Centre Database (2019[6]) and (Tusholske et al., 2021[102]).

There is an inverse relationship between rising temperatures and GDP, with growing heat stress resulting in a loss of jobs and productivity (ILO, 2019[82]). Garcia-Leon et al. (2021[103]) estimate that economic losses triggered by heat waves in Europe in the years of 2003, 2010, 2015 and 2018 amount to 0.3-0.5% of European GDP, compared to the average loss in GDP between 1981 and 2010. The losses have been larger in heat-prone areas and places where work takes place outdoors. In a study of US counties, Deryugina and Hsiang (2014[104]) find that income per capita declines as temperatures increase: a day with an average temperature of 29°C decreases annual income by 0.065% compared to a day with an average temperature of 15°C. Evidence also suggests that higher temperatures have a stronger impact on developing countries. Dell et al. (2012[105]) find that, on average, a 1°C rise in temperatures in a given year reduces economic growth by 1.3 percentage points, but only in poor countries.

This relationship between GDP and temperatures is also observed across cities of developing countries. Figure 2.9, and the corresponding tables in Annex 2.A1, show the results of an analysis exploring the connection between the frequency of extreme heat events and GDP on cities of different sizes, and differentiates between cities with high and low average temperatures. Results worth highlighting include:

- There is a negative relationship between the number of extreme heat events and GDP at city level across time (after controlling for city characteristics such as population and build-up). However, the strength of this relationship is more acute in cities with low temperatures, i.e. the effect is significantly larger in cities characterised by low temperatures, independently of their size. For instance, a 1% increase in the frequency of these events is associated with a decrease of 0.37% in the GDP of low-temperature cities of 50 000 to 100 000 inhabitants, while for high-temperature cities of the same size the effect is -0.10%. This difference can be seen across cities of all sizes.
- The largest effect of extreme heat events is observed in cities that are both large and characterised by low temperatures. In cities with low temperatures and more than 1 million inhabitants, a 1% increase in the frequency of extreme events is associated, on average, with a decrease of 0.65% in GDP. From 1987 to 2016, the frequency of extreme heat events in low-temperature cities with more

than 1 million inhabitants grew annually by 0.1%, which would translate into an average annual drop in GDP of 0.065%.

- In high-temperature cities, the negative effect of extreme heat events on GDP is observed only in cities with fewer than 500 000 inhabitants. Moreover, the impact is more acute in cities with a population of 50 000 to 100 000 than in cities with a population of 100 000 to 500 000. In the former, a 1% increase in the frequency of extreme heat events is associated with a 0.1% drop in GDP, and in the latter with a drop of 0.06%. Given that the frequency of these events in these cities has grown annually by around 0.68%, this would translate into an annual drop in GDP of 0.07% and 0.04%, respectively.

The lower impact on GDP of extreme heat events in high-temperature places can be due to adaptation to heat. First, people in warm places seem to show a higher tolerance to extreme heat. Singh et al. (2018[106]) use Regional Internet Search Frequencies for air conditioning in India as an indicator of thermal discomfort, and find that people living in places with high average temperatures have a higher tolerance of heat. This adaptation or tolerance can be physiological, behavioural of psychological. Second, the fact that extreme heat events are more common in high-temperature places will increase the likelihood of these cities taking active measures to mitigate heat. A review of different articles about heat adaptation shows that, in low- and middle-income countries, the most common extreme heat responses are behavioural or cultural adaptations by individuals and communities, with little institutional involvement (Turek-Hankins et al., 2021[107]). Other factors can be linked to the fact that economic activities taking place in high-temperature cities are already intended for hot weather. For instance, outdoor activities might not take place in the warmest hours of the day, and people performing indoor activities might have ventilation devices already available, such as fans. In high-temperature cities, the larger effect in those with fewer than 500 000 inhabitants can be partly explained by their tighter relationship to rural areas and the primary sector. Agriculture accounted for 83% of global working hours lost to heat stress in 1995, and it is estimated to have accounted for 60% in 2013 (ILO, 2019[82]). This follows from the fact that agricultural work is mostly outdoors and requires a high physical effort that is impaired under heat stress.

Extreme heat events are a threat to a city's economy and the well-being of its citizens regardless of the baseline climate, and the frequency of these events has been growing faster in high-temperature places. In order to offset the consequences of extreme heat events, cities need to take adaptation measures that protect their citizens and economic activities as well as those of surrounding areas. However, adaptation strategies should be planned carefully, as many initiatives that prioritise immediate and short-term climate risk reduction can reduce the opportunity for transformational adaptation. Moreover, maladaptation can lock in the vulnerability of the people that are intended to be protected, while being difficult and costly to change once implemented (Dodman et al., 2022[108]).

Figure 2.9. Effects of extreme heat events on the GDP of cities in developing countries

By city with high/low temperature and by city size

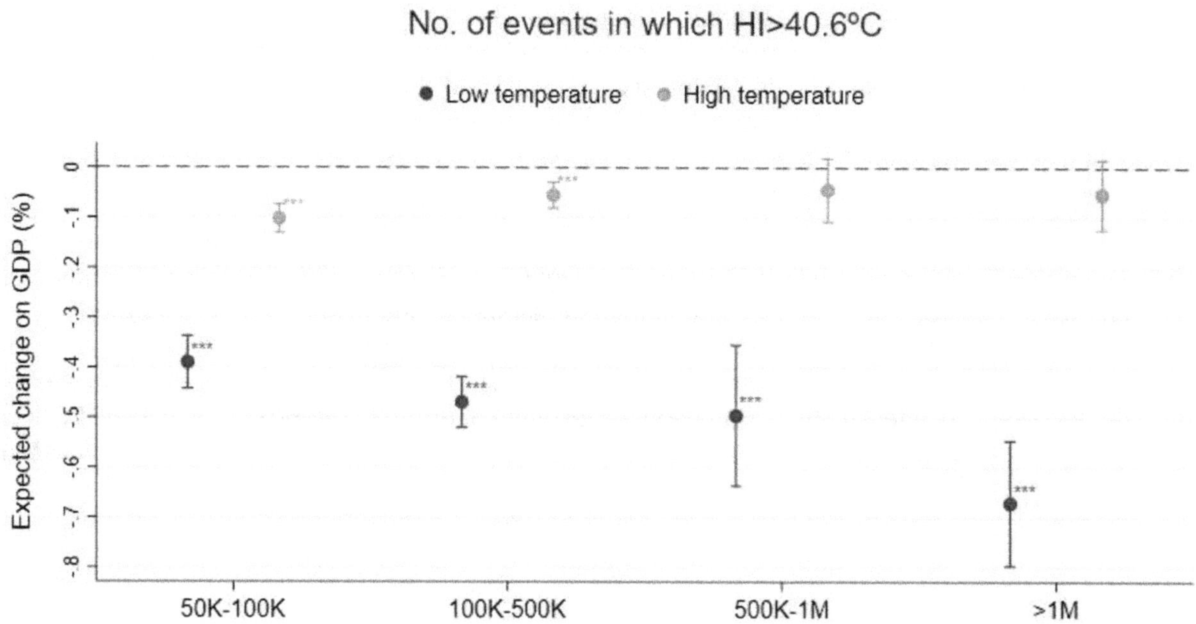

Note: Author's own calculations using GHS Urban Centre Database (2019[6]) and (Tusholske et al., 2021[102]). The sample does not include cities in high-income countries.

Source: Estimates of a panel econometric model regressing the log of GDP on the log of number of days that exceeded a HI>40.6°C, interacted by city size and whether the city is high or low temperature. Other variables included as controls are log of population, log of built up area and log of average temperature (calculated over the last 5 years). Results based on a fixed-effects estimator and standard errors clustered by city. Year fixed effects are included. Data for the periods 1990, 2000 and 2015.

Water stress and droughts will be more frequent in cities of developing countries

Droughts are extreme events in which precipitation levels, soil moisture and groundwater fall below normal for several months or even years. The intensity, frequency and land coverage of droughts are influenced by global climatic patterns, as well as by local factors. For this reason, it is difficult to quantify the extent to which climate change has influenced this phenomenon. However, increasing evidence suggests that, during the last 50 years, anthropogenic emissions have contributed to more frequent warm events. Rising global temperatures since the 1970s have altered atmospheric circulation patterns and contributed to higher evaporation of land moisture, surface water and plant soils, which in turn have intensified droughts overall (Dai, 2011[109]). Moreover, dry soils and diminished plant cover can further reduce rainfall in a dry area, creating positive feedback and making droughts more persistent (C2ES, 2021[110]).

Droughts are increasingly affecting water scarcity in urban areas. Since 2000, 79 of the world's largest urban areas have experienced urban droughts. Urban areas located in arid, semi-arid and humid regions are more susceptible to droughts. Climate change not only exacerbates the frequency and extent of droughts, but is also making it harder for cities to cope with water scarcity since it tends to deplete commonly used water reservoirs such as dams (Zhang et al., 2019[111]). At the same time, while cities are experiencing increasing droughts and higher temperatures, they also face higher demand for water due to rising urbanisation and increasing economic activities (Flörke, Schneider and McDonald, 2018[112]). Global water demand is expected to increase by up to 55% by 2050 (OECD, 2012[113]).

Rising global temperatures combined with fast and unplanned urban growth risk increasing the exposure of cities to water stress and droughts. Growth in urban population implies an increasing demand for water and very often the depletion of natural resources. This will impose increasing strains on local governments seeking to manage declining freshwater resources. Furthermore, urban sprawl exposes vulnerable dwellers to limited access to water or polluted water sources (Gebre and Gebremedhin, 2019[114]). Water stress is already occurring in fast-growing small and medium-sized cities in Nepal and India. In Nepal, the cities of Dharan and Dhulikhel have been experiencing fast population growth, and this coupled with the increasing effects of climate change and urban sprawl has depleted ground water resources (The Straits Times, 2019[115]). In India, the city of Chennai experienced drought with severe water shortages in 2019, leading it to import 2.5 million litres of water (The Straits Times, 2019[115]).[11]

Changes in precipitation patterns are also expected to affect groundwater reserves and recharge rates, putting additional pressure on urban dwellers. Persistent droughts and low precipitation can lead to higher depletion of groundwater reserves due to an increase in demand as well as the extraction of groundwater for irrigation systems, especially in low-income countries (OECD, 2014[57]). In regions like Africa, a decline in groundwater supply can affect 90 million people living in rural areas, while in Asia, changes in water supply are expected to impact food security affecting 60 million people (Dasgupta et al., 2014[51]). Box 2.6 highlights the increasing strains on water resources caused by droughts and increasing water demand in South Africa's Eastern Cape Province.

Box 2.6. The effects of drought on cities in South Africa's Eastern Cape Province

South Africa's Eastern Cape Provinces has a network of intermediary cities and small towns and is also one of the country's regions most vulnerable to drought. The province encompasses medium-sized cities such as Port Elizabeth, Nelson Mandela Bay, Buffalo City and East London (John, 2012[116]). It has been experiencing severe droughts since 2015. In 2019 it was declared a drought-disaster region following severe water shortages across both rural and urban areas (Mahlalela et al., 2020[117]). At the start of 2020, the region continued to face worsening drought conditions, with the area's supply dam at only 6% of its capacity (SABC, 2020[118]). Several urban areas in the region almost ran out of piped water (Mahlalela et al., 2020[117]). Cities in the region such as Port Alfred have faced prolonged water shortages, leading an increasing number of residents to rely on water tanks (SABC, 2020[118]).

Prolonged and intense droughts in Eastern Cape region are causing a series of negative socio-economic impacts. Droughts combined with increasing urbanisation and rising demand for water are affecting the well-being of people in the province (PMG, 2018[119]). The region's principal sources of livelihood, livestock and communal farming, are particularly vulnerable to droughts. A study conducted in 2014 in the region's O.R. Tambo district found that farmers lost or delayed the sale of their livestock due to droughts and often ended up with lower prices. The droughts also caused psychological stress among farmers, higher dependence on government grants, poverty and an overall lack of security (Muyambo, Jordaan and Bahta, 2017[120]).

Water stress and droughts present socio-economic and welfare losses, especially for urban dwellers. By 2050, more than 650 million urban dwellers living across 500 cities will face declining availability of fresh water, with a projected reduction in streamflow of more than 10% compared to current levels (UCCRN and C40, 2018[121]). Current estimates suggest that one in four cities faces water stress and that this trend will continue to increase (McDonald et al., 2014[122]).

Droughts and water stress cause health and economic risks, especially in cities of low and middle-income countries. They can cause public health issues such as diarrhoeal diseases, especially among children, and can lead to the faster spread of diseases, especially in densely populated areas with low water and sanitation services (Ashraf et al, 2016[123]). Droughts can also cause food insecurity (Kareem et al., 2020[124]), and are associated with economic and welfare loss. A study of 78 large Latin American cities between 2005 and 2014 concluded that droughts lead to a decline in employment and number of working hours, as well as negatively impacting informal employment (Desbureaux and Rodella, 2019[125]). The economic losses are attributed in particular to the negative effects of droughts on electricity supply, as hydropower is the main source of electricity in Latin America (Desbureaux and Rodella, 2019[125]).

Cities of different sizes face different exposure to flooding and storm surges

Flooding is one of the most prominent climate shocks affecting urban areas. Climate change is associated with urban flooding through three main channels: *a)* floods caused by increasing sea levels; *b)* floods from overflowing rivers and glacial melting; and *c)* floods caused by prolonged precipitation or storm surges, which result from an abnormal rise of water generated by a storm affecting coastal areas (Satterthwaite et al., 2007[42]). Flooding poses serious risks to a significant proportion of the urban population worldwide. In particular, floods are expected to increase in Asia, Africa and Latin America (UN-HABITAT, 2011[9]).

A larger share of the population in intermediary cities than in large cities is potentially exposed to riverine floods and storm surges. Figure 1.2 shows the share of cities potentially exposed to storm surges and riverine floods (left), and the share of population potentially exposed to storm surges and built-up areas potentially exposed to riverine floods (right), by city size in 2015. The figure shows that the share of cities potentially exposed to storms or floods increases with city size – but that the share of population and built-up area potentially exposed decreases with city size. For instance, only 4% of the cities in the smallest group were potentially exposed to storm surges, while almost 90% of their population was potentially exposed to this type of climate shock. In contrast, 17% of the cities in the largest group were potentially exposed to storm surges, which concerned 41% of their population. A similar pattern is observed in the case of riverine flooding. In cities with 50 000 to 100 000 inhabitants, 26% of the population and 60% of their built-up areas were potentially exposed to riverine flooding, while in cities with more than 1 million inhabitants, almost half of the population but only 38% of their built-up areas were potentially exposed to riverine floods.

Figure 2.10. Exposure to riverine floods and storm surges, 2015

Share of cities potentially exposed to storm surges and floods (left) and share of population and built-up areas potentially exposed (right)

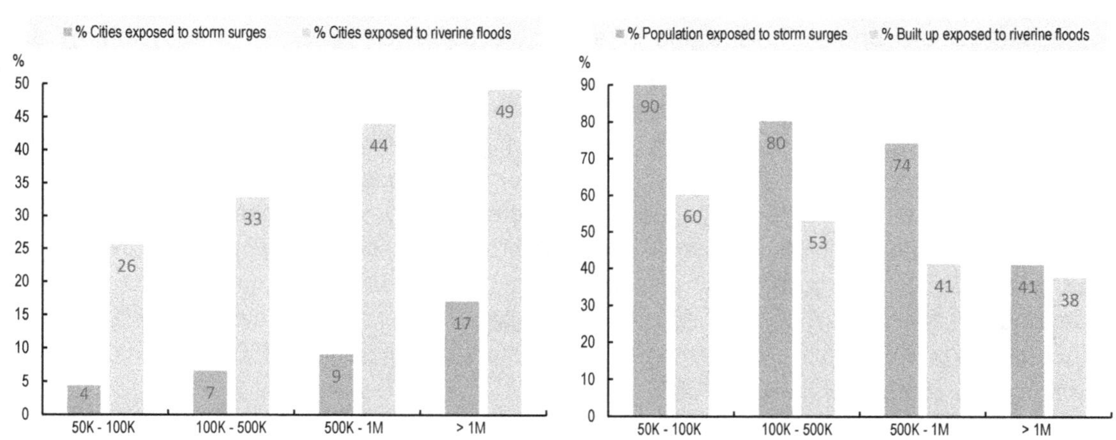

Note: The figure on the right side only considers cities with built-up areas and population potentially exposed to riverine flooding and storm surges. The sample does not include cities in high-income countries.
Source: Authors' own calculations using GHS Urban Centre Database (2019[6]).

As previously discussed, the vulnerability of a city is partly explained by its growing process. In many cities at potential risk of flooding and storms, the built-up area has expanded quickly, leading to a decrease in urban density and a reduction of green areas. This dynamic has previously been found to exacerbate the risks of floods, as was the case with Hurricane Harvey in Houston (Zhang et al., 2018[126]). Moreover, a reduction of green space increases the imperviousness of urban areas (i.e. the ability of urban areas to absorb water), which increases storm-water runoff and damages the urban water-cycle system (Salvadore et al., 2015[127]).

Poor urban planning, inadequate management of land use and lack of effective governance render urban areas susceptible to flooding. Geography and socio-economic factors characterising certain urban areas increase the risk of flooding: proximity to coastal areas, deforestation, concrete, poor-quality infrastructure and housing, and lack of an adequate drainage system (Satterthwaite et al., 2007[42]; Campbell-Lendrum and Corvalán, 2007[128]). Roads and concrete infrastructure prevent the absorption of water from rainfall into the ground. Inadequate drainage paired with poor waste management usually result in clogging, which prevents excess water from being absorbed into the drainage. This is exacerbated by the fact that, in many cities, drainage systems are not built within the urban fabric and the drainage is sometimes obstructed by buildings (Satterthwaite et al., 2007[42]). Box 2.7 uses the example of the low-lying city of Can Tho, Viet Nam, to illustrate how flooding can strain local water resources.

Box 2.7. Flooding in Can Tho, Viet Nam

Can Tho is the fourth largest city in Viet Nam, with around 1.4 million inhabitants. It is located in the Mekong Delta region on the southern bank of the Hau River (Huynh et al, 2020[129]). The city is particularly vulnerable to flooding, typhoons, storms and droughts, and the frequency of flooding has increased in recent years. Between 1900 and 1960, the region experienced four severe floods, while there were 11 between 1961 and 2011. Can Tho city alone experienced severe flooding events in 2011 and 2013. The exposure to extreme flooding is caused by a rise in sea level as well as land subsidence caused by groundwater exploitation (Quang Vinh Ky, 2018[130]).

The rise in flooding in Can Tho has severe implications, especially for the poorest and most vulnerable populations. It has created large economic losses in the agriculture and energy sectors as well as damaging water resources (Huynh et al, 2020[129]). Flooding caused by sea-level rise is particularly straining the city's water resources by increasing the salinity of freshwater resources, leading to a severe shortage of water to meet growing urban demand (Rajesh, 2018[131]).

Floods cause socio-economic losses and infrastructure damage. They can destroy energy and electricity networks, damage and contaminate water-storage services and disrupt transportation and road services (UN-HABITAT, 2011[9]). Most importantly, floods can raise health risks by increasing the likelihood of malaria, dengue and other water-borne diseases. For instance, high humidity, which increases with high temperatures and precipitation, contributes to the spread of the Aedes mosquito and dengue fever. Flooding induced by climate change is therefore expected to lead to an increase in dengue-endemic areas, both globally and in some developing regions, including China. The health problems associated with floods are often compounded by poor urban waste management, which usually results in waste getting into drinkable water (Campbell-Lendrum and Corvalán, 2007[128]). Floods in cities can be an important cause of death. To cite two examples, floods in Mumbai in 2005 caused more than 1 000 deaths, while more than 900 people died in severe flooding in Algiers in 2001 (Satterthwaite et al., 2007[42]).

Coastal cities face a major threat from rising seas

Rising sea levels present high risks to populations living in coastal cities. According to the IPCC's Sixth Assessment, the mean global sea level is expected to rise throughout the 21st century, increasing by 0.28-0.55 meters by 2100 under the very low GHG emissions pathway (IPCC, 2021[1]).[12] Estimates suggest that sea-level rise will affect 824 million people by 2030, and that this number will reach 1.2 billion by 2060 (Church et al., 2013[132]).

Sea level rise is one of the main consequences of increasing ocean heat and rising land temperatures. Global sea levels have been rising since the 20th century, mainly due to thermal expansion but also due to the fast melting of ice sheets in Greenland and Antarctica. These two factors have accounted for 75% of sea-level rise since 1971 (Cubasch et al., 2013[133]). Between 1901 and 1990, the global mean rate of sea-level rise was approximately 1.4 mm per year; between 1970 and 2015, the rate increased to 3.2 mm per year; and during the period 2006-15, it reached 3.6 mm per year (Oppenheimer et al., 2019[134]).

Global sea-level rise particularly threatens low-lying coastal areas and small islands. Low coastal areas in developing countries are particularly vulnerable due to fast population growth and built-up expansion, which have accelerated the anthropogenic subsidence of these areas. Anthropogenic subsidence is expected to outpace other sources of sea-level rise mentioned above.

Under both the 1.5°C and 2°C climate scenarios, and if no further adaptation plans are implemented, 136 coastal cities of more than 1 million inhabitants are at risk of flooding. Many of these urban centres are located in South and Southeast Asia (Hoegh-Guldberg et al., 2018[24]). Jevrejeva et al. (2018[135]) estimate that a rise of 2°C by 2040 means that more than 90% of global coastal lines will experience sea-level rise of above 0.2 m. According to their findings, people living in large coastal cities such as Lagos, Guangzhou and New York are particularly at risk and face limited time to establish adaptation measures.

A large share of the world's urban population lives in close proximity to coastal areas. In 2015, around 22% of city dwellers in developing countries lived in areas below 50 meters of altitude and within 5 kilometres of the coast.[13] This represents more than 635 million people. The share of cities with more than 1 million inhabitants located near the coast is much higher than the share of smaller cities. One-quarter of the big cities of the developing world are located in low-lying coastal areas, with 36% of the population, or 450 million people, residing in these cities (Figure 2.11). A much lower percentage of cities with fewer than 1 million inhabitants is located in these areas, but a sizeable share of the population is still at risk. For instance, 10% of cities with 100 000 to 500 000 inhabitants are located in low-lying coastal areas, and they count 11% of the population of cities of this size, or 107 million people.

Figure 2.11. Share of population living near coastal areas, by city size (2015)

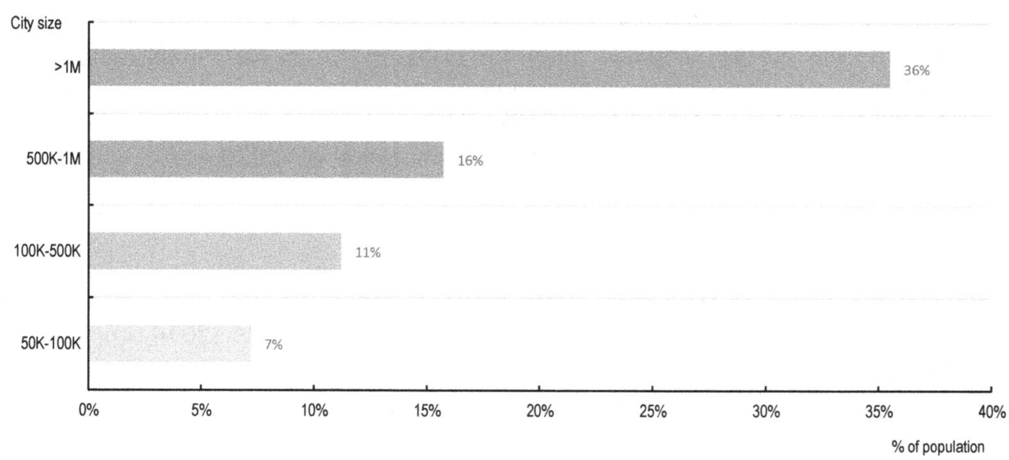

Note: Near coastal areas refers to cities with an average altitude of less than 50 meters above sea level and within 5 kilometres of the coast. The sample does not include cities in high-income countries.
Source: Authors' own calculations using GHS Urban Centre Database (2019[6]).

Globally, more than 570 cities, counting more than 800 million inhabitants, will be exposed to sea-level rise of 0.5 meters by 2050 (UCCRN and C40, 2018[121]). Rising seas will particularly affect Asian cities, as well as cities in deltaic areas (Church et al., 2013[132]). By 2050, 80% of the population affected by sea-level rise will be in Southeast and East Asia; among the most threatened countries in the region are China, India, Bangladesh, Indonesia and Viet Nam (Revi et al, 2014[21]). In Africa, sea-level rise is expected to reach 0.38m by 2080, and the average number of people affected will increase from 1 million per year in 1990 to 25 million by 2050, and potentially 70 million by 2080 (Douglas et al., 2008[136]). Coastal cities with low drainage infrastructure, such as Lagos (Nigeria), Mombasa (Kenya), Mumbai (India) and Dhaka (Bangladesh), will face major challenges in managing floods caused by sea-level rise (Revi et al, 2014[21]).

Low-lying coastal cities play a key role in Asia's urbanisation process and are a key element of the region's export-oriented economy and overall global trade. Increasing urban sprawl and population growth across coastal areas will further exacerbate the regions' vulnerabilities if adequate adaptation strategies are not implemented. Urbanisation causes land subsidence, especially in areas that are already below sea level, such as the Pearl and Mekong river deltas. Some of Asia's largest urban areas, including Bangkok, are already sinking at 4 cm per year, while in Jakarta land is subsiding at 6 cm per year (Fuchs, Conran and Louis, 2011[137]). In Asian cities such Khulna in Bangladesh, sea-level rise is already causing large challenges such loss of assets, damage and contamination of water and sanitation infrastructure (Box 2.8) (KFW, 2015[93]).

Box 2.8. Sea-level rise in Khulna, Bangladesh

Khulna, the third largest city in Bangladesh, is highly vulnerable to sea-level rise. With 663 000 inhabitants, Khulna is one of the country's most important economic centres (Roy et al., 2018[138]) and it hosts a large number of industries, including chemicals, food processing and packaging, and shipbuilding. Its vulnerability to rising seas is due to its geographic position – in the Ganges river delta, inland from the Bay of Bengal – as well as to rapid population growth and high levels of poverty and inequality. The city's infrastructure and water resources are under strain, and GHG emissions are increasing (Zermoglio et al., 2020[139]).

Khulna is vulnerable to a series of climate-induced threats, such as rising temperatures, changes in precipitation and flooding. The effects of sea-level rise and other climate-induced threats are particularly damaging as the city lacks effective urban planning and its dwellers face acute shortages of safe housing, infrastructure, safe drinking water, sewerage and other solid waste management systems (Roy et al., 2018[138]). Sea-level rise is putting additional strains on the city, as causing clogging in the draining systems and leading to contamination of water resources and the spread of water-borne diseases. Sea-level rise is also increasing the salinity levels of the city's groundwater sources, reducing freshwater availability for the growing number of urban dwellers (Zermoglio et al., 2020[139]).

Small and medium-sized cities in coastal areas may benefit economically from their geographic position, but they are increasingly exposed to sea-level rise. As highlighted by Roberts (2014[140]), coastal small and medium-sized cities tend to be economically dynamic, with diversified industries and sought-after housing markets. However, these cities are also disproportionately exposed to storm surges caused by sea-level rise, and tend to be more heavily polluted than inland cities. Because these cities are growing quickly, rising seas could create additional challenges for protecting vulnerable populations living in informal settlements (Roberts, 2014[140]). For example, Beira, Mozambique's second largest city, is highly vulnerable to rising sea levels. In 2019, the city was hit by Cyclone Idai, causing 1 000 deaths and large losses in assets and infrastructure (Williams, 2021[141]).

How are intermediary cities contributing to climate change?

Cities play a key role in national and international efforts to mitigate climate change. Urban areas, which cover merely 2% of the earth's surface, account for 60% of global GHG emissions (UN-Climate Action, 2018[142]), and 70% of total CO_2 emissions (IEA, 2021[143]). The high GHG emissions of cities stem from their high energy demand: indeed, urban areas account for 75% of global energy use (IEA, 2021[143]). This is expected to increase as urban demand for energy and infrastructure continues to grow. By 2050, energy demand from cities is expected to grow by 70% compared to 2013 levels, accounting for 66% of total global energy demand and increasing CO_2 emissions from the energy sector by 50% (IEA, 2016[144]).

Cities contribute to GHG emissions mainly through three gases: carbon dioxide (CO_2), methane (CH_4) and nitrous oxide (N_2O). These gases are the result of energy conversion, landfills and urban solid waste, as well as land conversion (from rural to urban areas). The emissions are also the by-product of energy production for meeting urban domestic demand, for manufacturing construction materials used in urban infrastructure and for the provision of food to city dwellers. Moreover, these emissions interact and may even reinforce each other. For instance, the higher concentration of carbon monoxide (CO) in cities, which is produced by transportation emissions, traps emissions such as CH_4 and prolongs their presence in urban areas (OECD, 2010[27]). Cities also produce additional gases that are specific to economic activities taking place in urban areas, such as ozone (O_3), one of the main GHGs and the third most important pollutant after CO_2 and CH_4, as well as sulphur hexafluoride (SF_6), which is emitted during the production of refrigerants and semiconductors (OECD, 2010[27]).

However, CO_2 remains the key driver of GHG emissions worldwide. Approximately 72% of the gases contributing to climate change in 2018 were fossil-fuel-related, with CO_2 emissions coming mainly from coal, oil, and natural gas combustion (Olivier and Peters, 2020[145]). The top emitters of CO_2 (and other GHGs) are China (which accounts for 30% of global CO_2), the United States (14%), the European Union (9%), India (6.9%), Russia (4.6%) and Japan (3.2%). Developing countries account for only 33% of CO_2 emissions, but they bear some of the most severe consequences of climate change. Overall, the potential for reducing GHG emissions is higher in non-OECD countries – where urban planning is either lacking or at early stages across a large number of urban areas – than in OECD countries (IEA, 2016[144]).

Cities in developing countries are becoming important contributors to GHG emissions

Emissions are rapidly accelerating in developing countries. OECD countries were the main contributors of CO_2 before the 1970s following an energy-intensive industrialisation process. But over the past 30 years, a large share of emissions has come from developing countries, especially in Asia. Since 2010, emissions from Asian countries account for the largest share (IPCC, 2014[72]). Figure 2.12 compares CO_2 emissions per capita in 1970 against their annual growth rates between 1970 and 2017 for different geographical regions. It shows that OECD countries in America and Europe had the highest levels of CO_2 emissions per capita in 1970, at 16.2 and 8.1 tonnes per person, respectively; in contrast, China emitted only 0.9 tonnes per person. The growth trajectories of emissions in these regions have since reversed: from 1970 to 2017, OECD countries in Europe and America experienced negative growth rates, while China's CO_2 emissions per capita expanded rapidly, with an average annual growth rate of 4.3%. Likewise, Asia and the Middle East started from a low level but caught up fast, with growth rates above 3% during the period.

Figure 2.12. Growth rates of CO_2 emissions per capita

Growth dynamics between 1970 and 2017 in major geographic regions

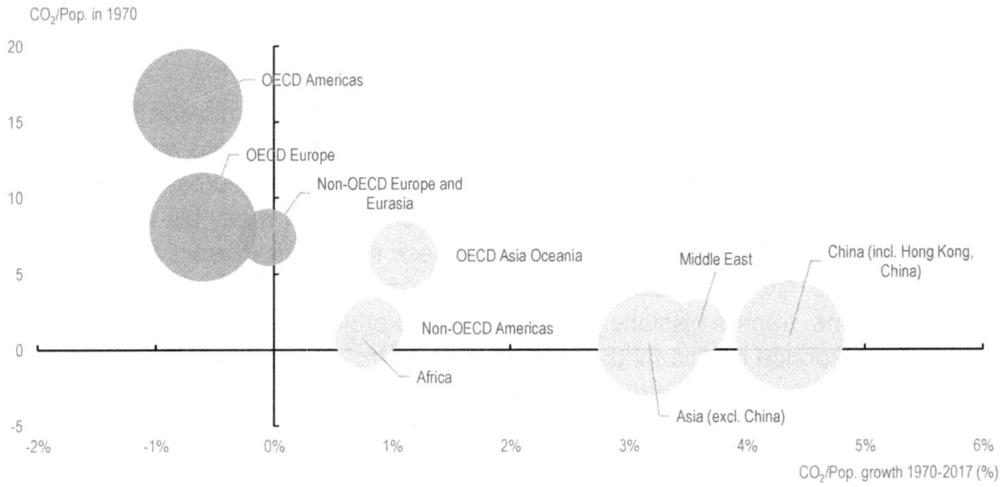

Note: The vertical axis represents CO_2 emissions per capita in 1970, i.e. the ratio of total CO_2 emissions from fuel combustion over the total population in the region expressed as million tonnes of CO_2 per 1 million population. The horizontal axis represents the average annual growth rate of total CO_2 emissions per capita between 1970 and 2017. The size of the bubble represents GDP in 2017 expressed in PPP.
Source: IEA (2018[146]).

Emerging regions are also shifting the global landscape of energy demand. Countries in Asia account today for two-thirds of the growth in global energy demand, with demand currently growing twice as fast in Southeast Asia as in China. At country level, India accounts for 30% of the growth in energy demand in the world, and by 2040 will account for 11% of the increase in global demand for energy (OECD/IEA, 2017[147]). As for China, in 2018 it had the highest growth in energy demand since 2012, and this accounted for one-third of total growth in global energy demand, according to the IEA (2018[146]).

As the economies of developing countries transform, the GHG emissions from their cities will continue to increase. Many developing countries have industrialised, with some becoming centres for global manufacturing. This process, coupled with fast urbanisation rates and growing wealth, has led to more emissions from urban areas in emerging economies. By 2030, emissions from cities in non-OECD countries will account for 81% of global energy use (OECD, 2010[27]).

Income differences within cities also affect emission rates. Affluent urban dwellers have a higher emissions rate due to higher energy consumption, use of private transport and consumption of goods characterised by highly embedded carbon. In India, for example, the annual CO_2 emissions of the richest 1% of the population are four times those of the poorest 38% (UN-HABITAT, 2011, p. 51[9]). Moreover, the livelihoods of many poor urban households depend on recycling and reuse of waste, which can yield negative emission levels. Although recycling produces emissions, negative emissions arise when the emissions "saved" exceed the emissions produced (Satterthwaite, 2009[148]).

Big cities produce most urban CO_2 emissions in developing countries. In 2015, cities of more than 1 million inhabitants produced around 13 million tons of CO_2 on average. This is almost five times more than the average amount of CO_2 produced by cities with a population of 500 000 to 1 million, 37 times more than cities of 100 000 to 500 000, and 132 times more than cities of 50 000 to 100 000.

Per capita CO_2 emissions are also lower in intermediary cities than in large cities. Figure 2.13 compares CO_2 per capita emissions in 2000 and 2015. It shows that, in 2015, an average person in an intermediary city produced 2.3 kilo tonnes of CO_2, compared to 3.7 kilo tonnes per person in large cities. It also shows that CO_2 emissions per capita increased over the period, with per capita emissions in intermediary cities rising by 2015 to the level in large cities in 2000.

Figure 2.13. CO_2 emissions per capita in intermediary and big cities, 2000 vs. 2015

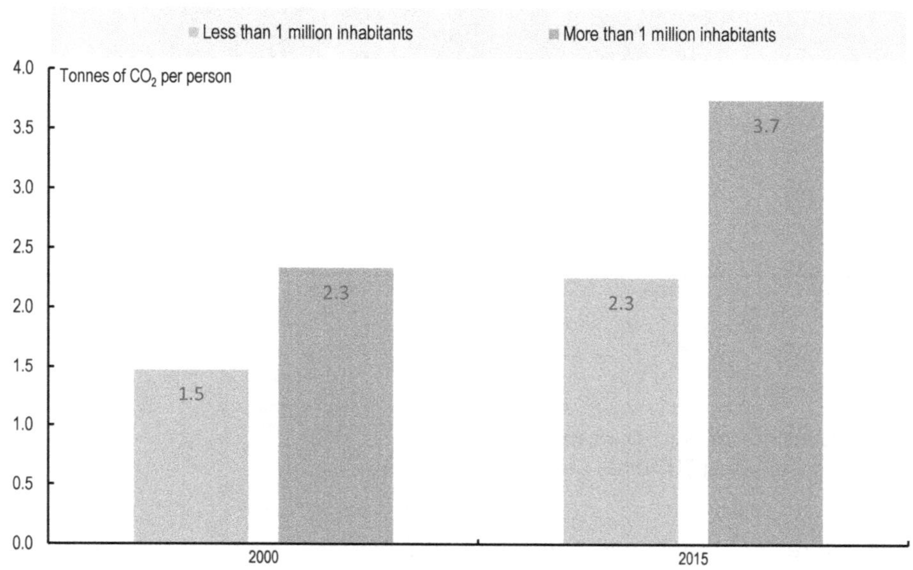

Note: Intermediary cities are those agglomerations with fewer than 1 million inhabitants in 2015. The sample does not include cities in high-income countries.
Source: Author's own calculations using GHS Urban Centre Database (2019[6]).

Large cities also account for the largest share of CO_2 emissions in most economic sectors. Excluding high-income countries, cities with more than 1 million inhabitants accounted for 55% of all CO_2 emissions in 2015 (Figure 2.14). However, as the figure shows, the contribution to CO_2 emissions by city size depends on the sector of activity: large cities produce close to two-thirds of CO_2 emissions in the transport and industry sectors, and more than half of the emissions in the residential sector, while intermediary cities account for the largest share of emissions in the energy and agriculture sectors.

Figure 2.14. Contribution of cities of different sizes to CO_2 emissions

Estimates by sector, 2015

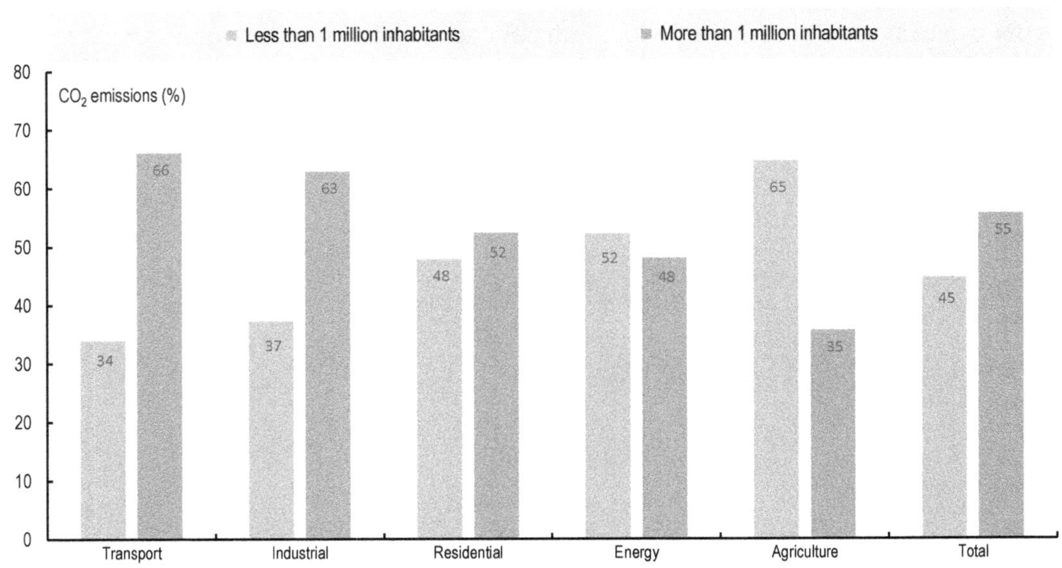

Note: The sample does not consider cities in high-income countries.
Source: Author's own calculations using GHS Urban Centre Database (2019[6]).

There are, however, regional variations in the share of CO_2 emissions by city size. Although big cities represent a small percentage of urban centres, they are responsible for the lion's share of urban CO_2 emissions. Figure 2.15 shows that only 5% of the cities in Latin America and the Caribbean have more than 1 million inhabitants, but they account for 68% of the region's urban CO_2 emissions, while small and medium-sized cities account for the rest (32%). In Sub-Saharan Africa, big cities represent 2% of urban centres but account for 62% of urban CO_2 emissions. In contrast, intermediary cities in some regions emit more CO_2 than big cities. This is the case of India, where intermediary cities (98% of all Indian cities) accounted for 57.5% of CO_2 emissions in 2015.

Figure 2.15. Percentage of cities with more than 1 million inhabitants and % of CO_2 emissions

Estimates by region for 2015

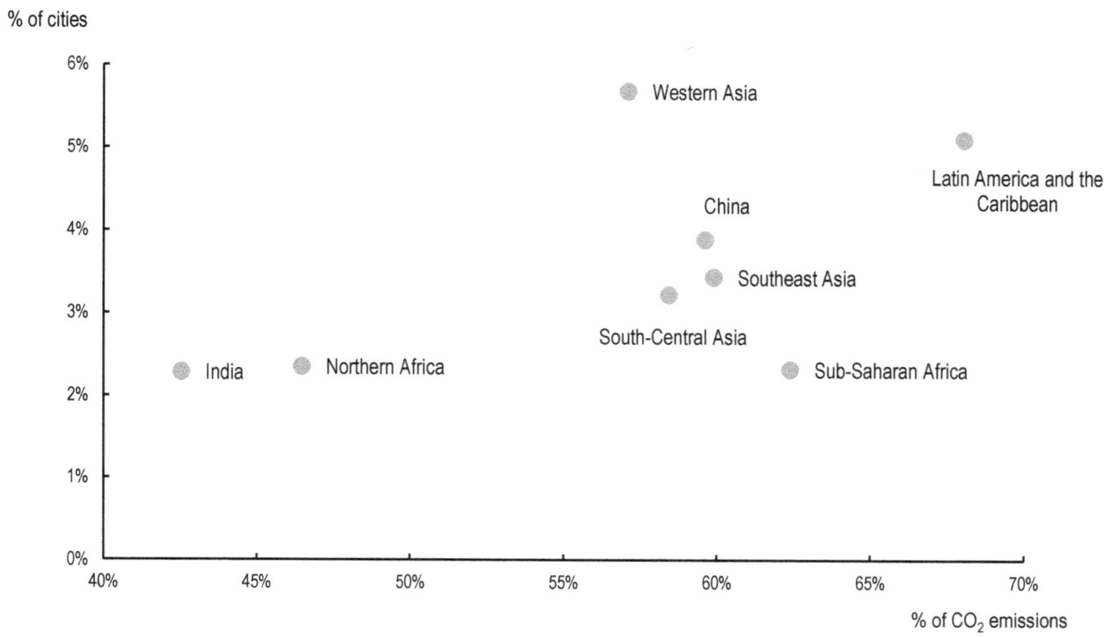

Note: The sample does not include cities in high-income countries.
Source: Authors' own calculations using GHS Urban Centre Database (2019[6]).

The contribution to CO_2 emissions by different sectors is fairly similar across intermediary cities.[14] Overall, the industry and energy sectors are the largest contributors to CO_2 emissions. Figure 2.16 shows that in big cities, the industrial sector emits the largest share, while in intermediary cities energy production contributes the most to CO_2 emissions. The transport and residential sectors account for a smaller but still relevant share of emissions across all city sizes. Agriculture is the smallest contributor to urban emissions. This does not mean that agriculture is not an important source of overall CO_2 emissions, but rather that is not such a relevant factor in urban CO_2 emissions.

There are important differences in sectoral emissions across regions. In China and India, the energy sector accounts for the highest share of emissions, particularly in intermediary cities. In other regions, such as Western Asia and Southeast Asia, the energy sector is not as relevant, but it is higher in intermediary cities. Latin America has the highest share of industrial and transport emissions, which are fairly similar across city sizes. Sub-Saharan Africa is a particular case as residential emissions account for a large share of CO_2 emissions, reaching 55% of total CO_2 emissions in cities with a population of 50 000 to 100 000.

Figure 2.16. Composition of emissions in cities of different sizes

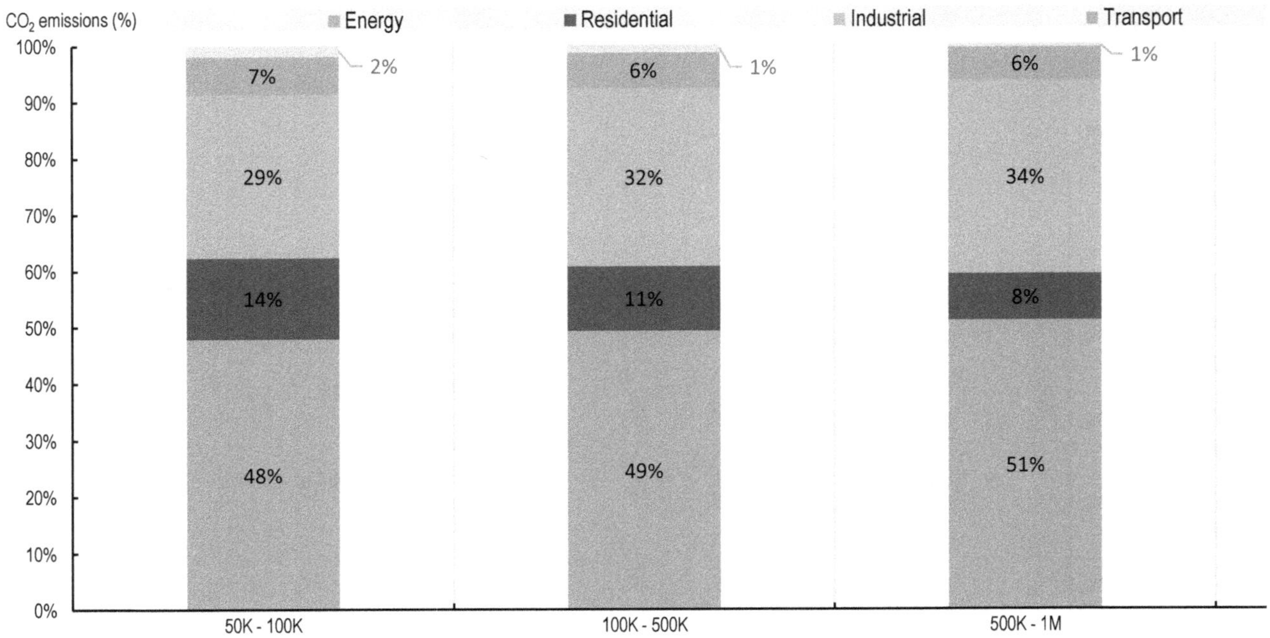

Note: The sample does not consider cities in high-income countries.
Source: Author's own calculations using GHS Urban Centre Database (2019[6]).

CO_2 emissions are evolving differently across cities of different sizes

Urban emissions of CO_2 have grown in all regions. From 2000 to 2015, CO_2 emissions from cities outside high-income countries increased by 4.6% on average. They grew across all regions, particularly in China (7.3%) and India (4.1%), while the lowest increase was in Sub-Saharan Africa (1.7%). Although CO_2 emissions grew more rapidly in big cities on average, regions followed different trends. In Western Asia, for instance, the smallest cities saw a 6.2% increase in emissions, while big cities' emissions grew by 2.4%.

Overall, CO_2 emissions from the energy sector grew fastest during the period 2000-15. This sector grew on average by 5.5%, followed by the industrial sector (4.9%) and transport (4.9%), while the residential sector (1.3%) and agriculture (1.6%) experienced the lowest growth rates.

Sectoral CO_2 emissions followed different trends depending on the size of the city. CO_2 emissions from the energy and transport sectors grew faster in smaller cities, reaching 6.6% and 5.1% respectively in cities of 50 000-100 000 and 100 000-500 000 inhabitants. CO_2 emissions from the residential, agriculture and industrial sectors grew more rapidly in larger cities (Table 2.2). As such, the energy sector contributed most to the growth of CO_2 emissions in cities with fewer than 1 million inhabitants and was responsible for 58% to 62% of the increase. In cities with more than 1 million inhabitants, the industrial sector was the main contributor to CO_2 emissions growth, with up to 46% of the increase between 2000 and 2015.

Table 2.2. Annual growth rate of CO_2 emissions

Growth rate between 2000 and 2015 by city size and sector

	Energy		Residential		Industrial		Transport		Agriculture	
City size	**Rate**	**Contribution**	**Rate**	**Contribution**	**Rate**	**Contribution**	**Rate**	**Contribution**	**Rate**	**Contribution**
50K-100K	6.6%	61.7%	0.6%	2.7%	4.1%	27.4%	5.1%	7.4%	1.5%	0.8%
100K-500K	5.1%	58.0%	0.6%	2.3%	4.0%	31.6%	5.0%	7.5%	1.6%	0.6%
500K-1M	5.1%	58.6%	0.9%	2.3%	3.9%	32.5%	4.7%	6.3%	1.8%	0.3%
>1M	5.7%	39.6%	1.9%	4.5%	5.5%	46.1%	4.9%	9.5%	1.7%	0.2%

Note: "Rate" refers to the annual average growth rate between 2000 and 2015, while "contribution" refers to the contribution to emissions growth by each sector during the same period. The sample does not include cities in high-income countries.
Source: Author's own calculations using GHS (2015) data.

Cities of more than 500 000 inhabitants tend to have a higher CO_2 intensity. The increase of CO_2 emissions in cities has historically been tied to economic development, since important industries relied on the burning of fossil fuels. To understand this relationship, the carbon intensity of GDP measures how much CO_2 is produced per dollar of GDP, or the carbon cost of economic development (Wang, Yang and Qi, 2020[149]). In developing countries, the CO_2 intensity of GDP decreased between 2000 and 2015, especially in intermediary cities. As a result, in 2015, CO_2 intensity was lower in cities with fewer than 500 000 inhabitants than in bigger cities.

Cities in developing economies have yet to break the link between economic growth and CO_2 emissions. A decrease of CO_2 intensity is known as decoupling. Decoupling refers to breaking the link between "environmental bads" (CO_2 emissions) and "economic goods" (GDP growth), and it can either be absolute or relative (OECD, 2002[150]). Absolute decoupling is usually described as the way to make economic growth environmentally sustainable, and it happens when countries manage to decrease their CO_2 emissions while their economy continues to grow. On average, however, cities in developing countries are undergoing relative decoupling, as their CO_2 emissions continue to grow, but at a much lower rate than GDP (Figure 2.17). This can be seen as a gain in efficiency, but it does not remove the link between economic growth and environmental impact (Ward et al., 2016[151]).

Figure 2.17. Growth rate of CO_2 intensity and its components

Growth rate between 2000 and 2015

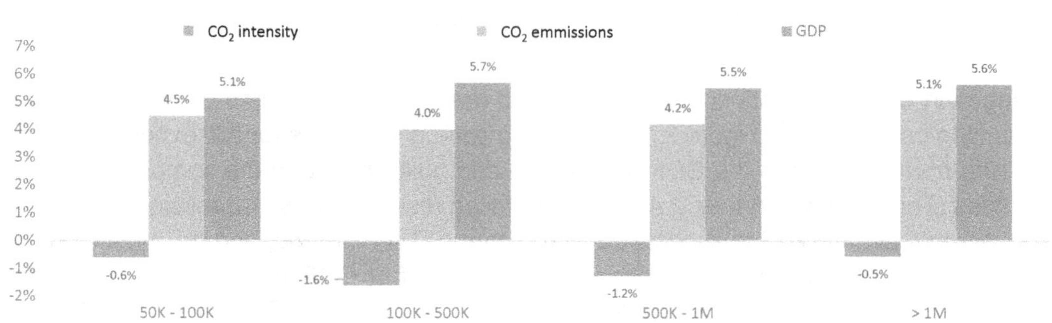

Note: The calculations exclude the observations where GDP is 0 due to missing values.
Source: Authors' own calculations using GHS Urban Centre Database (2019[6]). The sample does not include cities in high-income countries.

GDP, population and urban expansion contribute to growing CO_2 emissions in cities

CO_2 emission levels are strongly associated with the degree of urbanisation. As cities grow and their wealth increases, CO_2 emissions tend to be higher. Figure 2.18 shows the relationship between GDP and CO_2 levels in 2015 for the sample of cities outside high-income countries. It shows a positive trend that follows an S-shape. This shape seems to result from the relationship between GDP and CO_2 among different city groups, i.e. the strength of this relationship seems to grow with city size, only to eventually decrease among large cities with more than 1 million inhabitants. Figure 2.19 also shows the relationship between CO_2 emissions and both population and built-up land for the same sample of cities in 2015. The data suggest an overall linear relationship between these variables (expressed in logarithmic terms), and also suggest that the relationship between CO_2 and these variables is different among city groups.

Figure 2.18. CO_2 emission, GDP, population and built-up land across cities of different sizes

Data for cities in developing countries in 2015

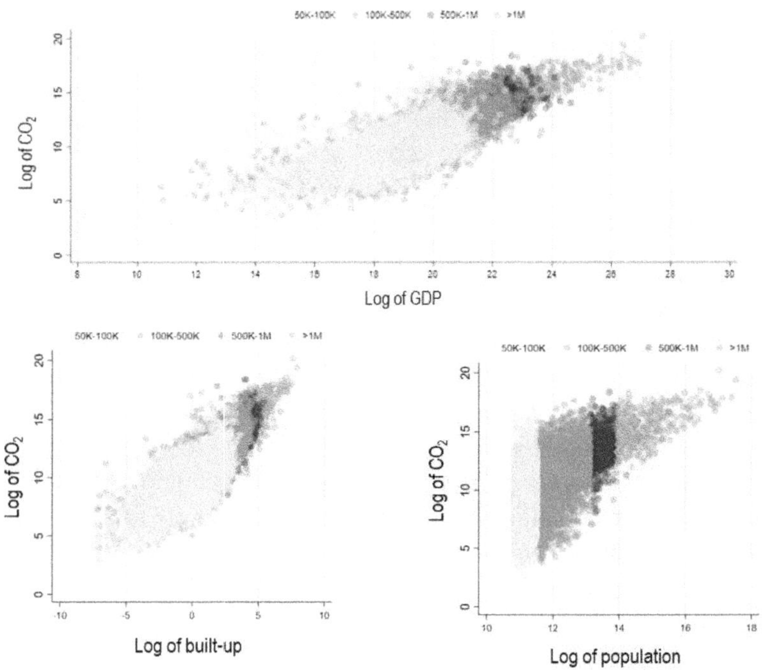

Note: Each circle represents a city. Colours account for different groups of cities depending on their size: 50 000-100 000 inhabitants (50K-100K), 100 000-500 000 inhabitants (100K-500K), 500 000-1 million inhabitants (500K-1M), and 1 million inhabitants or more (>1M). The sample does not include cities in high-income countries.

Source: Author's own calculations using GHS Urban Centre Database (2019[6]).

Changes in GDP, population, and built-up land area can be expected to affect the level of CO_2 differently, depending on city size.[15] Figure 2.19 shows regression estimates for the expected change in CO_2 emissions resulting from changes in the GDP, population and built-up land in the sample of cities outside high-income countries (Table 2.A.4 in Annex 2.A1 shows detailed results of these regressions). Three main points emerge. First, an increase in GDP is associated with higher CO_2 emissions, and this effect increases with city size.[16] In cities with more than 500 000 inhabitants, the effect of GDP on emissions is significantly larger than in smaller agglomerations. On average, an increase of 1% in GDP among cities with more than 1 million inhabitants is associated with a 0.38% increase in CO_2 emissions, while the rise in emissions is 0.13% among cities of 50 000 to 100 000. Second, higher levels of population are associated with higher CO_2 emissions in cities with less than 500 000 inhabitants. A 1% increase in population is associated with a 0.15% and a 0.22% increase in total CO_2 emissions among cities of 50 000 to 100 000 and 100 000 to 500 000 inhabitants, respectively. Third, changes in built-up area have a significant effect on CO_2 emissions only in cities of fewer than 500 000 inhabitants. In such cities, a 1% increase in built-up land is associated with an increase of 0.18% in CO_2 emissions in cities of 50 000 to100 000 inhabitants and an increase of 0.15% in cities of 100 000 to 500 000 inhabitants.

Figure 2.19. Expected change in CO_2 emissions from changes in GDP, population, and built-up land

Estimates for cities of different sizes (developing countries)

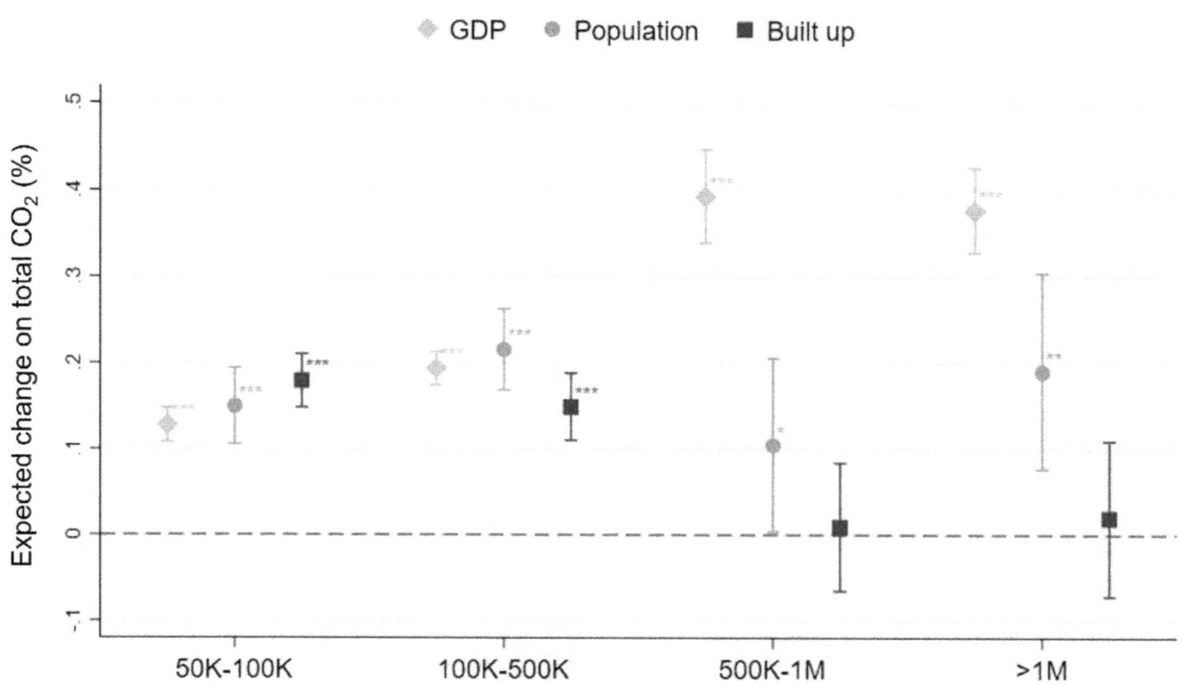

Note: Estimates of a panel econometric model regressing CO_2 emissions (total) on: GDP, population, and built-up land, the three variables interacted with city size. Base category is cities above 1 million inhabitants. All variables included expressed logarithmic terms. Results based on a fixed-effects estimator, considering year-effects, and standard errors clustered by city. Data for the periods 1990, 2000 and 2015. The sample does not include cities in high-income countries.
Source: Author's own calculations using GHS Urban Centre Database (2019[6]).

The extent to which changes in production and urbanisation affect CO_2 emissions also depend on the activity of a city's main economic sectors. In Annex 2.A1, Figure 2.A.1 shows the results from a series of econometric models focusing on emissions in the residential, transport and industry sectors. (Columns 2, 3 and 4 of Table 2.A.4 in Annex 2.A1 display the results of the regressions). Some general trends emerge from this analysis:

- Larger cities tend to have a stronger relationship between GDP and CO_2 in the transport and industrial sectors. For cities of more than 1 million inhabitants, a 1% increase in GDP is associated with a 0.5% increase in transport CO_2 emissions; in cities of fewer than 100 000 inhabitants, the increase is close to 0.3%. A similar pattern is found in CO_2 emissions from the industrial sector, where 1% increase in GDP ranges from 0.22% in cities with less than 100 000 inhabitants to 0.3% in cities with more than 1 million people. In contrast, an increase in GDP is associated with a slight decrease in residential CO_2 emissions in cities of fewer than 500 000 inhabitants: a 1% increase in GDP is associated with a decrease in residential emissions of around 0.03%.

- Population plays a key role in the increase of emissions in the residential sector among intermediary cities. Indeed, the estimated effect of a 1% increase in population is an increase in emissions of 0.24% in cities with less than 100 000 inhabitants to 0.46% in cities of 100 000 t0 500 000 inhabitants. In contrast, for transport emissions, the relationship between population and emissions is negative: a 1% increase in population is associated with a decrease in emissions of 0.21% to 0.29% across all city sizes.
- Built-up expansion is positively associated with higher CO_2 emissions, but only in cities of fewer than 500 000 inhabitants. The effect is particularly acute in the residential sector, where a 1% increase in built-up land is associated with an increase of 0.33% to 0.34% in CO_2 emissions in cities with fewer than 500 000 inhabitants.

These results are in line with literature studying the dynamics between urbanisation and CO_2 emissions. GDP has proved to be a significant driver of CO_2 emissions in cities in developing countries, as the Environmental Kuznet's Curve (EKC) theory suggests: as cities become richer, emissions grow until they reach a certain level of development, from which point emissions go down. Evidence on the existence of the EKC was found by Castells-Quintana et al. (2020[152]) and He et al. (2017[153]). Previous studies also suggest that built-up expansion drives up CO_2 emissions by converting land for commercial, residential or industrial purposes (Wang et al., 2018[154]; Zhou et al., 2015[155]) and through the carbon lock-in of infrastructure, as long-life capital stocks can lock in CO_2 emissions for very long periods (World Bank, 2010[97]).

Why climate mitigation efforts are particularly important for intermediary cities

Intermediary cities deserve special attention in terms of climate mitigation efforts for several reasons. First, emissions in small and medium-sized cities have grown constantly since 2000, particularly those from the energy and transport sectors. Second, urbanisation trends imply that these cities will continue to grow in the next years, most likely without proper planning and with a high risk of sprawl, and that some of them eventually will become large metropolitan areas. If not adequately planned, these cities risk being locked onto an unsustainable path and will face the challenges big cities face today.

Although emission levels are shaped by the way cities grow, the relationship between urban dynamics and CO_2 growth is far from clear. The multiple studies exploring the effect of a country's urbanisation[17] on CO_2 emissions in most cases find a positive relationship between the two (Parikh and Shukla, 1995[156]; Cole and Neumayer, 2004[157]; Wei, Yagita and Inaba, 2003[158]). Nevertheless, the relationship between the growth of cities and CO_2 emissions is far from simple, and is based on multiple factors. Some city-level studies highlight the role of urban density on CO_2 emissions, finding a relation between increasing population density in cities and decreasing CO_2 emissions per capita (Wang et al, 2020[159]; Castells-Quintana et al., 2015[160]). Other studies link higher density with higher emissions because of greater congestion (Gaigné, Riou and Thisse, 2012[161]). Some studies have focused on the effect of wealth on emissions, finding evidence of a Kuznet's Curve: wealth and emissions have an inverted U-shape relation (He et al., 2017[153]). The spatial distribution of cities and the number of urban centres has also been identified as a relevant factor. One major conclusion stands out from these studies: There are many factors related to urbanisation that influence CO_2 emissions, and many results are country- and metric-specific (i.e. depends on the measure used). This raises the importance of understanding the dynamics between urban trends and CO_2 emissions among cities in developing economies.

Intermediary cities are key in the achievement of a zero-carbon future that is in line with economic objectives and society's welfare. According to the Coalition for Urban Transitions (2019[162]), cities with fewer than 750 000 inhabitants have more than half of the carbon abatement potential of large agglomerations around the world. These carbon savings will come from improving commercial and residential buildings (58%) and enhancing the transport sector (21%), materials efficiency (16%) and waste management (5%). The good news is that this abatement will largely be possible through technically feasible measures that are already available in cities (such as decarbonising urban electricity grids, shifts in public transportation or improving the efficiency of heating and cooling systems in buildings). To bring these measures to scale and reach their full abatement potential, local governments will need to work closely with national and regional governments[18] and involve the community and protect citizens from the challenges that may arise from the transition. In this way, cities can become compact, connected and clean urban centres that attract investment, promote sustainable economic development by increasing productivity and innovation, and create a healthy and secure environment for their residents.

There is large scope for limiting the effects of urban expansion among intermediary cities in developing countries. A large number of these cities – especially medium-sized cities – face a significant lack of infrastructure. The fact that this gap will eventually be addressed brings an unprecedented opportunity for building low-carbon infrastructure and housing that takes account of climate hazards, facilitates energy efficiency and uses recycled or green materials in construction (Seto et al., 2014[163]; IPCC, 2018[164]). Likewise, many intermediary cities in developing countries lack urban planning and land management systems. The early urbanisation stage in some developing countries, especially in Africa, provides scope for implementing policies that promote the use of pedestrian space and green areas (such as parks), and that push for investment in low-carbon transportation systems, which can help to reduce urban emissions while improving the population's well-being (IPCC, 2018[164]).

Growth in intermediary cities and increased standards of living will translate into higher GHG emissions unless systemic changes are implemented. As populations, grow there will be higher demand for energy, infrastructure, transportation, housing and other public services. According to the IPCC (2014[4]), with the currently available technology and with the global population estimated to reach 9.3 billion by 2050, addressing the corresponding infrastructure demand will generate approximately 470 gigatonnes (Gt) of CO_2. A large share of the needed infrastructure will be built in intermediary cities in low- and middle-income countries (IPCC, 2014[4]; Seto et al., 2014[163]; Grubler et al., 2012[165]). Indeed, the growth in energy use will be highest in small and medium-sized cities, which are currently characterised by low and moderate final energy use. These cities are expected to increase their energy use by a factor of 6.1 (for fast-growing small cities) and 1.6 (for medium-sized cities), whereas energy use in the largest cities is expected to rise by a factor of 0.5 (Seto et al., 2014[163]; Grubler et al., 2012[165]). That the largest projected growth in energy use is in small cities with fewer than 500 000 inhabitants corresponds to the fact that these cities are expected to undergo the highest population growth, with very high elasticity in growth of energy demand (Seto et al., 2014[163]; Grubler et al., 2012[165]). These cities also have low capacity in the institutional, financial and technical resources needed to manage and mitigate climate threats, rendering them particularly important for targeted implementation strategies (Seto et al., 2014[163]).

Future GHG emissions in intermediary cities will differ highly across regions, based on population size as well as the economic structures of these urban centres. City-level GHG emissions depend on geography, economic structure and specialisation, and energy use (Seto et al., 2014[163]). A significant share of manufacturing industries and production are located in urban areas, which drives their GHG emissions upward (UN-HABITAT, 2011[9]). For example, many Asian intermediary cities have a large industrial base and are the growth engines of their respective regions. In Hai Phong,[19] a major industrial city in Viet Nam, CO_2 emissions from energy sources are accounted for 13.2 million tonnes in 2010 and were estimated to increase to 49.6 million tonnes in 2020 (OECD, 2016[166]). Similarly, in the Malaysian cities of Jahor Bahru and Pasir Gudang (located within Isklandar, a special economic zone), CO_2 emissions increased from 5 million tonnes to 18.5 million tonnes between 2000 and 2012 (OECD, 2018, p. 42[167]). As for Africa, Godfrey and Zhao (2015[168]) note that 69 African cities of more than 500 000 inhabitants, from across 35 countries, emitted 240 million tonnes of CO_2 2012. By 2030, the total emissions of CO_2 are projected to increase by 61%, to 386 million tonnes, for cumulative CO_2 emissions of 6 billion tonnes between 2012 and 2030 (Godfrey and Zhao, 2015[168]).

System innovation for intermediary cities: Towards sustainable policy solutions

A shift in perspective is required to address the systemic challenges brought by climate change and increasingly volatile ecosystems, as well as to achieve the global development goals. This implies thinking of climate actions not as partial measures but as a whole system. It calls for transforming unsustainable systems towards lower energy demand and for shifting from traditional measures of development (mainly GDP) towards improved well-being outcomes (OECD, 2021[12]). This shift in perspective is referred to as a well-being lens. Applying a well-being lens to climate actions can help to catalyse systemic changes that are sustainable *by design* and are better able to build synergies between improved environmental quality and the attainment of well-being goals. Through this approach, the benefits (and costs) of a specific mitigation measure will be weighed according to their impact on health, education or security, and not just on economic welfare (OECD, 2019[169]).

Improving well-being outcomes is key for building resilience. Indeed, addressing the vulnerabilities of intermediary cities to climate change also implies addressing the underlying socio-economic conditions of these cities. A large share of the population of intermediary cities is often characterised by low socio-economic conditions that heighten their vulnerabilities to climate change. Moreover, intermediary cities tend to be dependent on climate-sensitive sectors (such as agriculture) and to face large gaps in "risk-reducing" infrastructure (such as roads, waste and drainage systems, access to safe water, electricity, etc.) (IPCC, 2014[170]). Urban dwellers in informal settlements are particularly at a disadvantage due to their limited access to these services. Climate vulnerabilities in intermediary cities are largely shaped by the compounded factors of low socio-economic development and low institutional capacities. Climate risks serve as multipliers of threats in these agglomerations. As such, climate actions should take into consideration how multiple economic sectors are affected by climate change, and these actions should aim to strengthen the socio-economic conditions of urban dwellers. They should also tap into some of the opportunities characterising intermediary cities, such as access to education and training opportunities, as well as a strong linkage to bigger markets (UCLG, 2016[171]).

Applying a well-being lens to climate action can also facilitate better mitigation outcomes at the city and national levels. The IPCC's pathways for net-zero transitions largely depend on the prioritisation of policies. Attaining low energy demand or transformational pathways requires systemic changes that yield improved well-being outcomes. Yet most climate policies today tend to focus on decarbonising systems rather than addressing the systemic changes needed for net-zero transition. These approaches also depend on carbon removal technologies that are not in use yet. In contrast, applying a well-being lens to climate action would imply taking advantage of synergies across different objectives and planning in advance for possible trade-offs. The well-being lens builds on systems thinking, with the core aim of accelerating climate mitigation by *redesigning* systems that centre on well-being goals (such as health, accessibility, biodiversity, etc.). Indeed, the proposed well-being lens will lead to designing systems that are less reliant on energy and will ultimately lead to lower emissions while simultaneously attaining well-being outcomes (OECD, 2019[169]). The well-being lens also fosters better co-operation across key stakeholders and enables local governments to prioritise mitigation strategies more effectively, while changing the community's perception of environmental objectives (OECD, 2019[169]). Climate mitigation strategies are most effective when they are localised and effectively communicated to local stakeholders. This helps to maximise public engagement while also enabling longevity of climate actions.

Applying a well-being lens to local and national policies also calls for a shift from analysing parts to viewing systems as a whole. In other words, it implies building systems that are sustainable *by design* (OECD, 2019[169]). For instance, adopting systems thinking in food systems can enable policy makers to understand the complexity of these systems, including the distribution of activities across space and actors, and to see how food systems relate to climate change. What is required is a holistic approach that can capture the interconnected economic, ecological, social and spatial dimensions of urban systems.

Applying a well-being lens requires a three-step thinking process that can be applied to various sectors or systems. This includes: *envisioning* the desired outcome of a functioning and sustainable urban system; *understanding* the underlying factors and key stakeholders that sustain undesirable results; and *changing* policy packages, governance systems and budgeting in order to attain the desired outcome (Figure 2.20).

Figure 2.20. The well-being lens process

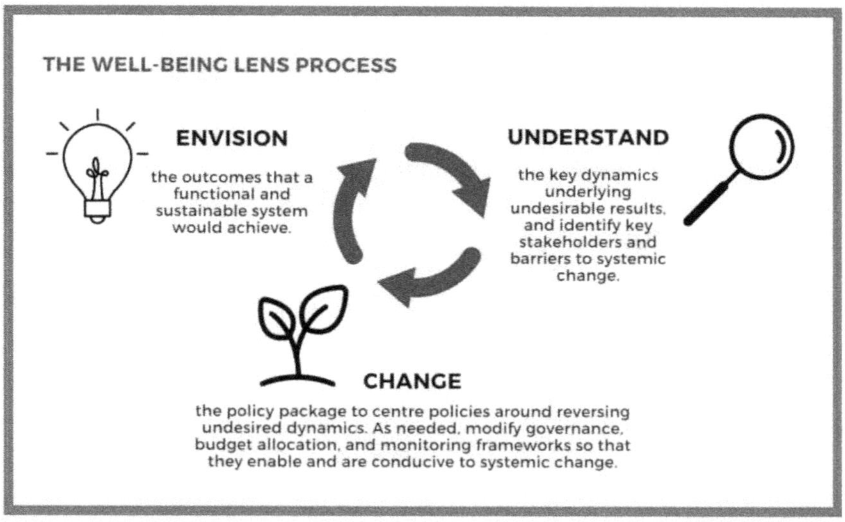

Source: (OECD, 2021[172]), What is the Well-Being Lens: An innovative process for net-zero strategies.

Conclusion

Intermediary cities play a critical role in addressing climate change, and they deserve a more relevant role in the international agenda. This chapter has highlighted that the growth dynamics of intermediary cities, paired with their underlying socio-economic characteristics, make these cities particularly important for climate action. Moreover, as intermediary cities grow, their GHG emissions will increase. Ignoring this can potentially undermine national and international efforts to curb global emissions. For these reasons, the inclusion of intermediary cities in local, national and international climate policies is critical today. If intermediary cities are endowed with adequate resources and targeted policies, they have the potential to contribute to the reduction of global GHG emissions and to act as a laboratory for innovative solutions. However, this calls for a shift in policy approaches.

Notes

[1] The Working Group I contribution to the Sixth Assessment Report published in 2021.

[2] The ratios were obtained through a Google Scholar search. For the overall comparison, the searches were: (i) "secondary city" OR "secondary cities" OR "intermediary city" OR "intermediary cities" OR "small city" OR "small cities" OR "medium cities" OR "medium city" vs (ii) "capital city" OR "capital cities" OR "metropolis" OR "megacity" OR "megacities" OR "big city" OR "big cities". For the climate change topic comparison; (iii) "climate change" AND ("secondary city" OR "secondary cities" OR "intermediary city" OR "intermediary cities" OR

"small city" OR "small cities" OR "medium cities" OR "medium city") vs (iv) "climate change" AND ("capital city" OR "capital cities" OR "metropolis" OR "megacity" OR "megacities" OR "big city" OR "big cities").

[3] To answer this question, we analyse recent estimates from the GHS Urban Centres Database (GHS-UCD) covering different time periods: 1990, 2020 and 2015. This dataset addresses some important caveats from other existing datasets (including the ones from the UNDESA presented above). First, this dataset is not based on administrative boundaries; instead, it uses a standardised definition for cities that improves international comparison. Second, it provides estimates of cities with at least 50 000 inhabitants (estimates from the UN do not account for cities with fewer than 300 000 inhabitants). This is particularly important for less developed regions, where large shares of the population reside in cities with fewer than 300 000 people.

[4] The 7% in annual GDP is calculated by adding up the annual external cost (USD 400 billion, cost of loss in fitness and public health), and the annual internal cost (USD 625 billion, costs borne by commuters), and as % of total US GDP in 2015 (USD 18 trillion).

[5] Based on projection of urban population to reach 3.5 billion across the 970 cities in the study, by 2050.

[6] In 2001 and 2019.

[7] Based on baseline period 1961-90.

[8] Compared to a world with 0°C temperature change.

[9] The estimations consider various climate-induced causes of death, including heat waves, coastal flooding, vector-borne diseases including diarrhoea (especially among children under the age of 15), malaria, dengue, as well as undernutrition and other related causes. The death rates are expected to vary highly based on future economic growth rates, underlying health conditions, socio-economic dynamics as well as public health systems and universal health coverage. However, the results do not capture climate-induced indirect causes of death.

[10] Cities are classified as warm or cold depending on whether their average temperature was above or below the median temperature in the sample in 1990.

[11] Chennai is a far larger city than what is considered an intermediary city in this study.

[12] Under the very low GHG emissions pathway leading to a rise in global temperatures of 1.4°C by 2081-2100.

[13] Urban areas that are located within 5 km of the coast and that have an elevation of less than 50 m are highly exposed to sea-level rise and coastal flooding.

[14] The sectors include: energy (power industry), residential (energy for buildings, solid and water waste), industry (combustion for manufacturing, oil refineries and transformation industry, fuel exploitation, industrial processes, solvents and products use), transport (road, off-road, shipping and aviation) and agriculture.

[15] CO2 emissions are modelled as a function of income, population, and built-up land, i.e. CO2 = f(GDP, Population, Built-up). This specification for the dependent variable was preferred over CO2 per capita in order to identify the effect of population on emissions.

[16] To test whether the effects of the four city sizes are significantly different, Wald tests have been performed.

[17] Defined as the percentage of the population living in urban areas.

[18] According to the same report, 72% of the mitigation potential identified depends directly or indirectly on collaboration with higher levels of government.

[19] An industrial city of 2 million inhabitants.

References

Abunyewah, M., T. Gajendran and K. Maund (2018), "Profiling Informal Settlements for Disaster Risks", *Procedia Engineering*, Vol. 212, https://doi.org/10.1016/j.proeng.2018.01.031. [43]

Arndt et al (2015), "The economic costs of climate change: A multi-sector impact assessment for Vietnam", *Sustainability (Switzerland)*, Vol. 7/4, pp. 4131-4145, https://doi.org/10.3390/su7044131. [81]

Ashraf et al (2016), "Infrastructure, Incentives, and Institutions", *American Economic Review*, Vol. 106/5, pp. 77-82, https://doi.org/10.1257/aer.p20161095. [123]

Baarsch, F. et al. (2020), "The impact of climate change on incomes and convergence in Africa", *World Development*, Vol. 126, https://doi.org/10.1016/j.worlddev.2019.104699. [76]

Bae, C. and W. Richardson (2004), *Urban Sprawl in Western Europe and the United States*, Routledge, California. [7]

Berdegué et al (2014), *Inclusive Rural-Urban Linkages*, https://rimisp.org/wp-content/files_mf/1431869344123InclusiveRural_UrbanLinkages_edited.pdf (accessed on 11 February 2021). [45]

Berry, P. et al. (2018), "Assessing Health Vulnerabilities and Adaptation to Climate Change: A Review of International Progress", *International Journal of Environmental Research and Public Health*, Vol. 15/12, https://doi.org/10.3390/ijerph15122626. [84]

Birkmann (2016), "Boost resilience of small and mid-sized cities", *Nature*, Vol. 537/1, pp. 605-609, https://www.nature.com/news/boost-resilience-of-small-and-mid-sized-cities-1.20667. [33]

Blackburn, S. (2014), "The politics of scale and disaster risk governance: Barriers to decentralisation in Portland, Jamaica", *Geoforum*, Vol. 52, https://doi.org/10.1016/j.geoforum.2013.12.013. [37]

Brueckner, J. (2000), "Urban Sprawl: Diagnosis and Remedies", *International Regional Science Review*, Vol. 23/2, pp. 160-171, https://doi.org/10.1177/016001700761012710. [18]

Burgalassi, D. and T. Luzzati (2015), "Urban spatial structure and environmental emissions: A survey of the literature and some empirical evidence for Italian NUTS 3 regions", *Cities*, Vol. 49, pp. 134-148, https://doi.org/10.1016/j.cities.2015.07.008. [10]

Busby, J. et al. (2018), "In harm's way: Climate security vulnerability in Asia", *World Development*, Vol. 112, pp. 88-118, https://doi.org/10.1016/j.worlddev.2018.07.007. [22]

C2ES (2021), *Drought and Climate Change*, Center For Climate and Energy Solutions, https://www.c2es.org/content/drought-and-climate-change/ (accessed on 11 July 2021). [110]

Cambaza, E. et al. (2019), "Outbreak of Cholera Due to Cyclone Kenneth in Northern Mozambique, 2019", *International Journal of Environmental Research and Public Health*, Vol. 16/16, p. 2925, https://doi.org/10.3390/ijerph16162925. [29]

Campbell-Lendrum, D. and C. Corvalán (2007), *Climate change and developing-country cities: Implications for environmental health and equity*, https://doi.org/10.1007/s11524-007-9170-x. [128]

Cao, C. et al. (2016), "Urban heat islands in China enhanced by haze pollution", *Nature Communications*, Vol. 7/1, https://doi.org/10.1038/ncomms12509. [100]

Cardoso, R. et al. (2017), "Assessment of Urban Heat Islands in Small- and Mid-Sized Cities in Brazil", *Climate*, Vol. 5/1, https://doi.org/10.3390/cli5010014. [101]

Carruthers, J. and G. Ulfarsson (2002), "Fragmentation and Sprawl: Evidence from Interregional Analysis", *Growth and Change*, Vol. 33/3, pp. 312-340, https://doi.org/10.1111/1468-2257.00193. [17]

Castells-Quintana et al. (2015), "Climate change and the geographical and institutional drivers of economic development", *Centre for Climate Change Economics and Policy Working Paper*, No. 198, University of Leeds and the London School of Economics and Political Science, Leeds and London, http://www.lse.ac.uk/grantham. [160]

Castells-Quintana, D., E. Dienesch and M. Krause (2020), "Density, Cities and Air Pollution: A Global View", *SSRN Electronic Journal*, https://doi.org/10.2139/ssrn.3713325. [152]

Chapman, S. et al. (2017), "The impact of urbanization and climate change on urban temperatures: a systematic review", *Landscape Ecology*, Vol. 32/10, pp. 1921-1935, https://doi.org/10.1007/s10980-017-0561-4. [95]

Christiaensen, L. and Y. Todo (2013), *Poverty Reduction during the Rural-Urban Transformation The Role of the Missing Middle*, http://econ.worldbank.org. [48]

Church et al. (2013), *Sea Level Change*, IPCC, Cambridge and New York, https://www.ipcc.ch/site/assets/uploads/2018/02/WG1AR5_Chapter13_FINAL.pdf. [132]

Clement, V. et al. (2021), *Groundswell: Acting on Internal Climate Migration - Part 2*, World Bank, Washington DC, http://www.worldbank.org. [64]

Coalition for Urban Transitions (2019), *Climate Emergency: Urban Opportunity*, Coalition for Urban Transitions, Washington DC and London, https://urbantransitions.global/en/publication/climate-emergency-urban-opportunity/ (accessed on 13 July 2021). [162]

Cole, M. and E. Neumayer (2004), "Examining the Impact of Demographic Factors on Air Pollution", *Population and Environment*, Vol. 26/1, https://doi.org/10.1023/B:POEN.0000039950.85422.eb. [157]

Cubasch et al. (2013), "Introduction", in *Climate Change 2013: The Physical Science Basis. Contribution of Working Group I to the Fifth Assessment Report of the Intergovernmental Panel on Climate Change*, Cambridge University Press, Cambridge (UK), New York (USA). [133]

Dai, A. (2011), "Drought under global warming: a review", *WIREs Climate Change*, Vol. 2/1, https://doi.org/10.1002/wcc.81. [109]

Dasgupta, P. et al. (2014), "Rural Areas", in Edward and Raholiao (ed.), *Climate Change 2014: Impacts, Adaptation and Vulnerability*, Cambridge University Press, Cambridge, https://www.ipcc.ch/report/ar5/wg2/. [51]

Dell, M., B. Jones and B. Olken (2012), "Temperature Shocks and Economic Growth: Evidence from the Last Half Century", *American Economic Journal: Macroeconomics*, Vol. 4/3, pp. 66-95, https://doi.org/10.1257/mac.4.3.66. [105]

Deryugina, T. and S. Hsiang (2014), *Does the Environment Still Matter? Daily Temperature and Income in the United States*, National Bureau of Economic Research, Cambridge, MA, https://doi.org/10.3386/w20750. [104]

Desbureaux, S. and A. Rodella (2019), "Drought in the city: The economic impact of water scarcity in Latin American metropolitan areas", *World Development*, Vol. 114, pp. 13-27, https://doi.org/10.1016/j.worlddev.2018.09.026. [125]

Dodman et al. (2022), "Cities, Settlements and Key Infrastructure", in *Climate Change 2022: Impacts, Adaptation and Vulnerability*, Cambridge University Press, Cambridge. [108]

Douglas, I. et al. (2008), "Unjust waters: Climate change, flooding and the urban poor in Africa", *Environment and Urbanization*, Vol. 20/1, pp. 187-205, https://doi.org/10.1177/0956247808089156. [136]

Ebi et al. (2018), *The 1.5°C Health Report: Synthesis on health and climate science in the IPCC SR1.5*, University of Washington, http://climatetracker.org/ipcc-report-on-health/. [25]

Edenhofer, O. et al. (eds.) (2014), *Climate change 2014: Mitigation of Climate Change: Working Group III contribution to the Fifth Assessment Report of the Intergovernmental Panel on Climate Change*, Cambridge University Press, Cambridge, United Kingdom and New York, USA. [4]

FAO (2017), *The State of Food and Agriculture. Leveraging Food Systems for Inclusive Rural Transformation*, FAO, Rome, http://www.fao.org/3/a-I7658e.pdf (accessed on 17 February 2021). [46]

FAO (2016), *The State of Food and Agriculture 2016: climate change, agriculture and food security*, Food and Agriculture Organisation, Rome, http://www.fao.org/publications/sofa/2016/en/. [52]

Filho, W. et al. (2019), "Assessing the impacts of climate change in cities and their adaptive capacity: Towards transformative approaches to climate change adaptation and poverty reduction in urban areas in a set of developing countries", *Science of The Total Environment*, Vol. 692, pp. 1175-1190, https://doi.org/10.1016/j.scitotenv.2019.07.227. [20]

Florczyk, A. (2019), *GHS Urban Centre Database 2015, multitemporal and multidimensional attributes*, http://data.europa.eu/89h/53473144-b88c-44bc-b4a3-4583ed1f547e (accessed on 13 July 2021). [6]

Florczyk, A. (2019), *GHS Urban Centre Database 2015, multitemporal and multidimensional attributes*, http://data.europa.eu/89h/53473144-b88c-44bc-b4a3-4583ed1f547e (accessed on 13 July 2021). [173]

Flörke, M., C. Schneider and R. McDonald (2018), "Water competition between cities and agriculture driven by climate change and urban growth", *Nature Sustainability*, Vol. 1/1, pp. 51-58, https://doi.org/10.1038/s41893-017-0006-8. [112]

Fuchs, R., M. Conran and E. Louis (2011), "Climate Change and Asia's Coastal Urban Cities", *Environment and Urbanization ASIA*, Vol. 2/1, pp. 13-28, https://doi.org/10.1177/097542531000200103. [137]

Gaigné, C., S. Riou and J. Thisse (2012), "Are compact cities environmentally friendly?", *Journal of Urban Economics*, Vol. 72/2-3, https://doi.org/10.1016/j.jue.2012.04.001. [161]

García-León, D. et al. (2021), "Current and projected regional economic impacts of heatwaves in Europe", *Nature Communications*, Vol. 12/1, https://doi.org/10.1038/s41467-021-26050-z. [103]

Garschagen, M. and P. Romero-Lankao (2013), “Exploring the relationships between urbanization trends and climate change vulnerability”, *Climatic Change*, Vol. 133/1, https://doi.org/10.1007/s10584-013-0812-6. [40]

Gasper et al (2011), “Social and economic impacts of climate change on the urban environment”, *Current Opinion in Environmental Sustainability*, Vol. 3/3, pp. 150-157, https://doi.org/10.1016/j.cosust.2010.12.009. [19]

Gebre, T. and B. Gebremedhin (2019), “The mutual benefits of promoting rural-urban interdependence through linked ecosystem services”, *Global Ecology and Conservation*, Vol. 20, https://doi.org/10.1016/j.gecco.2019.e00707. [114]

Godfrey and Zhao (2015), “The Contribution of African Cities to the Economy and Climate”, New Climate Economy, London, https://newclimateeconomy.report/workingpapers/wp-content/uploads/sites/5/2015/09/NCE-African-Cities-Economy-Climate_technical-note.pdf (accessed on 13 July 2021). [168]

Grubler, A. et al. (2012), “Urban Energy Systems”, in *Global Energy Assessment - Toward a Sustainable Future*, https://iiasa.ac.at/web/home/research/Flagship-Projects/Global-Energy-Assessment/Chapte18.en.html (accessed on 13 July 2021). [165]

Hassani-Mahmooei, B. and B. Parris (2012), “Climate change and internal migration patterns in Bangladesh: an agent-based model”, *Environment and Development Economics*, Vol. 17/6, https://doi.org/10.1017/S1355770X12000290. [67]

Henderson, J., A. Storeygard and U. Deichmann (2017), “Has climate change driven urbanization in Africa?”, *Journal of Development Economics*, Vol. 124, pp. 60-82, https://doi.org/10.1016/j.jdeveco.2016.09.001. [70]

Hertel et al. (2010), “The poverty implications of climate-induced crop yield changes by 2030”, *Global Environmental Change*, Vol. 20/4, pp. 577-585, https://doi.org/10.1016/j.gloenvcha.2010.07.001. [79]

He, Z. et al. (2017), “Impact of urbanization on energy related CO2 emission at different development levels: Regional difference in China based on panel estimation”, *Journal of Cleaner Production*, Vol. 140, pp. 1719-1730, https://doi.org/10.1016/j.jclepro.2016.08.155. [153]

Hoegh-Guldberg, O. et al. (2018), *Impacts of 1.5°C of Global Warming on Natural and Human Systems*, IPCC, https://www.ipcc.ch/sr15/. [24]

Hussein, K. and D. Suttie (2016), *Rural-urban linkages and food systems in sub-Saharan Africa*, International Fund for Agricultural Development, Rome, http://www.ifad.orgwww.ruralpovertyportal.orgwww.facebook.com/ifadinstagram.com/ifadnewswww.twitter.com/ifadnewswww.youtube.com/user/ifadTV. [47]

Huynh et al (2020), “Climate change vulnerability assessment for Can Tho city by a set of indicators”, *International Journal of Climate Change Strategies and Management*, Vol. 12/1, pp. 147-158, https://doi.org/10.1108/ijccsm-01-2018-0003. [129]

IEA (2021), *Empowering Cities for a Net Zero Future: unlocking resilient, smart, sustainable urban energy systems*, International Energy Agency, Paris, https://iea.blob.core.windows.net/assets/4d5c939d-9c37-490b-bb53-2c0d23f2cf3d/G20EmpoweringCitiesforaNetZeroFuture.pdf (accessed on 23 December 2021). [143]

IEA (2018), *Global Energy & CO2 Status Report: The latest trends in energy and emissions in 2018*, Internatinal Energy Agency, Paris, https://webstore.iea.org/global-energy-co2-status-report-2018. [146]

IEA (2016), *Energy Technology Perspectives 2016: Towards Sustainable Urban Energy Systems*, International Energy Agency, Paris, https://www.iea.org/reports/energy-technology-perspectives-2016. [144]

IFPRI (2020), *2020 Global Food Policy Report: Building Inclusive Food Systems*, International Food Policy Research Institute, Washington DC, https://doi.org/10.2499/9780896293670. [53]

ILO (2019), *Working on a warmer planet: The impact of heat stress on labour productivity and decent work*, International Labour Office, Geneva, http://www.ilo.org/publns. [82]

IPCC (2021), "Summary for Policy Makers", in IPCC (ed.), *Climate Change 2021: The Physical Science Basis*, Cambridge University Press, Cambridge, https://www.ipcc.ch/report/ar6/wg1/downloads/report/IPCC_AR6_WGI_SPM.pdf (accessed on 25 October 2021). [1]

IPCC (2018), "Summary for Policymakers", https://www.ipcc.ch/sr15/. [164]

IPCC (2014), *Chapter Climate Change 2014 Synthesis Report Summary for Policymakers Summary for Policymakers*, IPCC, Geneva, https://www.ipcc.ch/site/assets/uploads/2018/02/AR5_SYR_FINAL_SPM.pdf. [72]

IPCC (2014), *Climate change 2014: Mitigation of Climate Change: Working Group III contribution to the Fifth Assessment Report of the Intergovernmental Panel on Climate Change*, Cambridge University Press, Cambridge, United Kingdom and New York, USA. [170]

Jevrejeva, S. et al. (2018), "Flood damage costs under the sea level rise with warming of 1.5 °C and 2 °C", *Environmental Research Letters*, Vol. 13/7, https://doi.org/10.1088/1748-9326/aacc76. [135]

John, L. (2012), *Secondary cities in South Africa: The start of a conversation*, South African Cities Network, Cape Town. [116]

John, R. (2020), "Flooding in Informal Settlements: Potentials and Limits for Household Adaptation in Dar es Salaam City, Tanzania", *American Journal of Climate Change*, Vol. 09/02, https://doi.org/10.4236/ajcc.2020.92006. [44]

Kareem, B. et al. (2020), "Pathways for resilience to climate change in African cities", *Environmental Research Letters*, Vol. 15/7, https://doi.org/10.1088/1748-9326/ab7951. [124]

KFW (2015), *Climate-Focus-Paper: Cities and Climate Change*, https://climate-adapt.eea.europa.eu/metadata/publications/climate-focus-paper-cities-and-climate-change. [93]

Knittel, N. et al. (2020), "A global analysis of heat-related labour productivity losses under climate change—implications for Germany's foreign trade", *Climatic Change*, Vol. 160/2, https://doi.org/10.1007/s10584-020-02661-1. [83]

Knox, J. et al. (2012), "Climate change impacts on crop productivity in Africa and South Asia", *Environmental Research Letters*, Vol. 7/3, https://doi.org/10.1088/1748-9326/7/3/034032. [77]

Lecocq, F. and S. Zmarak (2007), "How Might Climate Change Affect Economic Growth in Developing Countries? A Review of the Growth Literature with a Climate Lens", *Policy Research Working Paper*, No. 4315, World Bank, Washington DC, http://econ.worldbank.org. [80]

Li, H. et al. (2018), “Interaction between urban heat island and urban pollution island during summer in Berlin”, *Science of The Total Environment*, Vol. 636, pp. 818-828, https://doi.org/10.1016/j.scitotenv.2018.04.254. [99]

Litman, T. (2014), *Analysis of Public Policies That Unintentionally Encourage and Subsidize Urban Sprawl*, http://www.lsecities.net. [11]

Li, Y. et al. (2018), “Projecting future climate change impacts on heat-related mortality in large urban areas in China”, *Environmental Research*, Vol. 163, pp. 171-185, https://doi.org/10.1016/j.envres.2018.01.047. [98]

Lobell et al. (2011), “Climate Trends and Global Crop Production Since 1980”, *Science*, Vol. 333/6042, pp. 613-616. [58]

Maharjan, K. and N. Joshi (2012), *Climate Change, Agriculture and Rural Livelihoods in Developing Countries with Reference to Nepal*, Springer Japan, Tokyo, https://doi.org/10.1007/978-4-431-54343-5. [56]

Mahlalela, P. et al. (2020), “Drought in the Eastern Cape region of South Africa and trends in rainfall characteristics”, *Climate Dynamics*, Vol. 55/9-10, https://doi.org/10.1007/s00382-020-05413-0. [117]

Manda, M. and E. Wanda (2017), “Understanding the nature and scale of risks in Karonga, Malawi”, *Environment and Urbanization*, Vol. 29/1, https://doi.org/10.1177/0956247817692200. [38]

Marplecroft (2018), *84% of world’s fastest growing cities face “extreme” climate change risks*, https://www.maplecroft.com/insights/analysis/84-of-worlds-fastest-growing-cities-face-extreme-climate-change-risks/. [28]

McDonald, R. et al. (2014), “Water on an urban planet: Urbanization and the reach of urban water infrastructure”, *Global Environmental Change*, Vol. 27, pp. 96-105, https://doi.org/10.1016/j.gloenvcha.2014.04.022. [122]

Mika, J. et al. (2018), *Impact of 1.5 K global warming on urban air pollution and heat island with outlook on human health effects*, Elsevier B.V., https://doi.org/10.1016/j.cosust.2018.05.013. [23]

Muyambo, F., A. Jordaan and Y. Bahta (2017), “Assessing social vulnerability to drought in South Africa: Policy implication for drought risk reduction”, *Jàmbá: Journal of Disaster Risk Studies*, Vol. 9/1, https://doi.org/10.4102/jamba.v9i1.326. [120]

Naya, D. (ed.) (2016), “Is Decoupling GDP Growth from Environmental Impact Possible?”, *PLOS ONE*, Vol. 11/10, p. e0164733, https://doi.org/10.1371/journal.pone.0164733. [151]

NCE (2018), *Unlocking The Inclusive Growth Story of the 21st Century: Accelerating Climate Action in Urgent Times*, http://www.newclimateeconomy.report. [14]

Ningrum, W. (2017), *Urban Heat Island towards Urban Climate*, Institute of Physics Publishing, https://doi.org/10.1088/1755-1315/118/1/012048. [96]

NOAA National Centers for Environmental Information (2020), *Climate at a Glance: Global Time Series*, https://www.ncdc.noaa.gov/cag/. [73]

Nyahunda, L., H. Tirivangasi and H. Tirivangasi (2019), “Challenges faced by rural people in mitigating the effects of climate change in the Mazungunye communal lands, Zimbabwe”, *Jàmbá-Journal of Disaster Risk Studies*, Vol. 11/1, pp. 1-9, https://doi.org/10.4102/jamba. [54]

OECD (2021), *Transport Strategies for Net-Zero Systems by Design*, OECD Publishing, Paris, https://doi.org/10.1787/0a20f779-en. [12]

OECD (2021), *What Is the Well-Being Lens: An Innovative Process for Net-zero Strategies*, OECD Publishing, Paris, https://www.oecd.org/climate-change/well-being-lens/well-being-lens-brochure.pdf (accessed on 20 October 2021). [172]

OECD (2019), *Accelerating Climate Action: Refocusing Policies through a Well-being Lens*, OECD Publishing, Paris, https://doi.org/10.1787/2f4c8c9a-en. [169]

OECD (2018), *Building Resilient Cities: An Assessment of Disaster Risk Management Policies in Southeast Asia*, OECD Green Growth Studies, OECD Publishing, Paris, https://doi.org/10.1787/9789264305397-en. [167]

OECD (2018), *Rethinking Urban Sprawl: Moving Towards Sustainable Cities*, OECD Publishing, Paris, https://doi.org/10.1787/9789264189881-en. [13]

OECD (2016), *The Economic Consequences of Outdoor Air Pollution*, OECD Publishing, Paris, https://doi.org/10.1787/9789264257474-en. [91]

OECD (2016), *Urban Green Growth in Dynamic Asia*, OECD Green Growth Studies, OECD Publishing, Paris, https://doi.org/10.1787/9789264266360-en. [166]

OECD (2014), *Climate Change, Water and Agriculture: Towards Resilient Systems*, OECD Studies on Water, OECD Publishing, Paris, https://doi.org/10.1787/9789264209138-en. [57]

OECD (2012), *OECD Environmental Outlook to 2050: The Consequences of Inaction*, OECD Publishing, Paris, https://doi.org/10.1787/9789264122246-en. [113]

OECD (2010), *Cities and Climate Change*, OECD Publishing, Paris, https://doi.org/10.1787/9789264091375-en. [27]

OECD (2002), *"Indicators to Measure Decoupling of Environmental Pressure from Economic Growth*, OECD Publishing, Paris, https://www.oecd.org/environment/indicators-modelling-outlooks/1933638.pdf (accessed on 11 July 2021). [150]

OECD/IEA (2017), *World Energy Outlook 2017*, International Energy Agency, Paris, https://www.iea.org/reports/world-energy-outlook-2017. [147]

OECD/UCLG (2016), *Subnational Governments around the world: Structure and finance*, OECD and UCLG, Paris, https://www.uclg.org/sites/default/files/global_observatory_on_local_finance_0.pdf (accessed on 13 July 2022). [39]

Okaka, F. and B. Odhiambo (2019), "Health vulnerability to flood-induced risks of households in flood-prone informal settlements in the Coastal City of Mombasa, Kenya", *Natural Hazards*, Vol. 99/2, pp. 1007-1029, https://doi.org/10.1007/s11069-019-03792-0. [32]

Oliveira, J. and P. Pereda (2020), "The impact of climate change on internal migration in Brazil", *Journal of Environmental Economics and Management*, Vol. 103, https://doi.org/10.1016/j.jeem.2020.102340. [66]

Olivier, J. and J. Peters (2020), *Trends in Global CO2 and Total Green House Gas Emissions - 2019 Report*, PBL Netherlands Environmental Assessment Agency, The Hague, https://www.pbl.nl/sites/default/files/downloads/pbl-2020-trends-in-global-. [145]

Oppenheimer, M. et al. (2019), "Sea Level Rise and Implications for Low-Lying Islands, Coasts and Communities", in Pörtner, D.C. Roberts, V. Masson-Delmotte, P. Zhai, M. Tignor, E. Poloczanska, K. Mintenbeck, A. Alegría, M. Nicolai, A. Okem, J. Petzold, B. Rama, N. (ed.), *IPCC Special Report on the Ocean and Cryosphere in a Changing Climate*, https://www.ipcc.ch/srocc/chapter/chapter-4-sea-level-rise-and-implications-for-low-lying-islands-coasts-and-communities/. [134]

Pandey, K. (2010), "Costs of Adapting to Climate Change for Human Health in Developing Countries", The World Bank, Washington DC, https://openknowledge.worldbank.org/bitstream/handle/10986/27750/581680NWP0Box31CDP0111010Health1web.pdf?sequence=1&isAllowed=y (accessed on 11 July 2021). [92]

Pareek, N. (2017), "Climate Change Impact on Soils: Adaptation and Mitigation", *MOJ Ecology & Environmental Sciences*, Vol. 2/3, https://doi.org/10.15406/mojes.2017.02.00026. [55]

Parikh, J. and V. Shukla (1995), "Urbanization, energy use and greenhouse effects in economic development", *Global Environmental Change*, Vol. 5/2, pp. 87-103, https://doi.org/10.1016/0959-3780(95)00015-g. [156]

Parker, L. et al. (2019), "Vulnerability of the agricultural sector to climate change: The development of a pan-tropical Climate Risk Vulnerability Assessment to inform sub-national decision making", *PLoS ONE*, Vol. 14/3, https://doi.org/10.1371/journal.pone.0213641. [59]

Parncutt, R. (2019), "The human cost of anthropogenic global warming: Semi-quantitative prediction and the 1,000-tonne rule", *Frontiers in Psychology*, Vol. 10/OCT, https://doi.org/10.3389/fpsyg.2019.02323. [89]

Paterson, S. et al. (2017), "Size does matter: City scale and the asymmetries of climate change adaptation in three coastal towns", *Geoforum*, Vol. 81, pp. 109-119, https://doi.org/10.1016/j.geoforum.2017.02.014. [35]

Pendall, R. (1999), "Do land-use controls cause sprawl?", *Environment and Planning B: Planning and Design*, Vol. 26/4, pp. 555-571, https://doi.org/10.1068/b260555. [15]

PMG (2018), *Western and Eastern Cape drought crisis*, Parliamentary Monitoring Group Water and Sanitation Meeting Summary, https://pmg.org.za/committee-meeting/25770/ (accessed on 12 July 2021). [119]

Podesta, J. (2019), *The climate crisis, migration, and refugees*, Brookings, Washington DC, https://www.brookings.edu/research/the-climate-crisis-migration-and-refugees/. [65]

Quang Vinh Ky (2018), *Planning for peri-urban development and flooding issues: The story of new urban areas in Can Tho City*, Institute for Social and Environmental Transition-International, Can Tho, https://www.preventionweb.net/publications/view/58096 (accessed on 12 July 2021). [130]

Rajesh, D. (2018), *Managing water amidst urban sprawl and climate change in Can Tho City*, Stockholm Environmental Institute, https://www.sei.org/featured/managing-water-amidst-urban-sprawl-climate-change-can-tho-city/ (accessed on 12 July 2021). [131]

Reardon, T. and D. Zilberman (2018), "Climate smart food supply chains in developing countries in an era of rapid dual change in agrifood systems and the climate", in *Natural Resource Management and Policy*, Springer, https://doi.org/10.1007/978-3-319-61194-5_15. [62]

Revi et al (2014), *Urban Areas in Climate Change 2014: Impacts, Adaptation, and Vulnerability*, IPCC, Cambridge, https://www.ipcc.ch/report/ar5/wg2/. [21]

Roberts et al. (2016), *Intermediary Cities: The Nexus Between the Local and the Global Co-creating the Urban Future*, UCLG, Barcelona, https://www.researchgate.net/publication/309401150. [34]

Roberts, B. (2014), *Managing Systems of Secondary Cities*, Cities Alliance/UNOPS, Brussels, https://www.researchgate.net/publication/273442050. [140]

Rohat, G. et al. (2019), "Projections of Human Exposure to Dangerous Heat in African Cities Under Multiple Socioeconomic and Climate Scenarios", *Earth's Future*, Vol. 7/5, pp. 528-546, https://doi.org/10.1029/2018EF001020. [31]

Rosenzweig, C. et al. (2015), *ARC3.2 Summary for City Leaders. Urban Climate Change Research Network*, Columbia University, New York, http://www.uccrn.org/casestudies. [94]

Roy, S. et al. (2018), *Bangladesh: National Urban Policies and City Profiles for Dhaka and Khulna*, Sustainable, Healthy and Learning Cities and Neighbourhoods (SHLC), http://www.centreforsustainablecities.ac.uk/research/bangladesh-national-urban-policies-city-profiles-dhaka-khulna/ (accessed on 12 July 2021). [138]

Rubiera-Morollón, F. and R. Garrido-Yserte (2020), "Recent Literature about Urban Sprawl: A Renewed Relevance of the Phenomenon from the Perspective of Environmental Sustainability", *Sustainability*, Vol. 12/16, p. 6551, https://doi.org/10.3390/su12166551. [8]

SABC (2020), *Drought worsening in large parts of Eastern Cape*, SABC News, https://www.sabcnews.com/sabcnews/drought-worsening-in-large-parts-of-eastern-cape/ (accessed on 12 July 2021). [118]

Salvadore et al. (2015), "Hydrological modelling of urbanized catchments: A review and future directions", *Journal of Hydrology*, Vol. 529, pp. 62-81, https://doi.org/10.1016/j.jhydrol.2015.06.028. [127]

Satterthwaite et al. (2007), *Adapting to climate change in urban areas: the possibilities and constraints in low- and middle-income nations*, International Institute for Environment and Development, London. [42]

Satterthwaite, D. (2016), "Small and intermediate urban centres in sub Saharan Africa", *Urban Africa Risk Knowledge*, No. 6, International Institute for Environment and Development (IIED), London, https://www.urbanark.org/background-paper-small-and-intermediate-urban-centres-sub-saharan-africa (accessed on 11 July 2021). [36]

Satterthwaite, D. (2009), "The implications of population growth and urbanization for climate change", *Environment and Urbanization*, Vol. 21/2, pp. 545-567, https://doi.org/10.1177/0956247809344361. [148]

Satterthwaite, D. et al. (2020), "Building Resilience to Climate Change in Informal Settlements", *One Earth*, Vol. 2/2, pp. 143-156, https://doi.org/10.1016/j.oneear.2020.02.002. [41]

Savini, F. and M. Aalbers (2016), "The de-contextualisation of land use planning through financialisation: Urban redevelopment in Milan", *European Urban and Regional Studies*, Vol. 23/4, pp. 878-894, https://doi.org/10.1177/0969776415585887. [16]

Seto et al. (2012), "Global forecasts of urban expansion to 2030 and direct impacts on biodiversity and carbon pools", *Proceedings of the National Academy of Sciences of the United States of America*, Vol. 109/40, pp. 16083-16088, https://doi.org/10.1073/pnas.1211658109. [5]

Seto, K. et al. (2014), "Human Settlements, Infrastructure and Spatial Planning", in Edenhofer, O. (ed.), *Climate Change 2014: Mitigation of Climate Change. Contribution of Working Group III to the Fifth Assessment Report of the Intergovernmental Panel on Climate Change*, Mitigation of Climate Change, Cambridge, and New York, https://www.ipcc.ch/site/assets/uploads/2018/02/ipcc_wg3_ar5_chapter12.pdf (accessed on 11 July 2021). [163]

Singh, T., C. Siderius and Y. Van der Velde (2018), "When do Indians feel hot? Internet searches indicate seasonality suppresses adaptation to heat", *Environmental Research Letters*, Vol. 13/5, p. 054009, https://doi.org/10.1088/1748-9326/aaba82. [106]

Sultan, B. and M. Gaetani (2016), "Agriculture in West Africa in the Twenty-first Century: climate change and impacts scenarios, and potential for adaptation", *Frontiers in Plant Science*, Vol. 7/1262, pp. 1-37. [78]

Swiss Re Institute (2021), *The economics of climate change; no action not an option*, Swiss Re Management, Zurich, https://www.swissre.com/dam/jcr:e73ee7c3-7f83-4c17-a2b8-8ef23a8d3312/swiss-re-institute-expertise-publication-economics-of-climate-change.pdf (accessed on 23 December 2021). [75]

Tacoli, C. et al. (2015), "Urbanisation, rural-urban migration and urban poverty", IIED, https://www.researchgate.net/publication/273888747_Urbanisation_Rural-Urban_Migration_and_Urban_Poverty. [71]

Tacoli, C. et al. (2014), *World Migration Report 2015. Urbanization, Rural-urban Migration and Urban Poverty*, Human Settlements Group International Institute forEnvironment and Development (IIED), London, https://www.iom.int/sites/default/files/our_work/ICP/MPR/WMR-2015-Background-Paper-CTacoli-GMcGranahan-DSatterthwaite.pdf (accessed on 17 February 2021). [63]

Tacoli, C. (2011), *Not only climate change: mobility, vulnerability and socio-economic transformations in environmentally fragile areas of Bolivia, Senegal and Tanzania*, IIED, London, https://pubs.iied.org/10590IIED/. [68]

Tacoli, C. and B. Vorley (2016), *Informal food systems and food security in rural and urban East Africa*, https://doi.org/10.1371/journal. [50]

The Straits Times (2019), *Water express delivers emergency supplies to drought-hit Indian city*, The Straits Times, Asia, https://www.straitstimes.com/asia/south-asia/water-express-delivers-emergency-supplies-to-drought-hit-indian-city (accessed on 25 October 2021). [115]

Tume et al. (2019), "Indigenous Knowledge and Farmer Perceptions of Climate and Ecological Changes in the Bamenda Highlands of Cameroon: Insights from the Bui Plateau", *Climate*, Vol. 7/12, p. 138, https://doi.org/10.3390/cli7120138. [30]

Turek-Hankins et al. (2021), "Climate change adaptation to extreme heat: A global systematic review of implemented action", *Oxford Open Climate Change*, https://doi.org/10.1093/oxfclm/kgab005. [107]

Turok, I. (2018), "Informing Africa's urban transformation: A response to Fox et al. and Potts", *Urban Studies*, Vol. 55/5, https://doi.org/10.1177/0042098017713575. [49]

Tusholske, C. et al. (2021), *Global High Resolution Daily Extreme Urban Heat Exposure (UHE-Daily), 1983-2016*, https://doi.org/10.7927/fq7g-ny13. [102]

UCCRN (2018), *The Future We Don't Want -- How Climate Change Could Impact the World's Greatest Cities*, UCCRN, C40, Acclimatise, Global Covenant of Mayors. [26]

UCCRN and C40 (2018), *The Future We Don't Want: How Climate Change Could Impact the World's Greatest Cities*, Columbia University, New York, https://uccrn.ei.columbia.edu/news/future-we-dont-want (accessed on 12 July 2021). [121]

UCLG (2016), *UCLG Frame document for Intermediary Cities: Planning and management of sustainable urban development*, United Cities and Local Governments , Barcelona, https://www.uclg.org/sites/default/files/uclg_frame_document_ic.pdf (accessed on 18 February 2021). [171]

UN-Climate Action (2018), *Cities and Pollution contribute to climate change: Cities and local action*, https://www.un.org/en/climatechange/cities-pollution.shtml (accessed on 22 June 2020). [142]

UNDESA (2018), *World Urbanization Prospects 2018 Highlights*, UNDESA, New York, https://population.un.org/wup/Publications/. [2]

UNDESA (2018), *World Urbanization Prospects: The 2018 Revision*, Online edition, https://population.un.org/wup/ (accessed on 23 April 2020). [3]

UN-HABITAT (2011), *Cities and Climate Change - Global Report on Human Settlements 2011*, Un-Habitat, London - Washington DC, https://unhabitat.org/cities-and-climate-change-global-report-on-human-settlements-2011. [9]

UNISDR (2016), *The Human Cost of Weather-Related Disasters 1995-2015*, UN Office for Disaster Risk Reduction, Geneva, https://www.undrr.org/about-undrr. [87]

Van der Geest, K. (2011), "North-South Migration in Ghana: What Role for the Environment?", *International Migration*, Vol. 49/SUPPL.1, https://doi.org/10.1111/j.1468-2435.2010.00645.x. [69]

Vermeulen, S., B. Campbell and J. Ingram (2012), *Climate Change and Food Systems*, https://doi.org/10.1146/annurev-environ-020411-130608. [61]

Wang et al (2020), "Convergence of carbon intensity: a test on developed and developing countries", *Environmental Science and Pollution Research*, Vol. 27/28, https://doi.org/10.1007/s11356-020-09175-4. [159]

Wang, F., F. Yang and L. Qi (2020), "Convergence of carbon intensity: a test on developed and developing countries", *Environmental Science and Pollution Research*, Vol. 27/28, pp. 34796-34807, https://doi.org/10.1007/s11356-020-09175-4. [149]

Wang, S. et al. (2018), "The effects of urbanization on CO2 emissions in the Pearl River Delta: A comprehensive assessment and panel data analysis", *Applied Energy*, Vol. 228, pp. 1693-1706, https://doi.org/10.1016/j.apenergy.2018.06.155. [154]

Watts, N. et al. (2015), "Health and climate change: policy responses to protect public health", *The Lancet*, Vol. 386/10006, https://doi.org/10.1016/S0140-6736(15)60854-6. [86]

Watts, N. et al. (2018), "The Lancet Countdown on health and climate change: from 25 years of inaction to a global transformation for public health", *The Lancet*, Vol. 391/10120, https://doi.org/10.1016/S0140-6736(17)32464-9. [85]

Wei, B., H. Yagita and A. Inaba (2003), "Urbanisation impact on energy demand and CO2 emission in China", *Journal of Chonging University*, Vol. 2/46, https://www.researchgate.net/publication/284385268_Urbanization_impact_on_energy_demand_and_CO2_emission_in_China/citation/download (accessed on 14 July 2021). [158]

WHO (2018), *Climate Change and Health*, https://www.who.int/en/news-room/fact-sheets/detail/climate-change-and-health (accessed on 8 July 2020). [90]

WHO (2014), *Quantitative risk assessment of the effects of climate change on selected causes of death, 2030s and 2050s*, World Health Organisation, Geneva, https://www.who.int/globalchange/publications/quantitative-risk-assessment/en/. [88]

Williams, S. (2021), "The sea is rising, the climate is changing: the lessons learned from Mozambique's deadly cyclone", *The Guardian*, https://www.theguardian.com/world/2021/jan/02/the-sea-is-rising-the-climate-is-changing-the-lessons-learned-from-mozambiques-deadly-cyclone (accessed on 25 October 2021). [141]

WMO (2019), *WMO Statement on the State of the Global Climate in 2019*, World Meteorological Organization, Geneva, https://library.wmo.int/doc_num.php?explnum_id=10211. [74]

World Bank (2010), *Cities and Climate Change: An Urgent Agenda*, World Bank, Washington DC, http://documents.worldbank.org/curated/en/194831468325262572/Cities-and-climate-change-an-urgent-agenda. [97]

World Bank, CIAT and CGIAR (2015), *Climate-Smart Agriculture in Nicaragua*, World Bank, Washington DC. [60]

Zermoglio, F. et al. (2020), *Climate vulnerability assessment: Impacts on health outcomes in Secondary Cities of Bangladesh*, USAID, New Wark, https://doi.org/10.13140/RG.2.2.22928.15368. [139]

Zhang, W. et al. (2018), "Urbanization exacerbated the rainfall and flooding caused by hurricane Harvey in Houston", *Nature*, Vol. 563/7731, https://doi.org/10.1038/s41586-018-0676-z. [126]

Zhang, X. et al. (2019), "Urban drought challenge to 2030 sustainable development goals", *Science of the Total Environment*, Vol. 693, https://doi.org/10.1016/j.scitotenv.2019.07.342. [111]

Zhou, Y. et al. (2015), "Effects of rural–urban development transformation on energy consumption and CO2 emissions: A regional analysis in China", *Renewable and Sustainable Energy Reviews*, Vol. 52, pp. 863-875, https://doi.org/10.1016/j.rser.2015.07.158. [155]

Annex 2.A. Additional figures and tables

Annex Figure 2.A.1. Expected change in cities' CO_2 emissions by sector due to changes in GDP, population, and built-up land

Estimates for cities of different sizes

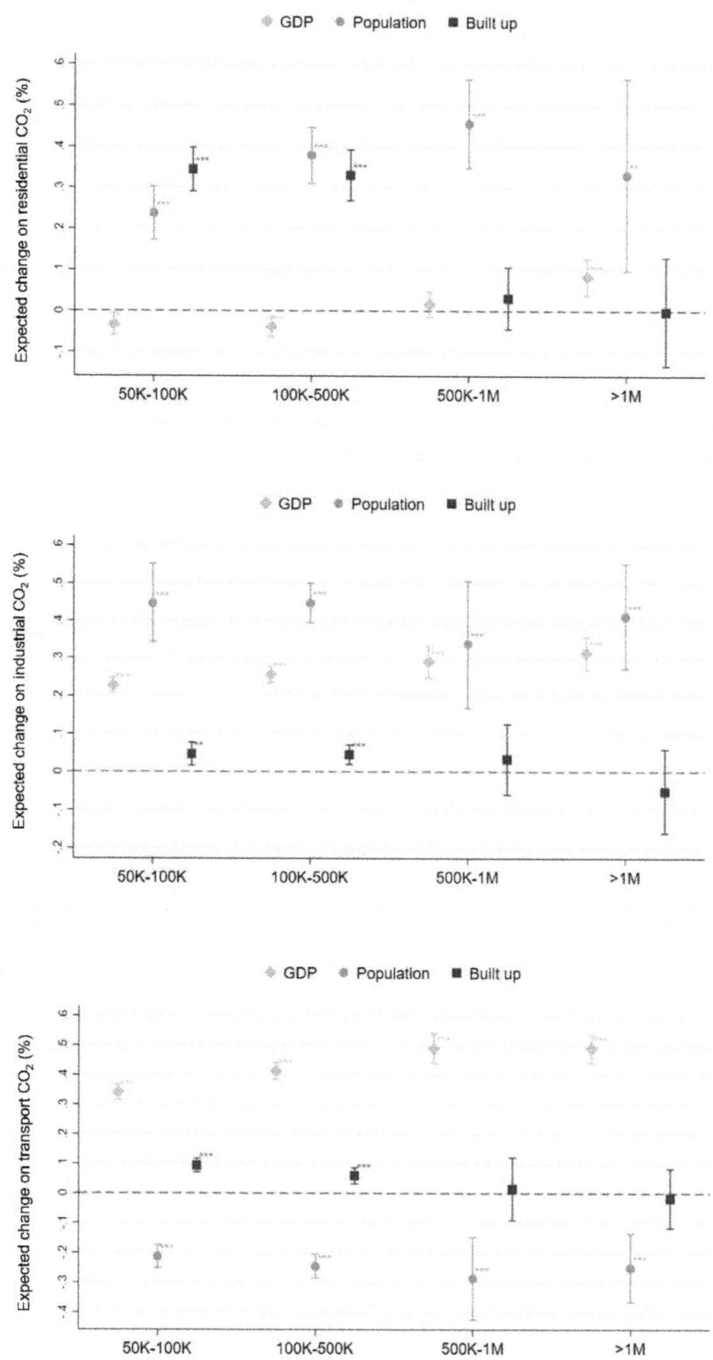

Note: Estimates of a panel econometric model regressing CO_2 emissions (residential, transport or industrial) on GDP, population, and built-up land, including their interactions with city size. Base category is cities above 1 million inhabitants. All variables included expressed logarithmic terms. Results based on a fixed-effects estimator, considering year-effects, and standard errors clustered by city. Data for the periods 1990, 2000 and 2015. The sample does not include cities in high-income countries.
Source: Author's own calculations using GHS Urban Centre Database (2019[173]).

Annex Figure 2.A.2. CO_2 emissions per capita across regions (2015)

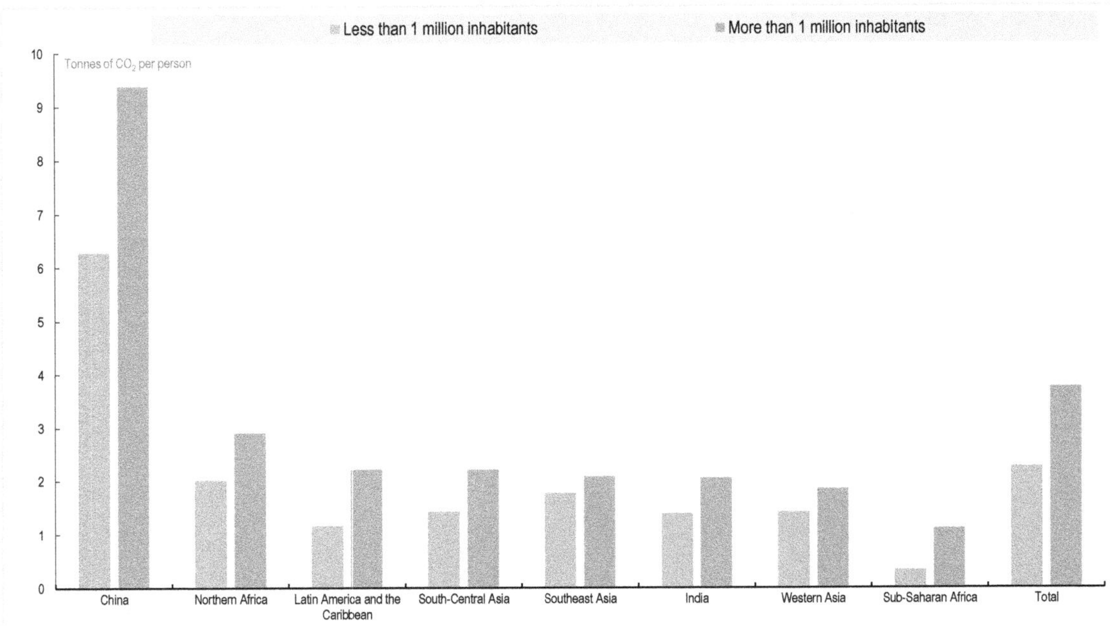

Note: Intermediary cities are those agglomerations with fewer than 1 million inhabitants in 2015. The sample does not include cities in high-income countries.
Source: Author's own calculations using GHS Urban Centre Database (2019[173]).

Annex Table 2.A.1. Description of logistic regression on the decrease of population density

Effects of city characteristics on density decrease

	(1) Density decrease	(2) Density decrease	(3) Density decrease
Time to capital	0.978 (-1.58)	0.976 (-1.51)	0.973 (-1.78)
Border	0.570 (-1.11)	0.584 (-0.96)	0.793 (-0.41)
River	1.005 (0.03)	1.019 (0.11)	1.051 (0.30)
Coast, 5Km	0.388*** (-4.23)	0.455*** (-4.29)	0.502*** (-3.78)
GDP, 2000		1.000 (-0.82)	1.000 (-0.31)
GDP, 2000-15		0.820** (-2.81)	0.839** (-2.89)
< 100K inhab.			5.260*** (8.21)
100K-500K inhab.			3.474*** (7.47)
500K-1M inhab.			1.920*** (4.02)
Country FE	Yes	Yes	Yes
No. Observations	6660	6660	6660
Pseudo R2	0.271	0.302	0.320

Note: Estimates of a logistic econometric model, where the dependent variable indicates whether a city has lost between 2000 and 2015. Covariates include the time to reach the capital city, whether the city is in an international border, whether the city is next to a river basin, whether the city is within 5 Km from the coast, the GDP level in 2000, the GDP growth rate between 2000 and 2015, as well dummy variables indicating whether the city had in 2015 less than 100 000 inhabitants, 100 000 to 500 000 inhabitants, and 500 000 to 1 000 000 inhabitants. All regression models include country fixed-effects. Results based on standard errors clustered by city. Year fixed effects are included. Data for the periods 1990, 2000 and 2015. Exponentiated coefficients; t statistics in parentheses. * $p < 0.05$, ** $p < 0.01$, *** $p < 0.001$.
Source: Author's own calculations using GHS Urban Centre Database (2019[173]).

Annex Table 2.A.2. Regression results and main effects of the effect of frequency of events in which the heat index was above 40.6°C on GDP, by average temperature below or above median and city size

	(1) Log of GDP	(2) Log of GDP	(3) Log of GDP
Log (Number of events over HI 40.6°C)	-0.649*** (-9.69)	-0.662*** (-9.86)	-0.671*** (-10.50)
High temperature X Log (Number of events over HI 40.6°C)	0.588*** (7.73)	0.604*** (7.94)	0.618*** (8.40)
50K-100K X Log (Number of events over HI 40.6°C)	0.284*** (3.96)	0.287*** (3.97)	0.282*** (4.08)
100K-500K X Log (Number of events over HI 40.6°C)	0.202** (2.83)	0.202** (2.81)	0.203** (2.95)
500K-1M X Log (Number of events over HI 40.6°C)	0.189 (1.92)	0.175 (1.76)	0.176 (1.83)
High temperature X 50K-100K X Log (Number of events over HI 40.6°C)	-0.325*** (-4.00)	-0.335*** (-4.10)	-0.331*** (-4.18)
High temperature X 500K-1M X Log (Number of events over HI 40.6°C)	-0.197* (-2.45)	-0.203* (-2.51)	-0.204** (-2.60)
High temperature X 500K-1M X Log (Number of events over HI 40.6°C)	-0.177 (-1.62)	-0.165 (-1.50)	-0.167 (-1.55)
Log of Built up		0.105*** (5.73)	0.104*** (5.69)
Log of Population		0.146*** (4.06)	0.145*** (4.02)
Log of average temperature (5 years)			4.622*** (6.12)
Constant	18.75*** (1204.99)	17.09*** (42.39)	0.628 (0.23)
City FE	Yes	Yes	Yes
Year FE	Yes	Yes	Yes
No. Observations	20830	20765	20744
N of Groups	7625	7615	7606
R-sq Within	0.707	0.716	0.717
R-sq Between	0.00455	0.287	0.00559
R-sq Overall	0.0505	0.308	0.0531

Main effects	(1) Log of GDP	(2) Log of GDP	(3) Log of GDP
Low temperature X 50K-100K	-0.365*** (-13.89)	-0.375*** (-13.80)	-0.390*** (-14.52)
Low temperature X 100K-500K	-0.447*** (-17.77)	-0.459*** (-17.36)	-0.469*** (-18.10)
Low temperature X 500K-1M	-0.460*** (-6.31)	-0.486*** (-6.60)	-0.496*** (-6.89)
Low temperature X >1M	-0.649*** (-9.69)	-0.662*** (-9.86)	-0.671*** (-10.50)
High temperature X 50K-100K	-0.102*** (-6.81)	-0.106*** (-7.35)	-0.102*** (-7.05)
High temperature X 100K-500K	-0.0565*** (-4.19)	-0.0587*** (-4.46)	-0.0551*** (-4.15)
High temperature X 500K-1M	-0.0492 (-1.51)	-0.0475 (-1.49)	-0.0442 (-1.37)
High temperature X >1M	-0.0611 (-1.73)	-0.0577 (-1.64)	-0.0533 (-1.50)
Observations	20830	20765	20744

Note: Estimates of a panel econometric model regressing the Log of GDP on: Log of number of days that exceeded a HI>40.6°C interacted by city size and whether the city is high or low temperature. Other variables included as controls are log of population, log of built-up area and log of average temperature (calculated over the last 5 years). Results based on a fixed-effects estimator and standard errors clustered by city. Year fixed effects are included. Data for the periods 1990, 2000 and 2015. t statistics in parentheses. * $p < 0.05$, ** $p < 0.01$, *** $p < 0.001$.
Source: Author's own calculations using GHS Urban Centre Database (2019[173]) and (Tusholske et al., 2021[102]).

Annex Table 2.A.3. Regression results and main effects of the effect of frequency of events in which the wet bulb was above 30°C on GDP, by average temperature below or above median and city size

	(1) Log of GDP	(2) Log of GDP	(3) Log of GDP
Log (Number of events over WB 30°C)	-0.559*** (-6.35)	-0.562*** (-6.39)	-0.585*** (-6.79)
High temperature X Log (Number of events over WB 30°C)	0.519*** (5.54)	0.527*** (5.61)	0.554*** (5.99)
50K-100K X Log (Number of events over WB 30°C)	0.258** (2.82)	0.254** (2.77)	0.244** (2.72)
100K-500K X Log (Number of events over WB 30°C)	0.113 (1.23)	0.0991 (1.08)	0.102 (1.14)
500K-1M X Log (Number of events over WB 30°C)	0.162 (1.28)	0.134 (1.07)	0.132 (1.08)
High temperature X 50K-100K X Log (Number of events over WB 30°C)	-0.302** (-3.09)	-0.305** (-3.10)	-0.293** (-3.04)
High temperature X 500K-1M X Log (Number of events over WB 30°C)	-0.115 (-1.19)	-0.106 (-1.08)	-0.107 (-1.11)
High temperature X 500K-1M X Log (Number of events over WB 30°C)	-0.182 (-1.37)	-0.150 (-1.14)	-0.145 (-1.13)
Log of Built up		0.0996*** (5.25)	0.0963*** (5.07)
Log of Population		0.157*** (4.20)	0.158*** (4.24)
Log of average temperature (5 years)			6.885*** (8.19)
Constant	18.73*** (1092.08)	16.94*** (40.38)	-7.609* (-2.53)
City FE	Yes	Yes	Yes
Year FE	Yes	Yes	Yes
No. Observations	19902	19842	19822
N of Groups	7455	7446	7437
R-sq Within	0.707	0.716	0.718
R-sq Between	0.00494	0.265	0.000221
R-sq Overall	0.0454	0.297	0.0118

Main effects	(1) Log of GDP	(2) Log of GDP	(3) Log of GDP
Low temperature X 50K-100K	-0.301*** (-11.95)	-0.308*** (-11.80)	-0.341*** (-12.88)
Low temperature X 100K-500K	-0.446*** (-18.24)	-0.463*** (-17.83)	-0.483*** (-18.87)
Low temperature X 500K-1M	-0.397*** (-4.33)	-0.429*** (-4.88)	-0.454*** (-5.27)
Low temperature X >1M	-0.559***	-0.562***	-0.585***

	(-6.35)	(-6.39)	(-6.79)
High temperature X 50K-100K	-0.0833***	-0.0857***	-0.0805***
	(-5.69)	(-6.15)	(-5.75)
High temperature X 100K-500K	-0.0424**	-0.0420**	-0.0357**
	(-3.12)	(-3.15)	(-2.68)
High temperature X 500K-1M	-0.0595*	-0.0511	-0.0448
	(-2.19)	(-1.83)	(-1.59)
High temperature X >1M	-0.0395	-0.0351	-0.0312
	(-1.25)	(-1.09)	(-0.95)
Observations	19902	19842	19822

Note: Estimates of a panel econometric model regressing the Log of GDP on: Log of number of days that exceeded a WB>30°C interacted by city size and whether the city is high or low temperature. Other variables included as controls are log of population, log of built up area and log of average temperature (calculated over the last 5 years). Results based on a fixed-effects estimator and standard errors clustered by city. Year fixed effects are included. Data for the periods 1990, 2000 and 2015. t statistics in parentheses. * $p < 0.05$, ** $p < 0.01$, *** $p < 0.001$.
Source: Author's own calculations using GHS Urban Centre Database (2019[173]) and (Tusholske et al., 2021[102]).

Annex Table 2.A.4. Effects of built-up land, population and GDP growth on CO_2 emissions (total, residential, transport and industrial), by city size

	Log of CO_2 total	Log of CO_2 residential	Log of CO_2 transport	Log of CO_2 industrial
Log of GDP	0.377***	0.0825***	0.489***	0.313***
	(15.09)	(3.68)	(20.25)	(13.83)
50K-100K* Log of GDP	-0.249***	-0.116***	-0.148***	-0.0857***
	(-9.69)	(-4.71)	(-5.77)	(-3.77)
100K-500K* Log of GDP	-0.183***	-0.122***	-0.0761**	-0.0572*
	(-7.10)	(-5.02)	(-2.92)	(-2.50)
500K-1M* Log of GDP	0.0161	-0.0669*	0.000862	-0.0243
	(0.44)	(-2.56)	(0.03)	(-0.82)
Log of Population	0.190**	0.331**	-0.250***	0.412***
	(3.26)	(2.77)	(-4.25)	(5.75)
50K-100K*Log of Population	-0.0401	-0.0937	0.0378	0.0348
	(-0.65)	(-0.76)	(0.61)	(0.41)
100K-500K*Log of Population	0.0258	0.0476	0.00525	0.0360
	(0.42)	(0.39)	(0.08)	(0.48)
500K-1M*Log of Population	-0.0855	0.125	-0.0357	-0.0740
	(-1.10)	(0.96)	(-0.39)	(-0.67)
Log of Built up	0.0190	-0.00195	-0.0166	-0.0508
	(0.41)	(-0.03)	(-0.32)	(-0.91)
50K-100K*Log of Built up	0.161***	0.346***	0.111*	0.0971
	(3.33)	(4.88)	(2.14)	(1.69)
100K-500K*Log of Built up	0.131**	0.332***	0.0762	0.0959
	(2.67)	(4.62)	(1.46)	(1.71)
500K-1M*Log of Built up	-0.0103	0.0328	0.0321	0.0835
	(-0.17)	(0.43)	(0.44)	(1.17)
City FE	Yes	Yes	Yes	Yes
Year FE	Yes	Yes	Yes	Yes
No. Observations	33608	33608	32844	33608
N of Groups	11393	11393	11138	11393
R-sq Within	0.515	0.225	0.760	0.623
R-sq Between	0.461	0.446	0.459	0.545
R-sq Overall	0.460	0.433	0.459	0.535

	(1)	(2)	(3)	(4)
Main effects	Log of CO_2 total	Log of CO_2 residential	Log of CO_2 transport	Log of CO_2 industrial
Log of GDP				
50K-100K	0.128***	-0.0333*	0.341***	0.227***
	(12.65)	(-2.44)	(25.41)	(23.27)
100K-500K	0.194***	-0.0392**	0.413***	0.256***
	(19.71)	(-3.22)	(28.69)	(22.92)
500K-1M	0.394***	0.0156	0.490***	0.289***
	(14.35)	(1.00)	(18.86)	(13.42)
>1M	0.377***	0.0825***	0.489***	0.313***
	(15.09)	(3.68)	(20.25)	(13.83)

Log of Population				
50K-100K	0.150***	0.238***	-0.212***	0.446***
	(6.65)	(7.16)	(-10.83)	(8.32)
100K-500K	0.216***	0.379***	-0.245***	0.448***
	(9.01)	(10.88)	(-11.98)	(16.54)
500K-1M	0.105*	0.456***	-0.286***	0.338***
	(2.03)	(8.27)	(-4.06)	(3.92)
>1M	0.190**	0.331**	-0.250***	0.412***
	(3.26)	(2.77)	(-4.25)	(5.75)
Log of Built up				
50K-100K	0.180***	0.344***	0.0945***	0.0463**
	(11.40)	(12.65)	(8.01)	(3.00)
100K-500K	0.150***	0.330***	0.0596***	0.0451***
	(7.54)	(10.45)	(4.34)	(3.44)
500K-1M	0.00871	0.0308	0.0155	0.0327
	(0.23)	(0.81)	(0.29)	(0.69)
>1M	0.0190	-0.00195	-0.0166	-0.0508
	(0.41)	(-0.03)	(-0.32)	(-0.91)
Observations	33608	33608	32844	33608

Note: Estimates of a panel econometric model regressing CO_2 emissions (total, residential, transport or industrial) on: GDP, population, and built-up, the three variables interacted with city size. Base category is cities above 1 million inhabitants. All variables included expressed logarithmic terms. Results based on a fixed-effects estimator, considering year-effects, and standard errors clustered by city. Data for the periods 1990, 2000 and 2015. t statistics in parentheses. * $p < 0.05$, ** $p < 0.01$, *** $p < 0.001$.
Source: Authors' own calculations using GHS Urban Centre Database (2019[173]).

3 The ripple effects of climate change on intermediary cities: Disruption of food systems and internal migration

This chapter describes the complex linkages between climate change, food systems, internal migration and intermediary cities. Given their close socio-economic and geographic links with rural areas, intermediary cities will face ripple effects of climate change. These include disruptions of food systems, and changes in the scale and pattern of rural-to-urban internal migration. The chapter presents policy actions that can help build resilience in both rural areas and urban centres. It argues that preparing for rapid urbanisation and strengthening food systems requires territorial planning that accounts for the interdependence between intermediary cities and rural areas. The chapter concludes by stressing the need for effective dialogue across all levels of government and the importance for local governments of forging partnerships to strengthen their capacities and resources.

Climate change is increasingly disrupting the rural-urban interface of developing countries. Extreme climatic events and climate variability threaten the livelihoods of urban and rural households, as well as the infrastructure they rely on, according to the Food and Agriculture Organization and other experts (FAO et al., 2018[1]; Vermeulen et al, 2012[2]). In addition to directly affecting urban and rural areas, climate change could also disrupt the ways in which these areas interact with each other, namely though food systems and internal migration.

This chapter discusses the relationship between internal migration, food systems, climate change and intermediary cities. It aims to unpack the intricate and complex channels through which climate change affects both food systems and internal migration, while also providing a better understanding of the potential implications for intermediary cities.

The chapter is structured as follows. The first section provides an overview of how climate change affects the rural-urban interface. The second assesses how climate change affects food systems and the ripple effects on intermediary cities. The third explores the relationship between climate-induced migration and intermediary cities. The final section proposes a way forward and possible policy implications.

Climate change and the rural-urban interface

The rural-urban interface encompasses intermediary cities, small towns and rural areas. It hosts 5.5-6 billion inhabitants worldwide (Berdegué et al., 2014[3]; Proctor, 2018[4]), as well as most of the world's 500 million smallholder farmers (FAO, 2017[5]). Indeed, as a majority of the global population resides in these areas, the rural-urban interface encompasses most of humanity. As a very dynamic area, it is key for the well-being of a large share of the population since it acts as a facilitator for continuous bi-directional movements of people and goods, as well as services (financial, environmental, etc.).

Intermediary cities are at the core of the rural-urban interface. They function as nodes that connect social and economic activities and provide the critical mass necessary for the development of social, economic and cultural processes taking place across the rural-urban interface (Berdegué et al., 2014[3]; OECD/PSI, 2020[6]). Intermediary cities are distinct in their functions and closeness to rural areas. They facilitate rural-urban linkages by giving rural populations access to infrastructure, transportation and public services as well as enabling access to markets for agricultural producers (Berdegué et al., 2014[3]). As such, intermediary cities are connected to rural areas through different channels that support the continuous flow of goods, services and people.

Food systems constitute a main channel tying together rural areas and intermediary cities, especially in developing countries. This is because activities within food systems are spatially distributed across rural and urban territories. Rural areas are most often the main site of agricultural production, while activities in the midstream (processing, wholesale, transportation) and downstream (distribution, retailing and restaurants) of food supply chains usually take place in intermediary cities, small towns and peri-urban areas (Berdegué et al., 2014[3]; Proctor, 2018[4]; Reardon and Zilberman, 2018[7]).

Another important channel linking intermediary cities and rural areas is internal migration. Population movements along the rural-urban continuum shape the development of both intermediary cities and rural areas. Indeed, between 2000 and 2010, rural-to-urban migration accounted for almost half of global urban population growth (Tacoli et al., 2014[8]). Overall, rural-to-urban migration strengthens the linkages between rural and urban areas (Berdegué et al., 2014[3]), as well as serving as a means of diversification of livelihoods and income.

Food systems and internal migration are intrinsically interlinked. Population movements along the rural-urban interface often reflect changes or transformations in food systems. In particular, food systems are a critical source of employment for a large share of rural migrants. Although the upstream segment of food systems (agricultural production) accounts for a significant share of total employment, the mid- and downstream segments of agricultural value chains are an increasingly important source of livelihood for rural migrants (Allen et al., 2018[9]; Dury et al., 2019[10]). As such, changes in food systems and their respective labour markets are closely correlated with migration trends and population dynamics in many developing countries (Berdegué et al., 2014[3]).

Rural-to-urban migration also plays a key role in the transformation of food systems. It leads to an increase in the demand for high-value-added and processed food, resulting in further transformations of food systems by prompting changes in agricultural production, food processing, distribution, storage, etc. (Tacoli and Agergaard, 2017[11]). At the same time, the growth of the "food away from home" sector and higher wages in urban areas are important pull factors for rural-to-urban migration (FAO, 2017[12]). Key characteristics of urban areas, such as agglomeration effects, spatial proximity and higher wages, have played key roles in the growth of "food away from home", making the sector attractive to urban and rural consumers alike and transforming food systems (OECD, 2021[13]), while also turning the industry into an attractive source of income diversification. As such, migration to intermediary cities creates large scope for farm and off-farm employment creation along agri-food value chains. Transformation of food systems can also facilitate seasonal or circular migration, which enables rural income diversification (Arslan, Egger and Winters, 2018[14]). Moreover, remittances resulting from internal migration can boost investment in the agricultural sector, further enabling rural households to hire seasonal wage labour to work in food production, including with high-value crops such as fruit and vegetables (Tacoli and Agergaard, 2017[11]). Thus, food systems and internal migration are closely interlinked, i.e. changes in one eventually lead to changes in the other.

Intermediary cities play a fundamental role in the transformation of both food systems and internal migration. These agglomerations provide the soft and hard infrastructure and the critical mass that is necessary to enable activities within food systems to take place; by doing so they facilitate mobility among rural households (Tacoli and Agergaard, 2017[11]). The growth in size and importance of intermediary cities is blurring the lines of rural and urban boundaries, further facilitating migration flows and transformation of food systems (Tacoli et al., 2014[8]). Moreover, the close links of intermediary cities to rural areas enable migrants to maintain their social ties and allow them to avoid the higher cost of migrating to larger metropolitan cities (Berdegué et al., 2014[3]). At the same time, the downstream activities of food systems found in intermediary cities provide a source of employment for women.

Climate change is expected to become a major disruptor of rural-urban dynamics

Climate change is expected to weaken rural-urban connectivity by disrupting the channels that connect these territories (Box 3.1). Indeed, climate change is proving to be a major disruptor of agricultural value chains. Climate phenomena can be classified as fast- and slow-onset events. Fast-onset events (such as floods, storms and cyclones) can lead to an immediate loss of livelihoods and basic infrastructure, which affects food systems and can force people to migrate. Food systems refer to the vast and interlinked networks of value-adding activities stretching from the farmer's gate to the consumer's plate: supply of production input, production, aggregation, processing, wholesaling, distribution and consumption (Nguyen H, 2018[15]; IFAD, 2021[16]). They also encompass the subsystems, policies and regulations that underpin the operation of the supply chains, including subsectors such as waste management and input supply (Nguyen H, 2018[15]). Their complex linkages make them particularly susceptible to climate-induced risks.

Box 3.1. How climate change disrupts the rural-urban interface

There is a growing consensus today that climate change disrupts linkages between rural and urban areas (Dasgupta et al., 2014[17]; UN-Habitat, 2017[18]; Jamshed et al., 2021[19]). Urban areas, especially small and medium-sized cities, are inherently dependent on surrounding rural areas for resources such as water, energy and food supply. Climate effects in rural areas such as droughts can trigger shortages in the supply of water and other resources to urban areas (Morton et al., 2014[20]). This was the case, for example, in Bulawayo, Zimbabwe's second largest city, where rural droughts led to city water shortages (Mkandla, Van der Zaag and Sibanda, 2005[21]). Similarly, flooding in rural areas of Pakistan has affected rural-urban linkages, increasing the price of transportation to cities and the cost of agricultural inputs such as fertiliser and seeds (supplied from cities). Moreover, as the floods negatively affected rural livelihoods, there was increased migration towards cities by rural people looking for work (Jamshed et al., 2021[19]).

Climate change will also affect service provision across the rural-urban interface. In climate disasters such as floods, droughts and storms, rural areas may be left at a disadvantage in terms of services as urban needs are often prioritised and have larger visibility by local and national governments (Morton et al., 2014[20]). This stems from the fact that rural areas tend to be less well equipped than urban areas for adapting to climate threats (Steinberg, 2014[22]). The effects of climate change such as flooding on rural-urban linkages can leave vulnerable populations trapped in poverty, with loss of livelihoods. Indeed, the socio-economic characteristics of individuals and households in the rural-urban interface play a large role in their resilience to climate change. In Pakistan, for instance, rural households with a higher level of education and income were better able to connect with cities after floods and had better access to finance, information, goods and services (Jamshed et al., 2021[19]).

Slow-onset events (rainfall variability, seasonal variations, rise in temperatures, etc.) also have large negative implications for food systems operating across the rural-urban interface. They lead to a decline in agricultural yield and income, affecting rural livelihoods and forcing rural dwellers to adopt coping strategies. Over a long period, this may become a push factor for rural migration (Arslan, Egger and Winters, 2018[14]). Moreover, climate change presents serious risks to infrastructure, which can consequently disrupt the mid- and downstream segments of food systems. Damage to transportation and wholesale and processing facilities can cause food waste, loss of livelihoods and overall interruption of activities along food value chains (Vermeulen et al, 2012[2]). Climate change thus acts as a multiplier of vulnerabilities (Mbow et al., 2019[23]). Figure 3.1 depicts the spatial distribution of food systems and migration flows along the rural-urban interface, as well as changes that can be induced by climate change.

Figure 3.1. The rural-urban interface and climate change

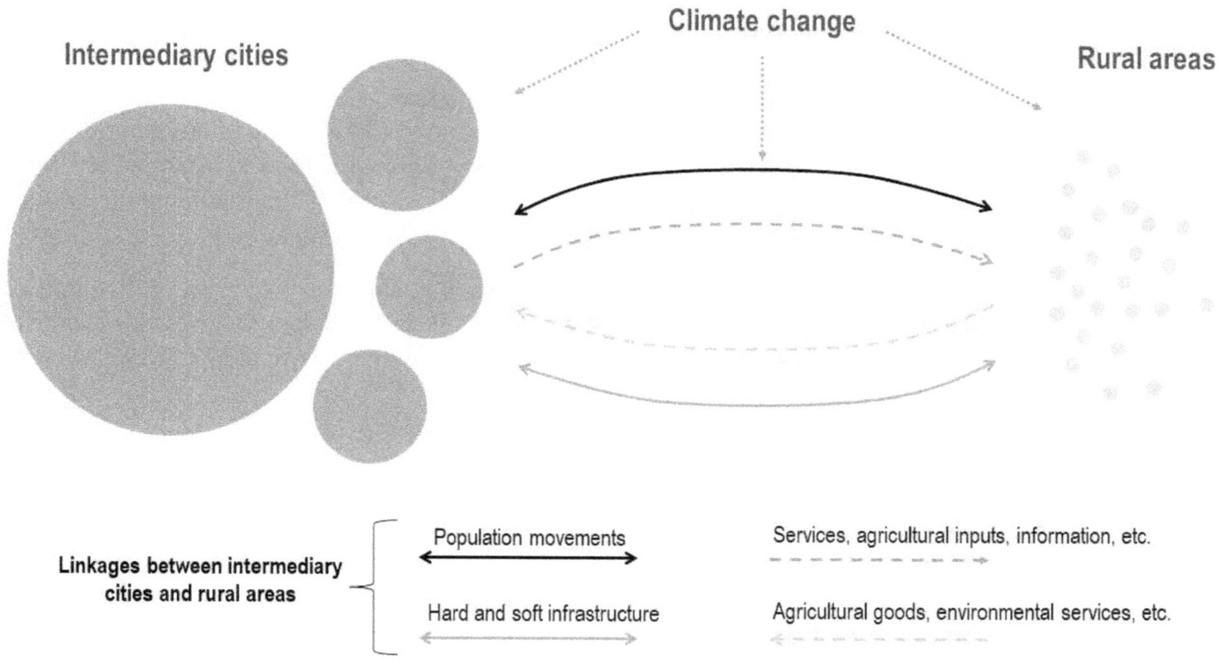

Note: The arrows in the figure connecting intermediary cities and rural areas refer to flows of people, goods, and services, as well as infrastructure linking both places. The green arrows coming out from climate change refer to climate shocks and changes in climatic patterns that affect intermediary cities, rural areas, and their linkages.
Source: Author's elaboration.

Intermediary cities, defined in this report as cities with a population of 50 000 to 1 million, will bear a significant share of the burden resulting from climatic shocks along the rural-urban interface. Intermediary cities, as well as many larger agglomerations, already face climate-induced challenges (rising seas, flooding, water stress, etc.) that impact the livelihoods and well-being of their population. However, intermediary cities in developing countries are usually characterised by weak governance, poor urban planning and limited infrastructure, with a large share of their inhabitants living in vulnerable socio-economic conditions (Roberts et al., 2016[24]; Roberts and Hohmann, 2014[25]). As outlined in Chapter 2 of this report, intermediary cities also tend to have lower levels of economic diversification and largely rely on one dominant sector such as agriculture, mining, etc. (Roberts et al., 2016[24]), which contributes to low local revenue mobilisation. Furthermore, intermediary cities often have limited capacity and authority to collect local revenue and invest in infrastructure and local services (Satterthwaite, 2016[26]), as in the case of Quelimane (Mozambique), described below in this chapter.

Not only are intermediary cities are particularly vulnerable to climate change, but they are also exposed to the effects of climate change on surrounding rural areas. In other words, intermediary cities will face the compounded effects of climate change across the rural-urban interface. For instance, as climate change prompts increasing flows of rural migrants, there will be higher demand for infrastructure, basic services and jobs. This could take place in parallel to an increase in the share of climate-vulnerable populations living in intermediary cities and disruptions of food supplies. Moreover, the institutional, financial and governance gaps characterising intermediary cities will be exacerbated by the effects of climate change. However, climate change may in some cases hinder migration towards intermediary cities. Indeed, Peri and Sasahara (2019[27]) find that rising temperatures slow the rates of rural-to-urban transition in poor countries, with climate change trapping rural populations in poverty through lower income from agriculture, thus reducing their capacity to migrate to urban areas (Peri and Sasahara, 2019[27]).

Intermediary cities, climate change and food systems

Climate change is becoming a major threat to food systems, particularly in developing economies. Because of the interconnectedness and complexity of food systems, disruptions caused by climate change may have exponential consequences that will impact not just other elements along the chain, but potentially the livelihoods of those living along the rural-urban continuum. Intermediary cities are placed at the core of food systems. Although they will be exposed to the indirect effects of climate change, intermediary cities can also function as key agents for development. Since the existing vulnerabilities of intermediary cities are likely to have a ripple effect on their vulnerable populations and their links with surrounding rural areas, adopting mitigation and adaptation strategies should be at the top of local agendas.

This section starts by conceptualising food systems and their interlinkages, highlighting the role of intermediary cities. It then reviews the effects of climate change on food systems and how this will impact intermediary cities. Finally, it provides insights into measures that could be implemented in urban areas to deal with this issue.

Conceptualising food systems

Food systems refer to the complex networks of actors and activities that operate along food supply chains. These include all the core activities that take place along food value chains, including production, aggregation, processing, distribution, consumption and disposal (Nguyen H, 2018[15]; IFPRI, 2020[28]; Reardon and Zilberman, 2018[7]). Food systems also embed wider subsystems or sectors (including energy, water, financial services, trade, health, etc.) that serve as feeders to activities along the supply chain. These subsectors include input-supply systems in the upstream segments of the chain (such as supply of fertilisers, seed, farming equipment, etc.), supply systems in post-farm-gate systems (financing and credit systems, transportation, road infrastructure, etc.), and feeders in the downstream activities of food systems (Reardon and Zilberman, 2018[7]). These can include governance and policies, infrastructure and the environmental and socio-economic dynamics underpinning the operation of activities along the downstream segments of food systems (Reardon and Zilberman, 2018[7]; Dury et al., 2019[10]; IFPRI, 2020[28]; Tendall et al., 2015[29]). The food economy can be further classified and measured through national accounts systems (Box 3.2). Most importantly, all these segments and subsystems are interlinked, and changes in one segment will automatically induce changes across the value chains (Reardon and Zilberman, 2018, p. 3[7]).

Box 3.2. Categorising the food economy

National accounts often categorise food-economy activities across three sectors: primary, secondary and tertiary. The primary sector entails production activities within the agricultural, mining, forestry or fisheries sectors; the secondary sector includes all processing and manufacturing of food intended for human consumption; and the tertiary sector encompasses post-production activities and logistics including transportation, distribution, wholesale and retail sales, and restaurant and street-food activities, among others (Allen et al., 2018[9]).

Tschirley et al. (2016[30]) further subcategorise activities and labour allocation within food systems across four segments: 1) food agriculture, entailing all activities within the primary sector; 2) food processing, including all activities the within the secondary sector; 3) food marketing (transport, logistics, wholesale, retailing) within the tertiary sector; and 4) food-away-from-home (restaurants, street food, catering services), also within the tertiary sector (Allen et al., 2018[9]; Tschirley et al., 2016[30]).

Food systems in developing countries are transforming rapidly

Food systems account for a significant share of the economy of developing countries and will continue to grow in the coming years. Over the past 30 to 40 years, the food economy has grown exponentially – eight fold in regions such as Africa, where it is expected to grow another six fold within the next four decades (Badiane and Makombe, 2015[31]; Haggblade, 2011[32]). Moreover, the food economy accounts for the lion's share of employment across developing countries, involving more than 2 billion workers globally (Dury et al., 2019[10]). In West Africa, for example, the food economy is the biggest source of employment, accounting for 66% of total employment, with a total of 82 million jobs (Allen et al., 2018[9]). Within the food economy, the agriculture sector remains the predominant source of employment, accounting for 70% of total employment in low–income countries, and 60% of total employment in Sub-Saharan Africa; as such, it plays a fundamental role in poverty reduction (World Bank, 2017[33]). Moreover, local food systems are an integral aspect of food security. Indeed, in Africa and Asia, 90% of urban dwellers rely on local food systems for the food they eat, and local food systems provide 50% to 80% of the diets of rural households (Reardon and Zilberman, 2018[7]; Reardon et al., 2016[34]).

In Western and Central Africa, agriculture accounts for the biggest share of the food economy (and of the total economy), according to OECD estimates. In countries like Chad and Niger, agriculture represents around 80% of the total economy (Figure 3.2). Nonetheless, activities in the mid- and downstream segments of food systems also play an increasingly important role (Dury et al., 2019[10]). In some developing regions, they account for a significant share of the manufacturing and service sectors (World Bank, 2017[33]).

Figure 3.2. Estimated share of the food economy by component, West Africa

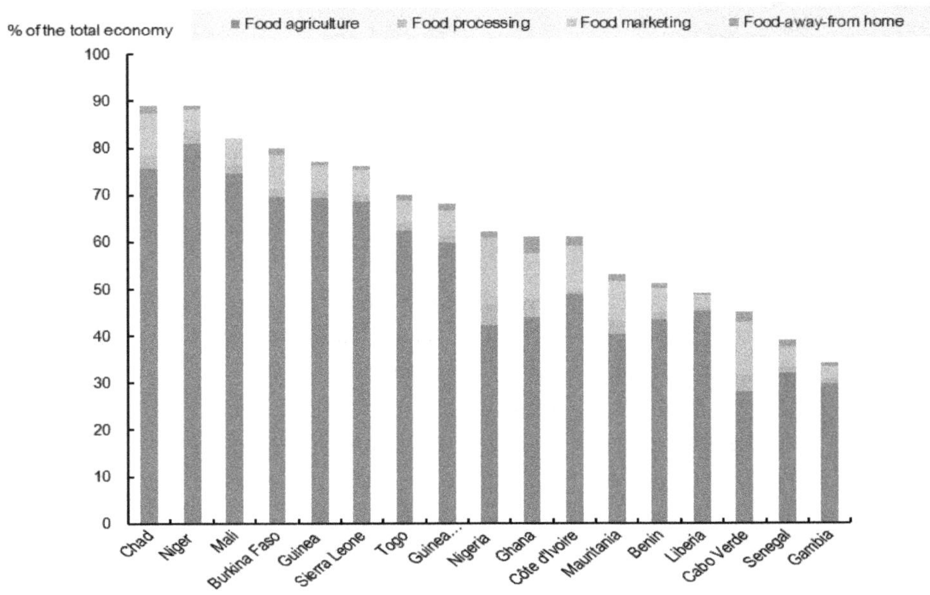

Note: Data estimates based on household surveys.
Source: Allen et al. (2018[9]).

Food systems are a key source of livelihood for women and other marginalised groups such as youth, although with different employment prospects across rural and urban areas. For instance, many rural youths in developing countries are engaged in the primary sector or in the production segments of agricultural value chains (OECD, 2018[35]). Overall, the agriculture sector accounts for 37% of rural youth employment in developing countries; in countries like Uganda and Tanzania, it can exceed 90% (Figure 3.3, top).

Urban areas, in contrast, provide differing prospects for youth employment. Urban areas in higher-income countries tend to see larger shares of youth employed in the downstream segments of food systems, with food processing as the main activity. In lower-income countries, food marketing is the dominant activity in urban areas (Figure 3.3, bottom) (OECD, 2021[13]). This indicates that as developing countries become richer, urban areas (especially intermediary cities) will be increasingly important sources of diversified employment in the food economy, especially for the marginalised. Indeed, small and medium-sized cities and towns are receiving increasing recognition for their role in employment and income diversification, within and outside of the food economy (Hussein and Suttie, 2016[36]; Agergaard et al., 2019[37]; Tacoli, 2017[38]; IFAD, 2010[39]). This is because they function as key nodes that consolidate off-farm activities (including the manufacturing sector) (Tacoli, 2017[38]), as will be further discussed below.

Figure 3.3. Rural and urban youth employment across food economy, by location and segment

Rural youth (top) tend to be less represented in diversified sectors than urban youth (bottom)

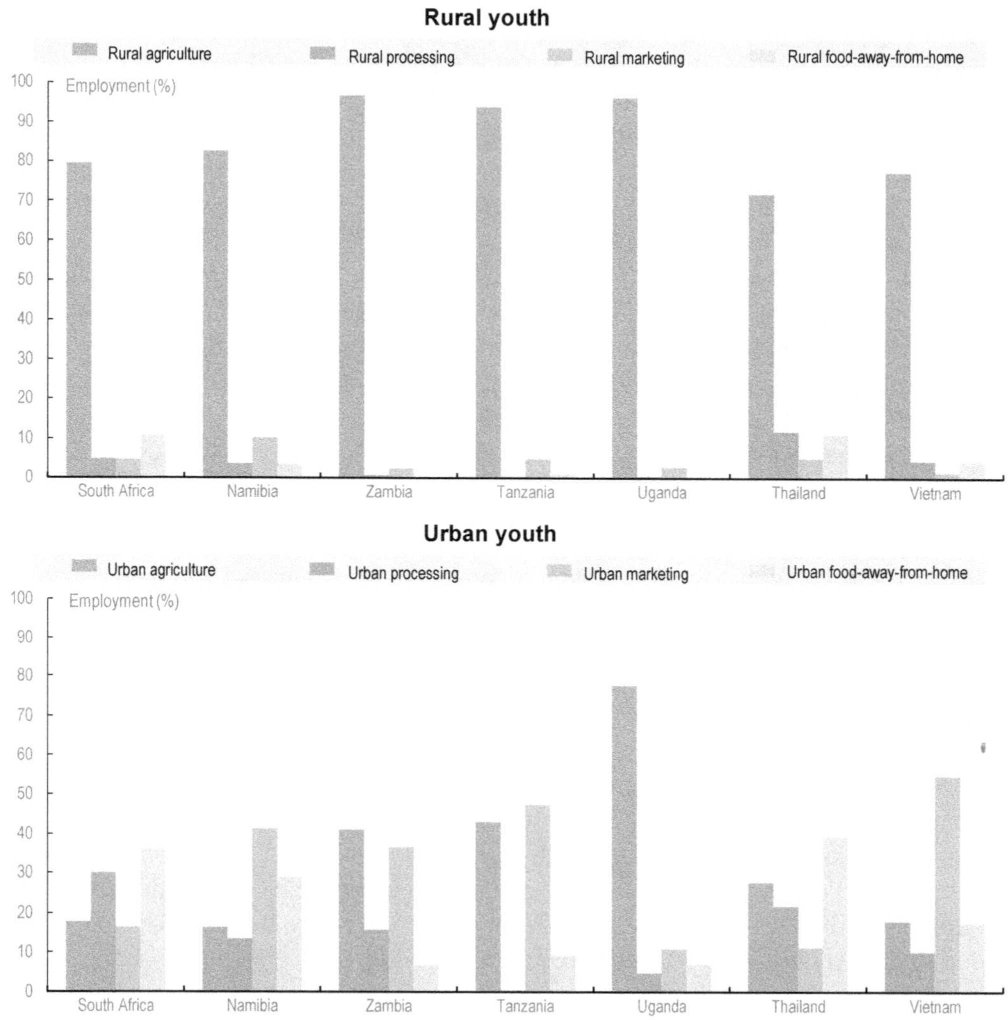

Notes: The seven countries were selected based on data availability.
Source: OECD (2021[13]).

The growth of the food economy in the past decades has enabled better access to wage employment, especially for women. In West Africa, the food economy accounts for 68% of total female employment in the region (Allen et al., 2018[9]). Downstream sections of food systems, although still relatively small, employ a higher number of young women than young men (Allen et al., 2018[9]). This is the case in the Niayes region of Senegal, where the food economy in 2020 accounted for 77% of female employment, of whom 63% were engaged in the marketing, 7% in processing and 25% in agriculture (OECD/SWAC, 2020[40]). The informal sector is also important in the creation and expansion of employment opportunities for women and youth (Box 3.3).

Box 3.3. The critical role of informal networks in food systems of developing countries

Informal networks play an integral role in food systems along the value chains linking rural and urban areas in developing economies. A large share of food activities are conducted within the informal sector, from agricultural production all across the value chain, including retail sectors (Vorley et al., 2020[41]; Allen and Heinrigs, 2016[42]). Informal networks are key providers of food and nutrition security. They provide livelihoods, especially for poor and marginalised groups (including women and rural and urban youth), and play an important role in meeting the growing demand for food in urban areas.

The accessibility and affordability of informal food systems makes them an important source of food security for low-income rural and urban households (Vorley et al., 2020[41]). Informal networks are integral to the "food away from home" segments of the food economy, as street-food vendors are key suppliers to (low income) urban dwellers, who are highly dependent on "ready to eat" food (Allen and Heinrigs, 2016[42]). In Southeast Asia, for instance, a large share of the urban poor, including consumers as well as traders, rely heavily on informal food sectors (Tacoli and Vorley, 2016[43]). In Southern Africa, a survey of 6 000 households conducted across 11 cities found that 70% of households rely on the informal food economy for their regular food purchases (Frayne B et al., 2010[44]).

The last 50 years have seen a transformation of food systems, particularly in developing countries. Some of the key determinants include changes in diets, urbanisation and the modernisation of food retail markets, including the use of new technology (Berdegué et al., 2014[3]; Reardon and Zilberman, 2018[7]). These interlinked determinants have primarily transformed the midstream (processing, wholesaling, etc.) and downstream (retail, fast food, etc.) segments of food systems. Changes in food systems have also been underpinned by "meta-conditioners" that facilitate the transformation process. These are national and international factors including: population and income growth; widespread liberalisation and privatisation policies; and increased investment in infrastructure across developing regions. These factors have led to increased participation of the private sector, changes in diets, higher labour-market participation, improved access to markets in urban areas and the development of supply chains (Reardon and Zilberman, 2018[7]). The transformation of food systems in some regions has implied the transformation of productive activities as well due to the way these activities are co-ordinated (Box 3.4).

Box 3.4. Transitioning from Food System 1.0 to Food System 2.0

With food systems evolving significantly over the years, Jennings et al. (2015[45]) have classified the transformations into Food System 1.0 and Food System 2.0. The defining characteristic of Food System 1.0 is the prevalence of informal actors, who work and conduct business in a generally localised and decentralised way. Most of the wastage produced in this paradigm is by production and aggregation activities. Smallholder and subsistence farmers are the main actors involved in production activities.

In contrast, Food System 2.0 is formal and centralised, with fewer actors involved than in Food System 1.0. Sophisticated global supply chains and increased efficiency help keep prices down and wastage low in the production and aggregation phase. The consumer produces most of the wastage (Jennings et al., 2015[45]).

Although developing countries are often characterised by Food System 1.0, they have been undergoing large transformations in recent decades, transitioning from fragmented and short supply chains to more complex supply chains that are growing in length and volume (Reardon and Zilberman, 2018[7]; Tschirley et al., 2015[46]).

Fast urbanisation is leading to the rapid expansion of supply chains, prompting large transformations in food systems. In the last 30 years, rural-urban supply chains have grown by 600% to 800% in Africa (Haggblade, 2011[32]) and by 1 000% in Southeast Asia (Reardon and Timmer, 2014[47]). This is underpinned by the fact that urban households tend to have higher incomes than their rural counterparts: food expenditure makes for a lower share of the household's budget, with higher food consumption per capita (Reardon and Zilberman, 2018[7]; Badiane and Makombe, 2015[31]). This is the case across emerging regions. Even in the least urbanised countries in Africa, cities dominate the food market. For instance, while only 25% of the population live in cities in Eastern and Southern Africa, urban areas account for 48% of food consumption (Badiane and Makombe, 2015[31]; Tschirley et al., 2015[46]). In West Africa, where the urban population grew from 5 million in 1950 to 133 million in 2010, spending on food accounts for 46% of the total expenditure of urban households, compared with 60% of the total expenditure of rural households (Allen and Heinrigs, 2016[42]). In Asian markets, urban food demand accounts for more than 65% of domestic food and depends on rural-urban food-supply chains (Reardon and Timmer, 2014[47]).

Changes in trade dynamics, consumer demand and urbanisation will contribute to structural transformation in low- and middle-income countries, and will continue to make food systems key sources of employment across developing economies. For example, between 2010 and 2025, transformation of food systems across six African countries (Ethiopia, Malawi, Mozambique, Tanzania, Uganda and Zambia) is projected to be the biggest source of employment (World Bank, 2017[33]). In the countries studied, employment in farming was expected to decline from 75% to 61%, while employment in the midstream and downstream segments will rise from 8% to 12% during the same period (World Bank, 2017[33]). Moreover, a study conducted by the OECD (2021[13]) highlights that provided adequate policies are implemented, employment in the food economy is expected to rise across 11 economies[1] in Sub-Saharan Africa from 2019 to 2030, with a 17% increase in the upstream (agricultural) segment and an increase in employment in the mid- and downstream segments from 21 million to 29 million. However, the relation of employment in the food economy to total employment will not change dramatically over the period, remaining at nearly 60% of total employment in the region (OECD, 2021[13]). In Thailand and Vietnam, employment in the food economy is expected to remain relatively stagnant, with a slight increase in Vietnam. Employment will decline in the agricultural sector and will increase slightly in the downstream segments of food systems, by 3% in Thailand and 4% in Viet Nam (Figure 3.4) (OECD, 2021[13]).

Figure 3.4. Projected change in employment across segments of food economy, 2019-30

Percentage change based on initial level

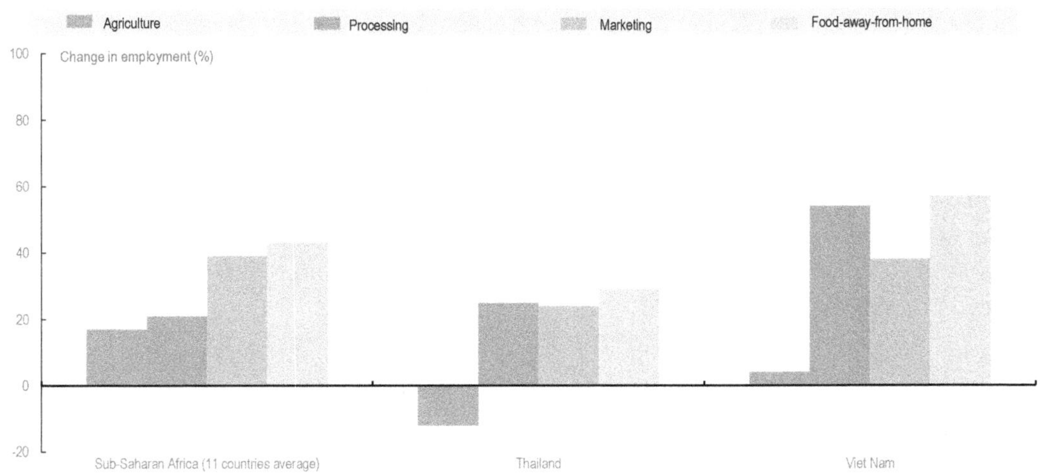

Source: OECD (2021[13]).

Intermediary cities are at the heart of food systems

Activities within food systems are dynamic and operate in continuous bi-directional movements across the rural-urban interface. Although it is easy to assume that food systems operate in only one direction, with rural areas as the location of production and urban areas as consumption centres, there are complex feedback loops that link these territories (see Figure 3.1 above). Often, rural areas source their agricultural inputs (such as fertilisers, pesticides, etc.) from production centres located in small and medium-sized cities (Berdegué et al., 2014[3]). Additionally, a large share of rural households are net food buyers, and rely on urban markets for their consumption of processed foods (Reardon and Zilberman, 2018[7]; IIED, 2015[48]). For example, in rural areas of Bangladesh, Indonesia, Nepal and Viet Nam, consumption of processed food (produced in urban or peri-urban areas) accounts for 59% of total rural consumption (Tacoli and Vorley, 2016[43]). In parallel, people living in urban areas can be involved in upstream activities. This is the case in West Africa, where urban dwellers may conduct agricultural activities in surrounding peri-urban or rural areas (Allen and Heinrigs, 2016[42]).

The intermediation role of intermediary cities places them at the heart of food systems. First, their closer linkages to rural areas enable rural households to have better access to local markets (FAO, 2017[5]). For instance, findings from Ethiopia highlight stronger agricultural linkages between rural areas and small cities than between rural areas and larger/metropolitan cities (Dorosh et al., 2012[49]). Second, unlike capital or metropolitan cities, intermediary cities are less dependent on internationally or nationally imported food, and tend to rely more on food provided from surrounding rural areas (Berdegué et al., 2014[3]). This further supports the transformation of local value chains. Third, the intermediation role of these cities acts as an entry point to agri-value chains for smallholder farmers, who are often excluded from formal supply chains

(Berdegué et al., 2014[3]; Tacoli and Agergaard, 2017[11]; Allen and Heinrigs, 2016[42]). Box 3.5 highlights the strategic role of intermediary cities in the transformation of food systems.

Box 3.5. Intermediary cities are a key factor in the transformation of food systems

The current transformation of food systems in developing countries is taking place along the rural-urban interface. Reardon and Timmer (2014[47]) situate this process in Asia across three zones: 1) "dynamic commercial zones", located within 8-10 hours of urban catchment areas; 2) "intermediary zones", including urban centres, that function as "economic pull" for the supply of goods from rural areas; and 3) "hinterland traditional, semi-subsistence zones", or remote rural areas with weak linkages to urban centres and markets (Reardon and Timmer, 2014[47]).

Intermediary cities, which are located in the "intermediary zones", are key in the transformation process. The evolution or transformation of food systems (partially due to rising urbanisation) is creating stronger and closer linkages between producers and consumers distributed across rural and urban territories. The development of networks of small towns and medium-sized urban centres has been an integral aspect of food system transformation. These urban centres serve as "nodes for the spatial organisation of trade and markets", and play a fundamental role in facilitating the integration of rural areas into market economies (Allen and Heinrigs, 2016, p. 5[42]). They host and link actors and activities along value chains, especially in the post-farm-gate or intermediate segments of the supply chain (Reardon and Timmer, 2014[47]). Urban markets have become particularly important for an increase in high-value and non-grain products, which are now transported along rural-urban supply chains (IFAD, 2016[50]).

It is important to note, however, that sustainable and inclusive transformation of food systems goes hand in hand with rural transformation. Indeed, intermediary cities and their urban consumers are highly reliant on rural areas for food, clean water, raw materials and environmental services. There is thus a growing interdependence as well as a blurring of boundaries between rural and urban areas (and people living in these territories) (Hussein and Suttie, 2016[36]), and this is an important factor in the ongoing transformation of food systems.

Their stronger linkages with smallholder farmers in surrounding rural areas place intermediary cities at the core of food systems. Smallholder farmers[2] account for more than a third (35%) of global food production (Lowder, Sánchez and Bertini, 2021[51]). In regions such as Sub-Saharan Africa, South Asia and East Asia and the Pacific, smallholder farmers account for 80% of the farms, representing 30%-40% of the total share of land (Lowder, Sánchez and Bertini, 2021[51]). For this reason, intermediary cities can highly benefit from their stronger linkages with food producers. These closer links are also key determinants of rural off-farm employment. Off-farm activities within agri-food systems (including food processing) tend to be established closer to urban centres (Berdegué et al., 2014[3]; Hussein and Suttie, 2016[36]). The development of road and service infrastructure (such as electricity) across these urban centres has enhanced their role as key locations for off-farm activities (Berdegué et al., 2014[3]; Badiane and Makombe, 2015[31]).

While urbanisation has had a transformative effect on food systems, it can also have detrimental effects if it is not appropriately planned. Unplanned urbanisation and urban sprawl can reduce the amount of land available for agricultural production and decrease the productivity of food systems (Box 3.6).

Box 3.6 The effects of urban sprawl on surrounding productive land

Urban sprawl can have negative implications for agriculture, and can consequently lead to issues of food security. This is a rising issue across various regions.

A study by Li (2018[52]) found that the metropolitan area of Buenos Aires (Argentina) had doubled over 20 years, expanding from 937.16 km^2 in June 1985 to 1 835.47 km^2 in July 2015, with 30.28% of the new urban land coming from existing cropland. Urban use of land has also increased rapidly in suburban areas of Jakarta (Indonesia), where the built-up area increased by 21.56% between 2001 and 2009, resulting in a decrease in forest area of 8.51% and a decrease in farmland of 5.78% (Nagasawa et al., 2015[53]). Similarly, the city of Bogotá (Colombia) expanded almost four fold over 29 years, from 151.2 km^2 in 1985 to 567.5 km^2 in 2014, and this expansion occurred at the expense of forests and farmland (Romero et al., 2020[54]) .This transformation impacts agricultural production and food security in the region, as the lands around Bogotá are among the most productive in the Andean region (Romero et al., 2020[54]).

In a study of urban sprawl in India, meanwhile, Pandey and Seto (2015[55]) note that urban expansion and the loss of agricultural land has increased steadily since 2006. They find that agricultural land loss has occurred near smaller cities more than large urban centres that urban conversion of agricultural land is concentrated in a few districts and states with high rates of economic growth, and that agricultural land loss is predominantly in states with higher agricultural land suitability. A separate study of urban sprawl in the Delhi periphery concludes that agricultural land loss could cause economic deprivation and increase poverty and socio-economic vulnerability (Das, 2017[56]; Abu Hatab et al., 2019[57]).

Climate change is disrupting food systems

As we enter the last decade of the Sustainable Development Goals (SDGs), the sustainability of global food systems is more important than ever. Building sustainable and resilient food systems is now being recognised in international policy arenas. For instance, the United Nations held its Food Systems Summit in 2021 with the aim of transforming global food systems and setting them on a path for the achievement of the SDGs. Climate change appeared in one of the five Action Tracks of the summit's agenda. There was recognition of the need to act on climate not only by reducing emissions from food systems, but also by promoting the protection of ecosystems and reducing food loss and energy use while ensuring nutritious diets (Caprile, 2021[58]). Similarly, 190 countries participating in the 26th Conference of Parties to the UN Framework Convention on Climate Change recognised the need to address agriculture and its link to climate change, with particular focus on the need to improve soil and nutrient management practices for building sustainable and resilient food production systems and contributing to global food security (UNFCCC, 2021[59]). While this reflects progress in addressing the climate vulnerability of global food supply systems, there is still a need to recognise and better articulate the vulnerability to climate change of the entire food supply chain in order to ensure resilient supply chains and food security.

Climate change will increasingly affect the dynamics of food systems. It acts as a "threat multiplier" and poses serious risks to the functioning and sustainability of food systems (IIED and Hivos, 2020[60]). Food systems are comprised of a network of complex and interdependent segments, which are critical for food security and the livelihoods of both rural and urban dwellers. Climate-induced threats in one segment can lead to a series of disruptions along the full supply chain (Reardon and Zilberman, 2018[7]). This can ultimately affect the availability, access, utilisation and long-term stability of food supplies (Reardon and Zilberman, 2018[7]). Figure 3.5 illustrates climate-induced changes along food supply chains and their socio-economic outcomes in intermediary cities.

Figure 3.5. Climate change and food systems

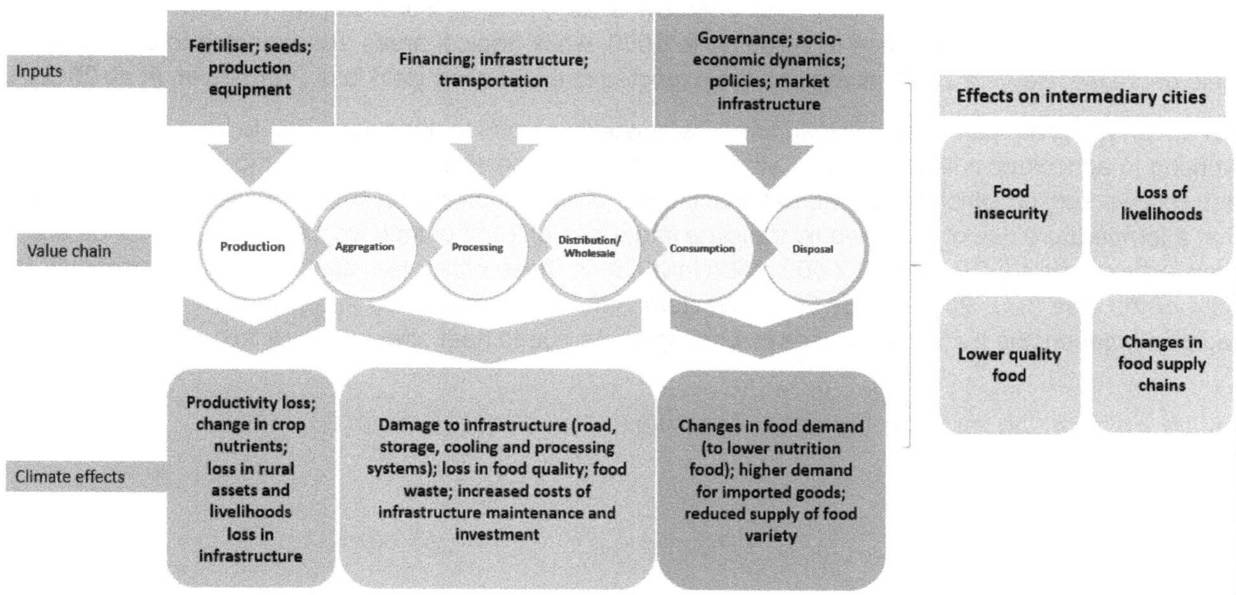

Source: Author's own elaboration.

Food systems will continue to be under pressure to feed the growing global population and to adapt to changes in food demand patterns. Estimates suggest that food supply will have to increase by 50% by 2050 to address these demands (FAO et al., 2018[1]).

Climate change will particularly affect regions and marginalised populations with low adaptive capacity. Poor and marginalised communities in developing countries are particularly vulnerable, as they are disproportionally exposed to food insecurity and loss of livelihood (Vermeulen et al, 2012[2]). Indeed, declining agricultural outputs will lead to a rise in food prices, causing significant strains on populations facing food insecurity.

Climate change will affect food systems by disrupting their production capacity and sustainability. This will result from a combination of issues, including a decrease in productivity in the primary sector and changes in the quality and types of crops. To assess the effects of climate change that will ultimately impact intermediary cities, the following section considers food systems by production (upstream activities) and post-production segments (midstream and downstream activities).

Climate change harms agricultural productivity

Climate change will lead to a decrease in crop yields in some regions. Crop yields are highly vulnerable to changes in temperature and water availability. Despite large regional variations, an overall increase in temperatures and reduced water availability are expected to lead to a decline in crop yields, especially across rain-fed farming systems (Myers et al., 2017[61]). Lizumi et al. (2018[62]) estimate the effects of climate change on the global average yields of maize, rice, wheat and soybeans for 1981-2010 (relative to the pre-industrial climate). Their findings indicate that climate change has had no significant impact on rice, but that it will significantly impact the yields of maize, wheat and soybeans. They estimate that, over the period, climate change decreased the global mean yield of maize by 4.1%, wheat by 1.8% and soybeans by 4.5%, relative to the pre-industrial climate. Estimates project that the decrease in yields will be more acute in South Asia, Sub-Saharan Africa and Southeast Asia (World Bank, 2010[63]). The reduction in crop yields is expected lead to significant economic losses. For instance, between 2005 and 2009, global yield losses amounted to USD 22.3 billion for maize, USD 6.5 billion for soybeans, USD 0.8 billion for rice and USD 13.6 billion for wheat (Lizumi et al., 2018[62]). However, losses in yields will vary considerably by region, CO_2 concentration and land fertility (Mbow et al., 2019[23]). For instance, temperate regions are expected to observe an increase in yields up to 2050, while tropical areas are expected to experience a yield decrease. Beyond 2050, all regions are expected to experience yield loss (Vermeulen et al, 2012[2]).

Moreover, rising temperatures will lead to a loss of working hours in agriculture due to heat stress. People working in agriculture will be the most affected by rising temperatures, especially those in countries with deficient working conditions. The International Labour Organization's most conservative estimates suggest that a temperature rise of 1.5°C would translate into a loss of 2.2% of total working hours worldwide and a drop in the world's GDP of USD 2 400 billion in 2030. In these estimates, agriculture alone accounts for 60% of the loss (ILO, 2019[64]). By 2030, Western Africa, Southeast Asia and Southern Asia will be the regions experiencing the largest losses in working hours due to heat stress (Figure 3.6).

Figure 3.6. Working hours lost in agriculture due to heat stress (% of total hours)

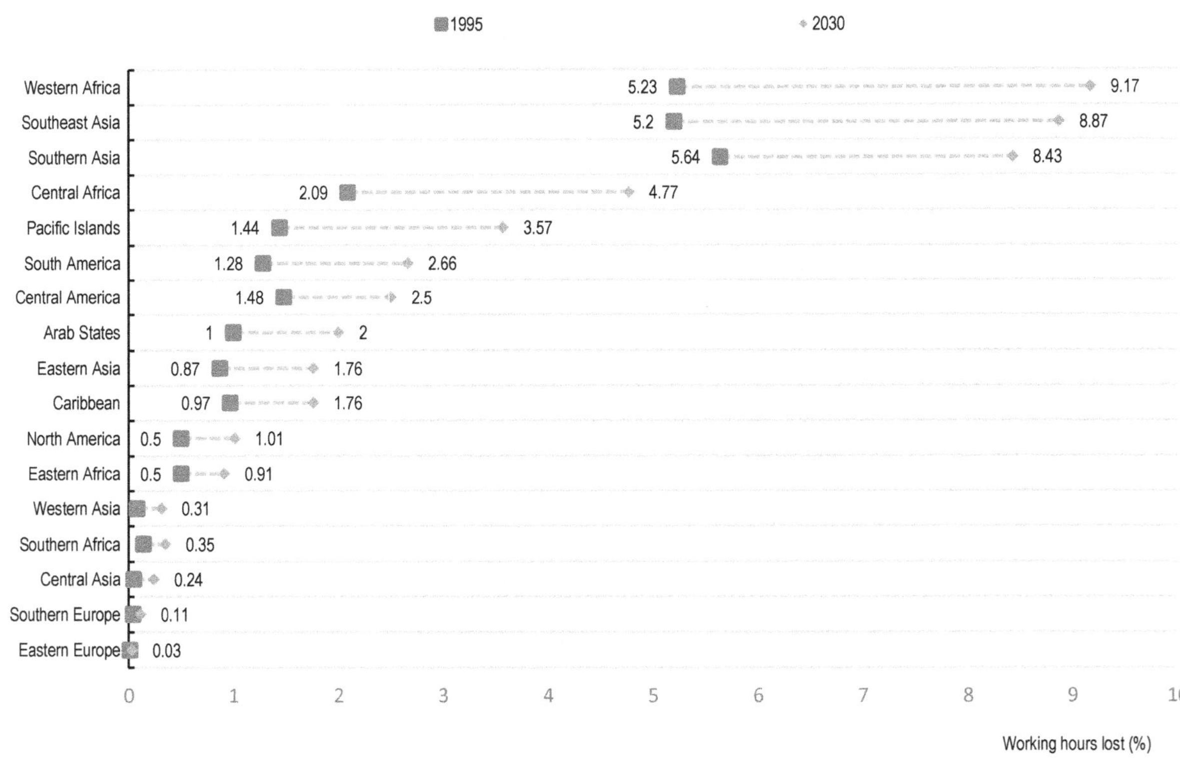

Note: Estimates based on the assumption that tropical countries tend to have cloudy days 40% of the time.
Source: ILO (2019[64]).

Climate change affects the predictability and quality of agricultural crops

Climate change can also cause unpredicted changes in the types of crops that can be produced under new climatic and unpredicted seasonal changes (Mbow et al., 2019[23]). Sudden extreme weather conditions cause loss of harvest and infrastructure, and they particularly impact producers with limited or no safety nets. For example, in the context of India, understanding the arrival of the monsoons plays a critical role in planning harvests. Climate change can cause variations in the arrival of the monsoons and cause floods and droughts, depending on the region (Loo, Billa and Singh, 2015[65]).

Beyond its impact on production, climate change can also change the nutritional composition of crops. The increase of pollutants in the atmosphere, such as ozone, black carbon, methane and CO_2, can damage crops and modify their nutritional level (especially crops such as wheat, rice, soybeans and green beans) (Mbow et al., 2019[23]). Increases in global temperatures are expected raise the concentration of these pollutants; it is estimated that an increase in ozone concentration can lead to crop damage of up to 20% by 2050 (Mbow et al., 2019[23]; Chuwah et al., 2015[66]). Climate change is known to increase the concentration of ozone in the atmosphere (EUC, 2010[67]), while ozone, a key component of GHG emissions, contributes to climate change by trapping heat in the atmosphere.

Climate shocks will also affect livestock and fisheries

Climate change will also cause considerable losses in other activities in the primary sector. Climate-induced changes such as rising temperatures and decreasing water availability will affect livestock production through their effect on feed supplies and spread of diseases, and will ultimately cause higher livestock mortality (Vermeulen et al, 2012[2]; Mbow et al., 2019[23]). Climate change may also lead to a large-scale redistribution of the catch potential of global fisheries, with an average increase of 30%-70% in high-latitude regions and a drop of up to 40% in the tropics (Cheung et al., 2010[68]). Although aquaculture was set to become a substitute or solution for declining global fisheries (Naylor et al., 2000[69]), the sector is particularly vulnerable to climate-induced threats, such as shortages of water and infrastructure, which that cause production losses, the spread of disease, development of toxic algae and parasites, thereby reducing farming capacities (Barange et al., 2018[70]).

Climate-induced damage will disrupt post-production along food supply chains

Post-production activities, operating along the midstream and downstream segments of supply chains, are also vulnerable to the long- and short-term effects of climate change.

Damage to essential infrastructure can cause losses along food system supply chains. Fast-onset climate effects (floods, hurricanes, typhoons and other disasters) can damage and disrupt power supply for food storage facilities and road and transportation infrastructure (FAO, 2008[71]). These risks can also affect post-production sub-segments along the supply chain, including damage to irrigation and drainage systems and to the power supply needed for production, processing and storage of food (Reardon and Zilberman, 2018[7]; FAO, 2008[71]). The extent of climate-induced damage or disruption is determined by a series of factors underpinning the operations of segments along the value chains (Box 3.7).

Box 3.7. Factors determining the vulnerability of food systems to fast-onset climate events

The vulnerability of food systems to short-term (or fast-onset) climate events depends on a series climate-risk "hotspots" along the value chains. These hotspots can be present along the various segments of food value chains as well as their subsegments (such as input systems for farming, irrigation, infrastructure, etc.). Reardon and Zilberman (2018[7]) outline characteristics that shape the vulnerability of food systems to climate risks. These include:

- type and resilience of the infrastructure that supports production systems, including drainage, irrigation and flood-control systems, which are crucial for controlling the risks to which supply chains are exposed.
- geographic distances along the supply chains, such as the distance between points of assemblage, processing, distributing, etc. Longer supply chains heighten the vulnerability of food systems, especially in circumstances with low urban food-supply diversification.
- perishability of products. Highly perishable products require fast delivery and adequate storage systems, leaving them vulnerable to climate shocks.
- extent of physical capital intensity along food-system segments. The use of robust physical capital (including irrigation systems, storage, transportation systems, etc.) can help reduce exposure to climate risks. Moving from traditional to modern food supply chains often increases the capital-to-labour ratio, with an overall decrease in climate vulnerabilities.
- location and asset specificity in intermediation production processes. Lack of interchangeable locations for crop production and logistics at intermediary segments can lock in supply chains to climate shocks.
- concentration of supply chains. Supply chains dominated by a few large firms, instead of larger numbers of small firms, can expose food systems to disruptions caused by climate change.
- variations in exposure to climate risks over time. This can be over one or multiple locations which may vary in their exposure to climate risks, and can exacerbate food system vulnerabilities.

Source: Reardon and Zilberman (2018[7]).

Climate change can also cause changes in the procurement patterns of supply chains. Long-term (or slow-onset) climate effects – changing temperatures, droughts, desertification, sea-level rise, ocean acidification – may lead to permanent changes and can change the procurement patterns of supply chains. Rising temperatures can increase the need for cooling and storage systems to maintain food quality, which implies more demand for energy (FAO, 2008[71]). Hotter weather can also cause food safety risks and wastage, especially along the supply chains of perishable goods (Vermeulen et al, 2012[2]). Changes in rainfall or droughts can cause shortages of water for food processing, and can create challenges for the transportation of goods. Other events, such as flooding, can cause pollution of water used for processing purposes (FAO, 2008[71]). Some of the repercussions of long-term climate effects can lead to significant long-term or permanent changes in the production segments and established supply-chain networks of food systems. For example, it is estimated that some areas of Nicaragua will lose 40%-60% of their suitability to grow coffee by 2050. This will affect the whole range of intermediaries who must adapt and change the connectivity of their supply chains (Laderach et al., 2011[72]). it could eventually lead to shifts in other economic activities because of low productivity and reduced profitability.

Climate-induced changes in food supply chains can cause an increase in the cost of public and private investment. Slow-onset climate events will lead to higher costs in terms of investment in alternative processing, storage or retail facilities; could cause businesses to decide to relocate to less risky areas; and could impose changes in logistics and procurement strategies. Regions or countries with inadequate or low-quality infrastructure will face large losses or rising maintenance costs (Vermeulen et al, 2012[2]). As such, responses to slow-onset climate events may lead to the adoption of innovations, migration, changes in trade and land-use strategies, and overall permanent changes in the midstream and downstream segments of food systems (Reardon and Zilberman, 2018[7]).

Food systems today are under larger pressure than ever due to the combination of climate change, increasing demand for food and the effects of COVID-19. This has been exacerbated by the Russia-Ukraine war, which has caused high price volatility in food staples including wheat, maize, soybeans and cotton (Rice et al., 2022[73]). Urgent actions to transform the current global food system are needed to cope with the unprecedented pressure on food systems and the disruptions in global value chains.

Developing countries will be disproportionally affected by the rising pressure on global and local food systems. Box 3.8 highlights some of the main challenges that COVID-19 has posed for food systems, especially in developing countries.

Box 3.8. COVID-19 has put additional strains on global food systems

COVID-19 has caused multidimensional challenges to global food systems and their governance. It has also set back progress towards the attainment of the SDGs, as many people have been pushed back into poverty (IFPRI, 2021[74]). Indeed, in 2020, the UN World Food Programme projected that the number of people facing hunger and food insecurity had nearly doubled over a year, rising from 135 million in 2019 to 265 million in 2020, mainly in low- and middle-income countries (WFP, 2020[75]). This puts national and local governments and global food systems under additional pressure as they seek to address the triple challenges of increasing hunger and malnutrition, climate-change-induced stress and an increase in global demand for food (IFPRI, 2021[74]; OECD, 2020[76]).

COVID-19 has caused losses of income and livelihood, disruption of food supply chains and decreases in nutrition and food security, as well as exposing and magnifying socio-economic inequalities across and within countries (IFPRI, 2021[74]). A survey conducted by the FAO (2020[77]) of 860 respondents, including municipalities, national governments and academic and non-governmental institutions, found that food supply chains had been negatively affected by containment measures implemented to reduce the spread of the virus, such as restriction of movements of goods, services and persons; closure of restaurants and food services; restrictions on the use of public transportation and public space for food markets; and labour shortages. Moreover, panic buying of large volumes of food by some urban dwellers further contributed to food insecurity and a rise in food prices (FAO, 2020[77]).

The spatial effects of COVID-19 are complex. Urban dwellers were most burdened overall by loss of income, shrinking economies and lockdown restrictions. Yet despite a buffer of protection for rural agricultural households, overall poverty increased both in rural and urban areas. This reflects the greater vulnerability of rural households of falling into poverty despite the lesser direct impact of the pandemic. Disruptions in flows of remittances across rural and urban areas, as well as internationally, also contributed to the increase in poverty in rural areas (IFPRI, 2021[74]). At the same time, geography and density played key roles in the ways urban areas were affected by interruptions in food supply chains. Larger and dense cities with more than 500 000 inhabitants were the most affected, while smaller towns and villages, with shorter supply chains and better proximity to production sites, were the least affected (FAO, 2020[77]).

Local governments played the main role in implementing COVID-19 restrictions and relief programmes. They faced enormous challenges in addressing the economic and social crisis created by the pandemic. More than 70% of municipalities surveyed by the FAO implemented COVID-19 measures and relief programmes with no or insufficient additional funding from national governments (FAO, 2020[77]).

With shocks caused by pandemics and climate disasters likely to be more frequent in future, it is now more urgent than ever to build food systems that are resilient, equitable and sustainable. The recovery process from the COVID-19 crisis should be taken as an opportunity to transform food systems globally (IFPRI, 2021[74]; OECD, 2020[76]). This entails building resilient food systems that anticipate and mitigate the effects of external shocks and that are flexible enough to adapt to changing global conditions (IFPRI, 2021[74]; OECD, 2020[76]). Improved public spending on health and other social protection systems, especially for vulnerable populations, is a key aspect of building resilience (IFPRI, 2021[74]).

Intermediary cities face ripple effects from the impact of climate on food systems

Intermediary cities are key actors in the complex dynamics between climate change and food systems. By virtue of their socio-economic and geographic closeness to rural areas, and the important role they play in the supply chains of food systems, intermediary cities face a series of indirect effects from climate change, which will cause large disruptions in the food economy and present a series of socio-economic challenges.

However, the effects of climate change are not linear. Instead, climate change will have ripple effects on the networks of activities connecting food systems, eventually affecting intermediary cities:

- Climate change can cause losses of livelihood and income for a large share of inhabitants of intermediary cities. Intermediary cities in low- and middle-income countries are heavily dependent on the primary sector (including agriculture, fishing, mining, etc.) for their local economy (Berdegué et al., 2014[3]; Roberts et al., 2016[24]) and are closely linked to the economies of their surrounding rural areas (Reardon et al., 2016[34]). These sectors are the source of livelihood for a large share of urban dwellers. In West Africa, for example, agriculture accounts for 34% of total employment in the region's urban food economy, and a large share of producers are in small and medium-sized cities (Allen et al., 2018[9]). Moreover, as highlighted above, post-production segments of food systems, including processing and "away-from-home" segments, are often located in intermediary cities, and act as a source of employment for a significant share of urban dwellers. The effects of climate change on food systems, such as drops in agricultural yield, livestock and fisheries, as well as reduced productivity due to heat stress or unsuitable crops, cause disruptions along supply chains and could mean large losses of livelihood for urban dwellers in intermediary cities.
- Climate-change effects on food systems can cause urban food insecurity. Intermediary cities and small towns highly depend on surrounding rural areas for the procurement of food for urban dwellers (Reardon et al., 2016[34]). Climate-induced threats cause unpredicted changes in the availability and suitability of crops used for consumption and pose major risks to post-farm-gate infrastructure. These threats can cause large losses in production value as well as food wastage, and can interrupt the food supply chain linkages between intermediary cities and their surrounding areas (Forster et al., 2015[78]). Such climate-induced disruptions can reduce food availability (Satterthwaite et al., 2010[79]), as well as causing increases and/or severe fluctuations in food prices in urban food markets (Tacoli et al., 2013[80]). This puts at stake both the availability and affordability of basic food and its nutritional quality (Mbow et al., 2019[23]).
- Climate-change effects on food systems can reduce the ability of urban dwellers to diversify their incomes through their links to rural areas. As highlighted above, urban dwellers in intermediary cities conduct their livelihoods in both urban and rural areas, and this affects their food security. For example, findings from two intermediary cities in Uganda (Mbale and Mbarra) highlight that

food-secure households tend to have strong links to surrounding areas in terms of livelihoods and social networks. Thus, the most food-secure urban households were those that were employed within urban areas in addition to having active rural lives and livelihoods (Mackay, 2019[81]).

- The impact of climate change on in intermediary cities will be more acute for vulnerable populations (women, youth, migrants), further aggravating inequalities. Losses of livelihood would disproportionally affect marginalised groups such as urban women and youth, as they tend to be overrepresented in sectors such as food-away-from-home or market stalls (OECD/SWAC, 2020[82]). Sudden price shocks can have a particularly negative impact on poor or marginalised urban dwellers who rely on irregular incomes and are unable to adjust to sudden price fluctuations (Tacoli et al., 2013[80]; Von Braun and Tadesse, 2012[83]). These compounded effects, along with a lower food supply, cause food inaccessibility and increase food insecurity and malnutrition among the most vulnerable groups (Tacoli et al., 2013[80]; Tefft et al., 2017[84]).

Intermediary cities, climate change and internal migration

Climate change is expected to disrupt rural livelihoods severely and trigger internal migration. Natural disasters or land degradation and water scarcity can prompt rural populations to migrate to intermediary cities, which are closer, culturally more similar and arguably less costly than large urban centres. Understanding the factors influencing migration decisions and the vulnerabilities of the migrants upon arrival is crucial. Intermediary cities can actively work to improve the well-being of rural migrants through local policies, which are likely to have positive spillovers on the cities as well.

The section starts by considering internal migration as a global phenomenon and its role in the growth of intermediary cities. It then assesses migration decisions and coping strategies in the event of shocks. It next focuses on the effects on migration of fast-onset and slow-onset climate effects and the indirect effects these could have on intermediary cities. Finally, a non-comprehensive list of local measures is presented to spark debate on the role of intermediary cities as agents of change.

Conceptualising internal migration

Internal migration is a key factor shaping countries' development processes. At the beginning of the millennium, there were an estimated 740 million internal migrants, three times the estimated number of international migrants (FAO et al., 2018[1]; UNDP, 2009[85]; Rigaud et al., 2018[86]). According to the UN Development Programme (UNDP) (2009[85]), internal migrants represented 10% of the global population, while international migrants represented 3% (FAO et al., 2018[1]; UNDP, 2009[85]). However, it is important to note that these internal migration estimates by the UNDP (2009[85]) were rather conservative. While methodologies have improved in recent years (Bell et al., 2015[87]), large difficulties remain in obtaining consistent definition and estimations of global internal migration (IOM, 2008[88]).

The interaction of international migration with climate change, while an important factor, is outside the scope of this report, for two reasons: first because this report focuses on the linkages between a country's rural and urban areas, and second because international migration has received much more attention in the literature than internal migration, despite being of smaller magnitude. Nevertheless, international migration also has an important role in shaping urbanisation in developing countries and in food systems. For instance, Venezuelan migrants have been employed in Colombian coffee plantations that were facing low labour supply, as rural youth in Colombia switched to different economic sectors, and internal migration to work on plantations had slowed down (Federacion Nacional de Cafeteros de Colombia, 2017[89]).

Patterns of internal migration vary across regions and even by gender. These patterns can be categorised as rural-to-rural, rural-to-urban, urban-to-rural and urban-to-urban migration. The FAO (2019[90]) has estimated the prevalence of these different types of movements within and across regions in various developing economies. Figure 3.7 shows the dynamics of these internal movements. Although the dynamics vary substantially among countries within one region, some patterns stand out. For instance, in regions such as Sub-Saharan Africa and South Asia, more people tend to migrate across rural areas than to urban centres, and especially women (in Burkina Faso, 85% of female migrants settle in a rural region). In Latin America and the Caribbean, in contrast, most of the migration is to urban areas, and these patterns are similar among men and women.

Figure 3.7. Internal migration patterns by gender

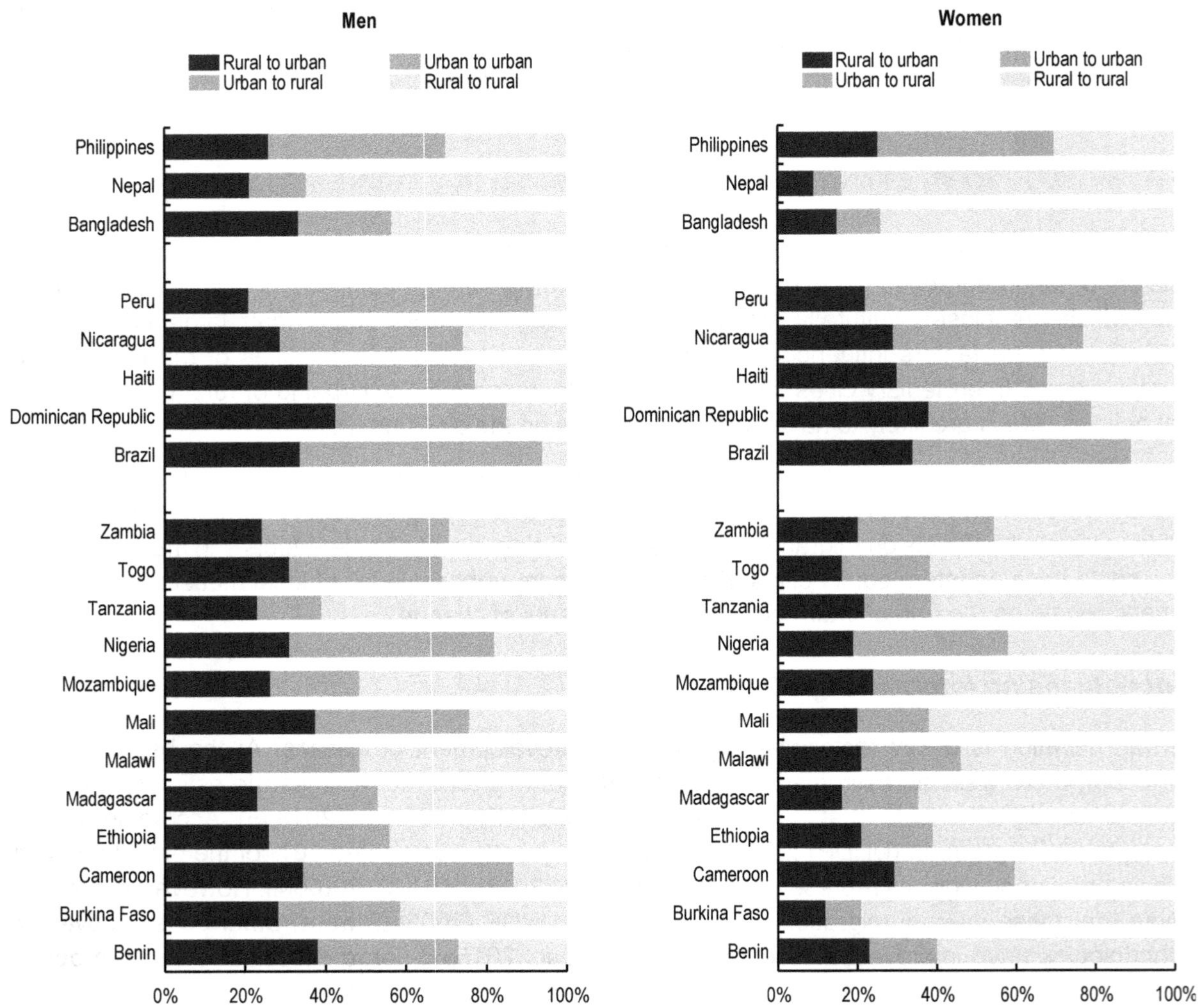

Note: Estimates by FAO using DHS survey data.
Source: FAO (2019[90]).

Despite differences in destination, an important share of internal migration originates from rural areas. Even in regions with high urbanisation, a sizeable share of migrants leave from rural areas. This is the case in Latin America and the Caribbean, which has an average urbanisation rate of 81% as of 2019 (UNDESA, 2018[91]) and where a high proportion of internal migrants nonetheless have a rural origin. In Haiti and the Dominican Republic, for instance, 58% of the movements of men originate in rural areas, while for Haitian women this statistic rises to 62%.

Climate change is a key driver of international or cross-border migration, and intermediary cities can be affected. Climate-driven international migration particularly affects countries in the Global South, such as

Bangladesh, Syria, Sudan and India, among others (Wesselbaum et al., 2021[92]). While more research and data is needed for better understanding of the links between climate change and international migration, internal migration from rural to urban areas is often the first step that migrants take before crossing international borders (Wesselbaum et al., 2021[92]).

Internal migration is a key driver of urbanisation

Internal migration to urban areas is a key element of urbanisation. While rural areas remain relevant as reception hubs in some regions (mostly due to rural-rural migration, and also a sizeable share of urban-rural movements in some cases), migration to urban areas represents an important share of internal migration across the board. Indeed, internal migration is one of the largest contributors to the growth of urban areas, along with natural population growth. For low- and middle-income countries, close to 40% of the urban growth rate stems from migration (Rigaud et al., 2018[86]; Tacoli et al., 2014[8]); see also (Montgomery, 2008[93]). Intermediary cities are projected to receive 400 million new inhabitants from 2014 to 2030, with more than 90% of this migration taking place in Asia and Sub-Saharan Africa – the equivalent of almost 70 000 rural migrants daily (Roberts et al., 2016[24]).

Rapid rural-to-urban migration has occurred particularly in countries that have undergone fast structural transformation, such as China, South Korea, Viet Nam and Thailand. For example, China's fast structural transformation process led to a decline of the rural population from 80% to 55% between 1992 and 2012, and the number of internal labour migrants reached 260 million, accounting for 19% of the country's total population (Lucas, 2015[94]). These changes took place in spite of Chinese government efforts to limit rural-to-urban migration through the *hukou* system. The development of infrastructure and communication services have been key drivers in the growth of rural-to-urban migration. As these services reduce the distances between rural and urban areas, rural households are now increasingly mobile and live along the rural-urban interface (FAO et al., 2018[1]).

Intermediary cities are often the preferred destination of migrants due to the low costs associated with moving to these urban centres. Migrants tend to look for better economic opportunities, and choose their destination based on factors including credit constraints and travel costs (Waldinger and Fankhauser, 2015[95]; IOM, 2008[88]). Indeed, migration costs (economic, social and psychological) are a key factor in rural migrants' choice of local and short-distance destinations. In Tanzania, for instance, lower migration costs were a key factor leading to migration towards small and medium-sized cities, as noted by Christiaensen et al. (2013[96]). Long-distance migration involves higher travel costs and greater difficulty in accessing information about the chosen destination (FAO et al., 2018[1]). Women can be especially constrained by migration costs, as they may not have access to personal transport (McOmber, 2020[97]).

Accessible information, pre-existing networks and cultural ties make intermediary cities attractive to migrants. Rural migrants may have better access to information regarding possible socio-economic opportunities in closer intermediary cities than in farther destinations. Pre-existing networks (like friends and relatives) may also play a role in incentivising migrants to travel to nearby cities and towns. Indeed, in rural Gujarat, India, the presence of family networks in urban areas was associated with the likelihood of rural out-migration for young men experiencing land scarcity and water depletion (Fishman et al, 2013[98]). Similar cultures, ethnicities, languages and social networks may play a role in keeping migration to shorter distances. The smaller the distance, the higher the likelihood of cultural similarities, making it easier for migrants to integrate, potentially exposing them to less xenophobia and possibly giving them a social safety net to fall back on (IOM, 2008[88]; Fishman et al, 2013[98]; Fafchamps and Shilpi, 2013[99]). Indeed, evidence in Nepal shows that much internal migration tends to be short distance, to nearby higher-density areas, because migrants prefer to go to areas with networks and similar language and culture (Fafchamps and Shilpi, 2013[99]; Burrows and Kinney, 2016[100]).

Rural migrants are more likely to relocate to informal settlements. Because of resource constraints and established networks, rural migrants are overrepresented in such settlements (Forefight, 2011[101]; Walter,

2015[102]; IDMC, 2017[103]; Bolay, 2020[104]; Mohit, 2012[105]). While informal settlements are most often associated with large metropolitan cities, especially in South Asia and Sub-Saharan Africa, the rapid, unplanned urbanisation now occurring in many intermediary cities in the developing world creates a ripe context for the spread of informal settlements (Roberts and Hohmann, 2014[25]; Williams et al., 2019[106]). These settlements often lack access to basic services such as electricity, running water, sanitation or waste management.

Internal migration can be a coping strategy for climate shocks

Internal migration can be considered a type of adaptation strategy that serves to manage risks, diversify income and smooth consumption levels in the face of shocks. Some experts see migration as a last resort coping strategy, one that denotes failure to adapt (IOM, 2020[107]; Banerjee, 2016[108]; Hummel et al., 2012[109]). However, this does not take into account that migration (including internal migration) is also a livelihood strategy, i.e. a way to accumulate assets (Hummel et al., 2012[109]; Tacoli, 2009[110]).

Migration does not necessarily denote the relocation of an entire household. Instead, households, especially rural households, can send one or more family members to migrate (Rigaud et al., 2018[86]; Stark and Bloom, 1985[111]; Rain, 2000[112]). This can be dynamic and does not have to be for an indefinite time period. There is extensive evidence of seasonal, or circular, migration, where an individual migrates away for a period of up to six months, and eventually returns home and re-integrates into the household's activities, as described in Box 3.9 (Hummel et al., 2012[109]; Findley, 1994[113]). Who migrates, where they migrate and for how long are questions determined by local socio-economic factors, as well as by patterns of vulnerability in places of origin (Tacoli, 2011[114]).

Box 3.9. Circular migration as a livelihood strategy

Circular or seasonal migration is an important coping strategy for many rural households seeking to diversify income and to reduce poverty, food insecurity and the effects of agricultural output fluctuations. Temporary migration is also an inherent part of the livelihoods and lifestyles of pastoralist groups.

Seasonal and circular migration as a coping mechanism is common across many regions and countries. In Lichinga, Mozambique, for example, non-linear migration patterns are frequent. The city of approximately 213 000 hosts more people in times of drought and excess rains than during the harvesting period, when men and women of working age often return to rural areas (UCLG, 2016[115]). A similar phenomenon is seen in Mzuzu and Blantyre in Malawi, which like many intermediary cities have larger daytime than nighttime populations (UCLG, 2016[115]; ARUP and Cities Alliance, 2016[116]). However, unlike in Lichinga, the elderly in Malawi are more likely to stay in rural areas (UCLG, 2016[115]). Findings from Mali, Ethiopia, Senegal, Argentina and India highlight that these migration strategies are seen as coping mechanisms, especially towards the end of the growing season (FAO et al., 2018[1]).

In India, despite seemingly low levels of urbanisation, people living in rural areas rely heavily on urban family members (Dyson, 2004[117]; Rigaud et al., 2018[86]). In Bangladesh, seasonal or circular migration is a common coping strategy when alternative measures are not available (Khandker et al., 2014[118]). In northern regions of Bangladesh, 36% of the extremely poor adopted seasonal migration in 2006 to mitigate or cope with hunger.

There are numerous benefits of circular or seasonal migration, especially for rural households. Having fewer household members can help reduce household expenses (Dillon et al., 2011[119]). Migration also facilitates the sending of remittances back to the household from different locations, particularly urban areas, helping to smooth consumption levels (Dillon et al., 2011[119]; Rosenzweig and Stark, 1989[120]). Migration that diversifies risk is occasionally deemed to be a result of income variability in a given location, as will be discussed in more depth below (Lilleør and Van den Broeck, 2011[121]).

Other coping strategies can complement or even substitute for migration from rural areas. In some cases, on-farm and off-farm strategies can serve as alternative adaptations to migration. Off-farm adaptation includes strategies such as starting small businesses or engaging in wage labour. This can diversify income streams and, depending on the business or employment, can diversify the sectors in which families or individuals are engaged, which is important as it can reduce the climate vulnerability associated with agriculture (FAO, 2016[122]). On-farm adaptation can include strategies such as climate-smart agriculture, agricultural intensification, crop adaptation, irrigation or changing species in livestock rearing (FAO, 2016[122]). Studies in Ghana show that on-farm adaptation such as irrigation and crop rotation may substitute for migration, as households that successfully implement these adaptations send fewer migrants (Antwi-Agyei, Stringer and Dougill, 2014[123]; Laube, Schraven and Awo, 2012[124]). As such, it is important understand that migration is not always the first or the preferred choice.

Climate change is expected to influence internal population movements

There is increasing evidence that climate change is a driver of internal migration in the developing world, and will continue to be in future (Rigaud et al., 2018[86]; Cattaneo et al., 2019[125]; IPCC, 2014[126]). Recent estimates suggest that, without action to reduce greenhouse gas (GHG) emissions, internal climate migrants could number 216 million by 2050 across regions including Sub-Saharan Africa, North Africa, South Asia, East Asia and the Pacific, Eastern Europe and Central Asia, and Latin America. This represents 3% of the projected total population of the six regions (Clement et al., 2021[127]). Migration trends may intensify after 2050 as climate impacts worsen in tandem with a rise in population across some regions (Rigaud et al., 2018[86]). Another study, drawing from case studies in Tanzania, Senegal and Bolivia, also finds that "climatic and environmental pressures" may cause hundreds of millions to seek shelter or leave their homes by 2050 (Tacoli, 2011[114]). However, accurately measuring the effects of climate change on internal migration is challenging and complex, due to the complex and interlinked factors that can prompt migration (Box 3.10). Estimations from recent studies on climate-induced migration, such as Clement et al. (2021[127]), are likely to be rather conservative because they may only consider slow-onset events driven by changes in water availability, crop production and sea-level rise caused by storm surges, and because they do not account for some regions, such as North America, Europe, the Middle East and small island states (Clement et al., 2021[127]).

Box 3.10. Measuring the impact of climate change on internal migration

Analysing the effects of climate change on internal migration for policy purposes is challenging. This is due to the following factors:

- Identifying who is a climate migrant is complex, as separating the effects of climate change from other migration drivers is challenging. This is because the decision to migrate is itself highly complex and is influenced by other interrelated factors, including economic, political, demographic, social and environmental factors (Rigaud et al., 2018[86]; Walter Kalin, 2010[128]; Brzoska and Fröhlich, 2016[129]). Making matters more complicated is the finding that people seldom move strictly due to climate conditions or even "altered ecosystem services" (IPCC, 2014[126]), with the exception of fast-onset events and displacement (Brzoska and Fröhlich, 2016[129]; Castles, 2002[130]).

- It is also difficult to predict what climate change-induced migration may look like. First, limitations in data and difficulties in methodology make it challenging to deduce the scale of existing internal migration ((Rigaud et al., 2018[86]; Tacoli, 2011[114]). It is also difficult to predict the locally specific effects of climate change, which may be dynamic and change from period to period depending on the region (Tacoli, 2011[114]).
- Despite the uncertainties, current research on the links between climate change and migration can play an important role in national, regional and municipal planning. As indicators of future migration, these links are best regarded as short-term estimates (Cattaneo et al., 2019[125]). Given the current unprecedented urbanisation in the developing world, anticipating trends in climate-influenced migration is important to help prepare areas for coming inflows of migrants.

In assessing the impact of climate change on migration decisions, it is important to understand the ways in which climate affects the household's environment. Climate change will cause rising temperatures, rainfall variability (too much or too little rainfall), degradation of soil quality and ecosystems and prolonged drought, and will result in extreme climate events such as storms and flooding (FAO, 2016[122]). As such, there is an important distinction to be made between fast-onset and slow-onset climate events (Rigaud et al., 2018[86]; IOM, 2008[88]; Cattaneo et al., 2019[125]). Fast-onset or extreme weather events include floods, storms, and cyclones, whereas slow-onset events include rainfall variability, seasonal variations and rising temperatures, among others (Table 3.1).

Table 3.1. Fast-onset and slow-onset climate events and migration

	Fast onset	Slow onset
Type of climate events	Extreme sudden climate events: floods, storms, cyclones, etc.	Long-term changes/shifts in climate: rainfall variability, seasonal variations, temperature rise, droughts, etc.
Direct vs. indirect effect on migration	Direct effect	Indirect through effects on existing social and economic drivers of climate change
Common type of migration	Involuntary internal displacement/fast migration trends	Slower pace migration trends, with permanent changes in livelihoods or locations
Migration distance	Short distance	Short distance, or longer distance based on migrant economic conditions
Migration period	Temporary	Permanent

Source: Author's elaboration.

Climate change is expected to impact rural livelihoods in many ways, and the speed with which households react to climate events depends on the nature of the event. Climate disasters increase the risk of fast displacement as they can cause the destruction of crops and livelihoods (IPCC, 2014[126]). On the other hand, slower events such as increasing temperatures can decrease crop productivity, reduce water availability and cause land degradation, among other impacts. This in turn can lead to resource constraints, create tension in communities and make it more difficult to engage in traditional livelihood activities (Selby et al., 2017[131]), which could delay the migration decision.

Changes in precipitation are expected to have a large impact on migration decisions. Recent evidence suggests that a decline or negative shock in rainfall is associated with an increase in internal and international migration (Zaveri et al., 2021[132]).[3] Estimates suggest that, between 1970 and 2000, declines in rainfall have accounted for 10% of the increase in migration globally. However, there are important nuances in the rainfall-migration nexus. The effects of changes in rainfall on migration patterns are highly dependent on a country's income level. Out-migration tends to take place primarily in rural areas in low-income countries, which tend to be highly reliant on agriculture as a source of livelihood and sustenance.

Climate change can also cause immobility. Slow-onset events harm agricultural productivity and curtail the available resources of households (Selby et al., 2017[131]), reducing their financial capacity to migrate

(Cattaneo et al., 2019[125]; Kleemans et al., 2014[133]; IPCC, 2014[126]; Robalino et al., 2013[134]). This is particularly relevant in low-income countries, where high temperatures have been found to have a negative effect on rural-to-urban migration, whereas in middle-income countries climate change has spurred migration. One possible mechanism behind this effect is that low rural income acts as an incentive to migrate, but that when it is too low it can act as a constraint (Peri and Sasahara, 2019[27]). Estimates suggest that the poorest households are less likely to migrate in circumstances of rainfall scarcity. As such, in circumstances of extreme poverty, declines in rainfall are more likely to trap populations than to induce migration (Zaveri et al., 2021[132]).

Migration trends and directions can also be disrupted by non-climate-related shocks. COVID-19 and the restriction measures implemented by governments caused large disruptions in internal migration trends, especially in developing countries. This process did not come without challenges since it especially impacted vulnerable internal migrants. Some of the main pandemic-related challenges faced by internal migrants are presented in Box 3.11.

Box 3.11. Effects of the COVID-19 pandemic on internal migrants in developing countries

COVID-19 and the restrictions imposed to contain the spread of the virus have posed and continue to impose enormous challenges on (vulnerable) internal migrants, especially in developing countries. Overall, far less research has been conducted on the effects of COVID-19 on internal migration than on food systems. Indeed, the shortage of adequate data and evidence on the numbers of internal migrants makes it challenging to gain accurate understanding of the effects on COVID-19 on their mobility and well-being. Yet studies of countries like India have demonstrated the deep effects on internal migrants of the sanitary and economic crisis caused by the pandemic (Gupta, 2020[135]).

COVID-19 disproportionality affected internal migrants due to their socio-economic vulnerabilities. Internal migrants tend to be overrepresented in informal sectors such as domestic work, seasonal work and street vending. As such, a large share of internal migrants lost their livelihoods and sources of income in the pandemic, and restrictions on mobility prevented them from returning to their places of origin, leaving them stranded in poor-quality and overcrowded housing or slums (Rajan et al., 2020[136]). COVID-19 and restrictive measures also led to an exodus of migrants from urban to rural areas.

India faced some of the largest challenges in protecting its internal migrants. India had an estimated 600 million internal migrants in 2020 (Rajan et al., 2020[136]). Out of this total, 200 million were interstate and inter-district migrants, with internal migrant workers accounting for two-thirds (or 140 million) of the interstate migrants (Gupta, 2020[135]; Rajan et al., 2020[136]). Indian internal migrants, who are often from lower-income quintile groups and disadvantaged caste groups, are often excluded from social safety nets, and thus face significant challenges from short-notice lockdowns and restrictions on mobility (Rajan et al., 2020[136]). During the pandemic, India's internal migrants found themselves stranded in urban areas with no source of income and no transportation for their journeys back to their families. Women internal migrants faced disproportionate challenges, as four in ten women lost their livelihoods within two months of the COVID-19 outbreak (Rukimini, 2020[137]). Some 30% of the migrants who left Indian cities are not expected to return post-pandemic, and their absence is expected to cause significant economic losses (Gupta, 2020[135]). In African countries, such as Uganda, Madagascar and Kenya, meanwhile, migrants undertook long journeys back to rural areas, in some cases by foot, to avoid even more economic strains and, in many cases, hunger (The Citizen, 2020[138]).

COVID-19 brought to the surface the structural challenges that internal migrants have long faced and their disproportionate vulnerability to these challenges. Moreover, the loss of livelihoods among internal migrants will have rebound effects on larger population groups. Internal migrants are critical in the flow of remittances, especially to rural households, which rely heavily on remittances for their daily consumption (World Bank, 2021[139]). Going forward, establishing an adequate evidence base (i.e. data) on the numbers and conditions of internal migrants is the first step to improving their well-being. In addition, local and national governments should establish measures to protect vulnerable internal migrants and to integrate them into local and national safety-net programmes.

Intermediary cities are often the main destination of climate-induced migration

Urban areas will increasingly be the main destination of internal migration in the face of climate shocks. As climate negatively affects agricultural productivity, and earnings, rural migrants will be encouraged to look for opportunities elsewhere (Cattaneo et al., 2019[125]). Studies have highlighted the links between declining agricultural productivity and migration due to variations in temperature in both Sub-Saharan Africa (Marchiori et al., 2012[140]) and India (Viswanathan and Kumar, 2015[141]).

People who resort to migration in search of opportunities and better livelihoods usually move to urban areas. As the primary destination for population movements resulting from changes in rainfall patterns, cities face the double burden of providing water services to a growing population while coping with a decline in water supply. By 2050, water demand in cities is expected to rise by 80% from current levels (Flörke et al., 2018[142]). Cities with a large metropolitan area, such as Cape Town (South Africa), Chennai (India) and São Paulo Brazil, have attracted international attention for approaching a "day zero" of water availability: the moment when water taps have to be shut down for lack of water (Zaveri et al., 2021[132]). Water decline slows economic activity and development processes; in the most extreme cases, cities can lose up 12 percentage points in GDP (Zaveri et al., 2021[132]). However, the effects of a decrease in rainfall have nuances depending on geography and city size. For instance, cities in arid areas tend to be better equipped to handle abnormally lower rainfall than cities in humid areas. Similarly, large cities tend to be more resilient against lower rainfall than small cities (Zaveri et al., 2021[132]).

The effects of climate change on the dynamics of internal migration will have indirect effects on intermediary cities. Climate change will escalate pre-existing migration flows to close and familiar urban centres, exacerbating pressures on intermediary cities and their urbanisation process – first and foremost by increasing the demand for infrastructure, but also by expanding social and economic inequalities; creating health concerns (IOM, 2008[88]); and increasing the pressures facing institutions that are already under strain. Nevertheless, the inflow of migrants could also become an opportunity for development.

Understanding the different ways in which climate change will impact patterns of migration and the needs of migrants is essential for intermediary cities to prepare for new challenges. The next sections will consider the different types of migration caused by climate events and the vulnerabilities migrants face upon arrival. There is scope for intermediary cities to act on these dynamics in advance and improve the well-being of both urban dwellers and newcomers.

Fast-onset events in particular can spur migration towards intermediary cities

Fast-onset events affect developing economies disproportionately and are a major reason for internal displacements. According to the Internal Displacement Monitoring Centre (IDMC), the countries with the greatest number of new internal displacements in 2019 were India, Philippines, Bangladesh and China. Natural disasters triggered the displacement of the more than 17 million people who migrated in these countries in 2019. Of the total number of natural disasters that impacted the world in 2019, 96% were weather related. Figure 3.8 shows the number of new displacements due to weather-related events in developing countries. Storms were the major cause of these movements, followed closely by floods.

Figure 3.8. Weather-related displacements in 2019, by type of event

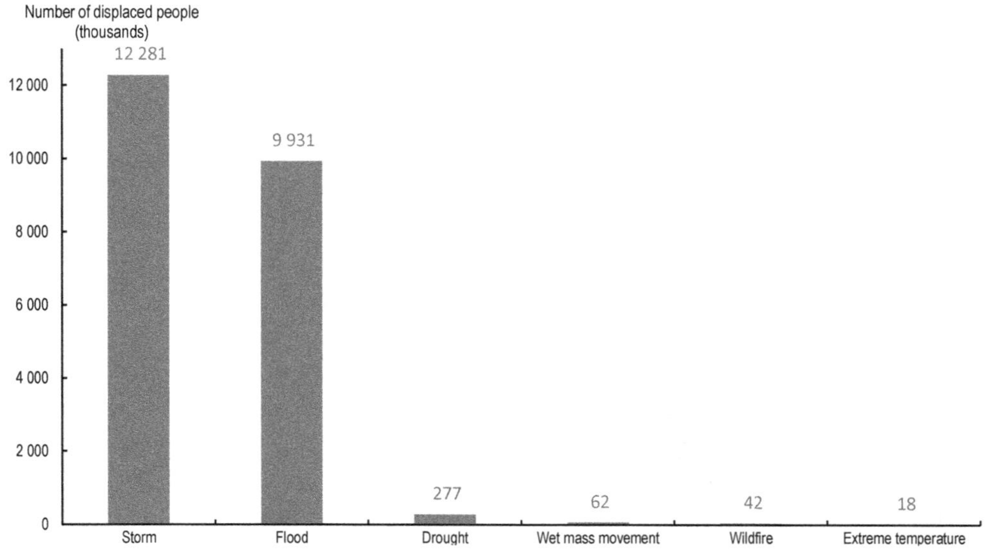

Note: Excludes geophysical events such as earthquakes.
Source: IDMC database.

Fast-onset events are linked to short-distance migration, with intermediary cities likely to be the destination of displaced people, particularly from nearby rural areas. In the face of extreme weather events, migrants are forced to make decisions very quickly and are likely to choose familiar places where they may have networks (Waldinger, 2015[143]; Brzoska and Fröhlich, 2016[129]). They may stay only temporarily at these destinations: there is strong evidence that many displaced migrants have an intent to return (Rigaud et al., 2018[86]; Burrows and Kinney, 2016[100]; Brzoska and Fröhlich, 2016[129]; Walter Kalin, 2010[128]; Black et al., 2011[144]; Castells-Quintana, Del Pilar Lopez-Uribe and Mcdermott, 2015[145]).

Depending on the extent of the damage caused by an extreme weather event, displaced migrants may slowly repopulate their original towns or villages after first living in a nearby city or town as an intermediary destination. This was observed in the United States following Hurricane Katrina, which struck New Orleans and its surrounding area in 2005 and forced many people to evacuate. Over a five-year period, New Orleans recovered its population as the displaced returned indirectly by migrating across one or more intermediary destinations (DeWaard et al, 2016[146]).

In some cases, intermediary cities receive migrants affected by fast-onset events in a delayed fashion. People may arrive in nearby cities and towns looking for work in the aftermath of the disaster, possibly because of loss of livelihood or debts from loans for damage repair. After severe rural flooding in 2014, Bangladesh saw an increase in migration, especially of males, for these reasons (Walter, 2015[102]).

Intermediary cities may also receive migrants from other urban areas in response to fast-onset events. For example, flooding due to rising seas and water scarcity affecting large coastal cities in South America may lead migrants to relocate to small and medium-sized cities (Warn and Adamo, 2014[147]). There is evidence in Costa Rica that less severe emergencies in metropolitan areas (those that do not result in death) can also increase migration to other metropolitan areas (Robalino et al., 2013[134]). Migration from large urban areas towards intermediary cities could be driven by the fact that many very large cities are severely stretched in terms of physical infrastructure, services, employment and housing.

Socio-economic factors play a role when migrants take refuge in intermediary cities during fast-onset climate events. Rural migrants may initially take up residence on the outskirts of urban centres due to the lower up-front costs. Since such settlements are often informal, this increases their vulnerability (IDMC, 2017[103]; Bolay, 2020[104]). Informal settlements are often poorly serviced, with no drainage systems or sewerage and little access to public services. Migrants who settle there, become vulnerable to events like floods and storms, making their displacement maladaptive (IOM, 2020[107]; McAdam and Ferris, 2015[148]).

Slow-onset events can spur migration towards intermediary cities for longer periods

Slow-onset climate events tend to influence internal migration indirectly via channels categorised as "economic" and "social", with migration taking place more slowly than with fast-onset events (Rigaud et al., 2018[86]; Lilleør and Van den Broeck, 2011[121]; Cattaneo et al., 2019[125]) (FAO et al., 2018[1]).

Economic channels" concern migration resulting from economic downturn. For instance, climate variability can reduce agricultural productivity and yields, which in turn decreases rural incomes. This is the case across rural areas of Sub-Saharan Africa, South Asia and Latin America, where agriculture – the basis of a large share of rural livelihoods – is highly vulnerable to climatic changes such as variability in rainfall or extreme wet or dry conditions, including droughts (Cattaneo et al., 2019[125]; Burke et al., 2015[149]; Dallmann and Millock, 2017[150]). These risks have the potential to decrease income in rural areas and eventually drive migration. Indeed, the people most vulnerable to climate change are those with income directly linked to agriculture (Cattaneo et al., 2019[125]). Box 3.12 highlights the subcategories in which migration can be triggered through economic channels.

Box 3.12. Climate induced-migration via economic channels

Income differentials between rural and urban areas is one of the main push factor for internal migration. Income differentials refer to wage differences between origin and destination, such as rural and urban areas (Cattaneo et al., 2019[125]). Research that builds on classic models of rural-to-urban migration found that expected increases in income associated with moving from rural to urban areas facilitate migration, even when considering the reality of widespread high unemployment in a destination city (Harris and Todaro, 1970[151]).

Climate change is affecting income differentials, which has contributed to spur urbanisation in the developing world. In Sub-Saharan Africa, evidence has shown that weather anomalies causing low agricultural productivity and rural earnings resulted in rural-to-urban migration, contributing to urbanisation (Marchiori et al., 2012[140]). A study in India showed that climate-induced losses in agricultural output led to interstate migration, working as a push factor for urbanisation (Viswanathan and Kumar, 2015[141]). The study indicated that migration patterns may vary depending on the main crops grown in the region, with the effect of out-migration for ubiquitous labour-intensive crops such as rice found to be higher than for wheat (Viswanathan and Kumar, 2015[141]). However, development and increased income can also facilitate mobility and migration. For example, development may be a factor in increased rural-to-urban migration in India from 1991-2001 compared to previous decades (Viswanathan and Kumar, 2015[141]).

Climate change could also spur migration through income variability. In this case, migration can occur in anticipation of or in response to changes or fluctuations in income over time (Cattaneo et al., 2019[125]). However, there is little evidence for climate-related income variability in rural areas contributing to migration. For example, a macroeconomic study of 39 Sub-Saharan African countries showed "negligible" impact of income variability on migration (Marchiori et al, 2017[152]); (Lilleør and Van den Broeck, 2011[121]; Cattaneo et al., 2019[125]). In contrast, a study on Nigeria found some evidence for income variability leading to migration. The study used household-level surveys in northern Nigeria to measure income variability through temperature and found that households had sought to smooth their consumption patterns both in response to and in anticipation of income variability caused by an idiosyncratic climate shock (Dillon et al., 2011[119]). Nigerian households were likely to send a male household member to migrate as a risk-management strategy to diversify income, with suggestive evidence for migration decisions ex-ante, in anticipation of a decrease in wages, and robust findings for migration decisions in response to risk and variation in wages (Dillon et al., 2011[119]).

"Social channels" concern conflicts that act as drivers of migration or result from migration. Conflict and climate change can interact with migration in various ways. Climate-induced migration can lead to resource scarcity in migrant destinations. This can spur tensions and competition for livelihoods, ultimately causing conflicts. Eruption of conflicts in migrant destinations can potentially trigger further migration through forced displacement. However, there is little agreement on the idea that climate change has a causal effect on conflict, and more specifically that climate-change-induced migration causes conflict (Burrows and Kinney, 2016[100]; Hsiang, Burke and Miguel, 2013[153]; Reuveny, 2008[154]). Box 3.13 highlights the ways in which climate change, migration and conflict can interact, especially in Sub-Saharan Africa.

Pre-existing networks and resource constraints are likely to influence the decision to migrate to urban areas in the case of slow-onset events. Unlike migration due to fast-onset events, when decisions must be made quickly, people migrating due to slow-onset events are likely to take account of travel costs, family ties and social networks. Moreover, while there is evidence, in India for example, of high rural-to-rural migration in times of drought, it may be that declining wages in rural areas mean that they offer fewer options than urban areas (Dallmann and Millock, 2017[150]).

Intermediary cities and towns near rural areas are likely to host rural migrants over a long period of time. Migrants whose livelihoods have been negatively affected will be motivated to leave rural areas (sometimes permanently) in search of new livelihoods. This is a continuation of a pre-existing practice of flocking to nearby cities and towns looking for ways to supplement income, diversify risk and secure nonfarm labour (Roberts and Hohmann, 2014[25]). If there are opportunities, then the migrants are likely to stay, especially if climate factors continue to constrain natural resources and diminish agricultural productivity (IOM, 2020[107]; UNEP, 2011[155]; Bolay, 2020[104]).

As a result of these interrelated factors, intermediary cities should expect an increase in the arrival of rural migrants looking for work. Upon reaching urban areas, rural migrants may look for work opportunities in construction and transport, including informal work; in work associated with natural resources, such as mining; or in farm-related employment such as agricultural processing and value-add services (McOmber, 2020[97]; Agergaard et al., 2019[37]; Christiaensen and Todo, 2013[96]). With greater reliance on self-employment in the midstream segments of food systems (Dolislager et al., 2020[156]), women who migrate to urban areas can be overrepresented in informal food markets in intermediary cities.

Due to resource constraints, migrants are likely to settle in the outskirts of town or informal settlements, where they face health risks including increased exposure to vector-borne diseases, such as malaria and dengue fever, and the risk of bodily injury. They may also lack access to transportation. Although migrants often choose to move to intermediary cities rather than large urban areas, mobility may be an issue while living on the edges of a city (Waldinger, 2015[143]; Bolay, 2020[104]). There is evidence that migrants in cities with less access to transportation services face higher costs and greater challenges (Waldinger, 2015[143]). They may find the city hard to navigate and have less access to nearby services.

Box 3.13. Climate change, internal migration, and conflicts

The links between climate change, internal migration and conflicts are complicated and vary significantly by local history and socio-economic circumstances. However, there is evidence that increasing pressure on environmental resources could result in mounting tension and migration. These findings are in line with neo-Malthusian theories that environmental and economic scarcities increase tensions and result in pressure or competition (McOmber, 2020[97]; Burrows and Kinney, 2016[100]). Extensive evidence in West Africa confirms the contribution of climate change to tensions due to pressure on natural resources. In some of these instances, the resource constraints themselves have been a result of climate change (Burrows and Kinney, 2016[100]). Dry conditions in Mali, Niger, and Nigeria resulted in shrinking land available to pastoralists, pushing them to search for land. This resulted in increased competition and tensions with agriculturalists, who were already increasing their land use to meet the growing food demand in the region (UNEP, 2011[155]; Dominic Azuwike, 2010[157]; Keith Moore, 2005[158]). In Mali and Nigeria, these tensions resulted, respectively, in low-level conflict and violence (UNEP, 2011[155]; Warner et al., 2009[159]; Mwiturubani and Van Wyk, 2010[160]).

Climate-induced migration driven by conflict is context specific. For instance, in the Lake Chad region, drought conditions pushed some agriculturalists to conduct fishing activities. This compounded the scarcity faced by existing fishermen as a result of the shrinking size of the lake, as well as overuse and population growth (UNEP, 2011[155]). It may have been exacerbated by new migrants to the area who arrived looking for work (UNEP, 2011[155]). A result was migration by those whose livelihood depended on the lake and those whose livelihoods were connected to business with fishermen (UNEP, 2011[155]).

In some instances, conflict can also limit the scope for migration responses to climate change. For instance, pastoralists in the Horn of Africa tried to respond to drought by migrating in search of better water resources but faced restrictions of movement due to conflict (ICRC, 2004[161]). McGuirk and Nunn (2020[162]) find that climate changes in Africa can lead to conflict between pastoralists and sedentary agricultural groups, particularly during rainy season. This is because changing rain patterns and rainfall shocks can push pastoralist groups to migrate to agricultural land before harvest time, which leads to crop damage due to premature grazing.

Overall, the climate change-conflict-migration pathway is more often than not associated with economic factors or resource scarcity. In this regard, climate change does not directly cause conflict but affects other variables that trigger conflicts. A leading counterargument against climate change-induced migration causing conflict is that there are a great many examples of migration without conflict, and that associating a security risk with migration may be political in nature and therefore requires caution (Burrows and Kinney, 2016[100]).

Climate-induced migration affects the urbanisation process of intermediary cities

The linkages between climate patterns and migration are manifold and complex. As discussed above, climate change can push people to relocate across the rural-urban continuum in search of employment, particularly from rural areas to cities, yet with slow-onset climate events people who would have otherwise migrated might postpone their decision or not migrate at all (Selby et al., 2017[131]). The effects of climate on migration also depend on the ability of people to migrate and the ability of a city to absorb migrants.

Climate-induced migration is expected to contribute to urban population growth in developing economies. Barrios et al. (2006[163]) find that shortages in rainfall are associated with an increase in urbanisation rates in Sub-Saharan Africa. However, there are nuances. Henderson et al. (2017[164]) find that drier conditions influence migration to urban areas only if the city can absorb the excess workers from agriculture into its manufacturing industry. If the city is not a manufacturing centre (less industrialised), drier conditions tend not to affect urbanisation levels.

The effect of changing climatic patterns on urban population will depend, among other things, on baseline climatic conditions. Recent evidence on capital cities suggests that the relationship between climate change and urban population depends on whether a city already experiences high temperatures and dry conditions: the effect of rising temperatures on urban population growth is higher in places that are already hot, and the effect of lower precipitation on population growth is higher in places that are already dry (Castells-Quintana, Krause and McDermott, 2021[165]).

Similar patterns are also observed in the case of intermediary cities. Figure 3.9 (left side) presents the results of an econometric analysis looking at the relationship between temperature and urban population among cities of different sizes in developing countries (detailed results in Tables 3.A.1 and 3.A.2 in Annex 3.A1). The figure shows that the relationship between temperatures and population growth follows a U-shape, suggesting that higher temperatures tend to have a stronger effect on population in places that are already warm, and that this relationship is more acute for intermediary cities.

Changing rain patterns also have an impact on the population of small and medium-sized cities. Figure 3.9 (right side) shows the relationship between precipitation and population. As in the case of temperature, this relationship is not linear. However, this relationship is only statistically significant for cities of fewer than 500 000 inhabitants and – in contrast to temperature – follows an inverted U-shape (detailed results in Tables 3.A.1 and 3.A.2 in Annex 3.A1). It suggests that in small and medium cities, higher levels of precipitation are associated with an increase in population.[4] The shape of the curve also indicates that dry places are more sensitive to changes in rain patterns, i.e. that more precipitation tends to have a positive and larger effect on population in dryer places.

Figure 3.9. Non-linear effect of temperature and precipitation on population of cities

By city size

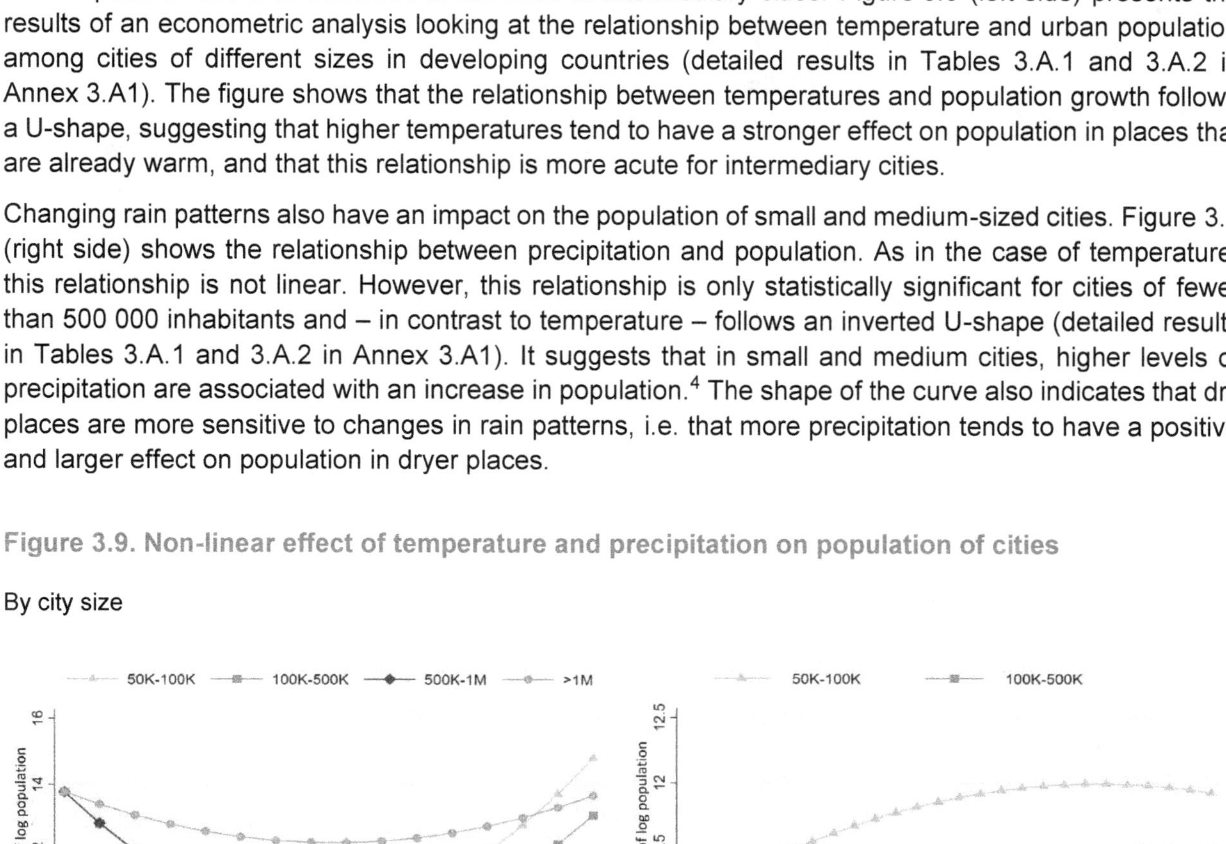

Note: Estimates of a panel econometric model, regressing population of cities on average temperature (or precipitation) in the last 5 years and its quadratic term, interacted with city size. Base category are cities above 1 million inhabitants. Population (dependent variable) expressed in logarithmic terms. Results based on a fixed-effects estimator and standard errors clustered by city. Year fixed effects are included. Data for the periods 1990, 2000 and 2015.
Source: Authors' computation using GHS Urban Centre Database (2019[166]).

Climate change can also influence the distribution of the population across a city's functional urban area (FUA). Functional Urban Areas refer to functional economic spaces that reflect population density and commuting flows, and that interconnect urban centres that are part of the same functional areas (OECD, 2018[167]). As argued throughout the chapter, cities need to be understood in the context of rural-urban linkages and interactions, as they are not individual entities but are deeply connected to their surroundings.

In the context of this analysis, urban share is considered as the ratio between a city's population in its high-density core and that of its total functional area. The FUA provides relevant information on the spatial structure of cities. A high value of the ratio indicates that more people are concentrating in high-density areas, while a low ratio means that the population of the FUA is more evenly distributed across high-density and low-density areas. The results in Tables 3.A.3 and 3.A.4 in Annex 3.A1 show that, in the case of cities of 50 000 to 100 000 inhabitants, rising temperatures have a negative relationship to urban share (albeit with decreasing returns). This suggests that, as temperatures increase, fewer people concentrate in high-density areas. This relationship is not statistically significant for bigger cities. Moreover, changes in precipitation do not seem to have a significant effect on urban share.

The effects of changing climate patterns on urban population are far from simple. The results above suggesting that an increase in temperatures will drive up population in warm cities is in line with the literature that relates higher temperatures to rural out-migration into urban areas (Arslan, Egger and Winters, 2018[14]). Moreover, these results reinforce previous findings about the complex effect of climate change on population, which can depend on baseline income levels (Zaveri et al., 2021[132]) as well as on baseline climatic conditions (Castells-Quintana, Krause and McDermott, 2021[165]). The analysis shows that the positive effect of higher temperature on urban population will only take place in those cities where average temperatures are already high. The effect of changing rain patterns on population is even more nuanced and the results suggest that this also depends on city size. Castells-Quintana, Krause and McDermott (2021[165]) find that drier conditions in already arid places drive up population in large cities. Focusing on smaller urban centres, as in this analysis, shows that an increase in precipitation levels has a positive effect on urban population only among cities with fewer than 500 000 inhabitants. This effect is more important for cities located in dryer places.

Strengthening the climate-change resilience of the rural-urban interface

Adopting territorial policies can be a critical step for building effective climate policies that account for rural-urban linkages. Building long-term resilience in the rural-urban interface, while tapping into the potential of cities for climate mitigation, calls for a shift in policy perspectives in both urban and rural areas. As global economies recover from the economic and sanitary crises created by COVID-19, and climate change becomes a pressing global concern, there is a need to adopt policy approaches that are people centred and place based, and to redefine policy goals to obtain wider well-being outcomes, such as improved health. Adopting territorial approaches for intermediary cities can help to achieve these goals, while strengthening rural-urban linkages and reducing regional and spatial inequalities (UN-Habitat, 2019[168]), as well as promoting policy coherence across sectors and territories (Hussein and Suttie, 2016[36]).

Adopting territorial approaches and building a resilient rural-urban interface cannot be successful without the full engagement of the national government and effective co-operation across all levels of government. Multi-level dialogue across all levels of governments (central, district or regional, and city or local) is key for designing policies that address the direct and indirect effects of climate change. Local governments play a critical role in implementing climate policies, as they have better awareness of the specific challenges faced. However, by unlocking resources and co-ordinating efforts, national governments play a fundamental role in supporting and scaling up local governments' climate actions. Many local governments that manage intermediary cities lack the technical and financial capacity, as well as the political autonomy, to maximise opportunities for adaptation and to implement actions to mitigate climate threats (Satterthwaite, 2016[26]). National governments have larger scope to support intermediary cities in establishing climate actions and unleashing the socio-economic gains that green growth strategies may provide (Coalition for Urban Transitions, 2021[169]). However, this will require closing the gap between local ambitions and national visions, while providing tailored support to implement strategies for disaster risk reduction. Box 3.14 highlights the challenges faced by local authorities in Quelimane, Mozambique, in their efforts to implement climate actions without support from the national authorities.

Box 3.14. Implementing climate actions in Quelimane, Mozambique

Quelimane, with approximately 400 000 inhabitants, is the fourth largest city in Mozambique. Its high vulnerability to increasingly frequent climate-change threats, especially floods, is causing large socio-economic challenges, including losses in agricultural production, land and water scarcity, infrastructure damage, etc. (Plataforma, 2020[170]). The local government has implemented climate actions to reduce the effects of extreme events. However, Quelimane's government faces challenges that diminish its capacity to intervene effectively, especially constraints in institutional capacity. These include:

- *inadequate legislative framework.* Local authorities do not have sufficient powers to deal with extreme climate-related events. This shows the need to strengthen legislative frameworks to enhance cities' capacity to respond to extreme events.
- *low human resources.* Local governments do not have the human resources needed to understand and create a policy framework for implementing actions to address climate threats.
- *lack of adequate dialogue and co-operation.* In most cases, local governments have no capacity to influence national goals and strategies and lack transparent dialogue with regional and national governments and international partners. National governments do not establish adequate spaces to enable local governments to access information or contribute to discussions at national level.
- *lack of access to information.* Despite being at the forefront of climate actions, local governments tend to have inadequate understanding of the relationship and dynamics between rural and urban areas, and are unprepared to manage pressing issues such as the increase in rural-urban migration, which contributes to the expansion of informal settlements and unemployment.

Source: Intervention by Mayor Manuel de Araujo of Quelimane, Cities Connect Expert Meeting, 2020.

As the Quelimane example makes clear, it is key that national governments provide the right incentives to city authorities to work collaboratively on a regional scale. Such collaboration allows leaders to tap into their own city's assets while also drawing upon the wider region's assets, scale and expertise (Jeffrey, 2017[171]). In order to build resilient urban systems, national governments should shift their approach from urban development to systems-based thinking. They ought to envision intermediary cities as part of the urban system and foster stronger partnerships, connectivity and collaboration across cities. This will enable local and national governments to better grasp the socio-economic potential of intermediary cities, as well as facilitating inclusive growth within urban systems. Collaborating with partners such as universities, the private sector, international organisations or other intermediary cities can bring valuable knowledge and experience.

The sections below build on the analysis and findings of Chapters 2 and 3 and propose a series of policy actions that can help to strengthen the resilience of the rural-urban interface while also tapping into the potential of intermediary cities for effective climate-mitigation actions.

Spatial planning is key for climate mitigation and adaption in intermediary cities

Effective spatial planning is one of the most important aspects of climate adaptation and mitigation in urban areas. According to the IPCC (2018[172]), a reduction of greenhouse gases requires transitions in four types of system: land and ecosystem; energy; urban and infrastructure; and industrial systems. Intermediary cities can play a transformative role across all four systems. Early and co-ordinated spatial planning, which links urban form and infrastructure, can shape land-use management and commuting and transportation patterns, which in turn can have a major effect on GHG emissions at city level. Early planning is key, as it avoids the high cost of changing already built urban infrastructure and established urban form (Satterthwaite et al., 2007[173]).

Integrated spatial planning – which incorporates efficiency in energy use, transportation, mixed density, urban sewerage and waste management infrastructure – has been used in policy strategies in some cities and can provide important lessons for other intermediary cities (UN-HABITAT, 2011[174]). Climate mitigation opportunities in low- and middle-income countries will depend significantly on the type of urbanisation process and energy mix in intermediary cities. The rapid built-up expansion of some intermediary cities, in addition to inadequate infrastructure and use of inefficient energy sources (such as wood fuels and other fossil fuel), may limit the mitigation potential of these cities. Yet spatial planning that accounts for integrated infrastructure and land-use planning can help to reduce urban sprawl and commuting distances, as well as discouraging reliance on private vehicles (UN-HABITAT, 2011[174]). Additionally, incorporating Functional Urban Areas (FUA) or a metropolitan approach to spatial planning can aid local and national governments to better co-ordinate and enable them to pool resources for joint investment. In turn, national governments can facilitate a metropolitan approach to spatial planning by facilitating and supporting horizontal co-ordination across lower-level governments (OECD, 2018[167]). Planning compact and high-density urban centres with better access to modern technology and sustainable energy sources can help to reduce GHG emissions. For example, European cities, which tend to be denser than North American cities, produce 50% less CO_2. Yet European cities produce double the emissions of Asian cities (Kamal-Chaoui and Robert, 2009[175]) despite being less dense (Gregor et al., 2018[176]). Higher density tends to lead to lower per-capita energy demand, lower CO_2 emissions from private transportation and higher demand for public transportation services (IEA, 2016[177]; IEA, 2018[178]).

Integrating infrastructure, housing and mobility policies into spatial planning

As intermediary cities increasingly become migration destinations, spatial planning should consider the implications of a growing local population. Beyond the usual patterns of rural-to-urban migration (including seasonal and circular migration), intermediary cities are also an important destination for displaced populations. Such displacements can result from climate change or conflicts. In Niger, for instance, small cities of 50 000 inhabitants such as Diffa, N'Guigmi, Chétimari and Mainé Soroa received approximately 250 000 displaced migrants due to conflicts in surrounding villages, by 2020 (Wetterwald and Thaller, 2020[179]). The fact that these cities had to host an unprecedented flow of people over a very short period of time put large strains on local basic services, such as housing, sanitation and water, that were already very limited (Wetterwald and Thaller, 2020[179]). With climate-induced displacement expected to continue in the next decades, as global temperatures continue to rise and precipitation patterns change, intermediary cities should prepare for increasing demand for infrastructure, housing and other public services. Overlooking urban population growth in city planning can lead to the expansion of informal settlements, as has occurred in a large share of African cities (Cities Alliance, 2019[180]), and thus increase the climate vulnerability of urban dwellers.

Intermediary cities in developing countries can use the early stages of infrastructure investment to implement instruments that reduce GHG emissions and that can accommodate their growing population. In intermediary cities in low- and middle-income countries, a large share of infrastructure has yet to be built. In Asia, for example, two-thirds of the infrastructure needed by 2050 is still pending (OECD, 2018[181]); this is also the case in Africa (AfDB/OECD/UNDP, 2016[182]). With proper planning, intermediary cities can invest in low-carbon infrastructure in order to reduce the risk of carbon lock-in and avoid a "build now and clean later" approach. Low-carbon infrastructure can contribute to local economic development while also improving the well-being of urban dwellers. It can adapt to and mitigate climate shocks in local food systems by reducing loss and waste in production, thus improving food security. For creating resilient connective infrastructure that is low carbon (such as public transportation services), this would involve building robust storage facilities and improving market stalls. Establishing spatial planning frameworks that aim to reduce urban sprawl and promote compact and accessible urban form can be key to reducing future GHG emissions, while also enhancing the well-being of urban dwellers. Other key elements of long-term urban climate resilience include building effective waste management systems and investment in clean energy supply (Broekhoff et al., 2018[183]).

Intermediary cities are also identified as high-potential areas for improved access to sustainable mobility. Findings from SEforAll (2020[184]) indicate that these urban areas present large opportunities for implementing sustainable mobility solutions and enhancing access to energy in parallel with population growth. However, this requires an integrated planning approach that links land use and transport planning, and that facilitates better mobility and energy use (SEforAll, 2020[184]). Integrating land use, transportation and infrastructure development can help shape travel demand towards lower-emission modes of transportation (Satterthwaite et al., 2007[173]). Investing in low-carbon transportation systems, low-carbon energy supply for domestic use and buildings, and waste management systems can enable local authorities to avoid the higher costs associated with polluting infrastructure (Satterthwaite et al., 2018[185]).

The building sector also provides opportunities for climate mitigation in intermediary cities. Buildings can have energy-saving potential through energy-efficient infrastructure, thermal insulation and recycling and reuse of materials. Adopting nature-based solutions can not only reduce the effects of urban heat islands (UHI), but can also help to reduce the effects of flooding and droughts and enhance water conservation (Satterthwaite et al., 2007[173]).This is particularly pertinent for intermediary cities as they prepare to host increasing numbers of urban dwellers, which will translate into higher demand for housing. Intermediary cities have a window of opportunity now to implement nature-based solutions to reduce the effects of UHI in the future.

Integrating food systems and migration into spatial planning

Integrating food systems into territorial planning is now more important than ever. Food systems are a critical aspect of urban and rural resilience in developing countries, as they are key sources of livelihoods and incomes. For this reason, accounting for food systems, their supply chains and their climate vulnerabilities is critical for building resilience in intermediary cities. This implies implementing strategies that go beyond rural and urban boundaries, and building coherent and sustainable frameworks that stretch across sectors (nutrition, health, social protection, environment, land management) and across rural, urban and peri-urban territories. As population growth and climate change put increasing strains on food systems and influence the flows of migrants along the rural-urban interface, implementing territorial planning that accounts for these changing dynamics is imperative. Intermediary cities would greatly benefit from territorial planning that takes into account their urbanisation process – in terms of both population and built-up expansion – and that addresses the food and nutrition security needs of urban and surrounding rural dwellers. As cities expand, arable agricultural land is increasingly being used for residential or industrial buildings, exacerbating risks of food insecurity and increasing displacement in developing countries (Cabannes Yves and Maricchino, 2018[186]).

Integrating food systems into territorial planning is an essential tool to ensure the food security of rural and urban dwellers. This implies ensuring affordability and facilitating access to nutritious food, especially for the most vulnerable (Cabannes Yves and Maricchino, 2018[186]), and fostering stronger and mutually beneficial linkages between rural and urban areas. This is particularly pertinent to intermediary cities, as they tend to account for a larger share of the urban poor than capital or metropolitan cities (Roberts and Hohmann, 2014[25]). In practice, integrating food systems into territorial planning implies promoting food production in local and surrounding areas and connecting producers in peri-urban and rural areas to urban markets through infrastructure and improved access to market services. This will promote the building of short supply chains and reduce food transportation needs and associated GHG emissions (Cabannes Yves and Maricchino, 2018[186]; Taguchi and Santini, 2018[187]). Short supply chains help to reduce food waste and water use as well as facilitating better access to nutrient food for local populations (Cabannes Yves and Maricchino, 2018[186]). They also help to strengthen rural-urban linkages and to improve food safety and the quality of nutrition. In order to enable land preservation around cities for agricultural production and food supply chains, intermediary cities also need to integrate land-use planning into their spatial and territorial planning that accounts for quickly transforming food systems, changes in food demand patterns and population growth (Cabannes Yves and Maricchino, 2018[186]).

An example of a programme for integrating food systems into spatial planning is the sustainable City Region Food System (CRFS) initiative, undertaken in 2015 by the FAO and RUAF (2015[188]). The programme promotes the need to go beyond city limits and integrate all elements of food systems into spatial planning. In Medellín (Colombia), one of seven cities to take part, the project had two main objectives: to strengthen and enhance regional value chains across the districts of Medellín and to improve the accessibility and availability of safe and varied food products to local populations (Dubbeling et al., 2017[189]). The programme led to the establishment of an inter-institutional taskforce, *Buen Vivir*.

Spatial plans must consider the needs of urban dwellers in informal settlements

Intermediary cities ought to address the needs of urban dwellers living in informal settlements. Growth in rural-to-urban migration has been one of the main causes of the expansion of informal settlements and precarious suburbanisation (Roberts and Hohmann, 2014[25]; Williams et al., 2019[106]; Satterthwaite et al., 2020[190]). Fast urbanisation will be conducive to the expansion of informal settlements unless effective planning is put in place. However, rural-to-urban migration (including seasonal and circular migration) is a critical aspect of livelihood diversification and poverty reduction strategies for urban and rural dwellers. As such, local, regional and national governments ought to implement policy measures that facilitate safe migration processes and invest in infrastructure and services that will contribute to the sustainable development of the rural-urban interface. For instance, local governments can invest in slum upgrading in areas that are not predisposed to environmental risk such as landslides or rising sea levels (Satterthwaite et al., 2020[190]). However, this requires generating information on population size, infrastructure needs and projected growth of demand within informal settlements. It is crucial to assess existing infrastructure stability and infrastructure needs (including waste management and water). Local governments ought to conduct surveys or collect other data to understand the needs of informal settlements and inform policy.

Spatial planning must include economic development and better access to services

Fostering inclusive and resilient economic development in rural and urban areas can strengthen local resilience to climate change. Well-managed economic development processes can help build adaptation capacities by contributing to improved human capital, increased income per capita and economic diversification, stronger institutions, local organisations, producer organisations, resilient infrastructure, etc. (Bowen, Cochrane and Fankhauser, 2012[191]; World Bank, 2010[192]). Fostering local economic development is a cost-effective way of strengthening local adaptation (World Bank, 2010[192]), as it can enable local governments to invest in climate-resilient infrastructure and locate development of assets or key infrastructure away from vulnerable areas (OECD, 2016[193]), as well as protecting local livelihoods from climate-induced losses (World Bank, 2010[192]).

The growth of intermediary cities presents opportunities for fostering local economic development and climate resilience. In some regions, especially in Southeast Asia, intermediary cities function as export processing zones, special economic zones or growth poles (Roberts and Hohmann, 2014[25]). Enabling rural-to-urban migration can make urban centres more dynamic with the addition of skilled and unskilled labour that can be absorbed into local economic activities. Establishing tailored policies that promote intermediary cities as poles for green growth and poverty reduction can help foster local and national economic growth and improve climate resilience. This was the case in Rwanda, where six intermediary cities – and the rural areas connected to them – were selected as poles of growth and poverty reduction, in line with the National Green Growth and Climate Resilient Strategy, established in 2011 (Republic of Rwanda, 2011[194]).

Tapping into the potential of food systems for local development and job creation

The ongoing transformation of food systems in developing countries can provide opportunities to integrate (rural) youth and rural migrants into the midstream and downstream sections of the food economy. Local governments can establish initiatives or regulations to incentivise enterprises and supermarkets working along food supply chains to create employment (Hussein and Suttie, 2016[36]). Labour-intensive value chains, such as horticulture, could provide opportunities for wage employment for rural youth (IFAD, 2014[195]; OECD, 2018[35]). The development of agro-industries and the growth in post-farm-gate activities (which often take place in small and medium-sized cities) can present attractive opportunities for rural youth. They also create an opportunity to provide education and training services, with more managerial and business services emerging along with the development of agro-business industries (OECD, 2018[35]). This can lead to mutually beneficial gains: rural youth can gain better access to income diversification mechanisms, while intermediary cities can experience growth in key areas and ensure the resilience of the food economy (Hussein and Suttie, 2016[36]) .

Addressing the needs of informal workers in food systems is integral for building resilient local economic development. As highlighted in this chapter, informality is prevalent in food systems, especially in African intermediary cities, and exposes informal workers to climate-related vulnerabilities. Despite the important role of the informal sectors in food systems – not only as key sources of livelihoods but also as key providers of food, particularly to poor populations in urban and rural areas – they often face bias from national and local policy makers and lack adequate support. For instance, in response to the COVID-19 pandemic, the South African government shut down informal open-air markets to reduce COVID transmission rates. However, this was highly detrimental to the poor urban population, who were reliant on informal markets and lacked the resources to buy large quantities of food from formal retail outlets (i.e. supermarkets) (Webb et al., 2021[196]). As such, local governments need to recognise the important role of informal traders or networks of activities for local food supplies, gain better understanding of their disproportionate vulnerabilities to climate-induced disruptions and provide support mechanisms to enhance their resilience and protect and strengthen livelihoods. Targeted policies including allocation of land-use permits, trading space and other key infrastructure, such as water, sanitation and waste management systems, are important actions to support livelihoods (Warren, 2018[197]).

The process of recovery from COVID-19 could serve as window of opportunity to support informal workers in intermediary cities. Unless appropriate policies are implemented, the economic and sanitary crisis brought on by the pandemic will exacerbate the challenges faced by informal workers (including migrants) and enterprises in intermediary cities. Roberts et al. (2020[198]) argue that the recovery from the pandemic could present opportunities to address and improve the informal economy. Strategies could include creating adequate spaces for informal businesses, helping them to integrate with regional markets and supply chains, and taking them into account in regulatory frameworks (Cities Alliance, 2020[199]).

Better access to urban services will strengthen the resilience of rural populations

Connecting rural populations to urban services is key to strengthening their long-term resilience and adaptation capacities. Better access to urban markets can enable rural producers to: increase their earnings and invest in more diversified economic activities (Hussein and Suttie, 2016[36]); access agricultural inputs and technology; better integrate into food supply chains; and reduce their climate vulnerabilities (FAO, 2019[90]). Intermediary cities are uniquely placed to do all this due to their close links to rural areas and their role as service providers and administrative centres for surrounding areas (Roberts and Hohmann, 2014[25]). Intermediary cities already facilitate access to agricultural extension services (Roberts and Hohmann, 2014[25]). This is important, as agriculture is and will be increasingly reliant on the services located in intermediary cities for both inputs and output markets (Berdegué et al., 2014[3]). As such, intermediary cities have large scope to help strengthen the resilience of rural livelihoods, by helping to build resilient production systems and by providing access to income-earning opportunities.

Intermediary cities can leverage their relations with rural areas to function as centres for marketing and processing, and to provide financial, advisory and knowledge services, all of which are needed to improve on-farm adaptation and mitigation strategies. This may be accomplished via government-run services or partnerships with the private sector, which could provide subsidised inputs. These services could be enhanced to integrate climate-resilience strategies such as climate-smart agriculture, intensification practices or crop/livestock rotation strategies (FAO, 2016[122]). Linking rural populations to urban services will lead to mutual benefits. Building stronger rural livelihoods can boost long-term resilience and reduce climate-induced migration to urban areas, reducing the pressure on urban services (Hussein and Suttie, 2016[36]). At the same time, improved livelihoods and incomes in rural areas will enable intermediary cities to benefit from larger markets for their goods and services.

Improving access to services such as education, training, transportation and communication is key for building urban and rural resilience. Provision of these services will also facilitate better integration into urban economies, such as better employment prospects, for future rural migrants. Access to communication and transportation also enables access to information regarding the employment or business opportunities available to rural dwellers (Hussein and Suttie, 2016[36]).

Integrating rural migrants into the local economy is a critical aspect of building local resilience. Rural migrants are highly vulnerable to climate change (as well as other systemic challenges, such as sanitary crises) in urban areas. Establishing migrant support systems, such as provision of work permits or health and education services, can help rural migrants both to address the immediate challenges they may face and to build resilience. This is particularly relevant for the large share of rural migrants who will likely be absorbed into the informal sector, especially those who are considered unskilled (Cattaneo et al., 2019[125]; Forefight, 2011[101]). Social protection services such as subsidised or low-cost health and education are important since migrants in informal settlements can face elevated health risks (Satterthwaite et al., 2020[190]; Bolay, 2020[104]). Investing in the human capital of rural migrants and integrating them into the local economy can help to strengthen their capacities to respond to climate events (World Bank, 2010[192]).

National governments play very important roles in the provision of social protection plans and safety nets for rural populations. Such services are largely beyond the mandates and administrative capacities of intermediary cities, whereas national or regional governments have more political capital and financial capacities to improve resilience in rural areas and to build stronger rural-urban linkages for long-term resilience. National or regional governments can implement policy actions that aim to strengthen rural livelihoods, through on-farm and off-farm strategies that build rural resilience in the face of fast- and slow-onset climate events. In Pakistan, for instance, social protection policies implemented by the national government, in addition to robust flood relief efforts, helped to manage the magnitude of the displacement caused by flooding events between 1991 and 2012 (Mueller, Gray and Kosec, 2014[200]; Cattaneo et al., 2019[125]).

Advance planning is needed to reduce the impact of climate disasters

Establishing proactive and long-term climate protocols can help to reduce mismanagement and facilitate effective recovery in climate disasters. As climate change weakens linkages and disrupts livelihoods across rural and urban areas, it will increase the vulnerability of local populations and weaken the consumption, production and livelihood linkages that connect intermediary cities with rural areas. This will increase strains in the provision of basic services in intermediary cities, such transportation, water and waste management. Protocols and action plans at the local level that reduce the potential impact of climate-induced disasters should focus on avoiding large economic losses and reducing local vulnerabilities.

Local governments, alongside national governments, need to strengthen disaster risk-management, rehabilitation and recovery systems. After climate disasters, it is a regular practice to conduct post-disaster assessments to review damage. Preparedness in the face of these events is crucial to ensure that climate disasters do not jeopardise the area's development. Although the involvement of the national government is essential to unlock resources, implementation should be delegated to local governments to ensure a quick response. This will also facilitate better assistance to key areas and sectors, as local governments are best positioned to understand a city's priorities (GFDRR, 2015[201]).

Planning emergency strategies to respond to climate disasters can reduce their negative impacts on well-being. Intermediate cities can play a special role in providing post-disaster services. To reduce the vulnerability of internally displaced people, they could provide access to safe housing in urban or peri-urban areas. Well-managed and well-placed safe housing, instead of makeshift housing, can reduce congestion and allow locals to continue to operate businesses, many of which are informal and rely on public spaces (Roberts and Hohmann, 2014[25]). Other strategies for managing climate risks, such as the use of technology for early-warning systems, early intervention systems (particularly in cases of slow-onset climate events, such as droughts), and social safety nets, have proven to be successful in reducing casualties and losses in countries including Mozambique, Niger, Kenya and Mauritania (European Commission, 2020[202]). Measures taken by the city of San Francisco, in the Philippines, provide an example of climate-disaster preparedness and are explained in more detail in Chapter 4.

Partnerships can help intermediary cities to strengthen their climate action

One challenge of implementing climate action lies in the fact that intermediary cities are highly heterogenous and there is no "one-size-fits-all" solution. For instance, as explained in Chapter 2, CO_2 emissions and urban expansion follow different trends depending on the region and size of a city. As such, cities of 50 000 to 100 000 inhabitants in India do not necessarily follow the same path as similar cities in Latin America, or even as bigger cities in the same country. Policies aimed at mitigating climate change should consider this heterogeneity and adapt policy formulas to fit the local context.

Building partnerships with national and international stakeholders can enable local governments to strengthen their climate actions. Partnerships can help local governments to address knowledge gaps regarding their vulnerabilities to climate change. International organisations have large scope for creating platforms for dialogue between national and local governments and the populations they represent, whether in urban centres or the rural areas connected to them. Similarly, strengthening relationships with networks of cities and municipalities (both nationally and internationally) can provide the means and the space for exchange of information and experiences, and overall mutual learning. For example, partnerships with knowledge-producing institutions, such as universities and research institutes, and with the private sector, can support the efforts of local governments to collect data (on climate, food systems, migration, etc.). Moreover, strong direct relations with international donors can enable local governments to access international funds (depending on their level of decentralisation and fiscal autonomy) and to build capacity to formulate and implement bankable climate projects.

Conclusion

Intermediary cities play a central role in the rural-urban interface. They are critical in food system supply chains, provide opportunities for livelihood diversification and serve as an important destination for internal migration. As climate change disrupts food systems, spurring rural-to-urban migration, intermediary cities will face ripple effects. They will have to provide jobs, infrastructure and services for a growing population while at the same time working on climate adaptation and mitigation. Given these complex linkages, forward planning is needed. But policies aiming to improve climate resilience will have limited outcomes if they do not take account of the inherent interdependence of rural areas and urban centres. Preparing for climate shocks that may overstrain cities and affect food security requires spatial planning, infrastructure and housing development, and wider provision of services. Local governments can tap into rapidly transforming food systems to increase job creation. By building national and international partnerships, local governments can strengthen their capacities and increase their resources.

Notes

[1] The countries of the study include: Côte d'Ivoire, Ghana, Mali, Namibia, Niger, Nigeria, Senegal, South Africa, Tanzania, Uganda and Zambia.

[2] Farms smaller than two hectares.

[3] The analysis by Zavesi (2021; 54) focuses on the "impact of repeated water shocks (e.g. decline in rainfall) that occur over a decade on out-migration rates".

[4] This result contradicts that of Castells-Quintana et al. (2021[165]), which finds that less precipitation leads to higher population in dry places. Nevertheless, the difference might lie in the use of a different sample, as this analysis only considers developing countries.

References

Abu Hatab, A. et al. (2019), "Urban sprawl, food security and agricultural systems in developing countries: A systematic review of the literature", *Cities*, Vol. 94, pp. 129-142, https://doi.org/10.1016/j.cities.2019.06.001. [57]

Acharya, S. et al. (eds.) (2017), *Marginalization in Globalizing Delhi: Issues of Land, Livelihoods and Health*, Springer India, New Delhi, https://doi.org/10.1007/978-81-322-3583-5. [56]

AfDB/OECD/UNDP (2016), *African Economic Outlook 2016: Sustainable Cities and Structural Transformation*, OECD Publishing, Paris, https://doi.org/10.1787/aeo-2016-en. [182]

Agergaard, J. et al. (2019), *Revisiting Rural–Urban Transformations and Small Town Development in Sub-Saharan Africa*, Palgrave Macmillan Ltd., https://doi.org/10.1057/s41287-018-0182-z. [37]

Allen et al. (2018), *Agriculture, Food and Jobs in West Africa*, OECD Publishing, Paris, https://doi.org/10.1787/dc152bc0-en. [9]

Allen, T. and P. Heinrigs (2016), "Emerging Opportunities in the West African Food Economy", *West African Papers*, No. 1, OECD Publishing, Paris, https://doi.org/10.1787/5jlvfj4968jb-en. [42]

Antwi-Agyei, P., L. Stringer and A. Dougill (2014), "Livelihood adaptations to climate variability: Insights from farming households in Ghana", *Regional Environmental Change*, Vol. 14/4, pp. 1615-1626, https://doi.org/10.1007/s10113-014-0597-9. [123]

Arslan, A., E. Egger and P. Winters (2018), *Migration, Demography, and Agri-Food Systems*, World Scientific, Singapore, http://www.worldscientific.com. [14]

ARUP and Cities Alliance (2016), *Uganda-Secondary Cities Future Proofing Cities*, Arup, London, http://file:///C:/Users/Haile_s/Downloads/Future%20Cities%20Africa%20%20Uganda.pdf (accessed on 18 February 2021). [116]

Badiane, O. and T. Makimber (eds.) (2015), *Beyond a Middle Income Africa: Transforming African Economies for Sustained Growth with Rising Employment and Incomes*, International Food Policy Research Institute (IFPRI), Washington DC, http://ebrary.ifpri.org/utils/getfile/collection/p15738coll2/id/130121/filename/130332.pdf (accessed on 17 February 2021). [31]

Banerjee, D. (2016), *Understanding the Effects of Labour Migration on Vulnerability to Extreme Events in Hindu Kush Himalayas: Case Studies from Upper Assam and Baoshan County*, University of Sussex, Sussex, http://sro.sussex.ac.uk/id/eprint/68118/1/Banerjee%2C%20Soumyadeep.pdf (accessed on 18 February 2021). [108]

Barange et al. (2018), *Impacts of climate change on fisheries and aquaculture: synthesis of current knowledge, adaptation and mitigation options*, Food and Agriculture Organization, Rome, http://www.fao.org/3/i9705en/i9705en.pdf (accessed on 17 February 2021). [70]

Barrios, S., L. Bertinelli and E. Strobl (2006), "Climatic Change and Rural-Urban Migration: The Case of Sub-Saharan Africa", *SSRN Electronic Journal*, https://doi.org/10.2139/ssrn.925652. [163]

Bell, M. et al. (2015), "Internal migration data around the world: Assessing contemporary practice", *Population, Space and Place*, Vol. 21/1, pp. 1-17, https://doi.org/10.1002/psp.1848. [87]

Berdegué et al. (2014), *Inclusive Rural-Urban Linkages*, https://rimisp.org/wp-content/files_mf/1431869344123InclusiveRural_UrbanLinkages_edited.pdf (accessed on 11 February 2021). [3]

Black, R. et al. (2011), "The effect of environmental change on human migration", *Global Environmental Change*, Vol. 21/SUPPL. 1, https://doi.org/10.1016/j.gloenvcha.2011.10.001. [144]

Bolay, J. (2020), *Urban Planning Against Poverty*, Springer International Publishing, Cham, https://doi.org/10.1007/978-3-030-28419-0. [104]

Bowen, A., S. Cochrane and S. Fankhauser (2012), "Climate change, adaptation and economic growth", *Climatic Change*, Vol. 113/2, pp. 95-106, https://doi.org/10.1007/s10584-011-0346-8. [191]

Broekhoff et al. (2018), "Building Thriving, Low-Carbon Cities: An Overview of Policy Options for National Governments", Coalition for Urban Transitions A New Climate Economy Special Initiative, London and Washington DC, http://www.coalitionforurbantransitions.org. [183]

Brzoska, M. and C. Fröhlich (2016), "Climate change, migration and violent conflict: vulnerabilities, pathways and adaptation strategies", *Migration and Development*, Vol. 5/2, pp. 190-210, https://doi.org/10.1080/21632324.2015.1022973. [129]

Burke et al. (2015), "Climate and Conflict", *Annual Review of Economics*, Vol. 7/1, pp. 577-617, https://doi.org/10.1146/annurev-economics-080614-115430. [149]

Burrows, K. and P. Kinney (2016), "Exploring the climate change, migration and conflict nexus", *International Journal of Environmental Research and Public Health*, Vol. 13/4, pp. 1-1, https://doi.org/10.3390/ijerph13040443. [100]

Cabannes, Y. (ed.) (2018), *Integrating Food into Urban Planning*, UCL Press, London. [186]

Caprile, A. (2021), *United Nations Food Systems Summit 2021: Process, challenges and the way forward*, European Parliament Research Service, Brussels, https://www.europarl.europa.eu/RegData/etudes/BRIE/2021/696208/EPRS_BRI(2021)696208_EN.pdf (accessed on 22 December 2021). [58]

Castells-Quintana, D., M. Del Pilar Lopez-Uribe and T. Mcdermott (2015), "Climate change and the geographical and institutional drivers of economic development", *Centre for Climate Change Economics and Policy Working Paper*, No. 198, University of Leeds and the London School of Economics and Political Science, Leeds and London, http://www.lse.ac.uk/grantham. [145]

Castells-Quintana, D., M. Krause and T. McDermott (2021), "The urbanising force of global warming: the role of climate change in the spatial distribution of population", *Journal of Economic Geography*, Vol. 21/4, pp. 531-556, https://doi.org/10.1093/jeg/lbaa030. [165]

Castles, S. (2002), "Environmental change and forced migration: making sense of the debate", *New Issues in Refugee Research*, No. 70, UNHCR, Geneva, http://www.unhcr.org. [130]

Cattaneo, C. et al. (2019), "Human migration in the era of climate change", *Review of Environmental Economics and Policy*, Vol. 13/2, pp. 189-206, https://doi.org/10.1093/reep/rez008. [125]

Cheung, W. et al. (2010), "Large-scale redistribution of maximum fisheries catch potential in the global ocean under climate change", *Global Change Biology*, Vol. 16/1, pp. 24-35, https://doi.org/10.1111/j.1365-2486.2009.01995.x. [68]

Christiaensen, L. and Y. Todo (2013), *Poverty Reduction during the Rural-Urban Transformation The Role of the Missing Middle*, http://econ.worldbank.org. [96]

Chuwah, C. et al. (2015), "Global impacts of surface ozone changes on crop yields and land use", *Atmospheric Environment*, Vol. 106, pp. 11-23, https://doi.org/10.1016/j.atmosenv.2015.01.062. [66]

Cities Alliance (2020), *Secondary cities Post-COVID 19: Achieving Urban Sustainable and Regenerative Development in Emerging Economies*, Cities Alliance, Brussels, https://www.citiesalliance.org/sites/default/files/2021-03/CA_SecondaryCitiesPostCOVID-19-FinalWeb.pdf (accessed on 31 July 2021). [199]

Cities Alliance (2019), *Connecting Systems of Cities*, Cities Alliance/UNOPS, Brussels. [180]

Clement, V. et al. (2021), *Groundswell: Acting on Internal Climate Migration - Part 2*, World Bank, Washington DC, http://www.worldbank.org. [127]

Coalition for Urban Transitions (2021), *Seizing the Urban Opportunity: how national governments can recover from COVID-19, tackle the climate crisis and secure shared prosperity through cities, insights from six emerging economies*, Coalition for Urban Transition, London, https://urbantransitions.global/wp-content/uploads/2021/03/Seizing_the_Urban_Opportunity_WEB-1.pdf (accessed on 9 December 2021). [169]

Dallmann, I. and K. Millock (2017), "Climate variability and inter-state migration in India", *CESifo Economic Studies*, Vol. 63/4, pp. 560-594, https://doi.org/10.1093/cesifo/ifx014. [150]

Dasgupta, P. et al. (2014), "Rural Areas", in Edward and Raholiao (ed.), *Climate Change 2014: Impacts, Adaptation and Vulnerability*, Cambridge University Press, Cambridge, https://www.ipcc.ch/report/ar5/wg2/. [17]

DeWaard et al (2016), "Population recovery in New Orleans after Hurricane Katrina: exploring the potential role of stage migration in migration systems", *Population and Environment*, Vol. 37/4, pp. 449-463, https://doi.org/10.1007/s11111-015-0250-7. [146]

Dillon et al. (2011), "Migratory responses to agricultural risk in northern Nigeria", *American Journal of Agricultural Economics*, Vol. 93/4, pp. 1048-1061, https://doi.org/10.1093/ajae/aar033. [119]

Dolislager, M. et al. (2020), "Youth and Adult Agrifood System Employment in Developing Regions: Rural (Peri-urban to Hinterland) vs. Urban", *The Journal of Development Studies*, Vol. 57/4, pp. 571-593, https://doi.org/10.1080/00220388.2020.1808198. [156]

Dominic Azuwike, O. (2010), *Nigeria's Changing Environment and Pastoral Nomadism: Redistribution of Paons and Gains*, University Owerri Nigeria, Imo State, https://refubium.fu-berlin.de/bitstream/handle/fub188/17881/Azuwike-NIGERIAS_CHANGING_ENVIRONMENT_AND_PASTORAL_NOMADISM-329.pdf?sequence=1&isAllowed=y (accessed on 18 February 2021). [157]

Dorosh, P. et al. (2012), "Road connectivity, population, and crop production in Sub-Saharan Africa", *Agricultural Economics*, Vol. 43/1, pp. 89-103, https://doi.org/10.1111/j.1574-0862.2011.00567.x. [49]

Dubbeling, M. et al. (2017), "Assessing and Planning Sustainable City Region Food Systems: Insights from Two Latin American Cities", *Sustainability*, Vol. 9/8, p. 1455, https://doi.org/10.3390/su9081455. [189]

Dury, S. et al. (2019), *Food systems at risk. New trends and challenges*, FAO, CIRAD, and European Comission, https://doi.org/10.19182/agritrop/00080. [10]

Dyson, T., R. Cassen and L. Visaria (eds.) (2004), *Twenty-first century India: population, economy, human development, and the environment*, Oxford University Press, New York, http://ukcatalogue.oup.com/ (accessed on 28 February 2021). [117]

EUC (2010), "Air Pollution and Climate Change", *Science for Environment Policy*, Vol. 1/24, https://ec.europa.eu/environment/integration/research/newsalert/pdf/24si_en.pdf (accessed on 22 December 2021). [67]

European Commission (2020), *Disaster Preparedness: A compendium of experiences*, European Comission, Brussels, https://ec.europa.eu/echo/system/files/2020-09/disaster_preparedness_-_a_compendium_of_experiences.pdf (accessed on 11 January 2022). [202]

Fafchamps, M. and F. Shilpi (2013), "Determinants of the Choice of Migration Destination", *Oxford Bulletin of Economics and Statistics*, Vol. 75/3, pp. 388-409, https://doi.org/10.1111/j.1468-0084.2012.00706.x. [99]

FAO (2020), *Cities and local governments at the forefront in building inclusive and resilient food systems*, FAO, https://doi.org/10.4060/cb0407en. [77]

FAO (2019), *FAO migration framework: migration as a choice and an opportunity for rural development*, Food and Agriculture Organization of the United Nations, Rome, http://www.fao.org/3/ca3984en/CA3984EN.pdf (accessed on 17 February 2021). [90]

FAO (2017), *The future of food and agriculture: Trends and challenges*, Food and Agriculture Organization, Rome, https://www.fao.org/3/i6583e/i6583e.pdf (accessed on 20 December 2021). [12]

FAO (2017), *The State of Food and Agriculture. Leveraging Food Systems for Inclusive Rural Transformation*, FAO, Rome, http://www.fao.org/3/a-I7658e.pdf (accessed on 17 February 2021). [5]

FAO (2016), *The State of Food and Agriculture 2016: climate change, agriculture and food security*, Food and Agriculture Organisation, Rome, http://www.fao.org/publications/sofa/2016/en/. [122]

FAO (2008), *Climate Change and food security: A Framework Document*, http://www.fao.org/3/a-au035e.pdf (accessed on 11 February 2021). [71]

FAO & RUAF (2015), *City Region Food Systems: Building sustainable and resilient city regions*, FAO, Rome. [188]

FAO et al. (2018), *The Linkages between Migration, Agriculture, Food Security and Rural Development*, http://www.fao.org/3/CA0922EN/CA0922EN.pdf (accessed on 12 February 2021). [1]

Federacion Nacional de Cafeteros de Colombia (2017), *Ensayos sobre Economía Cafetera*, https://federaciondecafeteros.org/app/uploads/2019/12/Economi%CC%81a-cafetera-No.-32-Final-mayo-2020.pdf (accessed on 23 December 2021). [89]

Findley, S. (1994), "Does Drought Increase Migration? A Study of Migration from Rural Mali during the 1983–1985 Drought", *International Migration Review*, Vol. 28/3, https://doi.org/10.1177/019791839402800306. [113]

Fishman et al (2013), *Patterns of Migration, Water Scarcity and Caste in Rural Northern Gujarat*, International Growth Centre(IGC), London, https://www.theigc.org/wp-content/uploads/2015/02/Fishman-Et-Al-2013-Working-Paper.pdf (accessed on 17 February 2021). [98]

Florczyk, A. (2019), *GHS Urban Centre Database 2015, multitemporal and multidimensional attributes*, http://data.europa.eu/89h/53473144-b88c-44bc-b4a3-4583ed1f547e (accessed on 13 July 2021). [166]

Flörke et al. (2018), "Water competition between cities and agriculture driven by climate change and urban growth", *Nature Sustainability*, Vol. 1/1, pp. 51-58, https://doi.org/10.1038/s41893-017-0006-8. [142]

Forefight (2011), *Migration and Global Environmental Change*, The Government Office for Science, London, http://www.bis.gov.uk/foresight/our-work/projects/current-projects/global-migration (accessed on 18 February 2021). [101]

Forster, T. et al. (2015), *Strengthening Urban Rural Linkages Through City Region Food Systems*, UNCRD and UN-Habitat, Rome, http://file://main.oecd.org/Homedir2/Haile_S/Cities%20Connect/Literature%20review%20CC%20and%20ICs/indirect/Strengthening_Urban_Rural_Linkages_through_CRFS.pdf (accessed on 17 February 2021). [78]

Frayne B, W. et al. (2010), *The State of Urban Food Insecurity in Southern Africa*, Queen's University and AFSUN, Kingston and Cape Town, https://www.alnap.org/help-library/the-state-of-urban-food-insecurity-in-southern-africa (accessed on 17 February 2021). [44]

GFDRR (2015), *Guide to Developing Disaster Recovery Frameworks*, World Bank Group, UNDP, European Union, https://www.gfdrr.org/sites/default/files/2017-09/Disaster%20Recovery%20Framework%20Guide.pdf (accessed on 18 February 2021). [201]

Gregor et al. (2018), *Similarities and diversity of European cities: A typology tool to support urban sustainability*, Environment Agency Austria, Vienna, http://file:///C:/Users/Haile_s/Downloads/etc-uls_report_2018-3-citytypology_final.pdf (accessed on 15 July 2022). [176]

Gupta, A. (2020), "30% of migrants will not return to cities: Irudaya Rajan", *The Times of India*, https://timesofindia.indiatimes.com/india/30-of-migrants-will-not-return-to-cities-irudaya-rajan/articleshow/76126701.cms (accessed on 20 October 2021). [135]

Haggblade, S. (2011), "Modernizing African agribusiness: Reflections for the future", *Journal of Agribusiness in Developing and Emerging Economies*, Vol. 1/1, pp. 10-30, https://doi.org/10.1108/20440831111131532. [32]

Harris, J. and M. Todaro (1970), "Migration, Unemployment and Development: A Two-Sector Analysis", *The American Economic Association*, Vol. 60/1, pp. 126-142, https://www.jstor.org/stable/1807860 (accessed on 18 February 2021). [151]

Henderson et al. (2017), "Has climate change driven urbanization in Africa?", *Journal of Development Economics*, Vol. 124, pp. 60-82, https://doi.org/10.1016/j.jdeveco.2016.09.001. [164]

Hsiang, S., M. Burke and E. Miguel (2013), "Quantifying the Influence of Climate on Human Conflict", *Science*, Vol. 341/6151, https://doi.org/10.1126/science.1235367. [153]

Hummel et al. (2012), *Climate Change, Environment and Migration in the Sahel - Selected Issues with a Focus on Senegal and Mali*, Institute for Social-Ecological Research, Universitat Bayreuth Universitat Wien, http://www.micle-project.net/fileadmin/redaktion/Download/micle-wp1-2012-en.pdf (accessed on 18 February 2021). [109]

Hussein, K. and D. Suttie (2016), *Rural-urban linkages and food systems in sub-Saharan Africa*, International Fund for Agricultural Development, Rome, https://www.ifad.org/documents/38714170/39135332/Rural-urban+linkages+and+food+systems+in+sub-Saharan+Africa.pdf/f5801ff5-2fb8-4b0d-ae77-976aa3e116d3?eloutlink=imf2ifad. [36]

ICRC (2004), *Regional Livestock Study In the Greater Horn of Africa*, ICRC, Nairobi. [161]

IDMC (2017), *Global Report on Internal Displacement*, Internal Displacement Monitoring Centre, Geneva, https://www.internal-displacement.org/global-report/grid2017/pdfs/2017-GRID.pdf (accessed on 18 February 2021). [103]

IEA (2018), *Global Energy & CO2 Status Report: The latest trends in energy and emissions in 2018*, International Energy Agency, Paris, https://webstore.iea.org/global-energy-co2-status-report-2018. [178]

IEA (2016), *Energy Technology Perspectives 2016: Towards Sustainable Urban Energy Systems*, International Energy Agency, Paris, https://www.iea.org/reports/energy-technology-perspectives-2016. [177]

IFAD (2021), *Transforming food systems for rural prosperity*, International Fund for Agricultural Development (IFAD), Rome, https://www.ifad.org/documents/38714170/43704363/rdr2021_overview_e.pdf/503cf76b-2a61-1d7e-44bd-7b4bf3739b85?t=1631621451944 (accessed on 20 December 2021). [16]

IFAD (2016), *Rural Development Report 2016 - Fostering inclusive rural transformation*, International Fund for Agricultural Development (IFAD), Rome, https://www.ifad.org/documents/38714170/40724622/Rural+development+report+2016.pdf/347402dd-a37f-41b7-9990-aa745dc113b9?t=1632401149187 (accessed on 20 December 2021). [50]

IFAD (2014), *Sustainable inclusion of smallholders in agricultural value chains*, IFAD, Rome, https://www.ifad.org/documents/38714170/40311826/Commodity+value+chain+development+projects.pdf/504a1102-7bc7-47e8-a46c-003333fe9335 (accessed on 16 July 2022). [195]

IFAD (2010), *Rural Poverty Report 2011: New realities, new challenges, new opportunities for tomorrow's generation*, International Fund for Agricultural Development (IFAD), Rome, https://reliefweb.int/sites/reliefweb.int/files/resources/0761B50B87EC879BC12577F10051867C-IFAD_Dec2010.pdf (accessed on 20 December 2021). [39]

IFPRI (2021), *2021 Global food policy report: Transforming food systems after COVID-19*, International Food Policy Research Institute, Washington, DC, https://doi.org/10.2499/9780896293991. [74]

IFPRI (2020), *2020 Global Food Policy Report: Building Inclusive Food Systems*, International Food Policy Research Institute, Washington DC, https://doi.org/10.2499/9780896293670. [28]

IIED (2015), "Reframing the debate on urbanisation, rural transformation and food security", *Food and Agriculture*, The International Institute for Environment and Development (IIED), London, http://pubs.iied.org/17281IIED. [48]

IIED and Hivos (2020), *A food systems assessment of the Sustainable Diets for All programme in Uganda and Zambia*, International Institute for Environment and Development (IIED) and HIVOS, London, https://hivos.org/program/sustainable-diets-4-all/ (accessed on 20 December 2021). [60]

ILO (2019), *Working on a warmer planet: The impact of heat stress on labour productivity and decent work*, International Labour Office, Geneva, http://www.ilo.org/publns. [64]

IOM (2020), *World Migration Report 2020*, International Organization for Migration, Geneva, https://publications.iom.int/system/files/pdf/wmr_2020.pdf (accessed on 18 February 2021). [107]

IOM (2008), *Migration and Climate Change*, International Organization for Migration, Geneva, http://www.iom.int. [88]

IPCC (2018), "Summary for Policymakers", https://www.ipcc.ch/sr15/. [172]

IPCC (2014), *Climate change 2014: Mitigation of Climate Change: Working Group III contribution to the Fifth Assessment Report of the Intergovernmental Panel on Climate Change*, Cambridge University Press, Cambridge, United Kingdom and New York, USA. [126]

Jamshed, A. et al. (2021), "How do rural-urban linkages change after an extreme flood event? Empirical evidence from rural communities in Pakistan", *Science of The Total Environment*, Vol. 750, p. 141462, https://doi.org/10.1016/j.scitotenv.2020.141462. [19]

Jeffrey, S. (2017), *Delivering change - How city partnerships make the most of public assets*, Centre for Cities, London, https://www.centreforcities.org/reader/delivering-change-city-partnerships-make-public-assets/ (accessed on 11 January 2022). [171]

Jennings, S. et al. (2015), "Food in an Urbanized World: The Role of City Region Food Systems in Resilience and Sustainable Development", *UN Food and Agriculture Organization* April, pp. 1-92, https://doi.org/10.1109/ULTSYM.2017.8092797. [45]

Kamal-Chaoui, L. and A. Robert (2009), *Competitive Cities and Climate Change*, OECD Publishing, Paris, https://www.oecd.org/regional/regional-policy/44232251.pdf (accessed on 15 July 2022). [175]

Khandker, S. et al. (2014), "Who Benefits Most from Rural Electrification? Evidence in India", *The Energy Journal*, Vol. 35/2, https://doi.org/10.5547/01956574.35.2.4. [118]

Kleemans, M. et al. (2014), "Migration Choice under Risk and Liquidity Constraints", *Job Market Paper*, University of California Berkeley, https://doi.org/10.22004/ag.econ.200702. [133]

Laderach, P. et al. (2011), "Predicted Impact of Climate Change on Coffee Supply Chains", in *The Economic, Social and Political Elements of Climate Change*, Verlag Berlin Heidelberg, Berlin, https://doi.org/10.1007/978-3-642-14776-0_42. [72]

Laube, W., B. Schraven and M. Awo (2012), "Smallholder adaptation to climate change: Dynamics and limits in Northern Ghana", *Climatic Change*, Vol. 111/3, pp. 753-774, https://doi.org/10.1007/s10584-011-0199-1. [124]

Lilleør, H. and K. Van den Broeck (2011), "Economic drivers of migration and climate change in LDCs", *Global Environmental Change*, Vol. 21/SUPPL. 1, https://doi.org/10.1016/j.gloenvcha.2011.09.002. [121]

Li, S. (2018), "Change detection: how has urban expansion in Buenos Aires metropolitan region affected croplands", *International Journal of Digital Earth*, Vol. 11/2, pp. 195-211, https://doi.org/10.1080/17538947.2017.1311954. [52]

Lizumi, T. et al. (2018), "Crop production losses associated with anthropogenic climate change for 1981–2010 compared with preindustrial levels", *International Journal of Climatology*, Vol. 38/14, pp. 5405-5417, https://doi.org/10.1002/joc.5818. [62]

Loo, Y., L. Billa and A. Singh (2015), "Effect of climate change on seasonal monsoon in Asia and its impact on the variability of monsoon rainfall in Southeast Asia", *Geoscience Frontiers*, Vol. 6/6, pp. 817-823, https://doi.org/10.1016/j.gsf.2014.02.009. [65]

Lowder, S., M. Sánchez and R. Bertini (2021), "Which farms feed the world and has farmland become more concentrated?", *World Development*, Vol. 142, p. 105455, https://doi.org/10.1016/j.worlddev.2021.105455. [51]

Lucas, R. (2015), "Internal Migration in Developing Economies: An Overview", No. 6, KNOMAD, Dhaka, http://www.KNOMAD.org. [94]

Mackay, H. (2019), "Food sources and access strategies in Ugandan secondary cities: an intersectional analysis", *Environment and Urbanization*, Vol. 31/2, pp. 375-396, https://doi.org/10.1177/0956247819847346. [81]

Marchiori et al (2017), "Is environmentally induced income variability a driver of human migration?", *Migration and Development*, Vol. 6/1, https://doi.org/10.1080/21632324.2015.1020106. [152]

Marchiori et al. (2012), "The impact of weather anomalies on migration in sub-Saharan Africa", *Journal of Environmental Economics and Management*, Vol. 63/3, pp. 355-374, https://doi.org/10.1016/j.jeem.2012.02.001. [140]

Mbow, C. et al. (2019), "Food security", in Benkeblia, N. et al. (eds.), *Climate Change and Land: an IPCC special report on climate change, desertification, land degradation, sustainable land management, food security, and greenhouse gas fluxes in terrestrial ecosystems*, Cambridge Press, Cambridge, https://www.ipcc.ch/srccl/chapter/chapter-5/. [23]

McAdam, J. and E. Ferris (2015), "Planned relocations in the context of climate change: Unpacking the legal and conceptual issues", *Cambridge International Law Journal*, Vol. 4/1, pp. 137-166, https://doi.org/10.7574/cjicl.04.01.137. [148]

McGuirk, E. and N. Nunn (2020), *Transhumant Pastoralism, Climate Change, and Conflict in Africa*, National Bureau of Economic Research, Cambridge, MA, https://doi.org/10.3386/w28243. [162]

McOmber, C. (2020), "Women and climate change in the Sahel", *West African Papers*, No. 27, OECD Publishing, Paris, https://doi.org/10.1787/e31c77ad-en. [97]

Mkandla, N., P. Van der Zaag and P. Sibanda (2005), "Bulawayo water supplies: Sustainable alternatives for the next decade", *Physics and Chemistry of the Earth, Parts A/B/C*, Vol. 30/11-16, pp. 935-942, https://doi.org/10.1016/j.pce.2005.08.040. [21]

Mohit, M. (2012), "Bastee Settlements of Dhaka City, Bangladesh: A Review of Policy Approaches and Challenges Ahead", *Procedia - Social and Behavioral Sciences*, Vol. 36, pp. 611-622, https://doi.org/10.1016/j.sbspro.2012.03.067. [105]

Montgomery, M. (2008), "The Urban Transformation of the Developing World", *Science*, Vol. 319/761, http://www.sciencemag.org. [93]

Moore, K. (ed.) (2005), *Conflict, social capital and managing natural resources: a West African case study*, CABI, Wallingford, https://doi.org/10.1079/9780851999487.0000. [158]

Morton, J. et al. (2014), "Cross-chapter box on urban-rural interactions – context for climate change vulnerability, impacts, and adaptation", in Field, C. and V. Barros (eds.), *Climate Change 2014: Impacts, Adaptation, and Vulnerability*, Cambridge University Press, Cambridge and New York, https://gala.gre.ac.uk/id/eprint/14371/ (accessed on 22 December 2021). [20]

Mueller, V., C. Gray and K. Kosec (2014), "Heat stress increases long-term human migration in rural Pakistan", *Nature Climate Change*, Vol. 4/3, https://doi.org/10.1038/nclimate2103. [200]

Mwiturubani, D. and J. Van Wyk (2010), *Climate change and natural resources conflicts in Africa*, Institute for Security Studies, Nairobi, https://issafrica.s3.amazonaws.com/site/uploads/Mono170.pdf (accessed on 18 February 2021). [160]

Myers, S. et al. (2017), "Climate Change and Global Food Systems: Potential Impacts on Food Security and Undernutrition", *Annu. Rev. Public Health*, Vol. 38, pp. 259-77, https://doi.org/10.1146/annurev-publhealth. [61]

Nagasawa, R. et al. (2015), "Urban Expansion and Its Influences on the Suburban Land Use Change in Jakarta Metropolitan Region (JABODETABEK)", *Urban Planning and Design Research*, Vol. 3/0, p. 7, https://doi.org/10.14355/updr.2015.03.002. [53]

Naylor, R. et al. (2000), "Effect of aquaculture on world fish supplies", *Nature*, Vol. 405/6790, pp. 1017-1024, https://doi.org/10.1038/35016500. [69]

Nguyen H (2018), "Sustainable food systems - Concept and framework", Food and Agriculture Organisation, Rome, http://www.fao.org/3/ca2079en/CA2079EN.pdf (accessed on 17 February 2021). [15]

OECD (2021), *Jobs for Rural Youth: The role of local food economies*, OECD Publishing, Paris, https://doi.org/10.1787/19900295. [13]

OECD (2020), *COVID-19 and Global Food Systems*, OECD Publishing, Paris, https://read.oecd-ilibrary.org/view/?ref=134_134299-gywwih2rh3&title=COVID-19-and-Global-Food-Systems&_ga=2.156185278.445084324.1626867873-2134157237.1593514553 (accessed on 20 October 2021). [76]

OECD (2018), *Building Resilient Cities: An Assessment of Disaster Risk Management Policies in Southeast Asia*, OECD Green Growth Studies, OECD Publishing, Paris, https://doi.org/10.1787/9789264305397-en. [181]

OECD (2018), *OECD Urban Policy Reviews: Viet Nam*, OECD Urban Policy Reviews, OECD Publishing, Paris, https://doi.org/10.1787/9789264286191-en. [167]

OECD (2018), *The Future of Rural Youth in Developing Countries: Tapping the Potential of Local Value Chains*, OECD Publishing, Paris, https://doi.org/10.1787/9789264298521-en. [35]

OECD (2016), *OECD Regional Outlook 2016: Productive Regions for Inclusive Societies*, OECD Publishing, Paris, https://doi.org/10.1787/9789264260245-en. [193]

OECD/PSI (2020), *Rural Development Strategy Review of Ethiopia: Reaping the Benefits of Urbanisation*, OECD Development Pathways, OECD Publishing, Paris, https://doi.org/10.1787/a325a658-en. [6]

OECD/SWAC (2020), *The Future of Rural Youth in Developing Countries: Tapping the Potential of Local Value Chains*, OECD Publishing, Paris, https://doi.org/10.1787/9789264298521-en. [40]

OECD/SWAC (2020), *Youth and Women's Employment in the Food economy*. [82]

Pandey, B. and K. Seto (2015), "Urbanization and agricultural land loss in India: Comparing satellite estimates with census data", *Journal of Environmental Management*, Vol. 148, pp. 53-66, https://doi.org/10.1016/j.jenvman.2014.05.014. [55]

Peri, G. and A. Sasahara (2019), *The effects of global warming on rural-urban migrations*, VOX CEPR, https://voxeu.org/article/effects-global-warming-rural-urban-migrations (accessed on 21 December 2021). [27]

Plataforma (2020), *Project 10/12: Milan (Italy) - Quelimane (Mozambique)*, https://platforma-dev.eu/project-1012-milan-italy-quelimane-mozambique/ (accessed on 11 October 2021). [170]

Proctor, F. (2018), *Food Systems at the Rural-Urban Interface*, https://hungrycities.net/wp-content/uploads/2018/07/Felicity-Proctor.pdf (accessed on 17 February 2021). [4]

Rain, D. (2000), *Eaters of the Dry Season: A Circular Migration System in the West African Sahel*, Westview Press, Boulder, CO. [112]

Rajan et al. (2020), "The COVID-19 Pandemic and Internal Labour Migration in India: A 'Crisis of Mobility'", *The Indian Journal of Labour Economics*, Vol. 63/4, https://doi.org/10.1007/s41027-020-00293-8. [136]

Reardon et al. (2016), *Growing Food for Growing Cities: Transforming food systems in an urbanizing world*, https://www.thechicagocouncil.org/research/report/growing-food-growing-cities (accessed on 11 February 2021). [34]

Reardon, T. and C. Timmer (2014), *Five inter-linked transformations in the Asian agrifood economy: Food security implications*, Elsevier, https://doi.org/10.1016/j.gfs.2014.02.001. [47]

Reardon, T. and D. Zilberman (2018), "Climate smart food supply chains in developing countries in an era of rapid dual change in agrifood systems and the climate", in *Natural Resource Management and Policy*, Springer, https://doi.org/10.1007/978-3-319-61194-5_15. [7]

Republic of Rwanda (2011), *Green Growth and Climate Resilience: National Strategy for Climate Change and Low Carbon Development*, https://www.greengrowthknowledge.org/sites/default/files/downloads/policy-database/RWANDA%29%20Green%20Growth%20and%20Climate%20Resilience%20-%20National%20Strategy%20for%20Climate%20Change%20and%20Low%20Carbon%20Development.pdf (accessed on 6 October 2021). [194]

Reuveny, R. (2008), "Ecomigration and violent conflict: Case studies and public policy implications", *Human Ecology*, Vol. 36/1, pp. 1-13, https://doi.org/10.1007/s10745-007-9142-5. [154]

Rice, M. et al. (2022), *The Russia-Ukraine war is exacerbating international food price volatility*, IFPRI, https://www.ifpri.org/blog/russia-ukraine-war-exacerbating-international-food-price-volatility (accessed on 13 July 2022). [73]

Rigaud, K. et al. (2018), *Preparing for Internal Climate Migration Groundswell*, http://www.worldbank.org. [86]

Robalino et al. (2013), *The effect of hydro-meteorological emergencies on internal migration*, Environment for Development, http://www.efdinitiative.org. [134]

Roberts and Hohmann (2014), "The Systems of Secondary Cities: The neglected drivers of urbanising economies", *Sharing Knowledge and Learning from Cities*, No. 7, Land Equity International and Cities Alliance, http://www.citiesalliance.org. [25]

Roberts et al. (2016), "Intermediary Cities: The Nexus Between the Local and the Global Co-creating the Urban Future", in *Co-Creating the Urban Future: The Agenda of Metropolis, Cities and Territories*, UCLG, Barcelona, https://www.researchgate.net/publication/309401150. [24]

Roberts, D. et al. (2020), "Durban's 100 Resilient Cities journey: governing resilience from within", *Environment and Urbanization*, Vol. 32/2, https://doi.org/10.1177/0956247820946555. [198]

Romero, C. et al. (2020), "Assessing Anthropogenic Dynamics in Megacities from the Characterization of Land Use/Land Cover Changes: The Bogotá Study Case", *Sustainability*, Vol. 12/9, p. 3884, https://doi.org/10.3390/su12093884. [54]

Rosenzweig, M. and O. Stark (1989), "Consumption Smoothing, Migration, and Marriage: Evidence from Rural India", *Journal of Political Economy*, Vol. 97/4, https://doi.org/10.1086/261633. [120]

Rukimini, S. (2020), "How Covid-19 locked out women from jobs", *mint*, https://www.livemint.com/ (accessed on 23 December 2021). [137]

Satterthwaite et al. (2010), "Urbanization and its implications for food and farming", *The Royal Society*, Vol. 365/1554, pp. 2809-2820, https://doi.org/10.1098/rstb.2010.0136. [79]

Satterthwaite et al. (2007), *Adapting to climate change in urban areas : the possibilities and constraints in low- and middle-income nations*, International Institute for Environment and Development, London. [173]

Satterthwaite, D. (2016), “Small and intermediate urban centres in sub Saharan Africa”, *Urban Africa Risk Knowledge*, No. 6, International Institute for Environment and Development (IIED), London, https://www.urbanark.org/background-paper-small-and-intermediate-urban-centres-sub-saharan-africa (accessed on 11 July 2021). [26]

Satterthwaite, D. et al. (2020), “Building Resilience to Climate Change in Informal Settlements”, *One Earth*, Vol. 2/2, pp. 143-156, https://doi.org/10.1016/j.oneear.2020.02.002. [190]

Satterthwaite, D. et al. (2018), *Responding to climate change in cities and in their informal settlements and economies*, IIED and IIED- América Latina, London, https://pubs.iied.org/G04328/. [185]

SEforAll (2020), *Switching Gears: Enabling Access to Sustainable Urban Mobility*, Sustainable Energy for All, Washington DC, https://www.seforall.org/publications/switching-gears-enabling-access-to-sustainable-urban-mobility (accessed on 13 July 2021). [184]

Selby, J. et al. (2017), “Climate change and the Syrian civil war revisited”, *Political Geography*, Vol. 60, pp. 232-244, https://doi.org/10.1016/j.polgeo.2017.05.007. [131]

Stark, O. and D. Bloom (1985), “The New Economics of Labor Migration”, *The American Economic Review*, Vol. 75/2, pp. 173-178, https://www.jstor.org/stable/1805591 (accessed on 28 February 2021). [111]

Steinberg, F. (2014), “Rural–Urban Linkages: an urban perspective”, *Working Group: Development with Territorial Cohesion, Territorial Cohesion for Development Program*, No. 128, RIMISP, Santiago, https://www.rimisp.org/wp-content/files_mf/files_mf/1421181729R_U_Linkages_Urbanperspective.pdf (accessed on 22 December 2021). [22]

Tacoli (2011), *Not only climate change: mobility, vulnerability and socio-economic transformations in environmentally fragile areas of Bolivia, Senegal and Tanzania*, IIED, London, https://pubs.iied.org/10590IIED/. [114]

Tacoli et al. (2014), *World Migration Report 2015. Urbanization, Rural-urban Migration and Urban Poverty*, Human Settlements Group International Institute forEnvironment and Development (IIED), London, https://www.iom.int/sites/default/files/our_work/ICP/MPR/WMR-2015-Background-Paper-CTacoli-GMcGranahan-DSatterthwaite.pdf (accessed on 17 February 2021). [8]

Tacoli, C. (2017), *Why small towns matter: urbanisation, rural transformations and food security*, International Institute for Environment and Development (IIED), London, https://pubs.iied.org/sites/default/files/pdfs/migrate/10815IIED.pdf (accessed on 20 December 2021). [38]

Tacoli, C. (2009), “Crisis or adaptation? Migration and climate change in a context of high mobility”, *Environment and Urbanization*, Vol. 21/2, pp. 513-525, https://doi.org/10.1177/0956247809342182. [110]

Tacoli, C. and J. Agergaard (2017), “Urbanisation, rural transformations and food systems: The role of small towns”, IIED, London. [11]

Tacoli, C. et al. (2013), *Urban poverty, food security and climate change*, Human Settlements Group, International Institute for Environment and Development (IIED), https://pubs.iied.org/sites/default/files/pdfs/migrate/10623IIED.pdf (accessed on 11 February 2021). [80]

Tacoli, C. and Vorley (2016), *Informal food systems and food security in rural and urban East Africa*, https://doi.org/10.1371/journal. [43]

Taguchi, M. and G. Santini (2018), *Better food systems for better rural-urban linkages*, pp. 7-9, http://7RURAL 21 04/18BETTER FOOD SYSTEMS FOR BETTER RURAL-URBAN LINKAGES (accessed on 18 February 2021). [187]

Tefft, J. et al. (2017), *Food Systems for an Urbanizing World*, World Bank Group; Food and Agriculture Organization of the United Nations, Washington DC and Rome, http://www.fao.org/3/I8346EN/i8346en.pdf (accessed on 17 February 2021). [84]

Tendall, D. et al. (2015), *Food system resilience: Defining the concept*, Elsevier, https://doi.org/10.1016/j.gfs.2015.08.001. [29]

The Citizen (2020), "Coronavirus fears spark urban-rural exodus across Africa", *The Citizen*, https://www.thecitizen.co.tz/news/africa/Coronavirus-fears-spark-urban-rural-exodus-across-Africa/3302426-5507414-ro6i7o/index.html (accessed on 20 October 2021). [138]

Tschirley et al. (2016), "Agrifood Youth Employment and Engagement Study", in *Agri-food Youth Employment and Engagement Study (AGYEES)*, Michigan State University, East Lansing, Michigan, https://www.isp.msu.edu/files/4814/7249/7008/AgYees_Report_FINAL_web.pdf (accessed on 18 February 2021). [30]

Tschirley, D. et al. (2015), "The rise of a middle class in east and southern Africa: Implications for food system transformation", *Journal of International Development*, Vol. 27/5, pp. 628-646, https://doi.org/10.1002/jid.3107. [46]

UCLG (2016), *UCLG Frame document for Intermediary Cities: Planning and management of sustainable urban development*, United Cities and Local Governments, Barcelona, https://www.uclg.org/sites/default/files/uclg_frame_document_ic.pdf (accessed on 18 February 2021). [115]

UNDESA (2018), *World Urbanization Prospects: The 2018 Revision*, Online edition, https://population.un.org/wup/ (accessed on 23 April 2020). [91]

UNDP (2009), *Human development report 2009 - Overcoming barriers: human mobility and development*, United Nations Development Programme, New York, http://hdr.undp.org/sites/default/files/reports/269/hdr_2009_en_complete.pdf (accessed on 17 February 2021). [85]

UNEP (2011), *Livelihood security: climate change, migration and conflict in the Sahel*, United National Environment Programme, Geneva, https://postconflict.unep.ch/publications/UNEP_Sahel_EN.pdf (accessed on 18 February 2021). [155]

UNFCCC (2021), *COP26 sees significant progress on issues related to agriculture*, UN Climate Change News, https://unfccc.int/news/cop26-sees-significant-progress-on-issues-related-to-agriculture (accessed on 20 December 2021). [59]

UN-HABITAT (2011), *Cities and Climate Change - Global Report on Human Settlements 2011*, Un-Habitat, London - Washington DC, https://unhabitat.org/cities-and-climate-change-global-report-on-human-settlements-2011. [174]

UN-Habitat (2019), *Urban-Rural Linkages: Guiding Principles Framework for Action to Advance Integrated Territorial Development*, Un-Habitat, Nairobi, http://www.unhabitat.org. [168]

UN-Habitat (2017), *Implementing the New Urban Agenda by Strengthening Urban-Rural Linkages*, United Nations Human Settlement Programme (UN-Habitat), https://unhabitat.org/sites/default/files/download-manager-files/Urban%20Rural%20Linkages%20for%20implementing%20the%20New%20Urban%20Agenda_08112017.pdf (accessed on 22 December 2021). [18]

Vermeulen et al (2012), *Climate Change and Food Systems*, https://doi.org/10.1146/annurev-environ-020411-130608. [2]

Viswanathan, B. and K. Kumar (2015), "Weather, agriculture and rural migration: Evidence from state and district level migration in India", *Environment and Development Economics*, Vol. 20/4, pp. 469-492, https://doi.org/10.1017/S1355770X1500008X. [141]

Von Braun, J. and G. Tadesse (2012), "Global Food Price Volatility and Spikes: An Overview of Costs, Causes, and Solutions", *ZEF- Discussion Papers on Development Policy*, No. 161, Centre for Development Research, Bonn, http://www.zef.de. [83]

Vorley et al. (2020), *Sustainable diets for all - Sustainable diets in the informal economy*, https://sustainablediets4all.org/document/sustainable-diets-in-the-informal-economy/ (accessed on 17 February 2021). [41]

Waldinger, M. (2015), "The effects of climate change on internal and international migration: implications for developing countries", No. 217, Centre for Climate Change Economics and Policy and Grantham Research Institute on Climate Change and the Environment, London School of Economics and Political Science, http://www.lse.ac.uk/grantham. [143]

Waldinger, M. and S. Fankhauser (2015), *Climate change and migration in developing countries: evidence and implications for PRISE countries*, Grantham Research Institute on Climate Change and the Environment, London School of Economics, http://www.lse.ac.uk/grantham/. [95]

Walter Kalin (2010), "Conceptualising Climate-Induced Displacement", in *Climate Change and Displacement: Multidisciplinary Perspectives*, Hart Publishing, London, https://doi.org/10.5040/9781472565211.ch-005. [128]

Walter, P. (2015), *Floods and Rural-Urban Migration in Bangladesh*, http://earthobservatory.nasa.gov/IOTD/view.php?id=84299. [102]

Warn and Adamo (2014), "The Impact of Climate Change: Migration and Cities in South America", No. 2, International Organisation of Migration, Geneva. [147]

Warner, K. et al. (2009), *In Search of Shelter: Mapping the Effects of Climate Change on Human Migration and Displacement*, United Nations University, CARE, CIESIN-Columbia, https://www.researchgate.net/publication/233979877. [159]

Warren, S. (2018), "Current urban food governance and planning in Africa", in Battersby, J. and V. Watson (eds.), *Urban Food Systems Governance and Poverty in African Cities*, Routledge, New York, https://doi.org/10.4324/9781315191195. [197]

Webb et al. (2021), *COVID-19 and Food Systems: rebuilding for resilience*, Global Panel on Agriculture and Food Systems for Nutrition, Rome, https://sc-fss2021.org/wp-content/uploads/2021/06/FSS_Brief_COVID-19_and_food_systems.pdf (accessed on 11 January 2022). [196]

Wesselbaum et al. (2021), *Climate Change and International Migration: The Role of Foreign Aid*, Georgetown Journal of International Affairs, https://gjia.georgetown.edu/2021/02/24/climate-change-and-international-migration-the-role-of-foreign-aid/ (accessed on 23 December 2021). [92]

Wetterwald and Thaller (2020), "Urban planning in times of displacement: secondary cities in Ukraine and Niger", *Forced Migration Review* 63, https://www.fmreview.org/sites/fmr/files/FMRdownloads/en/cities/cities.pdf (accessed on 11 January 2022). [179]

WFP (2020), *COVID-19 will double number of people facing food crises unless swift action is taken*, World Food Program, https://www.wfp.org/news/covid-19-will-double-number-people-facing-food-crises-unless-swift-action-taken (accessed on 20 October 2021). [75]

Williams, D. et al. (2019), "Vulnerability of informal settlements in the context of rapid urbanization and climate change", *Environment and Urbanization*, Vol. 31/1, pp. 157-176, https://doi.org/10.1177/0956247818819694. [106]

World Bank (2021), *COVID-19 Crisis through a Migration Lens*, KNOMAD World Bank, Washington DC, https://openknowledge.worldbank.org/bitstream/handle/10986/33634/COVID-19-Crisis-Through-a-Migration-Lens.pdf?sequence=5&isAllowed=y (accessed on 20 October 2021). [139]

World Bank (2017), *Future of Food - Shaping the Food System to Deliver Jobs*, The World Bank Group, Washington DC, http://www.worldbank.org. [33]

World Bank (2010), *Cities and Climate Change: An Urgent Agenda*, World Bank, Washington DC, http://documents.worldbank.org/curated/en/194831468325262572/Cities-and-climate-change-an-urgent-agenda. [192]

World Bank (2010), *World Development Report 2010: Development and Climate Change*, World Bank, Washington DC, https://doi.org/10.1029/2003RG000143. [63]

Zaveri, E. et al. (2021), *Ebb and Flow, Volume 1*, The World Bank, https://doi.org/10.1596/978-1-4648-1745-8. [132]

Annex 3.A. Additional figures and tables

Annex Table 3.A.1. Linear and quadratic effect of average temperature and average precipitation on population in cities

	(1) Log of Population	(2) Log of Population	(3) Log of Population	(4) Log of Population	(5) Log of Population	(6) Log of Population
Average temperature	-0.204** (-2.60)	-0.203* (-2.00)			-0.200* (-2.54)	-0.188 (-1.85)
50K-100K* Avg temp.	-0.317*** (-3.50)	-0.343** (-2.84)			-0.309*** (-3.41)	-0.325** (-2.70)
100K-500K* Avg temp	-0.314*** (-3.54)	-0.418*** (-3.48)			-0.311*** (-3.49)	-0.410*** (-3.42)
500K-1M* Avg temp	-0.303* (-2.46)	-0.386** (-2.69)			-0.300* (-2.47)	-0.379** (-2.67)
Average temperature^2	0.00668*** (3.63)	0.00863*** (3.75)			0.00686*** (3.73)	0.00912*** (3.98)
50K-100K* Avg temp^2	0.0118*** (4.94)	0.00999*** (3.40)			0.0115*** (4.81)	0.00917** (3.14)
100K-500K*Avg temp^2	0.00981*** (4.15)	0.0100*** (3.38)			0.00967*** (4.09)	0.00970** (3.27)
500K-1M* Avg temp^2	0.00790* (2.07)	0.00815* (2.21)			0.00782* (2.08)	0.00793* (2.17)
Average rain			-0.000976 (-0.38)	0.00184 (0.47)	0.00108 (0.41)	0.00443 (1.11)
50K-100K* Average rain			0.0103** (3.14)	0.0115* (2.23)	0.00780* (2.38)	0.00796 (1.55)
100K-500K* Average rain			0.00415 (1.43)	0.00343 (0.78)	0.00199 (0.68)	0.00124 (0.28)
500K-1M* Average rain			0.00559 (1.06)	0.00259 (0.48)	0.00423 (0.81)	0.000284 (0.05)
Average rain^2			0.00000249 (0.34)	-0.00000800 (-0.72)	-0.00000377 (-0.50)	-0.0000150 (-1.33)
50K-100K* Average rain^2			-0.0000261** (-2.78)	-0.0000166 (-1.13)	-0.0000219* (-2.33)	-0.00000582 (-0.40)
100K-500K* Average rain^2			-0.00000930 (-1.15)	0.000000382 (0.03)	-0.00000487 (-0.60)	0.00000894 (0.74)
500K-1M* Average rain^2			-0.0000154 (-1.10)	0.00000167 (0.12)	-0.0000123 (-0.85)	0.0000111 (0.75)
Constant	13.54*** (42.81)	14.23*** (24.91)	10.81*** (143.47)	10.53*** (86.98)	13.00*** (37.47)	12.98*** (20.81)
City FE	Yes	Yes	Yes	Yes	Yes	Yes
Year FE	Yes	Yes	Yes	Yes	Yes	Yes
No. Observations	34934	34934	34934	34934	34934	34934
N of Groups	11681	11681	11681	11681	11681	11681
R-sq Within	0.203	0.196	0.190	0.190	0.204	0.197
R-sq Between	0.0294	0.0147	0.241	0.196	0.0539	0.0400
R-sq Overall	0.0134	0.00596	0.0501	0.0767	0.0299	0.0232

Note: Average temperature measured in degrees Celsius and average precipitation measured in mm. Columns 1,3, 5 include average temperature and average rainfall calculated over the past 5 years. Columns 2,4,6 include average temperature and average rainfall calculated over the past 10 years. Estimates of a panel econometric model regressing population of cities on: average temperature and its quadratic term (identified by ^2), and average rainfall and its quadratic term (identified by ^2). Variables interacted with city size. Base category is cities above 1 million inhabitants. Dependent variable expressed in logarithmic terms. Results based on a fixed-effects estimator and standard errors clustered by city. Year fixed effects are included. Data for the periods 1990, 2000 and 2015. t statistics in parentheses. * p < 0.05, ** p < 0.01, *** p < 0.001.
Source: Author's own calculations using GHS Urban Centre Database (2019[166]).

Annex Table 3.A.2. Main effects of linear and quadratic effect of average temperature and average precipitation by city size, on population in cities

	(1) Log of Population	(2) Log of Population	(3) Log of Population	(4) Log of Population	(5) Log of Population	(6) Log of Population
Average temperature						
50K-100K	-0.520*** (-11.30)	-0.546*** (-8.43)			-0.508*** (-11.08)	-0.513*** (-7.92)
100K-500K	-0.518*** (-12.21)	-0.621*** (-9.71)			-0.511*** (-11.96)	-0.598*** (-9.35)
500K-1M	-0.507*** (-5.28)	-0.589*** (-5.72)			-0.499*** (-5.35)	-0.566*** (-5.60)
>1M	-0.204** (-2.60)	-0.203* (-2.00)			-0.200* (-2.54)	-0.188 (-1.85)
Average temperature^2						
50K-100K	0.0185*** (11.77)	0.0186*** (9.39)			0.0183*** (11.70)	0.0183*** (9.27)
100K-500K	0.0165*** (10.78)	0.0187*** (9.11)			0.0165*** (10.77)	0.0188*** (9.19)
500K-1M	0.0146*** (4.34)	0.0168*** (5.72)			0.0147*** (4.46)	0.0170*** (5.90)
>1M	0.00668*** (3.63)	0.00863*** (3.75)			0.00686*** (3.73)	0.00912*** (3.98)
Average rain						
50K-100K			0.00932*** (4.61)	0.0134*** (4.00)	0.00888*** (4.47)	0.0124*** (3.76)
100K-500K			0.00318* (2.29)	0.00526** (2.67)	0.00307* (2.26)	0.00566** (2.90)
500K-1M			0.00461 (1.00)	0.00443 (1.18)	0.00531 (1.17)	0.00471 (1.24)
>1M			-0.000976 (-0.38)	0.00184 (0.47)	0.00108 (0.41)	0.00443 (1.11)
Average rain^2						
50K-100K			-0.0000236*** (-4.10)	-0.0000246** (-2.58)	-0.0000257*** (-4.42)	-0.0000208* (-2.22)
100K-500K			-0.00000680* (-2.11)	-0.00000762 (-1.70)	-0.00000863** (-2.59)	-0.00000607 (-1.39)
500K-1M			-0.0000129 (-1.09)	-0.00000633 (-0.69)	-0.0000160 (-1.29)	-0.00000391 (-0.41)
>1M			0.00000249 (0.34)	-0.00000800 (-0.72)	-0.00000377 (-0.50)	-0.0000150 (-1.33)
Observations	34934	34934	34934	34934	34934	34934

Note: Average temperature measured in degrees Celsius and average precipitation measured in mm. Columns 1,3, 5 include average temperature and average rainfall calculated over the past 5 years. Columns 2,4,6 include average temperature and average rainfall calculated over the past 10 years. Estimates of a panel econometric model regressing population of cities on: average temperature and its quadratic term (identified by ^2), and average rainfall and its quadratic term (identified by ^2). Variables interacted with city size. Base category is cities above 1 million inhabitants. Dependent variable expressed in logarithmic terms. Results based on a fixed-effects estimator and standard errors clustered by city. Year fixed effects are included. Data for the periods 1990, 2000 and 2015. t statistics in parentheses. * p < 0.05, ** p < 0.01, *** p < 0.001.
Source: Author's own calculations using GHS Urban Centre Database (2019[166]).

Annex Table 3.A.3. Linear and quadratic effect of average temperature and average precipitation on urban share

	(1) Log of % urban share	(2) Log of % urban share	(3) Log of % urban share	(4) Log of % urban share	(5) Log of % urban share	(6) Log of % urban share
Average temperature	0.0264	0.0315*			0.0256	0.0316*
	(1.37)	(2.39)			(1.33)	(2.40)
50K-100K* Avg temp.	-0.0369	-0.0536***			-0.0373	-0.0528***
	(-1.85)	(-3.71)			(-1.87)	(-3.65)
100K-500K* Avg temp	-0.0290	-0.0348**			-0.0291	-0.0343*
	(-1.49)	(-2.58)			(-1.50)	(-2.54)
500K-1M* Avg temp	-0.0320	-0.0300*			-0.0321	-0.0297*
	(-1.61)	(-2.08)			(-1.61)	(-2.05)
Average temperature^2	-0.000270	-0.000259			-0.000264	-0.000239
	(-0.79)	(-1.02)			(-0.78)	(-0.94)
50K-100K* Avg temp^2	0.000545	0.000862**			0.000568	0.000830**
	(1.52)	(3.00)			(1.58)	(2.90)
100K-500K*Avg temp^2	0.000470	0.000589*			0.000478	0.000570*
	(1.35)	(2.23)			(1.38)	(2.17)
500K-1M* Avg temp^2	0.000606	0.000587			0.000609	0.000573
	(1.64)	(1.96)			(1.65)	(1.92)
Average rain			-0.000164	0.000160	-0.000113	0.000206
			(-1.00)	(0.49)	(-0.70)	(0.63)
50K-100K* Average rain			-0.0000243	0.000172	-0.0000620	0.000145
			(-0.13)	(0.48)	(-0.32)	(0.40)
100K-500K* Average rain			0.000182	0.00000943	0.000119	-0.0000292
			(0.96)	(0.03)	(0.63)	(-0.08)
500K-1M* Average rain			0.0000275	-0.000266	-0.00000188	-0.000233
			(0.12)	(-0.69)	(-0.01)	(-0.61)
Average rain^2			0.000000138	-0.000000794	-0.000000106	-0.00000100
			(0.31)	(-0.82)	(-0.24)	(-1.06)
50K-100K* Average rain^2			-0.000000473	0.000000134	-0.000000243	0.000000359
			(-0.86)	(0.12)	(-0.45)	(0.34)
100K-500K* Average rain^2			-0.000000630	0.000000470	-0.000000404	0.000000719
			(-1.21)	(0.45)	(-0.79)	(0.70)
500K-1M* Average rain^2			-9.63e-08	0.00000127	-5.68e-09	0.00000139
			(-0.14)	(1.11)	(-0.01)	(1.26)
Constant	-0.142***	-0.143***	-0.129***	-0.156***	-0.119***	-0.173***
	(-4.56)	(-3.76)	(-31.15)	(-24.69)	(-3.72)	(-4.56)
City FE	Yes	Yes	Yes	Yes	Yes	Yes
Year FE	Yes	Yes	Yes	Yes	Yes	Yes
No. Observations	26503	26503	26503	26503	26503	26503
N of Groups	8838	8838	8838	8838	8838	8838
R-sq Within	0.137	0.138	0.137	0.135	0.139	0.138
R-sq Between	0.0137	0.0172	0.000139	0.0000283	0.0123	0.0201
R-sq Overall	0.0145	0.0176	0.00207	0.00149	0.0131	0.0205

t statistics in parentheses

* $p < 0.05$, ** $p < 0.01$, *** $p < 0.001$

Note: Average temperature measured in degrees Celsius and average precipitation measured in mm. Columns 1,3, 5 include average temperature and average rainfall calculated over the past 5 years. Columns 2,4,6 include average temperature and average rainfall calculated over the past 10 years. Estimates of a panel econometric model regressing urban share (% of people of the functional urban area living in the high-density centre) on: average temperature and its quadratic term (identified by ^2), and average rainfall and its quadratic term (identified by ^2), Variables interacted with city size. Base category is cities above 1 million inhabitants. Dependent variable expressed in logarithmic terms. Results based on a fixed-effects estimator and standard errors clustered by city. Year fixed effects are included. Data for the periods 1990, 2000 and 2015.

Source: Author's own calculations using GHS Urban Centre Database (2019[166]).

Annex Table 3.A.4. Main effects of linear and quadratic effect of average temperature and average precipitation by city size, on urban share

	(1) Log of % Urban in FUA	(2) Log of % Urban in FUA	(3) Log of % Urban in FUA	(4) Log of % Urban in FUA	(5) Log of % Urban in FUA	(6) Log of % Urban in FUA
Average temperature						
50K-100K	-0.0105* (-2.09)	-0.0221*** (-3.69)			-0.0117* (-2.31)	-0.0212*** (-3.55)
100K-500K	-0.00261 (-1.12)	-0.00326 (-1.10)			-0.00349 (-1.50)	-0.00267 (-0.90)
500K-1M	-0.00557 (-1.14)	0.00149 (0.25)			-0.00645 (-1.30)	0.00193 (0.32)
>1M	0.0264 (1.37)	0.0315* (2.39)			0.0256 (1.33)	0.0316* (2.40)
Average temperature^2						
50K-100K	0.000275* (2.43)	0.000603*** (4.56)			0.000304** (2.67)	0.000591*** (4.48)
100K-500K	0.000199** (3.15)	0.000331*** (4.63)			0.000213*** (3.35)	0.000331*** (4.62)
500K-1M	0.000335* (2.41)	0.000328* (2.06)			0.000344* (2.46)	0.000334* (2.10)
>1M	-0.000270 (-0.79)	-0.000259 (-1.02)			-0.000264 (-0.78)	-0.000239 (-0.94)
Average rain						
50K-100K			-0.000188 (-1.74)	0.000331* (2.06)	-0.000175 (-1.59)	0.000351* (2.20)
100K-500K			0.0000179 (0.19)	0.000169 (1.16)	0.00000573 (0.06)	0.000177 (1.24)
500K-1M			-0.000136 (-0.81)	-0.000107 (-0.51)	-0.000115 (-0.70)	-0.0000264 (-0.13)
>1M			-0.000164 (-1.00)	0.000160 (0.49)	-0.000113 (-0.70)	0.000206 (0.63)
Average rain^2						
50K-100K			-0.000000334 (-1.01)	-0.000000661 (-1.35)	-0.000000349 (-1.04)	-0.000000642 (-1.32)
100K-500K			-0.000000492 (-1.79)	-0.000000324 (-0.80)	-0.000000510 (-1.86)	-0.000000281 (-0.70)
500K-1M			4.19e-08 (0.08)	0.000000475 (0.79)	-0.000000112 (-0.23)	0.000000385 (0.67)
>1M			0.000000138 (0.31)	-0.000000794 (-0.82)	-0.000000106 (-0.24)	-0.00000100 (-1.06)
Observations	26503	26503	26503	26503	26503	26503

Note: Average temperature measured in degrees Celsius and average precipitation measured in mm. Columns 1, 3, and 5 include average temperature and average rainfall calculated over the past 5 years. Columns 2, 4, and 6 include average temperature and average rainfall calculated over the past 10 years. Estimates of a panel econometric model regressing urban share (% of people of the functional urban area living in the high-density centre) on: average temperature and its quadratic term (identified by ^2), and average rainfall and its quadratic term (identified by ^2), Variables interacted with city size. Base category is cities above 1 million inhabitants. Dependent variable expressed in logarithmic terms. Results based on a fixed-effects estimator and standard errors clustered by city. Year fixed effects are included. Data for the periods 1990, 2000 and 2015.

Source: Author's own calculations using GHS Urban Centre Database (2019[166]).

4 Climate policies across intermediary cities in developing countries

This chapter presents a review of climate actions taking place across intermediary cities in Latin America, Asia and Africa. It highlights the critical role of local government in building climate resilience and identifies factors that have enabled successful climate actions. The chapter examines how disaster risk reduction and the upgrading of informal settlements can serve as entry points to climate action. It also examines factors that limit the capacity of local governments to establish adequate climate actions, including knowledge gaps, inadequate infrastructure, lack of financing, limited human capacity and fragmented governance structures. The chapter concludes with key policy lessons and reiterates the importance of coherent dialogue across all levels of governments for building resilient cities and communities in the face of climate change.

Introduction

This chapter has two main objectives: to highlight the critical role of local governments in establishing successful climate actions, and to help reduce knowledge gaps about climate actions in intermediary cities. The chapter identifies key enabling factors that have led to successful climate actions, based on findings from Africa, Asia and Latin America. It also spotlights the bottlenecks facing local governments in developing countries in the face of rising climate threats.

Cities are increasingly recognised as important agents for economic development, and for meeting the Sustainable Development Goals (SDGs) and the Paris Agreement. Indeed, no global meeting is complete without a mayor or two, while the number of city networks highlights that city/local government concerns continue to increase. Overall, as also shown by the COVID-19 sanitary crisis, city governments play critical roles in establishing a conducive environment for resilience and development, and for identifying and implementing actions to address climate change. In this regard, climate actions focusing on intermediary cities could pay a big dividend.

At present, Information on policies or strategies for addressing climate change in small and medium-sized cities is limited at best. As the urban agenda gains importance, more surveys and initiatives focus on the actions of local governments on climate adaptation and mitigation. However, there are two important caveats. First, most of these studies primarily focus on high-income regions. Second, city studies analysing climate policies in developing countries tend to concentrate on large cities. Yet there is enough evidence to suggest that small and medium-size cities face important constraints in their ability to establish climate policies. In particular, they are challenged by a lack of adequate infrastructure, a financing gap and limited human capacity. Moreover, intermediary cities usually lack the economies of scale and institutional capacity needed for adaptation investments (Revi et al., 2014[1]). This is usually linked to their low national and international profile and to the fragmented governance structures that characterise intermediary cities.

A series of messages stem from this study. First, with the exception of some intermediary cities in Latin America, climate change has often been on the margins of local policies and planning across many of the cities reviewed. Indeed, climate policies are rarely systematically integrated into local plans; rather, they tend to be established sporadically. Second, local governments are critical actors in establishing climate actions. Indeed, in the most successful cases of climate actions – such as in Manizales, Colombia, and Rosario, Argentina – local actors have been the main drivers of the local climate agenda and often are ahead of their respective national governments. Third, there is a strong overlap in strategies or policies that aim to target climate vulnerabilities and those addressing wider socio-economic goals, such as health, infrastructure, etc. Some of the common entry routes for climate policies, such as disaster risk reduction and upgrading of informal settlements, are effective because they target improving the basic needs of vulnerable urban dwellers. They are most effective if they also address the risk-reducing infrastructure needs of urban dwellers, such as provision of health care, safe and sufficient piped water, all-weather access roads, electricity, etc. However, provision of these services tends to be uncoordinated and managed by different departments, reducing the scope for integrated, resilient urban services.

The chapter is structured as follows. The first three sections outline case studies of climate actions in intermediary cities across Latin America and the Caribbean (LAC), Asia, and Africa, respectively. The next section highlights common entry points to climate actions: disaster risk reduction (DRR) and informal settlement upgrading and their overlapping functions. The following section outlines common enabling factors that facilitate successful climate actions and anchor climate change policies in the local development process. The final section offers key lessons and a way forward. In general in this study, intermediary cities are defined as those having 50 000 to 1 million inhabitants. It is important to note that some of the case studies presented here concern cities with more than 1 million inhabitants. This is because these cities play an intermediation role, as well as serving as pertinent examples of climate actions in cities across the three regions.

How intermediary cities in Latin America are responding to climate change?

Intermediary cities are important agents for development in highly urbanised developing regions like Latin America and the Caribbean. In 2020, 81% of LAC's population lived in urban areas, making it the world's second most urbanised region (after Northern America). Contrary to Asia and Africa, the region has long been heavily urbanised: its urban population came to outnumber its rural population in the early 1960s. In 2020, more than half of the urban population in LAC resided in cities of fewer than 1 million inhabitants (Figure 4.1). Moreover, cities with fewer than 1 million inhabitants in LAC are still growing and are expected to account for up to 32% of urban population growth in the region, by 2035 (UNDESA, 2018[2]). In regions like LAC, where structural transformation is advanced, intermediary cities play an important role as manufacturing hubs, platforms for global value chains and tourist centres. Yet, in a region characterised by high inequality and limited governance capacity, the contribution of these cities to national and subnational development risks being hindered by negative climate shocks.

Figure 4.1. Urban population in LAC (1980-2035) and expected urban population growth (2020-50)

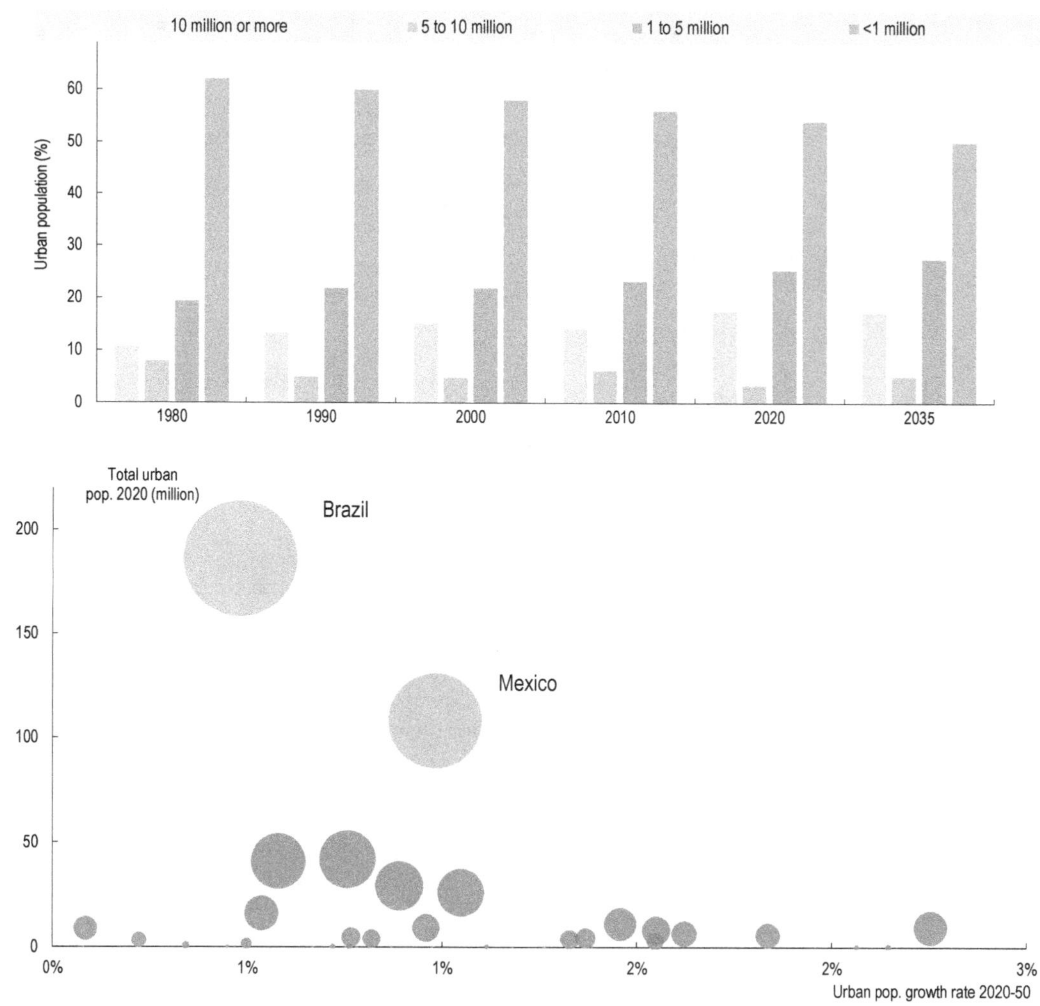

Note: In the bottom figure, the vertical axis shows the total population in urban areas in 2020, while the horizontal axis shows the expected annual growth rate of urban population between 2020 and 2050. The size of the circles represents the expected urban population in 2050.
Source: UNDESA (2018[2]).

What does existing evidence tell us about climate actions in LAC's intermediary cities? Overall, large efforts have been made to build climate resilience, but there is still a long way to go. The cities studied in this section stand out for being ahead of their national governments and other cities in advancing integrated urban, environmental and territorial planning, and on DRR and climate change policies. They also stand out for passing ordinances and generating monitoring and data collection systems. Moreover, these cities have been ahead in working across sectors and engaging with multiple actors. In most cases, academia has been a strong partner, as has civil society including social movements and community organisations. The case studies also show how certain themes begin to interconnect and integrate, and demonstrate the relevance of good governance and city leaders. However, and despite increasing attention to climate resilience and pledges made by many mayors, climate policies in the region have often lagged, with slow implementation. This situation is not exclusive to intermediary cities, but the possibility of achieving more balanced development is often challenging for them. For instance, a study applying a climate vulnerability index (looking into exposure, sensitivity and adaptive capacity) found that, from a group of 70 intermediary cities in the region, 27 had medium vulnerability and 36 high vulnerability (Novillo, 2018[3]).

The experience of selected intermediary cities in LAC in developing climate actions will be discussed below. In many of these cities, climate action has evolved from the key areas of DDR, urban planning and territorial policy. Table 4.1 presents an overview of the cities and their approach to climate change.

Table 4.1. Climate actions in Latin America's intermediary cities

City	Population	Climate threats	Selected climate actions/approaches	Main actors in climate change
Manizales (Colombia)	342 620	floods, landslides, heavy storms	- integration of environmental planning and DRR into local urban planning (Biomanizales) - territorial planning - local environmental action plan (Bioplan) Manizales territorial development plan (2017) - regional integrated climate change management plan (PIGCC)	local government; civil society; academia; regional environmental authority (Corpocaldas)
Santa Fe (Argentina)	Half a million	floods and increase in heavy precipitation, extreme temperatures	- integration of DRM into the new urban development plan - relocations and/or provision of land security and tenure regularisation for built-up areas in no-risk zones - participation in city networks - political coherence	local government; academia; local DRM office; local housing department
Rosario (Argentina)	1.5 million	floods, extreme heat and precipitation	- integrated and cross-sectoral urban development strategy along DRR and environmental planning etc. - building public-private partnerships for increasing funding capacities - policy coherence with transparency, accountability and participatory approach to climate actions - participation in city networks	local government; civil society; private sector; NGOs
Santo Tomé (Argentina)	66 133	floods	- partnerships: the *Plan Base* (2013-14); a plan for the development of projects to support sustainable urban development, in collaboration with UNESCO and UCLG - participatory planning project with Climate Resilient Cities Initiative aiming to promote participatory decision making in local actions and build capacity	provincial government; city mayor; international organisations
Portoviejo (Ecuador)	280 029	floods, droughts, landslides, tsunamis and mudslides	- integrated (and multisectoral) Urban Master Plan - Actual Territorial Model: mapping information on local natural resources, infrastructure gap, hazard prone areas, etc. - Mobility Plan for the Canton (2014-19) for improving public transportation systems and mobility	local government and international organisations; Office of Environmental Management and Risks
Santa Ana (El Salvador)	264 091 (2013)	droughts, floods, soil degradation,	- emergency response approach - participant in the Climate Resilient Cities Initiative	local government; international

		forest fires, volcanic eruptions		organisations; civil society
Santana, Abaetetuba, Ponta de Pedras and Mazagão – Amazon Delta and Estuary Region (Brazil)	99 000 (Santana), 83 000 (Abaetatuba), and 30 000 each (in Ponta de Pedras and Mazagao)	flooding, sea-level rise	- participant in the Climate Resilient Cities Initiative (2016-19)	local government; international organisations

Note: Most cities face heavy storms, heatwaves, and an increase in extreme temperatures and precipitation.
Source: Author's elaboration.

Disaster risk reduction is a key climate policy in Latin American intermediary cities

Manizales (Colombia)

Manizales, an intermediary city in Colombia, is one of the most interesting examples in terms of implementation of climate actions. In 2017, the city had 398 830 inhabitants (Alcadía de Manizales, 2017[4]). The city, which sits in the Andes about halfway between the capital, Bogotá, and the Pacific, is subject to various climate risks, including flooding, severe winds, landslides, thunderstorms, forest fires, etc. (Hardoy and Barrero, 2016[5]).

Established in an area of steep mountain ridges and seismic instability, Manizales has a long history of managing disasters. The eruption of the Nevado de Ruiz volcano in 1985 was a turning point. Since the early 1990s, Manizales has been integrating environmental planning and DRR into its urban planning. The city plans integrate long-standing local urban environmental policy (Biomanizales) and the local environmental action plan (Bioplan), and have involved many stakeholders, both as a legal obligation and as a strategy (UNDRR, 2019[6]). Academia has been a fundamental partner in the process. Given its well-documented experience, Manizales has in many ways shaped and guided national urban environmental policy. The city is widely known for its achievements (Hardoy and Barrero, 2016[5]) and is internationally recognised as a reference in urban resilience (Cardona, 2019[7]).

Over the decades, the work of the Manizales local government in building resilience has had its ups and downs. At times, momentum and local government support have wavered; however, an active and committed academic sector and civil society sustained the work and accumulated decades of learning. For instance, authorities have learned that DRR is only possible when there is a convergence between scientific and technical work, in addition to political and administrative will and community acceptance (Carrizosa, 2018[8]). Support from Corpocaldas, the regional environmental agency, has also been important. The last update of the Territorial Development Plan of Manizales (2017[9]) integrates robust technical-scientific data and political support (Carrizosa, 2018[8]). Key to the process developed in Manizales has been access to good information and generation of knowledge. Indeed, a detailed understanding of the territory allowed local authorities to calculate risk and guide urban development.

The climate-adaptation workstream in Manizales has several components. It is based on the idea that good DRR, environmental sustainability and territorial planning all contribute to adaptation and reduction of vulnerability. Some of the activities include:

- generating very good databases, an automatic hydrometeorological monitoring system and a risk management index to guide decision making
- relocation of population in at-risk areas. This has been ongoing for over 30 years with a wide variety of approaches, led by different institutions and programmes. Some programmes are more participatory than others, and they have had various outcomes (Chardon, 2021[10]).

- a voluntary collective insurance scheme that subsidises insurance for low-income groups. The scheme is financed through property taxes and has been operating since 1999.
- an environmental surcharge defined by law, which the Municipal Council set at 2%. The tax income is transferred to Corpocaldas, which is responsible for its management and implementation (UNDRR, 2019[6]).
- tax incentives for property-owners who reduce their vulnerability to risks.
- awareness campaigns, strong linkage with the education system and an active community that participates in different initiatives.
- structural work such as slope stabilisation. This has transformed hazard-prone areas into areas with "mitigable risk", where construction with restrictions is allowed, combined with a network of eco-parks, water management, etc.
- continuous strengthening of the Guardians of the Slope (Guardianes de Ladera). This is a long-standing programme that trains women living in or near high-risk zones to maintain slope vegetation, control drainage channels, monitor slope stabilisation work, report problems and changes in land use, keep an updated register of families living there at high risk and raise the awareness of their neighbours.

Although mitigation issues figure in the city's Development Plan, climate-change mitigation has not been a priority line of work in Manizales. However, mitigation is indirectly involved in the environmental coherence of its policies and actions. Sound environmental policies that contribute to mitigation include the protection of environmentally fragile areas and river basins, the development of the eco-park network, reforestation of mountain slopes and river basins, active education of residents, solid waste management, etc. Most of these activities are incorporated in the municipal budget and developed in collaboration with the private sector, universities and civil society organisations (Hardoy and Barrero, 2016[5]). Work has been done to identify the carbon footprint and water footprint of different activities in order to help generate awareness and guide decision making. Corpocaldas has been working on mitigation with projects of REDD+ (the United Nations-backed framework Reducing Emissions from Deforestation and forest Degradation); carbon markets; and CDM (the UN's Clean Development Mechanism). Recently it developed an Integral Climate Change Management Plan for the region (*Plan Integral de Gestión del Cambio Climático del Departamento de Caldas*). The plan involves the integration of DRR, adaptation and resilience, and low-carbon development and actions for climate empowerment and governance. Various municipalities, including Manizales, have developed their climate agendas in line with the regional plan.

Santa Fe (Argentina)

Santa Fe is an intermediary city in Argentina with approximately half a million inhabitants. The city lies inland near the junction of the Salado and Paraná rivers and is surrounded by lagoons and marshes. This, combined with heavy precipitation, creates a severe risk of flooding (Maurizi and Fontana, 2019[11]).

Santa Fe has suffered many floods, but two in particular have spurred local action. In 2003, one-third of the city was flooded; this caught the city authorities completely unprepared. In 2007 the same city areas were flooded, exposing the lack of official action. Much of the recovery work fell to evacuees and other community members and institutions. They organised and mobilised to claim justice and compensation. An alternative political coalition built its platform around the impact of 50 years with no official urban land policies (Hardoy, Pandiella and Barrero, 2011[12]). Elections were held later in 2007. The mayor at the head of new city government coalition had been dean of the University of El Litoral (the regional university), and he brought with him a team of professors who moved from academia to public office. Among other priorities, they decided to incorporate disaster risk management (DRM) as "state public policy" in the new urban development plan, backed up by municipal ordinances and internal restructuring.

Santa Fe was managed by the same coalition for the following three four-year political administrations (2007-19). Political commitment was kept alive by political continuity and co-operation among sectoral and DRM representatives of the city. There was also increasing support in mayoral elections from low-income electoral districts (historically, among the most exposed and vulnerable to urban flood risk). The DRM Office has a cross-cutting role in mainstreaming disaster risk reduction in other sectoral departments of the municipal government. This was facilitated by the formal inclusion of the director of the DRM Office in regular cabinet meetings; joint organisation of DRM training for municipal employees with one of the public universities; and strong linkage between the DRM Office and the Department of Communications, which has been central for embedding the DRM approach internally and externally (UNDRR, 2019[6]). The Housing Department (*Agencia Santa Fe Habitat*) developed a strong programme to address vulnerability by providing land security and tenure regularisation to houses built in areas not at risk of flooding and generating programmes to relocate those in at-risk areas.

Moreover, Santa Fe adopted an integrated approach to addressing urban resilience, which helped the city gain renown and access to international funds. City officials developed ordinances and implemented value-capture tools to minimise flood risks (De la sala, 2019[13]). Santa Fe joined city networks as it became nationally and globally recognised for its DRR approach and urban planning. In 2014, the local government began to apply for international financing for DRR and resilience. This included being part of the 100 Resilient Cities programme of The Rockefeller Foundation and developing the city's Resilience Strategy, which allowed local leaders to tap into different types of support and guidance. They also received funds from the French Development Agency (AFD) to support nature-based solutions. They created reserves to limit the city's expansion over flood-prone areas, improving the absorptive capacity of the soil and increasing the quality of life of residents (Simet, 2018[14]). Santa Fe also got involved in the Mercociudades city network, developing training courses on resilience for other cities and presenting the city's experience at international events such as the UN's Habitat III housing conference in 2016.

Santa Fe's local strategies have enabled the city to access various funds in addition to municipal resources. Since 2008, the Department of Water Resources has had an annual budget for the operation and maintenance of the flood defence and pumping systems. The city's clear definition of a DRM public policy helped it to secure financing from higher political-administrative levels, especially for drainage infrastructure, relocation and upgrading of flood-prone settlements. As Santa Fe officials became important national and global players, it became easier to access programmes and funding.

Santa Fe's resilience strategy integrates various cross-cutting issues. The strategy includes social inclusion, integration of information, "living with water" and a metropolitan focus. Climate change mitigation does not appear as a high priority; however, local officials work on transportation, mobility and solid waste management as a means to improve overall city quality (Valsagna and Tejedor, 2017[15]). DRR efforts in Santa Fe were also supported by a very strong communication and awareness-raising campaign that has been sustained over the years. The campaign aimed to keep the past alive so that no one would forget to shape the future city, and to ensure that everyone understood the risks and the importance of flood defence and water drainage system. The awareness strategy also included training of mass-media professionals to ensure better communication.

Urban development underpins climate strategy in some Latin American cities

Many cities in Latin America have started to work on climate change via a more sustainable urban development approach. This has been driven both by local at-risk contexts and by international agendas, regional initiatives and national legislation that demanded engagement. So far not much has been written about these cities, but this is changing as more of them take part in regional and international initiatives and their cases become documented.

Rosario (Argentina)

Rosario is a large intermediary city, with approximately 1.5 million inhabitants. Similar to other cities in the Province of Santa Fe, Rosario faces large flooding risks, as well as other threats including extreme heat and precipitation (Hardoy and Ruete, 2013[16]; Gobierno Provincia de Santa Fe, 2014[17]).

Long-term political commitment and effective urban governance have been important drivers of Rosario's resilience. Over the years, Rosario has shown commitment to decentralisation, transparency, accountability and participation, characterised by its long-term policies and governance systems (Seridan and Satterthwaite, 2016[18]). For more than 30 years, it has used a development paradigm that prioritises quality of life (Mastrángelo and Carbuccia, 2020[19]). Its long tradition of urban planning has evolved to include a broad vision of urban challenges and responses, a commitment to environmental sustainability and a strategic plan that involves multiple actors and sectors and encompasses the whole metropolitan area (Hardoy and Ruete, 2013[16]). What sustains everything is strong long-term political support by successive administrations.

Rosario's resilience is underpinned by a development strategy that is cross-sectoral, participatory and multistakeholder. The city administration has intertwined various lines of work, including urban planning, social development, health, DRR, environmental planning, education, mobility and solid waste management, among others, in an effort to embark on a sustainable development pathway (Barlett and Satterthwaite, 2016[20]). Here are some highlights of Rosario's planning approach and success in implementation:

- Successive plans are developed in a participatory way (including joint plans that have involved participation of various sectors and stakeholders, including the local population) and guide and structure the city's development (Mastrángelo and Carbuccia, 2020[19]).
- The plans are realistic and implementable because of their clear rules, innovative mechanisms for accessing funds, the establishment of public-private partnerships and agreements among different stakeholders.
- Attention is paid to a learning component, which adds flexibility in addressing challenges (Seridan and Satterthwaite, 2016[18]);
- The approach builds on strong institutions, civil society and the private sector.
- The city's decentralisation process increases proximity between local government and citizens.

Rosario's climate-action planning process is comprehensive and tailored to the needs of the city. The city administration, in partnership with local non-governmental organisations (NGOs) and universities, began to develop its climate strategy in 2009 (Mastrángelo and Carbuccia, 2020[19]). The plans and programmes developed over the years not only carry multiple environmental benefits but also tend to be anticipatory, not just reactive (Seridan and Satterthwaite, 2016[18]). The city also participates in city networks and regional and global meetings, and has subscribed to different climate initiatives.

Rosario's climate planning process is guided by interdisciplinary, participative, scientific and technical knowledge. It aims to set the city on a path of sustainable, socially balanced and inclusive development. In 2015, through local decree No. 9.424, the city established a local climate action plan to guide and align local policies, which led to the development of the *Plan Local de Respuesta Climática* (Local Climate Response Plan).[1] The plan cut across all local policies (territorial planning, mobility, DRR, public services, energy efficiency and renewable energy, sustainable construction, public spaces, urban agriculture, etc.). In this way, most of the local climate action agenda consisted of policies that were already being implemented by different city offices. These offices consider future actions that need to be accelerated, strengthened, amplified or re-oriented, or complemented with other actions aiming to move forward on decarbonisation and resilience.

Within the climate planning process, mitigation and adaptation projects were developed. Technical teams of the municipality were tasked with identifying ongoing actions and developing new projects, and the impact was quantified, evaluated and complemented with the inputs of multiple actors of civil society via a participatory process. Starting from 2016, initiatives undertaken in Rosario (Mastrángelo and Carbuccia, 2020[19]) include:

- awareness raising and capacity building, for civil servants and the community in general
- development of climate-change impact scenarios (2035, 2065 and 2100) and establishment of monitoring mechanisms
- establishment of clear linkages between climate-change impacts, health and vector-borne diseases such as dengue, zika and chikungunya; basic infrastructure; and services
- generation of a GHG emissions inventory
- elaboration of a Local Risk Map that combines the spatial distribution of climate hazards with social and physical vulnerability.

Local authorities in Rosario established wide-ranging actions under both adaptation and mitigation lines of work. In terms of climate adaptation, special attention is paid to city water management. This includes management of water and sanitation, drainage, water retention devices, building code and restrictions on land use in flood areas. Attention is also focused on management of public spaces, DRR (including early warning systems and a network of municipal meteorological stations), strengthening the health system and monitoring vector-borne diseases. In terms of mitigation, the city addressed urban mobility. It created bike lanes and a public rental bike system; promoted public transportation and improved the quality and type of fuel/energy used in public vehicles; created exclusive lanes; reconfigured sidewalks; discussed use of private vehicles; and rethought the urban freight transportation system. Other actions included sustainable solid waste management (separation, recycling, composting, disposal), energy efficiency and certification of sustainable constructions, and promoting the use of renewable energy (Mastrángelo and Carbuccia, 2020[19]). In 2021, Rosario won The World Resource Institute's Ross Centre Prize for Cities for its urban and peri-urban agriculture programme and social inclusion. Launched in the wake of Argentina's economic crisis in 2001, the programme aimed to promote sustainable food production, restore land, control urban sprawl and improve climate resilience (WRI, 2021[21]).

Portoviejo (Ecuador)

Portoviejo, with close to 280 000 inhabitants, is one of the most vulnerable urban areas in Ecuador. The city is located inland from the Pacific coast in the Province of Manabí, which is highly susceptible to floods, droughts, landslides, mudslides and tsunamis (Fernandez et al, 2015[22]).

The post-earthquake situation of 2016 was taken as an opportunity to re-create Portoviejo and innovate. It was also an opportunity to rethink the city's design, including its relationship with the Portoviejo River. As aid arrived, the local government began to guide investments in public works and used support received from international organisations to quickly develop projects for implementation. The city government began to accelerate plans and develop new ones with the idea of making Portoviejo the best Ecuadorian city to live in (Municipio de Portoviejo, 2019[23]).

Local government climate actions got underway with the hiring consultants to develop an Urban Master Plan ((Gobierno Municipal del Cantón Portovejo, 2017[24])). Work took place at three levels: *1)* the city and its surrounding area, to understand uses of land and propose ideas to treat different needs such as vacant areas, urban borders, the river corridor, etc.; *2)* the form of the city, by dividing it into areas to understand mobility, densities, building heights, infrastructure and services, etc.; and *3)* special plans for the different neighbourhoods. This was developed in phases that included diagnosis, revision and integration of different sectorial plans; the design of the Urban Master Plan (which included the River Portoviejo Master

Plan); and special plans for different sectors. The local government continued with several lines of work,[2] including a Multi-Hazard Protection Plan and Integral Improvement Plans.[3]

One of the city's main goals was to start implementing the Portoviejo river corridor master plan in stages. The plan aimed to integrate the city with the river, restore and recover the natural morphology of the riverbanks, integrate/incorporate the idea of resilience to better withstand shocks and stresses, and promote the socio-economic development of the different areas along the river. This also involved work to adjust to specific local ordinances.

Driven by the need for integral analysis of the territory and its dynamic, Portoviejo's local leaders are working hard to integrate information and generate good diagnoses. In addition to the Urban Master Plan, they generated the Actual Territorial Model (*Modelo Territorial Actual*), which combines information on natural resources, urban structures and economic-productive activities. The resulting map and matrix showed main challenges, such as lack of infrastructure, exposure to hazards and deforestation; opportunities related to cultural, natural heritage and tourism; administrative and commercial opportunities; and fertile land for agricultural development. The planning was done in a participatory way, leading to the creation of the Desired Territorial Model (*Modelo Territorial Deseado*), a vision of the city plan that is included in Plan Portoviejo 2035, a development and territorial plan. This is multiscale planning that corresponds to programmes and projects, with national and subnational levels aiming to promote sustainable development. Sustainability is promoted through risk-reduction and climate mitigation policies, equitable access to infrastructure and multilevel governance, all of which are integrated coherently with the urban planning process.

As in other cities in the region, the mitigation workstream in Portoviejo is concentrated mostly on improving mobility. Portoviejo's Mobility Plan for the Cantón (*Plan Mobilidad Sustentable Cantón Portoviejo 2014-19*) recognises the city's limitations and possibilities. It concentrates on improving the public transportation network, generating pedestrian corridors, removing barriers and generating bike lanes. The city is also working on improving green spaces with an integrated network of parks and green areas at different scales (Gobierno Municipal del Cantón Portovejo, 2017[24]).

Moreover, the local government has been effective at connecting with outside stakeholders and learning from other cities. It launched a programme of slope guardians (similar to that of Manizales) and developed special plans as a more effective means of getting needed approvals and funds, and of advancing in implementation, much like the city of Rosario. Part of the planning process has involved partnerships and collective efforts in which universities, local design professionals and architects' studios (both national and international) have worked together with teams from the Municipality of Portoviejo and Plan Ciudad Portoviejo to define a new vision for the city and the Portoviejo River watershed. Support has been received from Banco de Desarrollo de América Latina (CAF), and the French Development Agency (AFD), to establish a GHG inventory and evaluate climate trends within a regional initiative that is promoting low carbon and resilient development. The work aims to integrate climate aspects in projects, promote awareness-raising for local governments and generate climate co-benefits in urban projects.

Santo Tomé (Argentina)

Santo Tomé is a small intermediary city. It had 61 133 inhabitants as of the latest census in 2010 and is projected to grow to 81 000 by 2025. The city is located at the mouth of the Salado River and is prone to flooding. Nonetheless, the climate actions of Santo Tomé lag behind those of cities such as Santa Fe and Rosario (Hardoy et al., 2019[25]).

Santo Tomé's climate actions have mainly come in response to demands that originated from a lack of services and infrastructure. Local actions had little planning, with little incorporation of climate-change parameters. The city has developed a system of flood defences and pumping, but this is reaching the limits of its capacity. The city government has taken advantage of two participatory planning processes that called for integrated approaches to urban problem solving. Both originated from outside Santo Tomé:

- *The Plan Base (Base Plan)* was developed over 2013-14 as part of a provincial strategic planning process carried out with the support of United Cities and Local Governments (UCLG) and UNESCO. The planning tool aimed to support cities in crafting more sustainable and balanced urban development. It allowed project participants to analyse a set of variables and agree on ten strategic projects for the following ten years (Gobierno Provincia de Santa Fe, 2014[17]).
- *A participatory planning research action project within the Climate Resilient Cities Initiative*[4] sought to develop a practical decision-making process that would empower residents and facilitate discussions on the implementation of strategies that could contribute to resilient urban development and generate a commitment from local governments to do things differently. It also allowed the possibility to identify and agree on a range of feasible follow-up options (a portfolio of project drafts) (Hardoy et al., 2018[26]). The project included opportunities to build both internal and external capacities.

These two processes sparked the interest of the local government, particularly the mayor. Now in her second term, the mayor is committed to continue working on building climate resilience and seeking opportunities to further strengthen the municipality's integrated planning process. Some of the recommendations being followed today are:

- *Review processes and government plans.* This entails making sure to build climate resilience and to make this a common practice, regardless of the duration of mandates, short-term commitments or sectoral interests
- *Strengthen local governance.* This involves improving horizontal co-ordination between municipal departments, harmonising plans among sectors and between the municipal government and civil society actors, training of local stakeholders on how to hold spaces of meaningful participation where they can influence territorial development planning
- *Adapt the organisational structure.* To carry out resilience work, the municipality must have a work team dedicated to the comprehensive planning of the territory, with an understanding of disaster risks and resilience. This team must integrate, harmonise and strengthen public policies that favour resilience, such as working on the adaptation of urban codes, land use and application of various existing urban instruments and their integration with plans for infrastructure and services. A new directorate was established after completion of the project, with the Director of Hydraulics assuming responsibility for climate-resilience planning and monitoring to ensure that all plans, processes and interventions made sense from a hydraulic point of view. This involved the incorporation of new trained staff, technical resources and strong political support.
- *Generate useful information bases.* All municipal information generation is to be integrated in a spatially referenced information system. This did not exist prior to the project. With the support of the provincial government, the city managed to get the human and technical resources needed to start building the information base.
- *Begin to build a portfolio of key projects.* The portfolio, which is to include a resilience lens, could be pulled out as soon as funding opportunities arise.

Santa Ana (El Salvador)

Santa Ana is an intermediary city in El Salvador that is expanding without effective planning or integrated climate strategies. The city is surrounded by hillsides and the River Lempa; as of 2013, its inhabitants numbered 264 091 (Hardoy et al., 2019[25]). The population of Santa Ana, a quickly growing city with rapid built-up expansion, is increasingly exposed to risks such as floods, droughts, soil degradation, forest fires and volcanic eruptions (Hardoy et al., 2019[25]).

Although the city is part of the participatory planning project of the Resilient Cities Initiative, it lacks a comprehensive approach to climate change. Problems include a lack of territorial planning; the expansion of low-density peripheral housing to at-risk areas that are also key natural service providers; and a lack of integrated river basin management. Nevertheless, the city has an emergency response approach. As in the case of Santo Tomé, Argentina, the Resilient Cities Initiative facilitated discussions between stakeholders and helped in the generation of a set of recommendations and a portfolio of projects. What was particularly interesting in the case of Santa Ana was the strong engagement of civil society and the decision to develop a climate-change roundtable composed of local actors (established in May 2017). Local officials and technicians from the municipality, academia and civil society attended project workshops and wanted to extend the conversation on climate-resilient development. The roundtable met over several months, started to develop projects and was key in terms of providing credibility to participatory processes and the exchange between actors and municipal institutions. Their aim was to become a permanent consulting group to guide decision making. However, when local authorities changed, the roundtable lost support and possibilities to engage with city authorities (Hardoy et al., 2018[26]).

Santana, Abaetetuba, Ponta de Pedras and Mazagão (Brazil)

Santana, Abaetetuba, Ponta de Pedras and Mazagão are cities in Brazil's Amazon Delta and Estuary (ADE) region. The ADE region is a highly climate-variable area formed by one of the largest estuarine areas in the world. It is also the most densely populated area within Amazonia (Cavalcante and Almeida, 2018[27]). Research shows that approximately 1.2 million people (41% of the area's population) face flood risks due to lack of planning, occupation of lowlands and lack of investments (De Lima et al., 2020[28]). The region includes large urban centres such as Belém (with 1 485 000 inhabitants in the city and 2.5 million in the metro area) and Macapá (with a population of 474 706 in 2017), both of which are state capitals. The region also includes complex networks of small and medium-sized urban centres. Although many cities retain some rural characteristics, the urbanisation process has made them some of the fastest growing localities in Amazonia.

Santana, Abaetetuba, Ponta de Pedras and Mazagão, of varying population size, are highly vulnerable to climate-induced threats. Santana (State of Amazonia), with a population of 99 000 (101 262 inhabitants in the municipality) and Abatatuba (State of Para), with a population of 83 000 (141 100 inhabitants in the municipality), are in the lower population range of intermediary cities. Ponta de Pedras and Mazagão are smaller towns, with a population of around 30 000 each. These cities and towns share common characteristics such as a livelihood and culture tied to the local environment. They also share common rising climate vulnerabilities resulting from sea-level rise, regional migration and socio-economic crises. Underlying low socio-economic conditions, such as lack of access to potable water, sanitation and drainage services, are some of the main concerns. In the north of Brazil, only 45.3 % of the population has access to water through a network, and 20.8% have no water treatment.

Addressing the needs of these cities and building their climate resilience is essential. They need adequate investments, which in turn require better political co-operation, innovation, good urban planning and inclusive governance. Building resilience and continuing to provide services and employment opportunities will depend on the implementation of DRR and climate-change policies (De Lima et al., 2020[28]). The participation of Santana, Abaetetuba, Ponta de Pedras and Mazagão in the Climate Resilient Cities Initiative is helping them to find solutions to some of the climate-related challenges they face.

The Climate Resilient Cities Initiative (2016-19) in the four localities involved interviews with key informants and focus groups with local leaders, residents, government actors and faculty and students from local universities (Cavalcante and Almeida, 2018[27]). As with the initiative's other projects, tools and material were shared and made available to everyone. Some of the outputs of the projects include:

- *building a data set* with rainfall and temperature collected for more than three decades in climatological stations located in the delta and near the cities involved in the project and with insights into the longer-term changes in climate variables in a highly dynamic context. This data assists in characterising ongoing processes of climate change and variability, and in identifying the frequency and intensity of weather anomalies in or near the cities.

- *constructing a vulnerability index* (based on census sector data/smallest aerial survey units) and applying a multicriteria analysis (exposure, socio-economic sensitivity, infrastructure). This was complemented with interviews with government technicians to create vulnerability maps for the cities.
- *identification of varying resilience options*. While residents commonly change their livelihood strategies to respond to and recover from damaging floods, rainstorms and dry spells, policy makers tend to focus their actions on relief assistance to victims of catastrophic events such as landslides. Residents noted that they were better prepared to deal with catastrophic floods and droughts than with severe rainstorms that occur annually. Residents use rural and urban resources through sophisticated family, ethnic and neighbourhood social networks and collective action.
- *developing a mobile application*, AquiAlaga, to connect generators and users of local risk information and allow them to transmit and obtain information almost immediately. Many of the hydroclimatic events that affect livelihoods and the environment in small towns are not formally identified as catastrophic events, so disaster relief agencies end up providing no support to residents. However, information and records of the frequency, intensity and severity of storms, droughts and floods, as well as the impact on livelihoods and the environment, are abundantly documented and shared by residents through social media and the use of cell phones. The application is used in Belém, Abaetetuba, Ponta de Pedras, Santana and Mazagão. In collaboration with the Amazon Protection System (SIPAM), the application was improved and integrated into the Natural Disaster Prevention and Warning System of the Ministry of Defence. This is an important step, together with building data sets and vulnerability maps, as municipalities often do not have their own monitoring system and instead depend on federal, state and neighbouring municipal monitoring systems. However cities are often not able to generate data on events that will affect them in particular (AquiAlaga, n.d.[29]).
- *developing a rainwater collection prototype* for families living in vulnerable areas in Abaetetuba. Neighbours, health agents and local leaders were involved in the project. The system collects and treats rainwater. It has economic benefits compared to the construction of deep wells, all the more so compared to the construction of a water supply system in a flood area. Three families can share the prototype. It is expected that local authorities will eventually support its implementation.

How intermediary cities in Asia are responding to climate change?

Asia accounts for the largest urban population in the world. As of 2020, 51% of Asia's population, or 2.4 billion people, were living in urban areas, of whom 54% lived in cities with fewer than 1 million inhabitants (UNDESA, 2018[2]). Asian intermediary cities tend to be larger than intermediary cities in other developing regions. They are very dynamic and are expected to account for up to 38% of urban population growth by 2030.

Figure 4.2. Urban population in Asia (1980-2035) and expected urban population growth (2020-50)

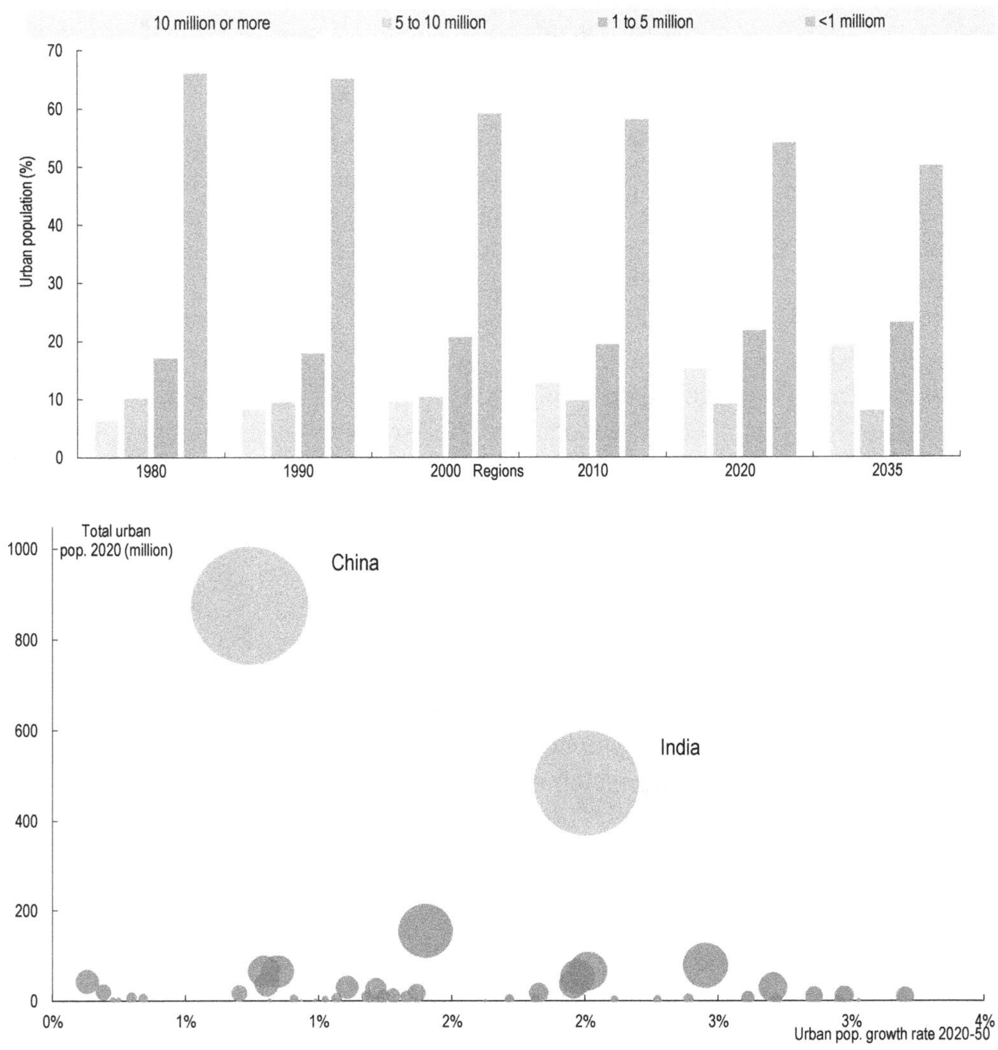

Source: UNDESA (2018[2]).

Note: In the bottom figure, the vertical axis shows the total population in urban areas in 2020, while the horizontal axis shows the expected annual growth rate of urban population between 2020 and 2050. The size of the circles represents the expected urban population in 2050.

In most of the case studies analysed in this section, and in contrast to Latin America and the Caribbean, climate action is the result of actions started by community-based organisations (with rare cases of local government participation) and international stakeholders. These initiatives have helped to clarify goals and promote the inclusion of climate-related outcomes into budgeting and planning. These actions, along with the upgrading of informal settlements, have been pillars for building resilience against climate change in the Asian intermediary cities studied in this chapter. Table 4.2 outlines the case studies presented in this section, along with an overview of their climate-change policies.

Table 4.2. Climate actions in Asia's intermediary cities

City	Population	Climate threats	Selected climate actions/approaches	Main actors in climate change
San Francisco (Philippines)	55 000	typhoons, heavy rainfall, increasing temperatures, sea-level rise, landslides, droughts, intense monsoons	- institutionalisation of disaster risk management systems in *puroks* (lowest levels of government) - adaptation programmes including water management systems with rain water catchment systems; adaptation planning in family farming systems	- local government units - *puroks* - local communities - national government
Bandar Lampung (Indonesia)	900 000 (with projected growth to 1.2 million in 2030)	tsunamis, floods, droughts, sea-level rise,	participant in the ACCCRN programme with the aim of building strategies for climate resilience: - creation of a multistakeholder platform, City Team, to carry out various projects - establishment of the City Resilience Strategy identifying financing and budgeting opportunities for local actions - City Action Plan	- local government - local civil society and NGOs - international organisations
Surakarta or Solo (Indonesia)	600 000	tropical monsoons, heavy rains, floods	- issuance of ID cards for informal settlement inhabitants to access emergency relief programmes - relocation policies for informal settlements at high risk - multilevel approach engaging various levels of administration which formed into working groups (Kelompk Kerja)	- representatives at different levels of government administration - local communities - local government

Source: Author's elaboration.

Local action helps to build climate-change resilience in intermediary cities in Asia

San Francisco (Philippines)

The coastal city of San Francisco, in Cebu province, is one of the municipalities of the Camotes islands in the Camotes Sea. In 2015, the city had roughly 55 000 inhabitants. Its principal economic activities are small-scale commercial and sustenance fishing, farming and animal husbandry. The people of San Francisco are mostly self-employed as small retailers or work in the services and tourism sectors (Bawagan et al., 2015[30]).

San Francisco is affected by typhoons and heavy rainfall that threaten its agricultural land and economic resources. Since it is located on a small island, San Francisco faces isolation from the rest of the province in the aftermath of climate disasters. It faces the risk of destruction of its weak infrastructure and housing, and a shortage of drinkable water. Climate change is expected to intensify climate risks such as rising temperatures, rising sea-levels and increased precipitation that could lead to landslides, droughts and changes in the intensity of monsoons (Bawagan et al., 2015[30]). There is also a growing strain on mangroves from illegal fishing and coastal development (Bawagan et al., 2015[30]).

Over the years, San Francisco has carried out innovative actions to build resilience against climate threats. It institutionalized DRM structures at the *purok* level (Johnson and Blackburn, 2014[31]). The *purok* is the lowest level of governance and plays a key role in disseminating and acting on disaster information, as well as in waste management, improving livelihoods and promoting education (Curato and Calamba, 2020[32]). *Puroks* are also key in ensuring nutrition and social cohesion (Cheng and Kim, 2019[33]). The system proved successful during Typhoon Haiyan in 2013, when collaboration between the local government unit and the *puroks* facilitated pre-emptive evacuation and prompt rehabilitation efforts (Cheng and Kim, 2019[33]). Despite the magnitude of the typhoon, zero casualties were reported in San Francisco, proving the effectiveness of the system and making the municipality a role model of the UN Making Resilient Cities Campaign. This form of organisation highlights the importance of involving local actors in DRM and recognising that their main asset was their strength as a community. Moreover, the system was not implemented in one go, showing that establishing and implementing community-based interventions is a long process that requires building relationships of trust and constant follow-up (Cheng and Kim, 2019[33]).

The local government of San Francisco has been implementing proactive measures to build local climate resilience. In 2018 the local government was awarded PHK 38.1 million (Philippine pesos) to implement climate adaptation programmes at the local level. The fund was part of the country's People's Survival Fund, an annual fund for the implementation of adaptation programmes by local governments. The fund was used to implement a water management programme with the aim of reducing dependence on groundwater and implementing rainwater catchment systems (SunStar Phillipines, 2018[34]). The local government also planned to implement a Climate Resilient Family Farm Planning programme aiming to strengthen the capacities of local farmers in their livelihood adaptation strategies (Office of the President of the Philippines, 2018[35]). San Francisco is one of the most active local governments in the Philippines, establishing climate actions through proactive partnerships and engagement with the national government as well as local communities.

Bandar Lampung (Indonesia)

Bandar Lampung is one of the most important cities on the island of Sumatra. The city extends for 27 kilometres along the southern coast and is characterised by wet and tropical weather. It is home to around 900 000 inhabitants, with the population projected to reach 1.2 million in 2030. Population growth is largely driven by transmigration (inter-island migration) and the city's proximity to Jakarta, located in the nearby island of Java (Lassa and Nugraha, 2015[36]).

Due to its geographic location, Bandar Lampung is exposed to tsunamis and volcanic activity. In 1883, the eruption of Krakatoa caused deadly tsunamis that severely hit the area where Bandar Lampung is now located. The lowlands suffered important damage, while the upper part was safer. These two areas later united into the city of Bandar Lampung, but social and economic inequalities still exist between the two areas. Moreover, the city is at high risk of extreme weather events like floods and droughts related to the El Niño Southern Oscillation (ENSO) phenomenon (Lassa and Nugraha, 2015[36]).

Bandar Lampung lacks coherent strategies for adapting to climate change. Informal settlements located along the coastline are at high risk of floods, tsunamis and sea-level rise. Additional challenges, such as poor solid-waste management and scarcity of fresh water, create tensions between usage for residential and agricultural purposes.

In 2009, Bandar Lampung became part of the Asian Cities Climate Change Resilience Network (ACCCRN) along with other Southeast Asian cities. Through the programme, the city developed ex-ante strategies for adaptation to climate change and for building resilience in the communities. The programme's multilevel approach involved international NGOs, think tanks and the local government. The City Team, a multistakeholder platform, was created to carry out the project (Taylor and Lassa, 2015[37]). The project had five phases: 1) shared learning dialogues; 2) vulnerability assessment; 3) pilot projects; 4) City Resilience Strategy; and 5) Action Plan. During the first year (phases 1 and 2), relevant stakeholders held multiple dialogues to build knowledge and mutual understanding, and to identify climate hazards and vulnerable populations. In the second year, the project determined its priorities and put pilot projects in place. The City Resilience Strategy identified financing opportunities, connecting recommendations to budgeting and thus helping with local policy decisions. Finally the Action Plan for the city was shaped (Taylor and Lassa, 2015[37]).

The programme's most relevant impact was to put climate change and environmental hazards on the decision table, as recommendations were taken up in the local medium-term planning agenda. Factors that influenced its success included: collaboration among different stakeholders through knowledge sharing; support from the local government, both in terms of environmental awareness and funding; and the increasing public interest in environmental issues (Taylor and Lassa, 2015[37]). The project has been successful in creating environmental sensitivity in the city and an increased fiscal capacity. However, there is no measurable evidence as to the reduction of vulnerability, and environmental spending is still modest (Lassa and Nugraha, 2015[36]). The sustainability and long-term success of this type of programme will rely on the incentives provided once outside stakeholders leave the project.

Upgrading of informal settlements builds resilience in intermediary cities in Asia

The upgrading of informal settlements has been the basis for urban resilience across many cities in Asia. Many examples come from initiatives by national federations of slum/shack dwellers, such as the National Slum Dwellers Federation (NSDF) in India and its sister organisation, Mahila Milan, and the Homeless People's Federation of the Philippines. Although the upgrading experiences described below are very different, what they have in common is support from grassroots organisations. These organisations have formed across each nation, typically as savings groups, and have built links with local government that often develop into partnerships.

Community organisation-based initiatives in Thailand and the Philippines

Large numbers of households in intermediary cities in Thailand have benefited from slum upgrading programmes led by local community organisations. A national government organisation, the Community Organisations Development Institute (CODI), funds and supports community organisations formed in Thailand by the inhabitants of informal settlements to plan and upgrade their settlement. For instance, actions by a programme called the Baan Mankong ("secure tenure") includes negotiating with the landowner to sell or lease the land to the inhabitants. If this not possible, support is also available for finding alternative sites. The importance of this example for this analysis is not only the high quality of the upgrading process (and its contribution to climate-change resilience), but also that many of the 100 000 plus households who have benefitted from the programme are in intermediary cities (Boonyabancha and Kerr, 2018[38]). It shows how the scale of such interventions is greatly increasing via work with hundreds of local partners, community organisations and local governments.

Many recipients of support from the Asian Coalition for Community Action (ACCA) for community-led upgrading are also intermediary cities. This programme, working in 215 cities in 19 nations, has catalysed community-driven upgrading in more than 1 800 small communities and more than 100 larger housing initiatives. In each city, community organisations choose what to do with their modest external funding, take action with it and bring city government officials to see what they have done. This often leads to a joint working group at the city level to provide a platform for community networks, city governments, civic groups, NGOs and academics to plan and manage the upgrading. In many of the cities, new local funds have been developed, jointly managed with the local government.

Another example of upgrading in intermediary cities is the Homeless Peoples' Federation of the Philippines. The programme has chapters in 33 cities throughout the country (ACHR/ACCA, 2014[39]). It has received support from ACCA, mostly for community-led upgrading of informal settlements, and most of the 24 cities or municipalities where the initiatives were located were intermediary cities (ACHR/ACCA, 2014[39]). For instance, Mandaue, a city of 362 654 inhabitants in the 2015 census, there is a long history of collaboration between community organisations (the Homeless People's Federation of the Philippines and the citywide urban poor alliance), a progressive mayor and a supportive local government. This partnership developed a large on-site upgrading project where 1 600 families got tenure and support for building new homes. It is also relocated 1 200 families living in dangerous areas around the city.

A multilevel approach in Indonesia

The Indonesian city of Surakarta (also known as Solo) is located in Central Java Province. It sits next to the Bengawan, an important river on the island. It is home to 600 000 inhabitants and has strategic political and economic importance in the region. The city features a tropical monsoon climate, with a lengthy wet season from October through June and consistent temperatures year round.

Along the Bengawan riverbank, large numbers of low-income populations live in informal neighbourhoods. Due to their closeness to the river and the fragility of the buildings, the frequent inundations impact them severely. Moreover, as they build their homes on public land and most lack land tenure, it is difficult for these informal dwellers to get an identity card, which is a requirement for accessing basic services such as education or health (Taylor, 2015[40]). These communities fall into a cycle of vulnerability, as they cannot afford to live in a safer place, but also cannot access basic services to improve their situation.

Following a number of climate disasters, the local government in Sukarata implemented a series of climate actions. In November 2007, seasonal rain caused flooding that led to severe infrastructure damage, particularly in the communities of the riverbank. The local government decided to pair emergency relief with a relocation policy that attempted to reduce the long-term vulnerability of the informal dwellers. It offered to relocate the riverbank communities to new land, offering cash grants for resettlement and expediting tenure for new plots of land (Weru et al., 2018[41]). They also launched a policy to distribute ID cards for those without them, allowing the recipients to access basic services. The programme proved to be quite successful, as interviews with the relocated population show that nearly 1 000 households were relocated and that families felt satisfied with the outcome. Nevertheless, those dwellers that did not have land tenure deemed the cash grant too low and did not resettle to a safer area (Taylor, 2015[40]) .

The initiative took a multilevel approach. It engaged different levels of administration and formed *Kelompok Kerja* (working groups), which proved to be essential to connect different stakeholders and make sure that the services were provided. The initiative also covered the costs of relocation of migrants from outside the city instead of focusing solely on Surakarta's citizens (Taylor, 2015[40]). This allowed the migrants to access basic services that would not have been available in other circumstances.

In 2009, a new initiative called Solo Kota Kita was born with the goal to "increase awareness of urban issues so residents can strengthen their voice in participatory budgeting (*musrenbang*)" (Solo Kota Kita, n.d.[42]). This initiative surveys and maps all of the neighbourhoods in Solo, including those along the riverbank. Citizens can then access detailed atlases of the city that include information on urban development, economic profile and the availability of public services. In this way, there is a better connection between the needs of citizens and investment in urban development by the local government.

International city networks play a key role in supporting local climate action

The Asian Cities Climate Change Resilience Network (ACCCRN)

The ACCCRN has been one of the leading initiatives on climate change in urban areas across Asia. The work of this network has included detailed studies of cities involved in climate-change adaptation, resilience-building initiatives and engagement with government to assess vulnerabilities and implement mitigation strategies. It began its work in 2008 in ten cities, and in 2012 support was extended to 46 more cities, most of them intermediary cities, with the involvement of Local Governments for Sustainability (ICLEI), an international NGO that promotes sustainable development. A working paper by Scott and Archer (2017[43]) drew on key lessons learned from 15 city resilience strategies from India, Bangladesh, Indonesia and the Philippines. In this sample, four of the 15 cities had populations of 1 million plus; eight had 50 000 to 1 million inhabitants; and three had fewer than 50 000. ACCCRN-India also worked in cities of different sizes, including working with Gorakhpur Environmental Action Group, a local NGO, to support resilience strategies in Gorakhpur, Basirhat, Saharsa and Jorhat.

Key findings from these studies highlight:

- the importance of engaging all key actors and institutions. One of the critiques of resilience thinking is that it does not pay sufficient attention to "people, power and politics'".
- the different ways in which planning processes include or exclude actors and institutions (Bahadur and Tanner, 2014[44]). This includes community and civil society groups selected in line with local hazards (e.g. communities susceptible to landslides) and forms of political organisation (e.g. trade unions). The inclusion of community groups in the early stages of resilience planning, as well as during the implementation phases, is critical.
- achieving scale. So far, 46 cities have benefited from the ICLEI–ACCCRN process and the various forms of support that accompany it. However, countless other cities remain in need of similar forms of support, and questions remain around how best to extend this. As such, it is worth reflecting on ways in which this initiative achieved scale and how it could be scaled up further in future.

The ICLEI–ACCCRN process raises questions with regard to embeddedness and transformation in climate actions. What steps need to be taken to ensure that resilience strategies, and the processes behind them, become genuinely embedded in the cities in ways that are transformational, reshaping local structures of political economy? To what extent can the process inform and change the way the city operates over decades to ensure that resilience-building initiatives evolve as the nature of climate threats changes and the city itself evolves?

How intermediary cities in Africa are responding to climate change?

Africa has one of the world's fastest growing urban population. In 2020, 44% of Africa's population was living in urban areas, and 63% of the urban population lived in cities with fewer than 1 million inhabitants (Figure 4.3). In contrast to Latin America and the Caribbean, where city governments have taken action (sometimes supported by the national government), Africa's experiences in local climate action are mostly the result of initiatives supported by international agencies.

Studies on intermediary cities in Africa and their climate vulnerabilities remain low, as in other developing regions. Ironically, there is now far less literature on intermediary cities and their role in supporting agricultural and rural development than there was during the 1980s (Rondinelli, 1982[45]), when there was a considerable amount of literature.

Although climate policies across intermediary cities remain isolated in the region, the case studies presented in this section show the different paths that can be followed. From national initiatives that look at the urban system to local governments that work on developing long-term climate objectives, these examples show the importance of local leadership and multilevel actions. As in the case of Asia, both informal settlement upgrading and international partnerships are key for triggering climate action.

Table 4.3 summarises the case studies presented in this section and highlights some of the key climate policies across intermediary cities in Africa.

Figure 4.3. Urban population in Africa (1980-2035) and expected urban population growth (2020-50)

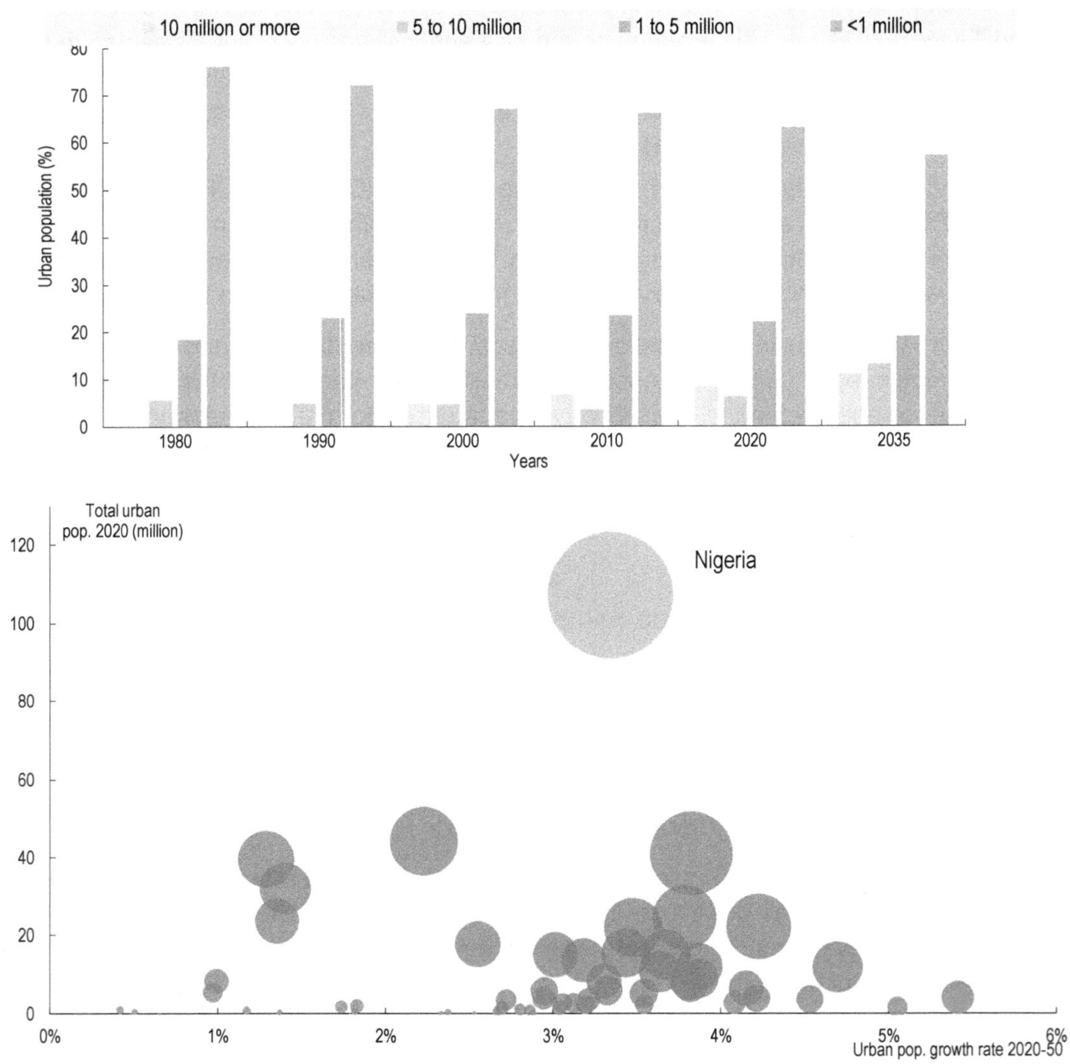

Note: In the bottom figure, the vertical axis shows the total population in urban areas in 2020, while the horizontal axis shows the expected annual growth rate of urban population between 2020 and 2050. The size of the circles represents the expected urban population in 2050.
Source: UNDESA (2018[2]).

Table 4.3. Climate actions in Africa's intermediary cities

City	Population	Climate threats	Selected climate actions/approaches	Main actors in climate change
Huye, Muhanga, Musanze, Nyagatare, Rubavu and Rusizi (Rwanda)	52 768 (Huye); 50 608 (Muhanga); 47 480 (Nyagartare); 149 209 (Rubavu); 102 082 (Musanze); 63 258 (Rusizi)	Increase in temperatures, intense precipitation, floods, prolonged dry seasons, droughts, desertification	- The six cities were selected as growth poles and a means for alleviating poverty. The cities are integrated into the National Urbanisation Policy (2015) - Rwanda's National Roadmap for Green Secondary City Development (2015): a plan to foster sustainable urban development, reduce urban sprawl and as a means to implement the national economic development plan. - revision of master plans to integrate green growth strategies	national government, international organisations
Kisumu (Kenya)	631 466 (2022, est.)	flooding, river pollution due to inadequate sewerage systems, soil erosion	- Kisumu County Climate Change Bill: providing regulatory frameworks for implementation of local climate actions - Kisumu County Climate Change Fund for local governments - Integrated Development Plan of Kisumu County (2018-22): aims to build local climate resilience through participatory actions - Kisumu Integrated Sustainable Solid Waste Management Project (2017)	county governor, national government
Beira, Nacala, Pemba and Quelimane (Mozambique)	500 000+ (Beira); 230 000 (Quelimane); 350 000 (Nacala); 125 635 (Pemba)	floods, coastal erosion, salinisation of coastal waters, loss in natural protection systems, rising sea levels, storm surges, loss of coastal land and wetlands	- Cities and Climate Change–Pilot Program for Climate Resilience (2014-19) (With World Bank) (Beira). - Mozambique Coastal Cities Adaptation Programme (CCAP) (2014-19) (with USAID), (Pemba, Quelimane and Nacala) - Quelimane Limpa (2018) - Quelimane Agricola (2015) - Quelimane- Milan city partnership	local government, international organisations, civil society, local communities, local NGOs
Durban (South Africa)	3.7 million	rising temperatures, urban heat island effects, droughts, floods and rainstorms, sea-level rise	- dedicated climate office across different levels of government (climate champions) and political climate change committee - mainstreaming climate change across rural, urban and peri-urban areas of the province - establishing technical task team for climate change - established Climate Action Plan (2019)	eTheckwini Municipality Climate Change Committee (EMCCC) and the Durban Climate Change Strategy (DCCS) Technical Task Team (TTT) headed by the mayor, mayor, provincial government
Karonga (Malawi)	63 000 (2018)	floods and droughts	- large challenges in establishing climate actions: low local capacity and absence of city government	rural council
Ambo Town (Ethiopia)	80 000 (2016)	floods, water stress, urban heat islands, winds, dust storms	- lack of local action plans by local government - ad-hoc climate adaptation strategies are adopted by local households such as harvesting rain water, maximising drainage systems, building flooding passages, etc.	urban households

Source: Author's elaboration.

Lack of funding and capacity hinders climate-resilience action in some cities in Africa

Although there is little documentation on government-led climate policies in intermediary cities in Africa, what is documented is the lack of capacity and funding for all aspects of development, including climate resilience. This includes lack of access to climate funds, as illustrated in the cases of Karonga, Malawi, and Ambo, Ethiopia.

Karonga (Malawi)

The city of Karonga is an example of the multidimensional challenges that local governments face in their capacities to address climate change. Karonga, with an estimated 63 000 inhabitants in 2018, faces large climate risks such as floods, droughts and earthquakes. Between 2009 and 2016, Karonga experienced floods at least once a year and sometimes more frequently (Manda and Wanda, 2017[46]). These climate risks put a large strain on the town's underdeveloped infrastructure, with poor water and sanitation services, poor solid waste management systems and expanding informal settlements (UN-Habitat, 2020[47]).

Karonga faces large challenges when it comes to managing climate risks. One of the most pertinent issues is that it lacks a local city administration or government. Despite its fast growth, the city has been managed by a rural council since the dissolution of its local council in 2009. This is a major problem, as the rural council is inadequate in managing the complex challenges faced by the city, and climate change is likely to exacerbate this (Manda and Wanda, 2017[46]). Premature deaths from indoor air pollution and tuberculosis are already high in Karonga, and frequent extreme climate events such as floods can cause additional health risks and overburden the council's capacities (UN-Habitat, 2020[47]; Manda and Wanda, 2017[46]). Informal settlements, which host the largest share of the city's population, are at particular risk of climate-induced threats.

Ambo (Ethiopia)

Ambo, with a population estimated at 80 000 in 2016, is one of the oldest municipalities in Ethiopia. It is governed by a municipal administration and has had a master plan since 1981 (Ogato et al., 2017[48]; Ogato, 2013[49]). Ambo is surrounded by rivers and serves as an important hub for transportation, administration and commerce for the zonal-level administration in the Oromia region (UN-Habitat, 2008[50]); see (OECD/PSI, 2020[51]) for institutional mapping of Ethiopia.

Ambo has seen increasing climate risks over the last decades. Disasters have included urban flooding, water stress, Urban Heat Island effect (increased urban heat), wind storms and dust storms (Ogato et al., 2017[48]). These climate shocks damage crops and infrastructure, including interrupting electricity supply, and also lead to soil erosion and an overall loss in economic activities while increasing public health risks (Ogato et al., 2017[48]; Ogato, 2013[49]).

Climate change and fast population growth are putting increasing strains on Ambo's infrastructure and local government capacities. Two factors heavily affect the city's climate resilience: poor land-use planning and management, and very limited capacity of the city authorities to improve in this area while also meeting other municipal responsibilities (Ogato et al., 2017[48]). Moreover, the city largely lacks adequate systems for waste management: half of the households are not equipped with toilet facilities, and rivers are often used as disposal points (UN-Habitat, 2008[50]). Fast population growth is straining Ambo's ability to supply adequate housing and to respond to growing needs (Ogato et al., 2017[48]; Ogato, 2013[49]). This is due to poor municipal financing, caused by low local revenues and an inadequate tax base, as well as limited administrative and human resources. Lack of political continuity is another constraining factor, as frequent changes in leadership reduce the scope for effective management of the city (UN-Habitat, 2008[50]).

Most of the climate action in Ambo has been carried out in uncoordinated initiatives. As highlighted by Ogato et al (2017[48]), households in Ambo are increasingly aware of the climate risks they face and have been adopting short-term adaptation methods to reduce losses resulting from climate change. They are using strategies such as harvesting rainwater during the rainy season, building flooding passages around homes, planting trees and maintaining existing drainage systems. Nonetheless, it is clear that Ambo, like many of the cities presented in this chapter, would highly benefit from more systemised, larger-scale interventions to reduce its climate vulnerabilities. Recommended actions include mainstreaming climate-change resilience in land-use management systems, increasing information on local climate risks and conducting vulnerability assessments (Ogato et al., 2017[48]).

Some national governments in Africa recognise the need to build resilient urban systems

Rwanda

Rwanda's strategy for building resilience across intermediary cities stands out since it is mainly driven by the national government. Rwanda has shown a strong commitment to building climate resilience and pursuing green growth, as demonstrated across its various national development and poverty reduction strategies. These include Rwanda's Green Growth and Climate Resilience Strategy (2011[52]), which aims to mainstream climate adaptation and mitigation across various sectors of development planning (Price, 2019[53]). The national government has also committed to foster sustainable urbanisation, alleviate poverty and facilitate economic transformation. It selected six intermediary cities – Huye, Muhanga, Musanze, Nyagatare, Rubavu and Rusizi – as engines of growth. The cities were chosen to support Kigali's dynamism based on their locations, growth trends, economic potential and links to rural areas.

Resilience is at the core of Rwanda's development strategy for intermediary cities. This is explicitly articulated in Rwanda's National Urbanisation Policy (2015[54]) and Urbanisation and Rural Settlement Sector Strategic Plan (2018[55]), both of which are aligned with Rwanda's Green Growth and Climate Resilience Strategy (2011[52]). Moreover, Rwanda has developed a National Roadmap for Green Secondary City Development (2015[56]), established in partnership with the Global Green Growth Institute (GGGI). This initiative was developed to complement the city master plans, with the objective of fostering sustainable urban development and reducing the scope for urban sprawl, congestion and informal settlement growth across the six selected intermediary cities (Price, 2019[53]). The roadmap was also developed as means to implement Rwanda's National Development Plan and Economic Development and Poverty Reduction Strategy 2 (EDPRS2) (2013[57]). The roadmap, funded by the Green Climate Fund, aims to consolidate land-use planning in the six cities (Price, 2019[53]). GGGI is also supporting the six cities in revising their master plans to adapt to their fast growth and to integrate green growth strategies (Price, 2019[53]; Gubic and Baloi, 2019[58]).

Rwanda has built strong partnerships with international organisations and made a large commitment to international climate actions. The GGGI has been a key partner to Rwanda in supporting the development of green growth programmes and as a key implementation agency of Rwanda's Climate Resilient Green Cities. This has provided support for private and public investment in green sectors.

In other African cities, local government takes the lead on long-term climate objectives

Kisumu (Kenya)

Kisumu, located near Lake Victoria, is the third largest city in Kenya. It is the regional capital of Kisumu County and a hub for industrial, commercial, administrative and transportation services, as well as serving as an internal port for the region (UN-Habitat, 2006[59]). Kisumu is a fast-growing urban centre; its 2009 population of 450 626 is expected to exceed 630 000 in 2022 (County Government of Kisumu, 2017[60]). Kisumu's economy mainly relies on agriculture, fisheries and livestock, which account for nearly half of household incomes. Other main sources tend to be wage employment in informal sectors.

Kisumu faces the compounded effects of climate change, while its changing socio-economic dynamic is straining local resources. Kisumu is highly prone to flooding due to its closeness to the lake. Lack of adequate sewerage or water management systems is polluting the lake , while surrounding areas face soil erosion and depletion of natural resources, mainly caused by increasing economic activities (UN-Habitat, 2006[59]). Only 25% of the waste in Kisumu County is collected for disposal, and solid waste management remains a large challenge (County Government of Kisumu, 2017[60]). At the same time, Kisumu has undergone large changes in agricultural practices, especially in surrounding rural areas. Farmers are increasingly practice agricultural activities closer to the lake, while the development of new industries in these areas is causing major environmental degradation in both the lake and surrounding rivers. The effects of climate change compounded with low socio-economic development are causing losses in the local economy and livelihoods.

The prevalence of the informal sector in Kisumu also heightens the vulnerability of its residents, with a large number of urban dwellers and rural migrants depending on the income and contribution of small groups of wage earners. This reduces the scope for local revenue mobilisation. Furthermore, a striking 60% of the residents of Kisumu city live in slums, with poor access to infrastructure and basic services (UN-Habitat, 2006[59]), leaving them highly vulnerable to climate threats and related public health issues.

Local authorities in Kisumu have sought to address the climate-induced threats facing the city in various ways. In 2020, The Kisumu County Climate Change Bill was established under the supervision of the Climate Change Council. The bill aims to provide a regulatory framework and implementation measures for local climate actions and reduction in GHG emissions (Republic of Kenya, 2020[61]). Under the bill, local governments in Kisumu County are required to mainstream climate adaptation and mitigation across different sectors, co-ordinate and finance local climate actions, disseminate climate information and preparedness strategies to the public, etc. Under the bill, financing for local climate actions is to take place through the pre-existing Kisumu County Change Fund (Republic of Kenya, 2020[61]).

Another effort towards mainstreaming climate adaptation and mitigation is the second Integrated Development Plan of Kisumu County (2018-2022) (2018[62]). The plan addresses important environmental and climate issues, such as reducing GHG emissions, climate adaptation, food and water security, and energy use. The plan aims to build resilience through participatory climate actions. Furthermore, the Kisumu Integrated Sustainable Solid Waste Management Project, launched in 2017, aims to raise awareness and improve local waste management. The initiative sought to build private-public partnerships and to support local entrepreneurship and business in finding solutions for solid waste management systems through capacity building and financing opportunities (County Government of Kisumu, 2017[60]) .

Lack of effective financing is one of the main challenges faced by Kisumu. The city remains highly dependent on national government revenue transfers, which account for 53% of its total revenue, with 35% coming from development partners (conditional grants) and 20% from locally collected revenue. Although Kisumu has access to programmes established by the national government to respond to disaster events. national transfers are insufficient and Kisumu's local government remains at the forefront of managing the short- and long-term effects of climate threats.

Overall, underdevelopment is the main factor limiting Kisumu's resilience. The county's long-term strategy relies on enhancing the overall development of the city by fostering productive economic activities as a precondition to mitigating climate effects, and further developing its own sources of financing. However, this cannot be done by local government alone. The support of the national government and development partners is paramount to achieve this objective.

Partnerships are important for building resilience across intermediary cities in Africa

ICLEI Africa

Some intermediary cities in Africa are part of initiatives and studies led by international organisations. ICLEI Africa has several programmes supporting local authorities in improving their adaptation and mitigation capacity, as well as disaster risk reduction. Many of these local authorities are in intermediary cities. The programmes include support for the Africa Water and Sanitation Local Authorities network, developing sustainable and equitable water and sanitation practices, and developing a roadmap for local authorities to move towards 100% renewables. Additional programmes include the AfriAlliance, which helps to prepare for the impact of climate change on water resources, and the Fortitude Initiative, enabling cities, towns and municipalities to co-produce and implement DRR strategies at the local level (ICLEI, n.d.[63]).

Beira, Nacala, Pemba and Quelimane (Mozambique)

Mozambique's coastal cities are at high risk of climate-induced threats. The country is highly vulnerable to sea-level rise and flooding; in 2019, Cyclone Idai killed 417 people in Mozambique alone (BBC, 2019[64]). The cities of Beira, Quelimane, Nacala and Pemba are among the largest coastal intermediary cities in Mozambique. They are fast-growing urban centres with over half a million inhabitants in Beira, and around 304 000 in Quelimane and 350 000 in Nacala (World Bank, 2020[65]). Pemba's population was estimated at 125 635 in 2007, with average annual growth of 3.66% (World Bank and Muzima, 2007).

Mozambique's intermediary cities have important functions in their surroundings and in national economic activities. Beira is an important port city that connects its rural hinterland, and neighbouring land-locked countries like Zimbabwe and Zambia, to the Indian Ocean (World Bank, 2020[65]). Similarly, Nacala and Quelimane are important destinations of rural-to-urban migration, which puts additional strains on their infrastructure, housing and urban services. Migration and population growth are leading to an expansion of informal settlements across the three cities (World Bank, 2020[65]).

Mozambique's coastal cities have low capacities to adapt to the high risk of climate threats. They face severe risks of flooding, coastal erosion, salinisation of coastal waters and losses in natural protection systems (World Bank, 2020[65]). The flood risk in Quelimane has been worsening over the past years, mainly due to an increasing loss of mangroves that reduces its natural protection system against flooding and salinisation of coastal waters (World Bank, 2020[65]; Araújo, 2021[66]). Beira, which is located near a cyclone-prone area, is highly susceptible to rising sea levels, storm surges and the risk of damage to the city's 3.4-meter seawall (GFDRR, 2011[67]). Rising sea levels will continue to present challenges, including losses of land and coastal wetlands, salinisation of fresh water and displacement of populations (USAID, 2014[68]). These climate risks can overwhelm the cities' infrastructure and transportation systems, increasing the loss of livelihoods.

Local governments across the three cities have implemented climate actions with the technical and financing support of international organisations. Projects like Cities and Climate Change–Pilot Programme for Climate Resilience (2012-19) with the World Bank (USAID, 2014[68]), and Mozambique Coastal Cities Adaptation Programme (CCAP, 2014-19) with USAID (2013[69]), are particularly pertinent as they aim to build resilience in these vulnerable coastal intermediary cities. The CCAP was a USD 14.9 million project implemented across Pemba, Quelimane and Nacala to pilot strategies for climate resilience. The project aimed to strengthen municipal capacities to mainstream climate adaptation across local planning processes and to supporting implementation of climate resilience strategies. It was implemented across selected informal settlements in collaboration with local governments, civil society, urban planners, academia and community leaders. The project also identified key priorities for building resilience, including enhancing policies for land-use planning, development of green infrastructure, vulnerability mapping, provision of improved sanitation and resilient housing, and improved municipal management (USAID, 2014[68]).

The partnership with the CCAP project facilitated a series of outcomes in Quelimane, Pemba and Nacala. it supported local governments in Quelimane and Pemba to develop medium-term Local Adaptation Plans. The plans integrated local vulnerability mapping and were incorporated into the local land registrations systems. They also helped to build partnerships and technical exchanges with partner cities such as Durban, South Africa, and to revive 13 hectares of mangroves in Quelimane (USAID, 2014[68]).

Beira's local government was one of the main implementing agents of the Cities and Climate Change pilot project. The USD 120 million project, financed by the World Bank's International Development Credit system, supported climate actions including rehabilitating a stormwater drainage system, (re)construction of drainage canals and construction of flood control stations and a water retention basin (World Bank, 2018[70]). The new drainage systems helped reduce the city's flooding risk by 70% (World Bank, 2018[70]). The Cities and Climate project also financed a nature-based solution to building climate resilience through Green Urban Infrastructure (GUI), which was used to rehabilitate the Chiveve River and enhance its drainage capacity. In the intervention, implemented by the government of Mozambique, GUI was used to enhance the environment of areas surrounding the river and create a green space for recreation, such as the building of a botanical garden, in a highly dense urban area (World Bank, 2020[65]).

The city of Quelimane has also been active in implementing climate actions through partnerships with international organisations and city-to-city partnerships. The municipality has taken action to reduce its climate vulnerability through investment in infrastructure such as roads, drainage systems and health and market facilities (Araújo, 2021[66]). Quelimane nurtured important partnerships to improve its local efforts and access international funding systems.

Quelimane Agricola and *Quelimane Limpa* are projects established in partnership with the city of Milan, Italy, and selected NGOs (such as Mani Tese). Quelimane Agricola, a three-year programme established in 2018, aimed to improve food safety, strengthen local agri-food systems, reduce food waste and soil degradation, and improve the resilience of local value chains (Araújo, 2021[66]). The project deployed strategies for improving the resilience of farming systems and increasing local profits, including training schemes; it also installed irrigation systems and promoted the use of mobile phones (Araújo, 2021[66]). Quelimane Limpa was launched in 2015 and ran for more than two years, with the objective of improving solid waste management and promoting sustainable farming and natural resource management (Plataforma, 2020[71]). The local government worked collaboratively with local populations and civil society, which led to the creation of microenterprises engaged in waste management, recycling and the development of a composting centre for the use of local farmers (Araújo, 2021[66]).

Upgrading of informal settlements can drive climate action in intermediary cities in Africa

As in Latin America and Asia, many initiatives to upgrade informal settlements are helping to build resilience to climate change across African cities. The number of intermediary cities that have federations of savings groups in informal settlements is of particular interest. These savings groups are taking action to address needs and reduce climate-related risks. The initiatives are based on community-managed savings groups (most savers and savings managers are women) that come together to form federations. These federations can work at a large scale to negotiate support from local governments and are members of Slum/Shack Dwellers International (SDI) (SDI, n.d.[72]). There are now 15 countries and hundreds of cities across Africa (and many others across Asia and Latin America) where the federations are active in upgrading informal settlements, fighting eviction threats and negotiating safe land sites for housing. Box 4.1 presents some examples of upgrading initiatives by slum/shack dweller federations that are seeking change at city level, including partnerships with local authorities.

Box 4.1. Upgrading initiatives across Africa

Zimbabwe: Despite a difficult and uncertain political environment, the Zimbabwe Homeless People's Federation has member savings groups in 71 cities and towns and many community-driven upgrading initiatives. The Federation is also working with the government to propose projects for enhancing the participation of the urban poor in city planning (Chitekwe-Biti et al., 2012[73]).

Tanzania: The Tanzanian Homeless People's Federation is currently operating in eight cities. Using savings as a core strategy, the federation has initiated enumeration exercises (a process of conducting household census in cooperation with local community in informal settlements (VPUU, 2019[74]) exchange programmes and upgrading projects, and has begun to broker deals with local governments (SDI, n.d.[72]).

South Africa: The South African Federation of the Urban Poor (FEDUP) has savings groups throughout South Africa's nine provinces and in many of its cities. Partnering with the Informal Settlement Network, FEDUP has memoranda of understanding with municipalities across South Africa. Development finance and social support for land, infrastructure and housing are managed jointly by the Community Organisation Resource Centre and the uTshani Fund (SDI, n.d.[72]).

Sierra Leone: The Sierra Leone Federation of the Urban and Rural Poor is present in five cities (SDI, n.d.[72]).

Namibia: The Shack Dwellers Federation of Namibia has member urban and rural saving groups throughout the country (SDI, n.d.[72]).

A particularly interesting upgrading initiative took place in Gobabis, Namibia. The upgrading, in Freedom Square, an informal settlement with 4 173 inhabitants on a 60-hectare site, involved the collaboration of the settlement's inhabitants with the local government and demonstrated what this approach can achieve. The upgrading cost about one-fifth as much as conventional approaches. It did not reach the whole settlement with full services, but some degree of coverage in basic services was attained, along with secure tenure. Other very positive benefits included the empowerment of those who took part, the technical skills acquired, social organising and engagement with municipal authorities. Another advantage was the consensus that was generated for the plans necessary for reblocking, or realignment of structures to allow basic services to be delivered, which can be very contentious.

Valuable lessons are provided by the upgrading of Freedom Square, along with other initiatives by the Shack Dwellers Federation of Namibia, working with the Namibian Housing Action Group and municipal authorities. What is interesting is not only what was done, but also how it was done and financed. The federation drew on methods developed and used by federations that are affiliates of Shack/Slum Dwellers International (SDI). For instance, community-driven enumerations (i.e. collecting household data) of informal settlements provide groups within the settlement the data needed to prepare plans for upgrading (and reblocking where needed). Then these are integrated into a settlement-wide map. In Freedom Square, the reblocking plan meant that most residents had to move, but all were accommodated on the site. Another benefit was that the initiative strengthened community organisations. But while Freedom Square received national government support, there is still insufficient state support for bottom-up initiatives in general.

The provision of local funds can also enhance the resilience of low-income households by supporting them to upgrade, acquire or build better housing. One example is the Akiba Mashinani Trust (AMT), which provides funding and financial services to the Kenyan Homeless People's Federation (Muungano wa Wanavijiji), a federation of autonomous savings groups with more than 60 000 members from informal settlements across Kenya. AMT provides a range of financial services: support for savings groups; livelihoods loans; consumption loans (to cover expenses such as school fees, medical costs and home improvements); and community project loans (for Muungano's social housing, sanitation and basic infrastructure projects). These loans finance in situ upgrading and house improvements, land acquisition for housing development and greenfield housing development, all of which contribute to housing and neighbourhood resilience. As of December 2016, 6 822 Muungano members had received financing from AMT for land and housing (Weru et al., 2018[41]).

Lessons from larger cities can help intermediary cities to identify future opportunities

Climate actions in larger cities can serve as lessons for intermediary cities in Africa. An example is the coastal city of Durban, South Africa, which was among the first cities to see the importance of city governments addressing climate-change issues and to develop appropriate policies for adaptation and mitigation. Durban, with 3.7 million inhabitants, faces climate risks including rising sea levels, rising temperatures, floods, droughts and heavy rainstorms. It is a city very well served for documentation contributed by both city government and experts outside local government. This includes a very detailed time-line identifying factors that helped or hindered the development of Durban's climate-change strategy (Roberts et al., 2016[75]). The city government's commitment to supporting locally rooted solutions meant that it withdrew from the 100 Resilient Cities initiative (Roberts et al., 2020[76]).

An assessment of city-based climate change policies and practices in a range of cities noted that Durban is a city from which we can learn on a number of fronts (Barlett and Satterthwaite, 2016[77]), including local political changes that brought more attention to climate-change issues and the policies adopted. Durban's climate-change strategy included:

- the necessary tools;
- identification of different options and their benefits and costs;
- integration of concern for climate change across urban, peri-urban and rural areas within the local government boundaries;
- assessment of the contributions of ecosystem services to adaptation, mitigation and disaster risk reduction and measures needed to protect and enhance these;
- attention to possibilities for enhancing employment through development of a green economy;
- the demonstration that local innovators, not national policies or international initiatives, are providing the knowledge on what needs to be done;
- the success of the environment sector in getting the attention of other sectors within city government by bringing the issues of job creation (within the green economy) and improved living conditions into climate change policy discussions;
- recognition and encouragement of local innovation and honesty around what is not yet achieved;
- the importance of climate change champions (both individual and institutional) at the local level (including the mayor) for facilitating key international networking opportunities. This strengthened support for the Durban Adaptation Charter, through which local governments around the world commit to local climate action that will assist their communities to respond to and cope with climate-change risks. It also helped to secure funding to operationalise the process.

The experience in Durban is informative about the focuses that best build support for climate-change adaptation within local governments, as well as about which measures work and where lessons can be drawn. It should be noted, however, that while Durban's government developed a capacity to act on climate-change adaptation and mitigation, it has other pressing development priorities that can make the needed commitment to adaptation and mitigation difficult (Roberts, 2008[78]; Roberts, 2010[79]; Roberts et al., 2012[80]; Cartwright et al., 2013[81]; Roberts and O'Donoghue, 2013[82]).

Entry points for climate action across intermediary cities

Intermediary cities in developing countries can start building resilience to climate change in two important ways: informal settlement upgrading and disaster risk reduction. Among the policy actions that help cities to build resilience, these two deserve special attention since they can also achieve other development objectives. These approaches are not only local but also have a lot in common when it comes to the issues they seek to address and the need for local competence and capacity to do so. However, the upgrading of settlements and DRR are often managed separately since they often fall under different departments that are not used to working with each other and that may see each other as competitors for scarce municipal funds. In extreme examples, cities with upgrading schemes can also have city infrastructure departments that are still bulldozing informal settlements. The following sections highlight the relevance of DRR and informal settlement upgrading for climate policies, as well as their overlapping objectives and how they help reduce climate risks among vulnerable populations (Figure 4.4).

Figure 4.4. Entry points for climate action and how they overlap

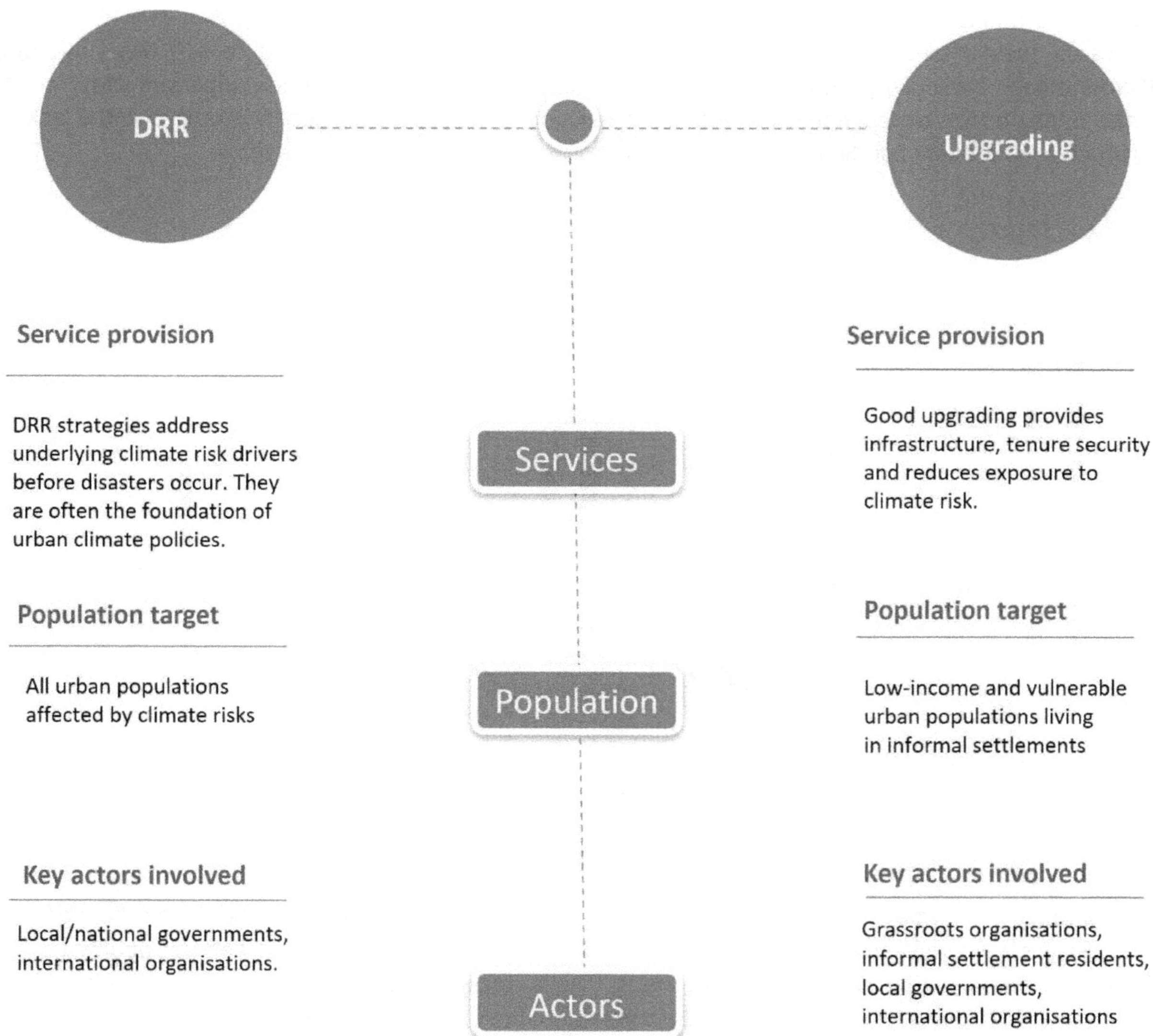

Source: Author's elaboration.

Building climate-change resilience via upgrading and relocation of informal settlements

Informal settlement upgrading programmes are key for reducing climate impacts. Yet they are often not considered to be climate policies. Upgrading projects in informal settlements have great importance because, if done well, they can reach many vulnerable groups and address risks that climate change would exacerbate. This is recognised by the International Panel on Climate Change (IPCC). Its list of risk-reducing infrastructure and services in relation to climate change is remarkably similar to the risks addressed by the upgrading of informal settlements. The IPCC's definition of risk-reducing infrastructure includes access to piped water that is safe, sufficient and affordable; good-quality sanitation and electricity; all-weather access roads; storm and surface drainage; street lighting; and risk-reducing services (including hospitals/health care, emergency services, road traffic management and the rule of law) (Revi et al., 2014[1]).

Hundreds of millions of urban dwellers live in informal settlements that have little if any of the risk-reducing infrastructure and services mentioned above. More than half the population of many cities lives in such settlements, most of which are at high risk from the impacts of climate change (Figure 4.5). Many informal settlements face particularly high risks from floods and landslides as they are on dangerous sites, which are also often chosen because there is less risk of eviction. Most have poor-quality buildings and a lack of infrastructure to prevent flooding, withstand heavy storms and cope with heat waves.

Figure 4.5. Countries with the highest percentage of urban population living in informal settlements (2018)

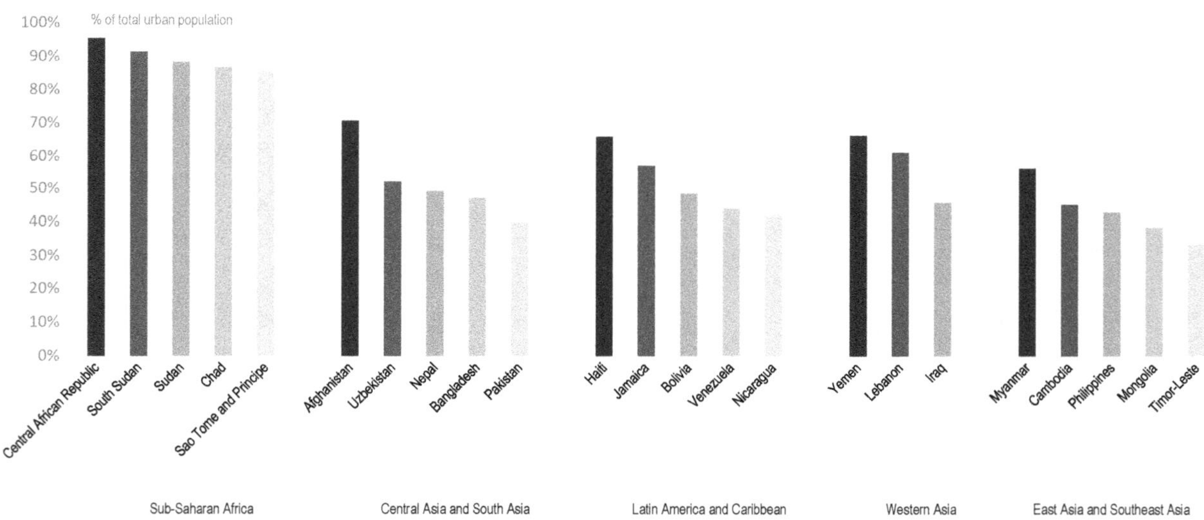

Source: UN-Habitat (2020[83]).

The upgrading of informal settlements is a key component of building local resilience. This is recognised by the IPCC's Fifth Assessment, which describes the importance of informal settlement upgrading for reducing extreme weather risks in high-risk areas. The assessment describes how it has become more common for local governments to work with community-based organisations in upgrading homes and settlements in DRR (UNDRR, 2009[84]; IFRC, 2010[85]), and the ways in which community-based climate adaptation is building on these experiences and capacities (Archer and Boonyabancha, 2011[86]). In growing numbers of cities in Latin America, Asia and Africa, informal settlement upgrading is increasingly recognised as a potential tool to reduce risks and vulnerabilities to climate threats. It is considered more effective when supported by local governments and civil defence response agencies (Archer and Boonyabancha, 2011[86]; Carcellar, Co and Hipolito, 2011[87]; Boonyabancha, 2005[88]).

The tendency for informal settlements to take shape on high-risk or dangerous sites calls for effective upgrading programmes. Informal settlements are often located on dangerous sites, including those at high risk of flooding or landslides, because these sites tend to be cheaper and often well located with regard to labour markets and services. In many cases, upgrading can greatly reduce risks, including climate-change-related risks, for instance through installing storm and surface drainage systems.

"Good" upgrading can be seen as a community-based adaptation strategy because it identifies and addresses risks related to climate change, usually with government support and often with tenure provided to residents. The reason for stressing "good" upgrading is that many upgrading schemes have serious deficiencies or limitations. There are large differences in what upgrading provides, what it costs per house served, who implements it, who pays for it and the extent to which it engages the population (and serves their needs). A review of informal settlements and upgrading by Satterthwaite et al. (2020[89]) notes that upgrading can vary from provision of basic infrastructure, such as public water services, to full supply of services and facilities. In some cases, the upgrading process can include income-generating activities, provision of land tenure for the inhabitants and support for improvement of settlements (Satterthwaite et al., 2020[89]). Where upgrading works well, it provides or improves all of the IPCC's risk-reducing infrastructure and services at household and community level and supports house improvement.

Upgrading projects can provide the foundation for resilience to climate change at household and community scale. Since upgrading schemes are generally focused on informal settlements, they also address the needs of low-income and vulnerable populations. Good upgrading schemes need to remove multiple risks (e.g. violence, unemployment, pollution, disease, etc). Upgrading schemes differ by region and are driven by different stakeholders. Most of the time, such initiatives focus on improving the quality of housing, which includes providing the risk-reducing infrastructure and services mentioned above. Examples from Asia highlight experiences of upgrading where grassroots organisations worked with local governments, and sometimes with national governments. Experiences in Africa are similar to a certain extent when upgrading has been driven by grassroots organisations and has sought the engagement and support of local governments.

Where upgrading is not possible, relocation can be an effective response to climate change

Residents of informal settlements usually prefer In situ upgrading, but what is to be done for sites where this is not possible? Relocation is often an alternative response. There is a long history of relocation moving residents to sites that are far from the city's labour markets, with inadequate public services (Buckley et al., 2016[90]). Nonetheless, there are now many examples of relocation programmes where the people being relocated helped to decide on the new site and its development. In Thailand, for instance, the Community Organisations Development Institute's secure tenure programme, described above, funded community organisations to negotiate to buy or lease the land they were on and, if this was not possible, CODI supported them to find a new site on which to develop their homes. In some intermediary cities in the Philippines, the Philippines Homeless People's Federation has worked with progressive mayors to find good relocation sites for those living on dangerous sites. In the city of Solo in Indonesia, funding was available to those living on dangerous sites to find new sites that they chose (Taylor, 2015[40]).

Examples from intermediary cities in Latin America can provide lessons for effective and participatory relocation strategies. City governments in Manizales, Colombia, and Rosario and Santa Fe, Argentina, developed programmes to work with local communities living in at-risk areas in order to generate appropriate solutions, including relocation. In Manizales, relocation of populations from at-risk areas has been taking place for more than 30 years using a variety of approaches, including in situ relocation. In many cases, this type of programme is developed in co-ordination with the national government. An internal report made for the city of Santa Fe summarises the results of 20 interviews with relocated families, from six different initiatives managed by different agencies or organisations, to capture their perceptions of the relocation process. In general, interviewees viewed the processes positively, highlighting safety, access to services and infrastructure, and the possibility to continue improving their houses. Depending on the programme, they pointed to aspects that could be improved, such as quality of construction, size, follow-up, participation and communication. Many of these recommendations have been included in more recent relocation programmes managed directly by the city, and as part of the country's Integrated Urban Programmes (*Programas urbanos integrales*). It is important to highlight that most examples of relocation programmes where the government worked with residents are from intermediary cities, where finding well-located sites is perhaps easier. Most examples also took place in cities with elected mayors who supported this.

The relevance of disaster risk reduction to city climate-change policies

Disaster risk reduction is an important element of climate-change policies. The IPCC's most recent assessment contains detailed coverage of DRR and its contribution to climate-change adaptation in urban areas. The assessment highlights the increased vulnerability and exposure to climate risks of growing urban populations, especially in low- and middle-income countries. This is seen in the rising number of localised disasters and extreme weather events across some urban areas (Revi et al., 2014[1]). Such events highlight the need for climate-change adaptation, and they have helped citizens and local governments gain awareness of the climate risks and vulnerabilities they face (UNDRR, 2009[84]).

Intermediary cities can draw from the rich and varied literature on DRR to develop local responses to climate-related risks. As described in the city case studies above, there is a large overlap between DRR strategies and climate policies. This can be seen in a review of what 50 cities did in response to the Making Cities Resilient Campaign led by the UN International Strategy for Disaster Reduction (UNISDR): half of the 50 cities studied were intermediary cities in the Global South (Johnson and Blackburn, 2014[31]).

Often local climate actions are drawn from DRR strategies. This is because DRR, resilience and climate-change adaptation all need to respond to underlying risk drivers. A review of DRR efforts that included many intermediary cities in Asia, Africa and Latin America notes that some cities expanded the mandate of existing bodies for emergency preparedness and response to include disaster risk, climate change and resilience (Johnson and Blackburn, 2014[31]). This involved activities such as institutionalising structures for disaster risk management at different city levels, including the lowest level of governance – the *purok* level in the case of San Francisco, Philippines. For Santa Tecla in El Salvador, citizen roundtables were involved in discussions and decision making. In Kisumu (Kenya), Overstrand (South Africa), Batticaloa (Sri Lanka) and Siquirres (Costa Rica), DRR efforts took the form of building technical capacities and partnerships with different stakeholders as well as improving basic infrastructure and control of flood waters. Additional actions include engaging communities to take on responsibilities for managing drains in front of their houses on a weekly basis (Moshi, Tanzania) and upgrading programmes (Kisumu, Moshi).

Across the cities reviewed in this chapter, the integration of a detailed understanding of DRR into urban plans and land-use management was seen as a priority. DRR efforts were seen as process that needed improved co-ordination between different sectors, as well as access to detailed local data on risks and commitment. For instance, having been affected by both civil war and the tsunami of 2004, Batticaloa (Sri Lanka) embraced DRR as an opportunity to reduce risks, alleviate poverty and empower communities, integrating development objectives and resilience.

Enabling environments for climate policies in intermediary cities

Underlying conditions can determine the success of climate policies. A review of examples of intermediary cities with climate-change policies allows us to identify a set of the underlying conditions, or enabling environments, that seem to facilitate the success of policies promoting urban resilience. These conditions have helped to anchor climate-change policies in the local development process and have often contributed to sustaining them in the long term. Figure 4.6 highlights seven broad conditions that have facilitated climate actions across the intermediary cities reviewed.

Figure 4.6. Enabling factors for climate actions in intermediary cities

Source: Author's elaboration.

Well-governed cities and good local governance are key for climate resilience

Well-governed cities and good local governance greatly reduce the impact of climate risks. Well-governed cities are more likely than other cities to have developed climate change policies (World Bank, 2015[91]). Success is highly dependent on the quality and capacity of city government, and often on the support received from higher levels of government. Decentralisation plays a key role in terms of the balance between delegated responsibilities that push for greater autonomy and the obligations acquired and resources allocated to fulfil them. The important role of good decentralisation for climate policies will be further discussed below.

Well-governed cities are usually those that have sufficient planning and implementation capacities and that are accountable to those they serve. Such cities are able to work to increase the share of the population served with risk-reducing infrastructure (all-weather roads, storm and surface drainage, piped water, sanitation, etc.) and services relevant to resilience (including health care, emergency services, policing/rule of law). They are also able to work to increase the proportion of population living in housing in safe locations and near education and employment opportunities (and that also meet health and safety standards). And they can plan for a city that is inclusive and in harmony with its surroundings, with planning for green spaces, use of nature-based solutions, better mobility, community markets, etc. Such planning requires very clear land-use, environmental and DRR policies. The cases covered in this chapter provide examples of how well-governed cities are capable of advancing integrated policies, including climate-change policies, but also examples of how poorly governed cities are not.

A key condition of good governance is putting participatory mechanisms in place so that local residents can be part of the decision-making process. Participation of local residents, and drawing on their knowledge and perceptions to inform policies and actions, are key. Good governance requires accountability, transparency and meaningful participation. Engagement with civil society has been fundamental to the success of most if not all of the city cases described here, and has ensured that policies and working approaches could withstand changes in city administrations. Figure 4.7 illustrates the characteristics and processes that contribute to well-governed cities.

Figure 4.7. Characteristics of well-governed cities

Source: Author's own elaboration.

A sizeable number of cities have developed and sustained participatory budgeting over the years. With varying scope and depth, more than 1 700 local governments in more than 40 countries are implementing participatory budgeting, in which citizens meet to discuss priorities for their neighbourhood or the city as a whole and oversee project implementation (Cabannes, 2014[92]). Reviewing the projects chosen through participatory budgeting shows the priority given to environmental issues and growing support for climate-change adaptation and mitigation (Cabannes, 2021[93]). Given the number of examples, it is likely that a high proportion of these cities are intermediary cities. Of 15 cities or areas chosen in a 2015 study for an in-depth look at the links between participatory budgeting and climate change, only two had more than 1 million inhabitants (Cabannes, 2015[94]).

Grassroot organisations have played a key role in shaping settlement upgrading processes and other city programmes and initiatives for building more resilient homes and neighbourhoods. Alone or with the support of other actors (NGOs, academia) and networks, engaged communities ensure that actions respond to local needs and concerns (UNDRR, 2019[6]), thus shaping how city officials plan and implement actions. As mentioned above, this includes many initiatives by federations of slum or shack dwellers that have been supported by Shack/Slum Dwellers International (SDI) and the Asian Coalition for Community Action (ACCA), implemented by the Asian Coalition for Housing Rights (ACHR).

A key enabling factor in many case studies of cities is the participation of informal settlement dwellers in local decision making. This is effective when informal dwellers are organised and clear about their demands, offer local governments their support and generate the data and maps needed to address their needs. Within the work of SDI and ACCA, it was community savings groups that formed city and national federations, and most savers and savings group managers are women. It is far easier for local governments to work with groups like these, with clear and realistic demands, leaders they can talk to in a non-confrontational manner (unless the informal dwellers are threatened with eviction and negotiation is not working), and capacities that local governments need (such as mapping informal settlements). Equally important is that community savings groups and their federations are trusted by informal dwellers.

The support of local universities has also contributed to research, sharing of knowledge and capacities, and facilitating continuity in local development planning processes. It is essential to develop institutions and teams that can undertake work like this and can design policies drawing on all areas of government as well as innovating and getting support from all sectors and agencies. Often environmental issues, and more specifically climate-change issues, have no institutional home within municipal structures. This makes it difficult to co-ordinate the work of different government areas and departments and give these themes the needed visibility and budget. It is easy to see how good governance, clear leadership and a strong group of collaborating actors form the basis from which cities build their climate policies.

Decentralisation can empower local governments to build city resilience

Decentralisation gives local governments the autonomy to establish local climate policies and actions. Decentralisation has been embraced as a means to achieve various goals, including deepening and strengthening democracy, improving a type of development more connected with local needs, reducing the state apparatus and making public management more efficient (Montecinos, 2005[95]). It has particular importance for intermediary cities in that roles and responsibilities should be passed down the urban hierarchy, along with the necessary resources and revenue-raising powers. This should include the powers, resources and capacities needed to develop and implement climate-change policies. Adequate decentralisation requires building effective multilevel governance systems, with the scope for consultation and participation of other relevant stakeholders, in order to facilitate climate actions that are sufficient and inclusive. Box 4.2 highlights main factors that can support local governments in their climate actions in a decentralised governance system in OECD countries.

Box 4.2. Multilevel governance mechanisms for climate actions in OECD countries

Subnational governments are critical for climate policy governance. However, they cannot achieve the goal of transition to zero emissions by 2050 without co-ordinated actions across different levels of government and adequate financing. Subnational governments are often left out of climate governance. Indeed, one of out of four countries that have submitted their nationally determined contributions under the Paris Agreement do not engage subnational governments in national efforts to reduce emissions.

What are the factors that can better enable subnational governments in OECD countries to take an active role in climate policy governance and facilitate transition to zero emissions by 2050?

- ***Adequate decentralisation*** is needed for effective participation of subnational governments. Across at least two-thirds of OECD countries, there are indications that there is increasing awareness and acceptance of the important role of subnational governments. However, the level of participation and integration of subnational actors in national climate strategies and frameworks remains limited. Moreover, subnational governments are limited in their capacities for implementing climate actions due to inadequate access to financing for climate actions.
- ***Place-based approaches to climate actions*** can be applied through effective dialogue across different levels of governments. Such dialogue can promote the integration of climate actions across regional and local development strategies as well as sectoral plans (land use, urban planning, etc.). Multilevel climate governance should reduce trade-offs on well-being outcomes across sectors by adopting a series of techniques to establish and measure short, medium and long-term targets as well as establishing monitoring and evaluation systems.
- ***Co-ordination across sectors and levels of government*** is essential for effective climate policy governance. This implies aligning and integrating policy actions across sectors (i.e. transportation, land use, spatial planning) for coherent strategies.
- ***Engaging non-state stakeholders in climate governance*** can strengthen government efforts. This involves engaging key actors from various sectors, including the private sector, civil society, academia and science.
- ***Establishing contractual instruments*** can help to foster place-based actions and meet national and international climate objectives. This may be achieved with a series of climate targets and agreements across different levels of government.

Source: OECD (2021[96]).

In decentralised governance systems, local authorities have greater autonomy regarding local development, but also greater obligations. In Latin America in particular, many responsibilities have been delegated to the municipal level, including in territorial planning, land-use management and DRR. The assumption behind decentralisation is that better choices can be made at the local level to respond to local needs, and that greater transparency and accountability can be achieved since decision makers and citizens are closer. However, decentralisation processes have not been without problems. Despite the laudable objectives, decentralisation has proceeded unevenly and often without the actual transfer of financial, technical and administrative capacities, and decision-making powers, to local governments.

Decentralisation can also generate territorial imbalances as local governments respond to local issues differently based on their administrative and financial capacities and human resources (López, 2015[97]). Most funds transferred from higher levels of government are earmarked for specific sectors (such as health, education or water management). Moreover, the possibility of raising income through local taxes varies depending on each municipality's capacity to so and the particular context of each country (Scott and Tarazona, 2011[98]). With some exceptions, there has been little effort to strengthen local capacities. In addition, party politics usually influence funding allocations.

In the process of addressing the SDGs, national governments in countries such as Argentina have been working with subnational levels. However, they found that this is not a simple process, even though it is seen as an opportunity to strengthen and complement existing local and territorial development plans. As a federal country, the national body responsible for co-ordinating the implementation of Agenda 2030 signs a co-operation agreement with focal points at provincial level to provide technical assistance. However, the organisation of Argentina's municipalities and institutions presents a great diversity of situations. The national constitution does not define a single municipal government regime. It is rather Argentina's provinces, through their own constitutions and laws, that organise the municipal regime (INDEC, n.d.[99]).[5] In this context, implementation of the SDGs is particularly complex as it depends on the institutional capacities and powers established by political regulations, as well as local planning and management capacities, technical teams and financial resources (Geddes, 2020[100]). It is also important to note that decentralisation has not necessarily been able to overcome rigidity in institutional structures, generate local capacities or solve citizens' needs more effectively (Montecinos, 2005[95]). Better collaboration between different levels of government has not always materialised (López, 2015[97]). Only the better-positioned cities, in terms of financial resources, professional civil servants, political commitment and a strong civil society, have been able to undertake the delegated responsibilities fully. These cities have often been able to address citizens' problems, showing coherence and the ability to work alongside multiple stakeholders.

Along with decentralisation, local governments can benefit from adopting a metropolitan governance approach. Metropolitan governance enables governments at all levels (as will as non-governmental stakeholders) to co-ordinate at different levels, including in service delivery, formulating policies and planning, and establishing mechanisms for governance of urban areas (Slack, 2019[101]). The metropolitan governance approach can help to reduce fragmented urban governance structures by enabling local stakeholders to establish plans jointly for infrastructure, land use and transportation, and to reduce bureaucratic costs, etc. (Slack, 2019[101]; OECD, 2015[102]). Metropolitan governance approaches are not always binding, and there are broad variations in the way they are adopted across cities, especially large metropolises. They can also be adapted to a specific policy area, such as spatial planning, transportation, infrastructure, etc. For instance, an OECD (2015[102]) study of metropolitan governance in OECD countries outlines the various forms of governance bodies across metropolitan areas. Some cities have informal co-ordination bodies that are mainly focused on exchange of information and that lack enforcement tools, while other urban areas have attained the status of "metropolitan cities", enabling them access higher levels of governance and larger competencies (OECD, 2015[102]). As intermediary cities in developing countries undergo spatial and economic transformation, adopting a metropolitan governance approach that is pertinent to their circumstances and long-term plans could provide large scope for improved local capacity, planning and management of resources.

Local champions play a key role in supporting sustainable development pathways

The city case studies indicate that local champions have been important in engaging key stakeholders and ensuring the durability of climate programmes. These champions have contributed to creating a more sustainable local development pathway where commitment to social and environmental issues becomes a cross-cutting theme in the local agenda. In practice, local champions are mayors who have managed to pass their vision along to the following administration, who have been capable of building strong technical city teams and who, up to a point, contribute to sustaining and building upon the line of work adopted. Many have also made room for grassroots leaders to engage with them and their government.

Local elected officials, city staff members and civil society leaders are important in the exercise of leadership (Carmin et al., 2011[103]). Often there is no clear national-level government leadership in DRR or climate change, forcing local champions to become active promoters. Manizales, Colombia, for instance, has managed over the years to consolidate a group of stakeholders (city officials, local universities, private sector) that, through consensus building, has shaped and sustained the city's DRR policies as well as territorial and environmental planning, and has integrated these into the city's climate-change policies (Hardoy and Barrero, 2016[5]). Another example is Rosario, Argentina, which has been governed by the same political alliance for more than 30 years, showing political continuity and institutional stability, and allowing the development of coherent long-term policies that integrate a social dimension (Almansi, 2009[104]). Local champions change, and it is not one individual, but groups of individuals, that contribute to sustaining a process. Santa Fe, Argentina, has recently seen how shifts in the administration may result in the loss of hard-won gains in DRR. However, it is the technical city team and the academic sector that, with their collective learning, sustain the process, often in co-operation with civil society and grassroots leaders.

Trigger factors enabling local climate actions and resilience

It is important to understand the type of events or contexts that drive cities to develop climate-change policies and actions. We noted earlier the careful and detailed timeline developed for Durban's climate-change policies and the interplay between influences within local government and external factors. As noted above, there are many overlaps between climate-change risks and DRR, so it is to be expected that many cities developed their climate-change policies from DRR policies, as shown by many of the cases covered in this chapter. Often a disaster event (or a succession of them) has persuaded cities to work on DRR, moving from emergency responses to an integral DRR strategy. This generates the capacity to plan with a risk lens and to take responsibility for city expansion into high-risk areas and difficulties in water management and basic service provision. This approach has required improved co-ordination capacities across sectors and actors, frequently operating at different levels, and has been useful for the process of developing and implementing climate-change policies.

There are also many cases of cities whose strength derives from a very clear urban, spatial and environmental planning tradition. This process involves generating a long-term vision, adopting a participatory approach in the shaping of that vision and providing trunk infrastructure, basic services, housing, safe land, etc. This approach has served as the basis for developing other policies, including climate-change policies.

Grassroots actions can also play an important role in local resilience building. Community and grassroots initiatives have taught authorities to do things differently, and have worked to provide services and infrastructure, along with local governments, to reduce development deficits and build resilience (Satterthwaite et al., 2018[105]). In doing so, they have contributed to shaping local agendas. The case study of Gobabis, Namibia, illustrates this well.

In addition to these internally driven changes and processes, there are also many cases of externally driven climate resilience initiatives. In some cases, externally generated programmes and initiatives have introduced the possibility of integrating DRR with territorial and environmental planning and climate change. Some have been capable of generating long-term local development work and becoming part of different city and international networks, or of generating alliances with particular international organisations or universities. Such networks and alliances provide technical support, training opportunities and spaces to share lessons, build capacities and take part in international discussions.

Local capacities and resources are key to building resilience

Local capacities and resources are fundamental for building resilience and facilitating climate actions. Human, technological, financial, political and social resources provide the foundation for initiating and sustaining climate planning (Carmin et al., 2011[103]). City teams and other relevant stakeholders need to develop capacities to address complex environmental problems and go beyond silo thinking. This is not only relevant to the technical areas of planning and implementation, but also key to being able to ask the right questions and discuss and develop appropriate solutions. Over the years, capacity building has prepared many stakeholders to learn, adjust and integrate policies to better address the challenges of climate change. But this is no easy process. Most cities in the Global South still face large constraints in terms of their human capacities and the availability of funding.

The lack of capacity to generate and process relevant data to guide decision making is generally a big constraint. Intermediary cities may lack the capacity to develop spatial analyses, climate scenarios and models or detailed emission inventories. Often local universities can be good partners. Technical appraisals and information generation are also becoming more integrated with participatory approaches that collect local knowledge and perceptions. These include enumerations in informal settlements that generate detailed data on houses, households and neighbourhoods, as illustrated in case studies in the section on Africa. They include methodologies developed to document and map informal settlements within "Know Your City" campaigns, which have reached 460 cities. They also include participatory planning processes developed within different initiatives and programmes. Sometimes the problem is not the absence of data but the lack of access to it and incompatibility in the formats in which data is found, which impedes its integration (Hardoy et al., 2019[106]; Hardoy et al., 2019[25]). There are also large barriers in the sharing of data across government offices and between government and research institutions and development agencies. Each city should assess the type of data and information needed to guide planning and decision making and how it will be shared and updated, understanding that this is a work in progress (UNDRR, 2019[6]).

Although the access of city governments to financial resources can be very limited, there are actions that can be taken to boost local funds. Funds available to local governments are usually limited, as transfers from higher levels of government are earmarked for specific sectors. However, as some of the examples have shown, many cities have been innovative in generating financial resources through local taxes, by partnering with civil society and the private sector, through value-capture mechanisms, and also by becoming better managers and developing capacities to prepare project proposals that could win the attention of international funders. Community savings groups and their federations can also provide resources to be invested locally. These funds can contribute to the finance of in situ upgrading and house improvements, land acquisition for housing development and greenfield housing development.

The support and policies of national governments are indispensable for strengthening the capacities and resources of local governments. Indeed, local governments have limited scope to build on their capacities and enhance their resources without national governments, as they may have limited autonomy to make the substantive changes that can enable them to unlock new resources and improve their technical capacities. The section below highlights the critical role of national policies and government frameworks for local capacities.

National policy support is crucial for building climate resilience

National governments are integral agents of building climate resilience in intermediary cities. As noted throughout the chapter, local governments in these cities are limited in their capacities, in terms both of technical and financial resources and of their autonomy to draft and implement effective climate policies. National governments tend to have far larger capacities to draft policies and legistlation that will influence the resilience of cities, and to help build coherent policies and strategies across the national and local levels. A study by the Coalition for Urban Transition (2019[107]) highlights that national governments have the primary capacity for climate mitigation actions in intermediary cities, with over 35% of mitigation potential in urban areas. Yet their limited financial and technical capacities for implementing mitigation actions imply that they need the support of national governments.

National governments are able to establish strategies and engage relevant stakeholders for building climate resilience in cities. National governments have better capacity and authority to implement policies that go beyond city boundaries and can mainstream or integrate climate standards across various sectoral policies, such as electricity, transportation, taxation regimes, etc. (Coalition for Urban Transitions, 2019[107]). Furthemore, national frameworks and strategies play a key role in driving and creating the right incentives for climate actions at city level. For example, ccountries such as the Philippines, Bangladesh, India and Indonesia have established national directives for climate actions, and integrate urban areas to different degrees. The Philippines requires urban areas to produce a local climate action plan under its Climate Change Act 2009, whereas Indonesia planned to mainstream adaptation and DRR into development planning, including in urban areas (Archer et al., 2017[108]). National governments, therefore, play an important role in delegating the capacities needed (financial, technical or human resources) for driving local climate actions (Archer et al., 2017[108]).

National governments can also learn from their local counterparts – those that are able to experiment in innovative strategies to build climate actions. In some of the case studies reviewed in this chapter, local authorities have been ahead of their respective national governments in implementing climate policies. This demonstrates that local governments can help drive national climate actions and strategies. Moreover, local governments have the opportunity to experiment with innovative actions, which can serve as a testing ground for national climate policies (Corfee-Morlot et al., 2009[109]). Table 4.4 highlights some of the most important actions for building local resilience that can be taken by national governments.

Table 4.4. National government roles in local climate actions

Policy coherence	Support	Enabling
Aligning climate policies both vertically and horizontally to reduce policy gaps and fragmentation	Supporting and scaling local climate actions	Establishing an enabling governance framework
• **Vertically:** Aligning climate policies across national, regional and local climate mandates and development planning for policy complementarity **(Coalition for Urban Transitions, 2019[107])**. • **Horizontally**: Embedding climate standards and policies across sectors and ministries; facilitating their interlinkages across levels of government – i.e. climate mainstreaming across sectors of transportation, electricity, etc. **(Archer et al., 2017[108]; Corfee-Morlot et al., 2009[109])** • Engaging **multiple actors** in climate policies: local and regional governments; civil society; national and international experts; donor institutions for technical assistance; creating an enabling environment for private sector participation in climate actions.	• **Creating incentives for experimentation** on new climate actions and help scale up successful strategies across national or local government climate actions (OECD, 2009; (Coalition for Urban Transitions, 2019[107]). • **Building local capacities in local actions** with cost-effective strategies such as integrating climate adaptation and mitigation in sectors like land use, transportation planning, etc. (Corfee-Morlot et al., 2009[109]) • **Actively and effectively engaging** with local governments in designing and implementing local climate actions that are cross-cutting (Coalition for Urban Transitions, 2019[107])	• **Adequate autonomy and capacity** to design and implement local climate policies at the local level (OECD, 2009). • **Adequate fiscal decentralization systems** that enable local governments to boost their revenues and build their credit worthiness to access capital markets; decentralised fiscal systems that support and enable local governments to create their own sources of revenue. These systems should create incentives for co-operation across sectors and local governments. National governments can also enhance local capacity for fiscal management and enable partnerships between local government and national financing institutions (Coalition for Urban Transitions, 2019[107]).

Source: Coalition for Urban Transitions (2019[107]), Archer et al. (2017[108]), and Corfee-Morlot et al. (2009[109]).

Colombia's DRR policies show how national governments can play a key role in facilitating co-ordinated policies and ensuring local government commitment. Colombia, a country at risk of many types of hazards (hydro-meteorological, geological, armed conflict, etc.), has over the years paid particular attention to managing risk and has built a good track record. A disaster risk management law requires that DRR be integrated with land use and environmental planning at all levels, and that a disaster risk lens be incorporated in all interventions related to housing, infrastructure, mobility, services, industry, agriculture, etc. Legislation makes politicians personally responsible for ensuring that their constituents are safe from disasters. In addition, municipalities must set an environmental surcharge of 1.5 to 2.5 per thousand of the appraised value of the assets that serve as the basis for property taxes; municipalities must invest this money in environmental protection (UNDRR, 2019[6]).

Colombia has made large efforts to integrate climate policies across national and local levels. Over the years, and especially since the IPCC's Fourth Assessment Report in 2007, Colombia has worked on modelling climate change scenarios, collecting data (UN-Habitat, 2012[110]) and consolidating the national institutional framework to manage climate change. Since 2010, climate actions have been incorporated in national development plans. The country has a Climate Change National System (SISCLIMA) to co-ordinate initiatives generated by different levels and sectors of government and by local communities, although the country's National Climate Change law was passed only in 2018.

Colombia is also very strong in territorial planning, which is key for integrating national and local climate actions. In 1997 the country implemented a law under which municipalities and districts have to develop local territorial development plans (*Planes de Ordenamiento Territorial*) with specific goals, strategies, programmes and norms to guide development, as well as environmental protection plans for catchment areas (PONCAS/POMAS). These plans have important climate adaptation implications as they regulate land use (Hardoy and Barrero, 2016[5]). Regional policies and plans are in line with national mandates and policies, and with the National Development Plan. Much of the national structure builds on the experience of Manizales. Colombia has regional environmental agencies (such as Corpocaldas, Corporisaralda, etc.) that are responsible for applying national environmental policies (including on climate change), and that manage natural resources and support municipal governments. Usually they are well staffed professionally and help local governments in climate-change planning, watershed management, DRR, etc.

Many other countries are also advancing their national legislation and developing co-ordination systems and plans. Ecuador, for example, introduced territorial planning (spatial planning) as a state policy following the adoption of a new constitution of 2008. The policy led to the implementation of a national system of decentralised participatory planning. All levels of government are expected to prepare territorial plans – but while many have done so, many others have no intention (or capacity) to implement the plans and developed them merely to comply (López, 2015[97]). Meanwhile, Ecuador developed a National Climate Change Strategy (2012-25) with the support of an Inter-Institutional Committee on Climate Change involving many ministries and secretaries. The strategy guides and co-ordinates actions and measures related to climate change. The country also has a Climate Change Plan, a tool designed to include climate change in all planning initiatives and that includes capacity building, mitigation and adaptation actions.

Similarly, the Philippines has made national commitments to combating climate change and incentivising better local actions. In 2009, it enacted the Philippine Climate Change Act (Republic Act No. 9729) and created a Climate Change Commission in the aim of mainstreaming climate change into government policy formulations, including establishing a framework strategy. Poor response during a series of typhoons led to renewed interest in climate change and its link with risk reduction (Cheng and Kim, 2019[33]). In 2010, the country adopted a National Disaster Risk Reduction and Management Act that provides for a comprehensive, all-hazard, multisectoral, interagency and community-based approach. Its objectives include building the resilience of communities and institutionalising arrangements to reduce risks, including projected climate risks, at all levels (province, city, municipality, *barangay*) (NDRRMC, n.d.[111]). The country also adopted a Strategic National Action Plan for Disaster Risk Reduction. The Philippines Climate Change Act clearly defined roles for cities and municipal governments, and cities report that national level DRR frameworks are enabling city level DRR (Johnson and Blackburn, 2014[31]).

International organisations play a fundamental role in promoting climate action

International agencies and networks have played a key role in supporting urban climate actions across developing regions. Despite limited evidence on intermediary cities, it is safe to say that international organisations are key players at conducting experiments for climate actions in cities (SEI, 2020[112]; Bulkeley and Castán Broto, 2013[113]). These agencies have the financial capacity to invest in experimental or pilot projects and are free from the political barriers that may constrain city actors. International organisations can also provide opportunities to access networks of experts or other cities, and to create platforms for peer learning and profile building (SEI, 2020[112]; Bulkeley and Castán Broto, 2013[113]).

Various international agencies have been promoting or supporting climate-change adaptation, mitigation, and/or DRR in cities across Africa, Asia and Latin America. They include UN agencies (UN-Habitat, UNDRR), United Cities and Local Governments (UCLG), Cities Alliance, 100 Resilient Cities and ICLEI, to cite some of the most important actors. C40 also plays an important role in supporting cities that aim to develop climate policies; however, it only focuses on large cities.

International organisations and city networks have been key in raising the urban agenda and bringing more attention to city/local authority issues. The inclusion of urban-related issues as part of the SDGs is a clear example of the work of these organisations. But while these institutions have been active in supporting cities, including intermediary cities, in developing climate-change policies, none can provide funding to support large capital projects. Box 4.3 below lists some of the most important international organisations in this sphere and their work on climate change.

Box 4.3. International organisations involved in global climate actions

- **United Cities and Local Governments (UCLG)** is a global network of cities and local, regional and metropolitan governments and their associations. UCLG aims to '"represent, defend and amplify the voices of local and regional governments to leave no one and no place behind". UCLG's work includes bringing knowledge of climate-change issues to members and supporting exchanges of experience. With more than 240 000 members in more than 140 UN Member States, this necessarily must include very large numbers of intermediary city governments.
- **Local Governments for Sustainability (ICLEI)** is a global network of more than 2 500 local and regional governments committed to sustainable urban development (ICLEI, n.d.[63]). The organisation operates across more than 125 countries and aims to "influence sustainability policy and drive local action for low-emission, nature-based, equitable, resilient and circular development" (ICLEI, n.d.[63]). The network, which is expanding and developing, has secretariats in all world regions, and its membership includes many intermediary cities.
- **100 Resilient Cities**, a programme that concluded in 2019, sought to support city governments in 100 cities in developing resilience to climate change. Most were cities with more than 1 million inhabitants in North America, Latin America and Europe; most of the rest in other regions were large cities. For instance, the only cities in India were Bangalore and Chennai, each with more than 10 million inhabitants, and Surat with more than 5 million. Most of the 100 cities with fewer than 1 million inhabitants were in high-income nations in Europe, North America and Oceania.
- **United Nations Office for Disaster Risk Reduction (UNDRR)** has supported governments to develop their policies on disaster risk reduction. It recognises the many overlaps with climate change adaptation and mitigation and, unusually for a UN agency, recognises the importance of city governments in this. More than 800 cities have used the tools of the agency's Making Cities Resilient Campaign to raise awareness and support the development of DRR and resilience strategy (UNDRR, n.d.[114]), and many more to commit to resilience.

Boosting climate actions in intermediary cities

This chapter has presented case studies discussing climate policies across intermediary cities in LAC, Asia and Africa. Most of the examples showcased have good governance or disaster risk reduction as their foundation. It is interesting to see how DRR policies and territorial/land-use policies have aligned and are often the backbone of climate-change policies. If more attention had been paid to these cities, intermediary cities would be making major contributions to national goals, including the SDGs and the Paris Agreement. There is therefore strong interest in enabling policies that can multiply the number of well-governed intermediary cities that are addressing climate change. Figure 4.8 maps the combination of factors that have contributed to successful local climate actions across the intermediary cities reviewed in this chapter, as well as highlighting the key policy needs for boosting urban resilience. The figure outlines policy instruments, enabling factors and key actors that have been critical enablers of climate action in intermediary cities. Yet, as the case studies reviewed in this chapter also highlight, additional factors are needed for boosting the resilience of intermediary cities. These include improved knowledge and data, boosting local capacity and climate proofing of local plans and investment.

Figure 4.8. Mapping factors for successful urban resilience

Based on factors that contributed to successful climate actions across the intermediary cities reviewed

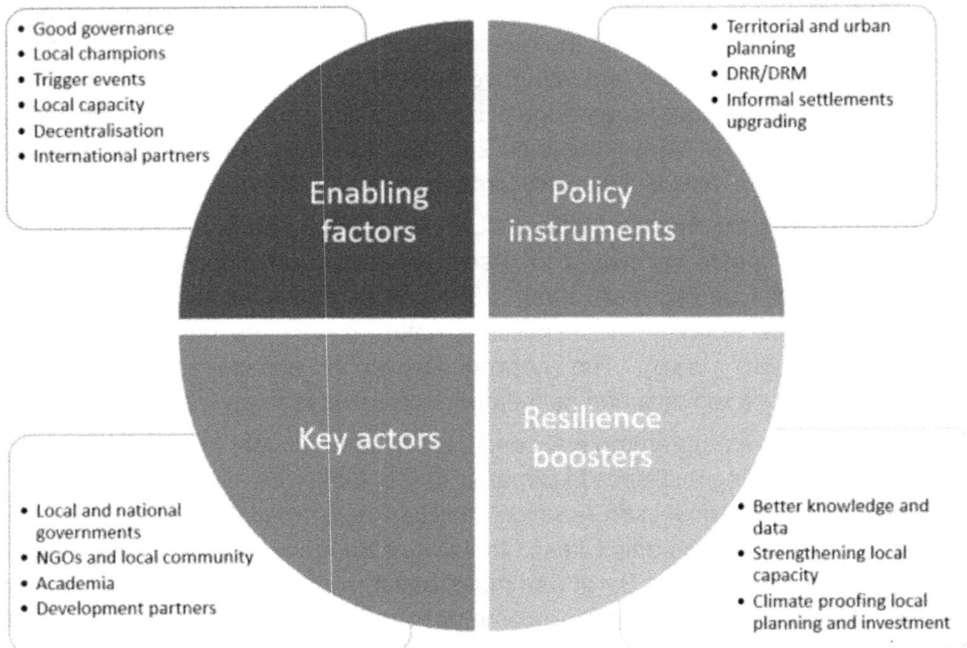

Source: Author's own elaboration.

Only limited numbers of studies of climate change have focused on intermediary cities in low- and middle-income countries. Most of what has been studied, registered and implemented regarding climate resilience in developing regions concerns large cities – often national capitals. Some reports and articles mention cities of different sizes, but they are used to illustrate a specific point. Moreover, they usually lack the depth and detail needed to understand cities' actual constraints and possibilities or how they are advancing in their climate actions. Yet intermediary cities in developing regions are diverse, and some have many years of experience in working on urban climate resilience. Building on this knowledge is a starting point to define a learning pathway that helps to identify strengths and the different sets of opportunities that cities have taken advantage of. Needless to say, it also allows identification of the challenges they face, as well as pointing to aspects that need to be further developed.

Figure 4.9 shows how separate agendas that are often regarded as competitors come together. Transformation is understood as the process in which urban centres have integrated their development, DRR and adaptation policies, along with the necessary investments addressing mitigation and sustainable ecological footprints (Barlette and Satterthwaite, 2016[115]).

Figure 4.9. Overlapping agendas of climate action

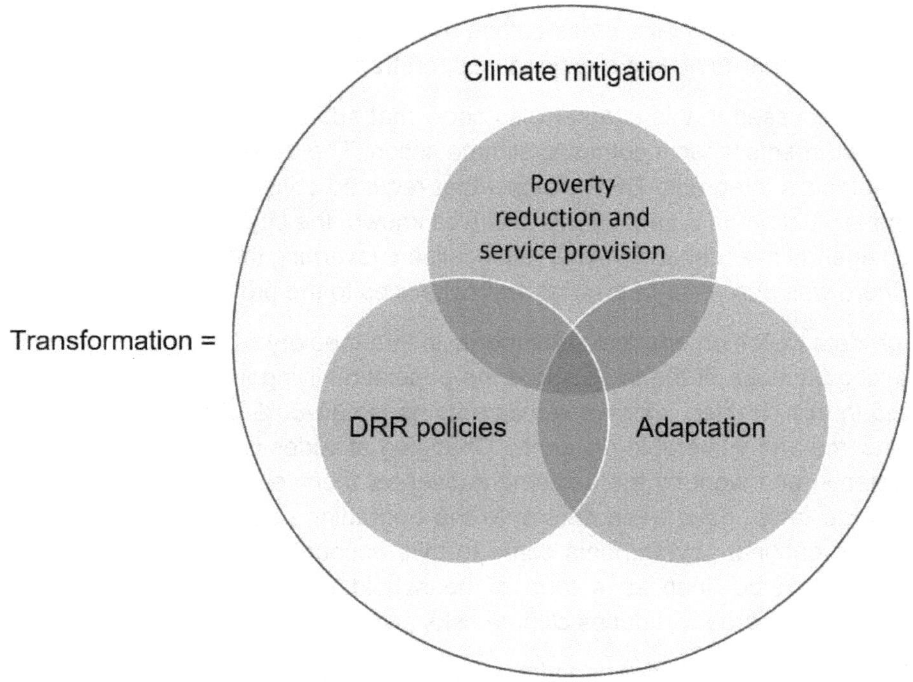

Source: (Barlette and Satterthwaite, 2016[115]).

Over the last 30 years, experience with DRR has delivered many lessons on climate-change policies, notably that a concern for risk reduction has many overlaps with adaptation. These lessons derive from city governments working to develop risk reduction on the ground (Johnson and Blackburn, 2014[31]) and developing innovative data collection methods on climate-related risks. Perhaps above all, DDR can inform and guide local policy. Meanwhile, climate-change adaptation has brought more attention to disasters and their causes, and a future perspective to guide plans and investments. Both depend on buy-in from local government departments with larger budgets and powers that enable action.

National governments play a fundamental role in supporting intermediary cities in building local resilience. This chapter has noted the importance of decentralisation and strong local democracy as key enabling factors for developing climate policies in intermediary cities in Latin America – but the only cities that have been fully able to undertake the responsibilities delegated under decentralisation are those that are better positioned in terms of financial resources, professional civil servants, political commitment and a strong civil society. Often these cities have been able to address citizens' problems with coherence and the capacity to work alongside multiple stakeholders. However, there are far more examples of intermediary (and other) cities without these capacities. Even so-called innovative cities are struggling with the scale of the problem and the constraints they face. This is why it is important for national governments to work with and support intermediary city governments.

These case studies also show that, while national laws and institutional frameworks provide guidance and support for climate action, they need to be complemented with coherent territorial planning. National laws alone do not guarantee that local governments will advance with their climate plans or improve the planning for their territorial development. In fact, even in countries such as Colombia, only a few cities have been able to develop local DRR, climate-change policies or territorial plans. In practice, the structure for this is not set up or lacks sufficient capacity to support local governments in working on themes such as climate change and territorial planning, which need cross-cutting approaches, new ways of thinking and the involvement of many actors across levels of government. However, examples exist of territorial planning being implemented by subnational authorities without national government engagement. For instance, the

Province of Santa Fe's decree No. 1872 of 2017 approved the development of territorial plans for municipalities and communes, and created a provincial register of territorial plans and an interministerial committee of territorial planning as a cross-cutting and co-ordinating body that oversees implementation. Most of this was done prior to having a national support framework in Argentina.

The experiences discussed in this chapter also show that subnational governments can advance faster than national governments when it comes to climate action. The case of Manizales served as an example for many of Colombia's integrated DRR policies that required coherence with urban, environmental and spatial-planning legislation. In a case that is less well known, the city of Rosario (Argentina) developed a coherent urban agenda over decades. When the coalition governing the city was also elected for governing the province, there was a transfer of lessons and capacities to the provincial level.

There is a large data deficit on informal settlements in intermediary cities in developing countries. This is particularly striking because of the large share the population living in these settlements. In some of the cities discussed in this chapter, informal settlements house 30-60% of the population, including most of the city's low-income and vulnerable residents. Changing attitudes in government regarding residents of informal settlements, and work by the settlement dwellers themselves to organise and bring their ideas and priorities to the table, have been central to the upgrading of these settlements. As the upgrading policies of city and national governments come to take account of risks related to climate change, the upgrading process can be seen as a form of household and community climate adaptation. When upgrading is done well, it greatly reduces climate risks and can have city-wide impact.

As discussed in this chapter, in order to address local challenges effectively there is a need to build local capacities (technical, human, financial, political). The case of Manizales shows that knowledge can be better produced locally by local technicians, researchers and citizens when there is capacity to do so. Some local actions that can help to build climate resilience in intermediary cities are listed below.

Policy transformations are needed to boost climate resilience in intermediary cities

Large gaps still exist in knowledge and data on intermediary cities. This inhibits the ability to understand the climate-resilience actions being taken by city governments and how best to support them. Nonetheless, existing literature and the examples presented in this chapter highlight strong commonalities that can be used to start thinking about and designing support mechanisms. The needed policy transformations can be grouped along three main axes:

1. **Strengthening the capacities of local stakeholders**

Local governments are often the first responders to local needs and climate disasters. As many responsibilities fall directly on local governments, it is necessary to work on shaping international agreements and national goals to local realities. National governments and international partners should support local governments in intermediary and other cities as they work to contribute to meeting global goals such as the SDGs and the Paris Agreement. Generating opportunities for city staff and senior politicians to participate in regional and international networks can help intermediary cities to become actors in the national and international arena. This can facilitate co-operation and attract further support.

Strong partnerships between local governments, communities and civil society are key for building local resilience. Productive partnerships can help strengthen local governments' capacities and ensure that they listen to and work with community organisations and recognise their capacities to define and generate appropriate solutions. Partnerships can also strengthen the long-term engagement of community organisations in working to build climate resilience. In terms of developing a climate-change policy, the experience of the mayor of Santo Tomé demonstrated the need to strengthen local governance by improving horizontal co-ordination between municipal departments and government and civil society actors, and by harmonising sectoral plans.

Local financing capacities can be strengthened by developing a more flexible local funding architecture to support climate-change action by local governments and civil society. The funding architecture should show that progress is possible even with very limited resources and should ensure that it is not only the large cities that get support. The system should include many different sources and be able to tap into them at different moments and for different needs. It must be able to close the gap between urgent funding for everyday needs and long-term funds for resilience and development planning. Box 4.4 outlines different components of such a funding architecture to support action at all levels.

Box 4.4. Sources for the funding architecture needed to support climate action at all levels

- **Independent external sources** (such as grants, loans, etc.) that are available and used for specific projects implemented by various actors (private and public).
- **Internal government funds** generated through local instruments such as local taxes, permit rights, land value capture, land value participation, betterment contribution, unearned land value capture, etc. These could be used to generate a local constant source of funding in support of climate-related actions (De la sala, 2019[13]). They can also be combined with incentives to promote specific investments (such as in green roofs, energy-saving equipment and use of renewable energy).
- **A local fund in each city** to support initiatives by community organisations. The scale and scope of such funds is much increased when there are community savings groups that bring their resources, form city-wide federations and seek partnerships with local governments, including local funds that become jointly managed with local government (see Akiba Mashatini Trust example).
- **Creation of a trust among local governments** to manage, support and implement climate adaptation and mitigation projects. This allows for the scale needed to mobilise local, national and international resources. It also provides the needed support and transparency to channel funds for projects. The trust receives contributions from members and from third parties (RAMCC, n.d.[116]).

2. Generating data to build a comprehensive understanding of local climate vulnerabilities

Building data and information systems is a necessary and important step for implementing effective climate actions. Developing a local geo-referenced database and integrating different knowledge sources that capture local specifics are actions that can help to improve government decisions. Manizales, for example, developed an integrated and geo-referenced information system to support local climate resilience. Building partnerships with key knowledge-generating institutions can boost understanding of the complex ways in which urban areas can be vulnerable to climate change. Such partnerships can also institutionalise knowledge across local governments. Drawing in local universities and professional groups with the knowledge and technical capacities to provide support in planning, training, data generation, scenario building, monitoring, evaluation, etc., can help to ensure coherence and continuity of policies, plans and planning processes.

3. Integrating climate proofing into local planning and investment

Local governments need to integrate climate proofing into local planning and investment across multiple sectors. Actions can include accelerating the incorporation of climate considerations when investing in settlement upgrading, housing programmes and long-lasting city infrastructure, which involves allocating important resources. Local and national actors can adopt and revalorise nature-based solutions, the use of green and blue infrastructure, and the links between urban, peri-urban and rural areas.

Elaborating a local approach to resilience that can be shared and demonstrated can help to increase the likelihood that it will be adopted and gain the support of relevant actors. This is illustrated by the importance given by the Asian Cities Climate Change Resilience Network (ACCCRN) to engaging all key actors and institutions in climate action, including community and civil society groups selected in line with local hazards (e.g. communities susceptible to landslides) and forms of political organisation (e.g. trade unions).

Conclusion

This chapter has outlined climate actions in intermediary cities across Asia, Africa and Latin America through a series of case studies. Climate change has often been on the margins of local policies across many of the cities reviewed. Indeed, in many cases, other policies, such as disaster risk reduction and the upgrading of informal settlements, have served as entry points that consequently enabled resilience building. Key catalysts in some of the cities reviewed include enabling factors that can be institutional, such as good governance and active support from the national government, or multi-stakeholder, with the active engagement of local actors, universities, civil society and local populations.

Intermediary cities in developing countries are still often overlooked in national and international climate policies despite the major challenges they face. This is perhaps because most studies of climate change and urban centres focus on large cities or cities in developed countries. As such, additional information and data are needed on intermediary cities in developing countries and their vulnerabilities to climate change.

Notes

[1] This is under revision by the new city administration that came into office in December 2019.

[2] Based on: Gobierno Municipal del Cantón (2017). Plan Maestro Urbano. Fase 1, Fase 2 A, Fase 2 B, Fase 3.; Department of Landscape Architecture and Environmental Planning University of California (2017) Portoviejo: The city and the River. Integrating Urban Design and Watershed Management on the Portoviejo River. Department of Landscape Architecture and Environmental Planning College of Environmental Design University of California, Berkeley; Gobierno Autónomo Descentralizado Municipal del Cantón Portoviejo (2020). Plan de Protección Multiamenaza and Bernal Chancay E. and García Arias M (2020) Presentation River Portoviejo Corridor, Climate Resilience and Urban Development, Virtual Planning Workshop, June 2020.

[3] The Multi-Hazard Protection Plan was a joint project between the Municipal Office of Territorial Development, the Office of Urban and Territorial Planning and the Office of Environmental Management and Risk. The integral improvement plans involve consolidated urban land, unconsolidated land and land destined for protection (because of risks and/or its importance for services to the area). The plans identify houses at risk, differentiate between mitigatable and unmitigatable risks, and design intervention accordingly. They aim to progressively integrate neighbourhoods and generate secure habitat conditions. Local officials have also worked on developing other plans such as Mi Barrio Lindo to work on urban borders.

[4] Climate Resilient Cities in Latin America Initiative, funded by the Climate and Development Knowledge Network, the International Development Research Centre and the Fundación Futuro Latinoamericano. The initiative involved six projects.

[5] In 2018, Argentina had 2 327 local governments, of which 1 206 were municipalities and the rest urban and rural communes, development commissions, municipal commissions, neighbourhood councils and autonomous government boards, according to the political-administrative organisation of each province.

References

ACHR/ACCA (2014), *ACHR/ACCA in the Philippines: Five community organizations, five strategies, same goal*, http://www.achr.net/countries-de.php?ic=4 (accessed on 10 March 2021). [39]

Alcadía de Manizales (2017), *Alcadía de Manizales*, https://manizales.gov.co/ (accessed on 10 March 2022). [4]

Alcadía de Manizales (2017), *Plan de Ordenamiento Territorial 2017 -2031*, https://manizales.gov.co/transparencia-y-acceso-a-la-informacion-publica/planeacion/plan-de-ordenamiento-territorial-2017-2031/ (accessed on 10 March 2022). [9]

Almansi, F. (2009), "Rosario's development; interview with Miguel Lifschitz, mayor of Rosario, Argentina", *Environment and Urbanization*, Vol. 21/1, https://doi.org/10.1177/0956247809103002. [104]

AquiAlaga (n.d.), *AquiAlaga*, https://appaquialaga.wixsite.com/odkpp (accessed on 5 October 2021). [29]

Araújo (2021), *The challenges and opportunities of implementing local climate action lessons from Quelimane, Mozambique*, Development Matters, https://oecd-development-matters.org/2021/02/04/the-challenges-and-opportunities-of-implementing-local-climate-action-lessons-from-quelimane-mozambique/ (accessed on 11 October 2021). [66]

Archer, A. et al. (2017), "Developing city resilience strategies: lessons from the ICLEI-ACCRN process", *Working Papers Series*, No. 41, IIED, ICLEI, The Rockefeller Foundation, https://www.researchgate.net/publication/316827587_Developing_city_resilience_strategies_lessons_from_the_ICLEI-ACCCRN_process (accessed on 10 March 2021). [108]

Archer, D. and S. Boonyabancha (2011), "Seeing a disaster as an opportunity – harnessing the energy of disaster survivors for change", *Environment and Urbanization*, Vol. 23/2, https://doi.org/10.1177/0956247811410011. [86]

Bahadur, A. and T. Tanner (2014), "Transformational resilience thinking: putting people, power and politics at the heart of urban climate resilience", *Environment and Urbanization*, Vol. 26/1, pp. 200-214, https://doi.org/10.1177/0956247814522154. [44]

Barlette and Satterthwaite (2016), “Conclusions on ways forward”, in Satterthwaite, D. and S. Bartlett (eds.), *Cities on a Finite Planet Towards transformative responses to climate change*, Routledge, London, https://www.routledge.com/Cities-on-a-Finite-Planet-Towards-transformative-responses-to-climate-change/Bartlett-Satterthwaite/p/book/9781138184107 (accessed on 11 October 2021). [115]

Barlett, S. (ed.) (2016), *Cities on a Finite Planet*, Routledge, London, https://www.routledge.com/Cities-on-a-Finite-Planet-Towards-transformative-responses-to-climate-change/Bartlett-Satterthwaite/p/book/9781138184107 (accessed on 11 October 2021). [77]

Bartlett et al. (2016), “Cross city analysis”, in *Cities on a Finite Planet*, Routledge, https://doi.org/10.4324/9781315645421. [20]

Bawagan, A. et al. (2015), *Shifting paradigms: Strengthening institutions for community-based disaster risk reduction and management*, University of the Philippines Diliman, Quezon City, https://ds.mainlib.upd.edu.ph/Record/UPD-00246506273 (accessed on 2 October 2021). [30]

BBC (2019), “Cyclone Idai: Scores more deaths reported in Mozambique”, *BBC Africa*, https://www.bbc.com/news/world-africa-47678743 (accessed on 10 October 2021). [64]

Boonyabancha, S. (2005), “Baan Mankong: going to scale with “slum” and squatter upgrading in Thailand”, *Environment and Urbanization*, Vol. 17/1, pp. 21-46, https://doi.org/10.1177/095624780501700104. [88]

Boonyabancha, S. and T. Kerr (2018), “Lessons from CODI on co-production”, *Environment and Urbanization*, Vol. 30/2, pp. 444-460, https://doi.org/10.1177/0956247818791239. [38]

Buckley et al. (2016), “Addressing the housing challenge: avoiding the Ozymandias syndrome”, *Environment and Urbanization*, Vol. 28/1, pp. 119-138, https://doi.org/10.1177/0956247815627523. [90]

Bulkeley, H. and V. Castán Broto (2013), “Government by experiment? Global cities and the governing of climate change”, *Transactions of the Institute of British Geographers*, Vol. 38/3, https://doi.org/10.1111/j.1475-5661.2012.00535.x. [113]

Cabannes, Y. (2021), “Contributions of participatory budgeting to climate change adaptation and mitigation: current local practices across the world and lessons from the field”, *Environment and Urbanization*, Vol. 33/2, pp. 356–375, https://doi.org/10.1177/09562478211021710. [93]

Cabannes, Y. (2015), “The impact of participatory budgeting on basic services: municipal practices and evidence from the field”, *Environment and Urbanization*, Vol. 27/1, https://doi.org/10.1177/0956247815572297. [94]

Cabannes, Y. (2014), “Contribution of participatory budgeting to provision and management of basic services: municipal practices and evidence from the field”, *Working Paper*, International Institute for Environment and Development, London, https://pubs.iied.org/sites/default/files/pdfs/migrate/10713IIED.pdf (accessed on 11 October 2021). [92]

Carcellar, N., J. Co and Z. Hipolito (2011), “Addressing disaster risk reduction through community-rooted interventions in the Philippines: experience of the Homeless People’s Federation of the Philippines”, *Environment and Urbanization*, Vol. 23/2, https://doi.org/10.1177/0956247811415581. [87]

Cardona, O. (2019), "Gestión del riesgo y adaptación en Manizales: Una estrategia de desarollo para lograr que una ciudad en transición sea resiliente, sostenible y competitiva", *Medio ambiente y Urbanización*, Vol. 90/1, pp. 127-168, https://www.ingentaconnect.com/contentone/iieal/meda/2019/00000090/00000001/art00009 (accessed on 8 March 2021). [7]

Carmin, J. et al. (2011), *Planning climate resilient cities: early lessons from early adapters*, https://www.researchgate.net/publication/273764560. [103]

Carrizosa, M. (2018), "Manizales, Colombia. Culture of Risk with a Scientific Backbone", in Carrizosa, M. et al. (eds.), *Facing Risk: New Urban Resilience Practices in Latin America*, CAF and Observatory on Latin America (OLA), The New School, https://scioteca.caf.com/handle/123456789/1431 (accessed on 8 March 2021). [8]

Cartwright, A. et al. (2013), "Economics of climate change adaptation at the local scale under conditions of uncertainty and resource constraints: the case of Durban, South Africa", *Environment and Urbanization*, Vol. 25/1, https://doi.org/10.1177/0956247813477814. [81]

Cavalcante, L. and O. Almeida (2018), *Mudanças climáticas em pequeñas cidades do Delta e Estuário Amazônicos: caminhos para a resiliencia*, NAEA, Belém, PA, https://livroaberto.ufpa.br/jspui/bitstream/prefix/570/1/Liovros_MudancasClimaticasPequenas.pdf (accessed on 10 March 2021). [27]

Chardon, A. (2021), "Resettling, re-enabling: the challenge of reconstructing a human habitat", in Johnson, C., G. Jain and A. Lavell (eds.), *Rethinking Urban Risk and Resettlement in the Global South*, UCL, London, https://doi.org/10.14324/111.9781787358287. [10]

Cheng, T. and T. Kim (2019), *Building community-based Resilience in the Municipality of San Francisco, Cebu, the Phillipines*, Global Delivery Initiative Know-How That Works, San Francisco, http://www.globaldeliveryinitiative.org/sites/default/files/case-studies/community-based_drrm_5-3-19_1.pdf (accessed on 10 March 2021). [33]

Chitekwe-Biti, B. et al. (2012), "Developing an informal settlement upgrading protocol in Zimbabwe – the Epworth story", *Environment and Urbanization*, Vol. 24/1, pp. 131-148, https://doi.org/10.1177/0956247812437138. [73]

Coalition for Urban Transitions (2019), *Climate Emergency: Urban Opportunity*, Coalition for Urban Transitions, Washington DC and London, https://urbantransitions.global/en/publication/climate-emergency-urban-opportunity/ (accessed on 13 July 2021). [107]

Corfee-Morlot, J. et al. (2009), "Cities, Climate Change and Multilevel Governance", *OECD Environmental working Papers*, No. 14, OECD Publishing, Paris, http://www.oecd.org/env/workingpapers. [109]

County Government of Kisumu (2017), *Kisumu Integrated Solid Waste Management Plan (KISWaMP) by horizon 2030*, County of Kisumu, Kisumu, https://www.kisumu.go.ke/wp-content/uploads/2019/08/Updated-KISWAMP-Feb-2018-.pdf (accessed on 8 October 2021). [60]

County of Kisumu (2018), *Kisumu County Integrated Development Plan II 2018-2022*, County of Kisumu, Kisumu, https://www.kisumu.go.ke/wp-content/uploads/2018/11/Kisumu-County-CIDP-II-2018-2022.pdf (accessed on 8 October 2021). [62]

Curato, N. and S. Calamba (2020), "Surviving Disasters by Suppressing Political Storms: Participation as Knowledge Transfer in Community-Based Disaster Governance", *Critical Sociology*, Vol. 46/2, https://doi.org/10.1177/0896920518796167. [32]

De la sala (2019), "Políticas de Suelo, Derecho Urbanístico y Cambio Climático: Instrumentos Urbanísticos-Tributarios como Medidas para Enfrentar al Cambio Climático WP19SD1SP", *Working Paper*, Lincoln Institute of Land Policy, Massachusetts, http://alterman.technion.ac.il;. [13]

De Lima, A. et al. (2020), "Climate hazards in small and medium cities in the Amazon Delta and Estuary: challenges for resilience", *Environment and Urbanization*, Vol. 32/1, https://doi.org/10.1177/0956247819874586. [28]

Fernandez et al (2015), "Assessing local vulnerability to climate change in Ecuador", *SpringerPlus*, Vol. 4/1, https://doi.org/10.1186/s40064-015-1536-z. [22]

Geddes, L. (2020), "La implementación de la Agenda 2030 en Argentina y en la Ciudad de Gualeguaychúa", *Medio Ambiente y Urbanización*, Vol. 92/14, pp. 237-250, https://www.ingentaconnect.com/contentone/iieal/meda/2020/00000092/00000001/art00010# (accessed on 11 October 2021). [100]

GFDRR (2011), *Climate Risk and Adaptation Country Profile: Mozambique Vulnerability, Risk Reduction and Adaptation to Climate Change*, Global Facility for Disaster Reduction and Recovery (GFDRR), Washington DC, https://www.gfdrr.org/en/publication/climate-risk-and-adaptation-country-profile-mozambique (accessed on 11 October 2021). [67]

Gobierno Municipal del Cantón Portovejo (2017), *Actualización del Plan de Ordenamento Territorial del Cantón Portoviejo*, https://www.portoviejo.gob.ec/md-transparencia/2017/julio-2017/Plan%20de%20Ordenamiento.pdf (accessed on 26 August 2022). [24]

Gobierno Provincia de Santa Fe (2014), *Plan Base de la Ciudad de Santo Tomé. Una herramienta participativa para el desarollo local*, Provincia de Santa Fe, Santa Fe, https://www.argentina.gob.ar/sites/default/files/plan_base_de_la_ciudad_de_santo_tome_.pdf (accessed on 10 March 2021). [17]

Gubic, I. and O. Baloi (2019), "Implementing the New Urban Agenda in Rwanda: Nation-Wide Public Space Initiatives", *Urban Planning*, Vol. 4/2, https://doi.org/10.17645/up.v4i2.2005. [58]

Hardoy et al. (2019), "Participatory planning for climate resilient and inclusive urban development in Dosquebradas, Santa Ana and Santa Tomé", *Environment and Urbanization*, Vol. 31/1, https://doi.org/10.1177/0956247819825539. [25]

Hardoy et al. (2018), "Planificación participativa para la resiliencia al clima en ciudades de América Latin: los casos de Dosquebradas (Colombia), Santa Ana (El Salvador), y Santo Tomé (Argentina)", *Medio Ambiente y Urbanización, IIED-America Latina*, Vol. 33/1, pp. 29-61, https://www.ingentaconnect.com/contentone/iieal/meda/2018/00000088/00000001/art00003 (accessed on 10 March 2021). [26]

Hardoy et al. (2016), "Rosario, Argentina", in *Cities on a Finite Planet*, Routledge, https://doi.org/10.4324/9781315645421. [18]

Hardoy and Barrero (2016), "Manizales, Colombia", in Barlett, S. and D. Satterthwaite (eds.), *Cities on a Finite Planet*, Routledge, Oxford, https://www.routledge.com/Cities-on-a-Finite-Planet-Towards-transformative-responses-to-climate-change/Bartlett-Satterthwaite/p/book/9781138184107 (accessed on 8 March 2021). [5]

Hardoy, J. et al. (2019), *Planeamiento participativo para la resiliencia al climate en ciudades de América Latina*, CDKN, FFLA, IDRC, https://www.crclatam.net/documentos/publicaciones/72-reporte-de-investigacion-planeamiento-participativo-para-la-resiliencia-al-clima-en-ciudades-de-am%C3%A9rica-latina/file.html (accessed on 10 March 2021). [106]

Hardoy, J., G. Pandiella and L. Barrero (2011), "Local disaster risk reduction in Latin American urban areas", *Environment and Urbanization*, Vol. 23/2, pp. 401-413, https://doi.org/10.1177/0956247811416435. [12]

Hardoy, J. and R. Ruete (2013), "Incorporating climate change adaptation into planning for a liveable city in Rosario, Argentina", *Environment and Urbanization*, Vol. 25/2, pp. 339-360, https://doi.org/10.1177/0956247813493232. [16]

ICLEI (n.d.), *African Members*, ICLEI-Local Governments for Sustainability, https://africa.iclei.org/iclei_member/ (accessed on 10 October 2021). [63]

IFRC (2010), *World Disasters Report 2010: Focus on urban risk*, International Federation of Red Cross and Red Crescent Societies, Geneva. [85]

INDEC (n.d.), *Instituto Nacional de Estadistica y Censos, Republica Argentina*, https://www.indec.gob.ar/ (accessed on 11 October 2021). [99]

Johnson, C. and S. Blackburn (2014), "Advocacy for urban resilience: UNISDR's Making Cities Resilient Campaign", *Environment and Urbanization*, Vol. 26/1, https://doi.org/10.1177/0956247813518684. [31]

Lassa, J. and E. Nugraha (2015), "From shared learning to shared action in building resilience in the city of Bandar Lampung, Indonesia", *Environment and Urbanization*, Vol. 27/1, https://doi.org/10.1177/0956247814552233. [36]

López, M. (2015), "El sistema de planificación y el ordenamiento territorial para Buen Vivir en el Ecuador", *Geousp – Espaço e Tempo*, Vol. 19/2, pp. 297-312, https://doi.org/10.11606/issn.2179-0892. [97]

Manda, M. and E. Wanda (2017), "Understanding the nature and scale of risks in Karonga, Malawi", *Environment and Urbanization*, Vol. 29/1, https://doi.org/10.1177/0956247817692200. [46]

Mastrángelo, D. and V. Carbuccia (2020), "Avances de la agenda climática en la ciudad de Rosario, Argentina", *Medio Ambiente y Urbanización*, Vol. 92/1, pp. 205-236, https://www.ingentaconnect.com/contentone/iieal/meda/2020/00000092/00000001/art00009#expand/collapse (accessed on 8 March 2021). [19]

Maurizi, V. and S. Fontana (2019), *Building capacity through risk communication strategies in Santa Fe city, Argentina*, UNDP and Catholic University of Córdoba, Tabasco, https://www.pagina12.com.ar/diario/elpais/1-34683-2004-04. [11]

Montecinos, E. (2005), “Los estudios de descentralización en América Latina: una revisión sobre el estado actual de latemática”, *Revista eure*, Vol. XXXI, pp. 77-88, https://scielo.conicyt.cl/pdf/eure/v31n93/art05.pdf (accessed on 11 October 2021). [95]

Municipio de Portoviejo (2019), *Plan Portoviejo 2035*, Gobierno Autónomo Decentralizado municipal del Cantón Portoviejo, Portoviejo, https://content.bhybrid.com/publication/df513425/mobile/ (accessed on 24 August 2022). [23]

NDRRMC (n.d.), *National Disaster Risk Reduction and Management Council - Office of Civil Defense*, https://ndrrmc.gov.ph/ (accessed on 11 October 2021). [111]

Novillo (2018), “Cambio climático y conflictos socioambientales en ciudades intermedias de América Latina y el Caribe (Climate change and environmental social conflicts in intermediary cities of Latin America and the Caribbean)”, *Letras Verdes, Revista Latinoamericana de Estudios Socioambientales* 24, pp. 124-142, https://doi.org/10.17141/letrasverdes.24.2018.3323. [3]

OECD (2021), *OECD Regional Outlook 2021*, OECD Publishing, Paris, https://doi.org/10.1787/17017efe-en. [96]

OECD (2015), *Governing the City*, OECD Publishing, Paris, https://doi.org/10.1787/9789264226500-en. [102]

OECD/PSI (2020), *Rural Development Strategy Review of Ethiopia: Reaping the Benefits of Urbanisation*, OECD Development Pathways, OECD Publishing, Paris, https://doi.org/10.1787/a325a658-en. [51]

Office of the President of the Philippines (2018), *PSF Bankrolls P192-Million Local Climate Change Adaptation Projects*, https://climate.gov.ph/news/46 (accessed on 2 October 2021). [35]

Ogato, G. (2013), “The Quest for Mainstreaming Climate Change Adaptation into Urban Development Planning of Ambo Town, Ethiopia”, *American Journal of Human Ecology*, Vol. 2/3, pp. 103-119, https://doi.org/10.11634/216796221302478. [49]

Ogato, G. et al. (2017), “Towards mainstreaming climate change adaptation into land use planning and management: The case of Ambo Town, Ethiopia”, in Filho, W. et al. (eds.), *Climate Change Adaptation in Africa capacity to adapt*, Springer, Cham, https://doi.org/10.1007/978-3-319-49520-0. [48]

Plataforma (2020), *Project 10/12: Milan (Italy) - Quelimane (Mozambique)*, https://platforma-dev.eu/project-1012-milan-italy-quelimane-mozambique/ (accessed on 11 October 2021). [71]

Price, R. (2019), “Climate compatible development and rapid urbanisation in Rwanda”*, K4D Helpdesk Report*, No. 660, Institute of Development Studies, Brighton, https://gain.nd.edu/our-work/country-index/. [53]

RAMCC (n.d.), *Red Argentina de Municipios Frente al Cambio Climatico*, https://www.ramcc.net/fideicomiso.php (accessed on 11 October 2021). [116]

Republic of Kenya (2020), *The Kisumu County Climate Change Bill 2020*, https://www.kisumu.go.ke/wp-content/uploads/2020/09/Climate-change-bill.pdf (accessed on 8 October 2021). [61]

Republic of Rwanda (2018), *Urbanisation & Rural Settlement: Sector Strategic Plan for National Strategy for Transformation*, Ministry of Infrastructure, Kigali, https://www.mininfra.gov.rw/fileadmin/user_upload/Mininfra/Publications/Policies/Urbanization__Human_Settlement_and_Housing_Development/Urbanisation__Rural_Settlements_Sector_Strategic_Plan_2018-24.pdf (accessed on 6 October 2021). [55]

Republic of Rwanda (2015), *National Roadmap for Green Secondary City Development*, Ministry of Infrastructure (MININFRA) and Global Green Growth Institute & Implementation (GGP&I), https://gggi.org/site/assets/uploads/2017/12/National-Roadmap-for-Green-Secondary-City-Development.pdf (accessed on 6 October 2021). [56]

Republic of Rwanda (2015), *National Urbanization Policy*, Ministry of Infrastructure, Kigali, https://bpmis.gov.rw/asset_uplds/files/National%20Urbanization%20Policy.pdf (accessed on 6 October 2021). [54]

Republic of Rwanda (2013), *Economic Development and Poverty Reduction Strategy II*, https://www.rsb.gov.rw/fileadmin/user_upload/files/EDPRS_2_Abridged_Version.pdf (accessed on 6 October 2021). [57]

Republic of Rwanda (2011), *Green Growth and Climate Resilience: National Strategy for Climate Change and Low Carbon Development*, https://www.greengrowthknowledge.org/sites/default/files/downloads/policy-database/RWANDA%29%20Green%20Growth%20and%20Climate%20Resilience%20-%20National%20Strategy%20for%20Climate%20Change%20and%20Low%20Carbon%20Development.pdf (accessed on 6 October 2021). [52]

Revi, A. et al. (2014), *Urban Areas in Climate Change 2014: Impacts, Adaptation, and Vulnerability*, IPCC, Cambridge, https://www.ipcc.ch/report/ar5/wg2/. [1]

Roberts, D. (2010), "Prioritizing climate change adaptation and local level resilience in Durban, South Africa", *Environment and Urbanization*, Vol. 22/2, https://doi.org/10.1177/0956247810379948. [79]

Roberts, D. (2008), "Thinking globally, acting locally — institutionalizing climate change at the local government level in Durban, South Africa", *Environment and Urbanization*, Vol. 20/2, https://doi.org/10.1177/0956247808096126. [78]

Roberts, D. et al. (2012), "Exploring ecosystem-based adaptation in Durban, South Africa: "learning-by-doing" at the local government coal face", *Environment and Urbanization*, Vol. 24/1, https://doi.org/10.1177/0956247811431412. [80]

Roberts, D. et al. (2020), "Durban's 100 Resilient Cities journey: governing resilience from within", *Environment and Urbanization*, Vol. 32/2, https://doi.org/10.1177/0956247820946555. [76]

Roberts, D. et al. (2016), "Durban", in Barlett, S. and D. Satterthwaite (eds.), *Cities in a Finite Planet*, Routledge, London. [75]

Roberts, D. and S. O'Donoghue (2013), "Urban environmental challenges and climate change action in Durban, South Africa", *Environment and Urbanization*, Vol. 25/2, https://doi.org/10.1177/0956247813500904. [82]

Rondinelli, D. (1982), "The potential of secondary cities facilitating deconcentrated urbanization in Africa", *African Urban Studies*. [45]

Satterthwaite, D. et al. (2020), “Building Resilience to Climate Change in Informal Settlements”, *One Earth*, Vol. 2/2, pp. 143-156, https://doi.org/10.1016/j.oneear.2020.02.002. [89]

Satterthwaite, D. et al. (2018), *Responding to climate change in cities and in their informal settlements and economies*, IIED and IIED-América Latina, London, https://pubs.iied.org/G04328/. [105]

Scott, H. and D. Archer (2017), “Developing city resilience strategies: lessons from the ICLEI-ACCCRN process”, *Working Paper Series*, No. 41, IIED, London, https://doi.org/10.13140/RG.2.2.18761.13928. [43]

Scott, Z. and M. Tarazona (2011), *Study on Disaster Risk Reduction, Decentralization and Political Economy Decentralisation and Disaster Risk Reduction*, ISDR, UNDP, OPM, https://www.preventionweb.net/english/hyogo/gar/2011/en/bgdocs/Scott_&_Tarazona_2011.pdf (accessed on 11 October 2021). [98]

SDI (n.d.), *Slum Dwellers International*, https://sdinet.org/ (accessed on 11 October 2021). [72]

SEI (2020), *Governing sustainability in secondary cities of the Global South*, Stockholm Environment Institute, Stockholm, http://www.sei.org. [112]

Simet, L. (2018), “Santa Fe, Argentina. Risk Management: Intersectoriality, Memory, and Global Platforms”, in Cohen, M., M. Gutman and M. Carrizosa (eds.), *Facing Risk. New Urban Resilience Practices in Latin America*, CAF and Observatory on Latin America (OLA), The New School, https://scioteca.caf.com/handle/123456789/1431 (accessed on 8 March 2021). [14]

Slack, E. (2019), *Metropolitan Governance: Principles and Practice*, Inter-American Development Bank, https://doi.org/10.18235/0001576. [101]

Solo Kota Kita (n.d.), *Project History*, https://solokotakita.org/en/about/history/ (accessed on 5 October 2021). [42]

SunStar Phillipines (2018), *Helping towns cope with climate change*, https://www.sunstar.com.ph/article/422882/Business/Helping-towns-cope-with-climate-change (accessed on 2 October 2021). [34]

Taylor, J. (2015), “A tale of two cities: comparing alternative approaches to reducing the vulnerability of riverbank communities in two Indonesian cities”, *Environment and Urbanization*, Vol. 27/2, pp. 621-636, https://doi.org/10.1177/0956247815594532. [40]

Taylor, J. and J. Lassa (2015), “How can climate change vulnerability assessments best impact policy and planning? Lessons from Indonesia”, *Asian Cities Climate Resilience*, No. 22, IIED, London, https://pubs.iied.org/sites/default/files/pdfs/migrate/10743IIED.pdf (accessed on 2 October 2021). [37]

UNDESA (2018), *World Urbanization Prospects: The 2018 Revision*, Online edition, https://population.un.org/wup/ (accessed on 23 April 2020). [2]

UNDRR (2019), *Words into Action guidelines: Implementation guide for local disaster risk reduction and resilience strategies*, United National Office for Disaster Risk Reduction, Geneva, https://www.preventionweb.net/files/57399_57399localdrrandresiliencestrategie.pdf (accessed on 8 March 2021). [6]

UNDRR (2009), *Risk and poverty in a changing climate*, United Nations Office for Disaster Risk Reduction, Geneva, https://www.undrr.org/publication/global-assessment-report-disaster-risk-reduction-2009 (accessed on 11 October 2021). [84]

UNDRR (n.d.), *Making Cities Resilient: My City is Getting Ready*, https://www.unisdr.org/campaign/resilientcities/ (accessed on 11 October 2021). [114]

UN-Habitat (2020), *Breaking Cycles of Risk Accumulation in African Cities*, United Nations Human Settlements Programme, Nairobi, https://unhabitat.org/sites/default/files/2020/03/un_report_2019_ebook_high_res.pdf (accessed on 5 October 2021). [47]

UN-Habitat (2020), *Urban Indicators Database*. [83]

UN-Habitat (2012), *The Impact of Climate Change on Urban Settlements in Colombia*, United Nations Human Settlements Programme (UN-HABITAT), Nairobi. [110]

UN-Habitat (2008), *Ethiopia: Ambo urban profile*, UN-Habitat, Ambo, https://unhabitat.org/sites/default/files/download-manager-files/Ethiopia%20Ambo%20Urban%20Profile.pdf (accessed on 5 October 2021). [50]

UN-Habitat (2006), *Kisumu Urban Sector Profile*, United Nations Human Settlement Programme, Nairobi, https://unhabitat.org/kenya-kisumu-urban-profile (accessed on 8 October 2021). [59]

USAID (2014), *Country Development Cooperation Strategy (CDCS)*, USAID, Maputo, https://www.usaid.gov/sites/default/files/documents/1860/CDCS_February_2019_Mozambique_update20202.pdf (accessed on 11 October 2021). [68]

USAID (2013), *Coastal City Adaptation Project (CCAP)*, Building More Resilient Mozambique, http://Mozambique Coastal Cities Adaptation Programme (CCAP, 2014-2019) (accessed on 11 October 2021). [69]

Valsagna, A. and M. Tejedor (2017), “De la gestión local de riesgos a la resiliencia. La experiencia de la Ciudad de Santa Fe”, *Medio Ambiente y Urbanización*, Vol. 86/1, pp. 43-69, https://www.ingentaconnect.com/contentone/iieal/meda/2017/00000086/00000001/art00003 (accessed on 8 March 2021). [15]

VPUU (2019), *What is Enumeration? Enumeration begins for informal settlement support programme*, Violence Prevention Through Urban Upgrading, http://vpuu.org.za/programmes/ict4d/enumeration-informal-settlements/ (accessed on 25 August 2022). [74]

Weru, J. et al. (2018), “The Akiba Mashinani Trust, Kenya: a local fund’s role in urban development”, *Environment and Urbanization*, Vol. 30/1, https://doi.org/10.1177/0956247817750963. [41]

World Bank (2020), *Mozambique: Upscaling nature-based flood protection in Mozambique’s cities*, The Wolrld Bank, Washington DC. [65]

World Bank (2018), *Helping Mozambique Cities Build Resilience to Climate Change*, https://www.worldbank.org/en/news/feature/2018/06/05/helping-mozambique-cities-build-resilience-to-climate-change (accessed on 11 October 2021). [70]

World Bank (2015), *Investing in Urban Resilience: Protecting and Promoting Development in a Changing World*, World Bank, Washington DC, https://www.gfdrr.org/sites/default/files/publication/Investing%20in%20Urban%20Resilience%20Final.pdf (accessed on 11 October 2021). [91]

WRI (2021), *Sustainable Food Production for a Resilient Rosario*, World Resources Institute Ross Centre, https://prizeforcities.org/project/sustainable-food-production-rosario (accessed on 5 October 2021). [21]

5 Financing low-carbon and resilient intermediary cities

This chapter highlights the challenges facing intermediary cities in accessing climate finance. Given the pressing nature of climate issues and the scale of investment required for mitigation and adaptation, urgent and innovative strategies are needed to address cities' financing needs. The chapter examines constraints on access to finance from two angles: the actors that implement climate investments in urban areas and the actual systems of financing. It presents a typology of climate financing mechanisms available to intermediary cities, provides examples of successful financing of urban climate projects in developing countries and recommends actions that can be taken by national and local governments to help intermediary cities mobilise urban climate finance.

Introduction

Intermediary cities host a large share of the world's population that is vulnerable to climate change. These small and medium-sized cities are also increasingly contributing to the greenhouse gas emissions that cause global warming. They face an urgent need of finance for climate action.

Yet climate finance for cities is facing an investment gap. A recent study estimated that investment in urban climate finance in 2017-18 amounted to USD 384 billion annually (Negreiros et al., 2021[1]). This is far below the trillions of dollars of investment in urban infrastructure that will be needed to meet the Paris Agreement targets – an estimated USD 4.5-5.4 trillion per annum from 2015 to 2030, the study notes.

As they seek to mobilise the finance necessary for addressing climate change, intermediary cities often have limited human and fiscal resources. This may be because of their size and generally lower per capita income. Figure 5.1 shows that GDP per capita in intermediary cities skews sharply lower than the national average and is well below the mean for larger cities.[1] The financing capacities of intermediary cities can also vary greatly within a country. This implies a need for flexibility in the structuring of finance for climate investments.

Figure 5.1. Differences in the city/country ratio of GDP per capita in intermediary and large cities

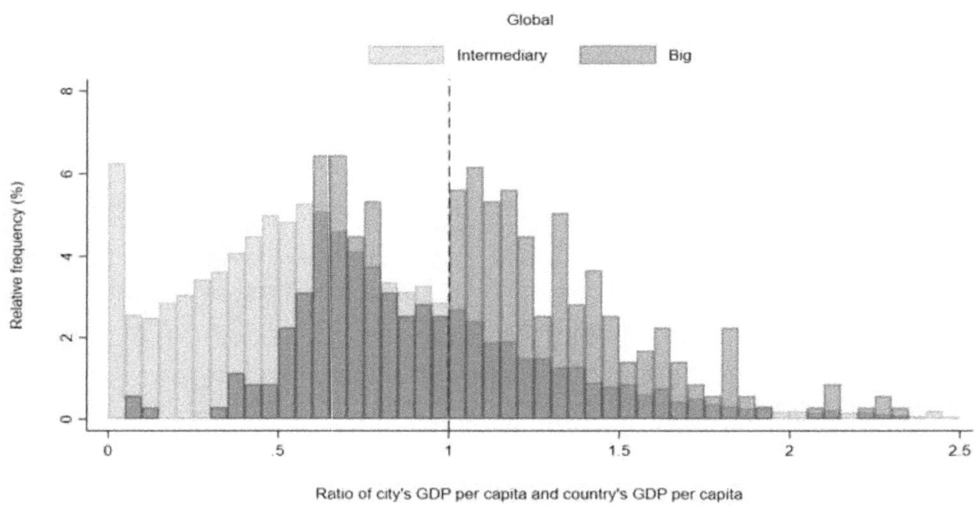

Source: Authors' computation using GHS Urban Centre Database (2019[2]).

What do we mean by urban climate finance? Climate finance is not limited to specialist financing or financing instruments that are labelled "green" or "climate", e.g. green bonds.[2] Rather, to be able to implement the scale of investment required to meet the Paris targets, all financial flows must be viewed as potentially climate finance. The idea is to reframe climate finance as mainstream financing that supports the transition of all aspects of urban investment into investments that either reduce greenhouse gas (GHG) emissions or build resilience, or both. Previous OECD publications have set out important areas of opportunity relating to repurposing and extending the revenue base, expenditure priorities and financing systems for city climate investment (OECD, 2019[3]). In this context, urban investment financing systems should:

- promote the concept that all urban finance must include climate objectives as an integral part of its operation, incentivising all urban infrastructure and services investment to be more environmentally sound;

- count as climate finance existing sources of finance and funding that are not from specialist/dedicated climate/green sources and that are used for climate-related investments (financing any eligible mitigation and/or adaptation projects);
- ensure that specialist climate finance (from dedicated climate finance sources) will leverage additional resources and be used to promote pilot initiatives addressing investments beyond the capacity of existing financing sources.

This chapter sets out the constraints and opportunities involved in providing urban climate finance to intermediary cities. It examines issues faced by the agencies that are making the investment decisions in cities (the "demand side" of the urban climate-finance market) and by the institutions that are potentially supplying the finance for these investments (the "supply side" of the market).

Given that existing revenue sources are insufficient for the investments required for climate action, even in larger cities, and that mobilising non-traditional finance for climate investment requires new capacities that challenge even larger cities and financial institutions, there is a clear need for national urban programmes that bolster demand-side capacities to formulate and structure bankable climate projects at the city level and that also structure supply-side enabling frameworks for appropriate financing mechanisms and instruments that provide access to needed finance by intermediary cities.

The key message of the chapter is that both sides of the market need to be strengthened, particularly when addressing the needs of intermediary cities.

Who are the users of climate finance in intermediary cities?

Before proceeding to examine the context of climate finance for intermediary cities, it is important to have a clear idea of which entities are to be financed. In the context of this chapter, the focus is on finance that facilitates the implementation of investment in climate-related activities (mitigation and adaptation) in urban centres and surrounding areas. The critical issue then becomes, who are the local users of climate finance? Which actors implement climate investments in urban areas? Collectively we will henceforth refer to these actors as "urban investment agents" (UIAs).They include:

- **local governments**. Often there are two or more local governments in an urban area. Many intermediary cities have outgrown their original administrative boundaries and cater to a significantly larger share of population, including rural population in adjacent jurisdictions. This raises issues of metropolitan government investment and burden sharing.
- **urban institutions**. City utilities may be public, private or public-private partnerships (PPPs)[3]. Often state or provincial-level entities such as development corporations and utilities operate within and across local government jurisdictions. For instance in some countries, such as in Indonesia, national institutions may play a large investment role in housing and upgrading.
- **manufacturing/processing firms and other services located in the city**. The primary GHG emissions of cities often come from enterprises and private-sector actors. Many of these firms and actors also process agricultural and other resources for surrounding rural areas, and have linkages to, and influence on, farming and other actors in these areas. Many of these actors will have an impact on emissions and are also impacted by climate change. Thus these actors will need to make investments to achieve needed mitigation and adaptation targets.
- **individuals and community organisations**. Individual decisions on issues such as mobility and the energy efficiency of housing can make a large impact on emissions. Further, the resilience of neighbourhoods is often determined by the capacity of community-based organisations operating at a neighbourhood level. Thus financial support of these actors can accelerate and complement climate action led by other actors.

Reaching the targets of the Paris Agreement will require the involvement of these local financial actors. Systems of urban climate finance have to take into account the needs of all actors within urban areas. Nationally determined contributions (NDCs) represent national government promises of aggregate cuts in emissions and increased climate resilience. In reality, these promises in the urban sphere will be fulfilled by investments undertaken by the actors listed above. NDCs do not necessarily cover all investments required for mitigation actions to meet the Paris targets, nor do they encompass the breadth of adaptation actions required in cities to respond to climate impacts. This further widens the scope of actors.

Eligible climate finance investments

How is climate investment defined from the viewpoint of the financial sector? A "taxonomy" defines which investments are eligible for climate finance and may provide criteria on how to judge their relative performance in different sectors. There are numerous such taxonomies. The Climate Bonds Initiative (CBI) Taxonomy (CBI, 2021[4]). one of the first, most developed and most used, is used to screen bonds and identify whether investment projects are eligible for green or climate financing. It "identifies the assets and projects needed to deliver a low-carbon economy and gives greenhouse gas screening criteria" (CBI, 2021[4]). The People's Bank of China (PBOC) taxonomy (PBOC, 2020[5]) was the first national taxonomy and is institutionalised in a broader "green finance" system. The EU's framework to facilitate sustainable investment (2020[6]), known as the Taxonomy Regulation, is considered the most sophisticated taxonomy in terms of breadth of coverage, which includes performance standards.

Figure 5.2 provides an overview of the sectors in which eligible investments may be found under the CBI taxonomy.

Figure 5.2. Climate Bonds Initiative taxonomy

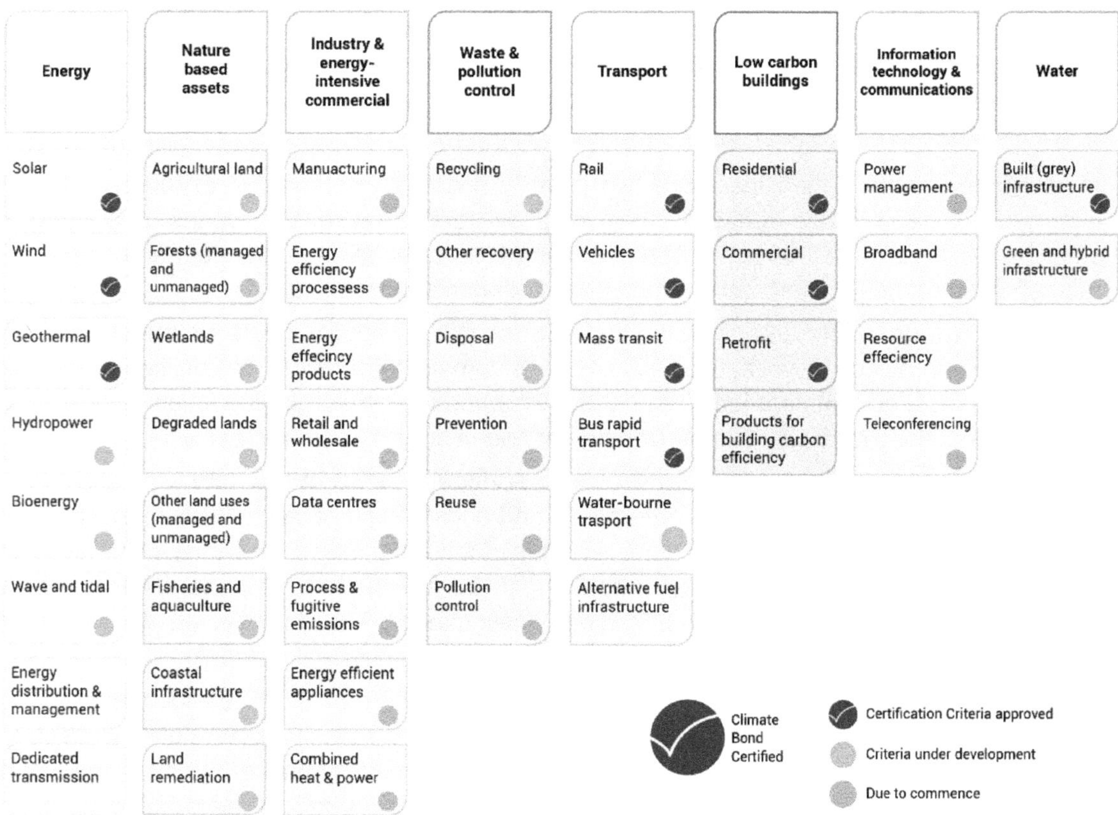

Source: Adapted based on https://www.climatebonds.net/standard/taxonomy; see also for further information, including eligible project types and eligibility criteria.

Taxonomies are structured according to the focus of their designers and can be both too detailed and too broad for easy application by city project sponsors. Further, current taxonomies underdefine the multiple investments involved in adaptation investment, particularly in relation to the consequences of sea-level rise, flood control and drainage, and this can be confusing. For example, it might be unlikely for a city to consider investing in "fisheries and aquaculture", yet the building of storm-surge barriers may involve just such industries. To an extent, this reflects a lack of clear business models for green investments. Further dialogue with financial regulators is needed on this issue. It should be noted, however, that as countries seek to draft taxonomies for sustainable or climate investment that match their circumstances, existing taxonomies such as the CBI taxonomy can be used.

Climate-related infrastructure development needs in intermediary cities

The OECD estimates that limiting the rise in global temperatures to less than 2°C by 2100 will require an annual investment of USD 6.9 trillion in global infrastructure between 2016 and 2030. Developing countries account for approximately two-thirds of the estimated investment needs, or about USD 4 trillion per year over the same period (OECD, 2017[7]). This amounts to an additional 10% in infrastructure spending (World Bank, 2019[8]). The associated annual incremental up-front costs of future infrastructure investments that are required to adapt to climate change consistent with the below 2°C scenario have been estimated at around 10%. This reflects costs in addition to business-as-usual infrastructure requirements and is in addition to mitigation costs. The World Bank estimates that there are significant benefits for such investment, with a net estimated benefit of USD 4 net for every USD 1 invested in resilience (World Bank, 2019[8]). However, achieving a sustained 20% increment over existing capital spending to meet adaptation and mitigation needs is an enormous task for many intermediary cities.

Given the pressing nature of climate issues and the scale of investment required, it is important:

- to address the key constraints on mainstreaming and upscaling climate finance
- to identify the challenges faced by intermediary cities around financing climate investments
- to examine whether these challenges are the same issues in all contexts.

As discussed in previous chapters, intermediary cities, defined in this report as cities of 50 000 to 1 million inhabitants, have often been a neglected area of national and regional economic and urban development and investment. As a result, there are growing levels of disparity and inequity between metropolitan regions and small and medium-sized cities in terms of development, fiscal transfers and productivity. In Indonesia, for instance, the per capita GDP of Jakarta, a city of 10 million, is more than four times greater than that of Denpasar, a city of 900 000 (BPS, 2020[9]).

Overall, the development of intermediary cities is hindered by poor infrastructure, inadequate human capital and weak urban governance, leading to a poor tax revenue performance. This is particularly the case for less developed regions: the average taxation yield of national GDP for local governments is 5.3% in Southeast Asia, 4% in Latin America, 3.2% in Africa and 1.5% in South Asia, compared with 13% in Europe (UCLG, 2008[10]). Moreover, spatial constraints relating to distance, remoteness and the complexities of a mixed formal/traditional tenure system present additional challenges for some intermediary cities particularly in Small Island Developing States (SIDS). For these reasons, industries in intermediary cities (including in most industrial clusters) often struggle to achieve scale, and may well face higher transaction costs for financing. This undermines their competitiveness and efficiency.

The macro context sets the scene for climate-related investment by urban investment agents in intermediary cities, but it is important to understand the scope of needed investment. Local government and other government agencies bear very little responsibility for carbon emissions and climate vulnerability, while investment decisions by local households and enterprises have a large influence on both. But the scope of city policies can be limited. Indeed, the larger-scale impact of enterprises based in the city with respect to emissions – broadly, Scope 3 emissions as defined by the International Panel on Climate Change (IPCC) (GHG Protocol, 2011[11]) – will not be amenable to action by city agencies. Action on the broader national climate impact of enterprises based in the city (Scope 3 emissions) will require action at the national level. Figure 5.3 shows the limits in intermediary cities on the scope and impact of direct climate investments by UIAs ("City operations" in the diagram).

Figure 5.3. Investment scope for climate-change finance

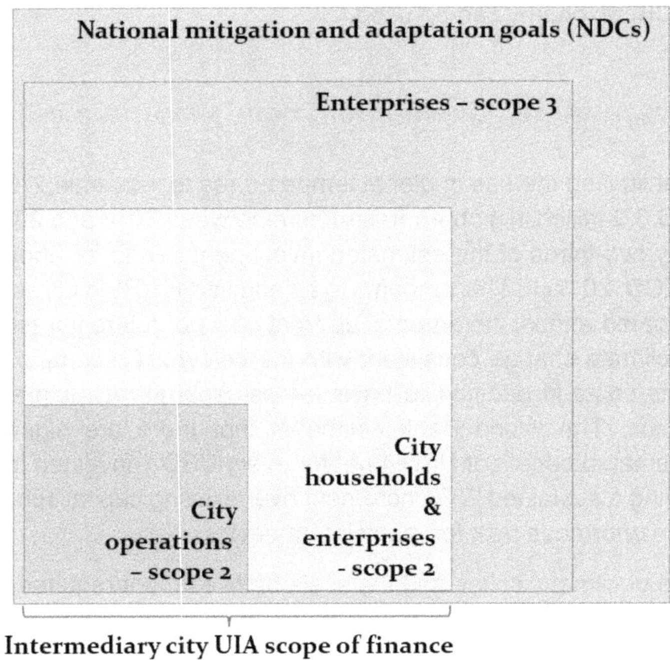

Source: Authors' own elaboration.

Intermediary cities are potentially bigger emitters proportionally than megacities and, as we have seen from OECD data (Figure 5.2, above), have fewer resources for addressing these emissions. This argues for much more focus on financial support for intermediary cities – especially when considering that adaptation investments are likely to be at least proportionally shared by these cities.

Objectives for urban climate investment in intermediary cities in a post-COVID world

The COVID-19 pandemic will exacerbate the constraints on the structuring of climate finance. This will particularly be the case in relation to own-source revenue used to finance investments or service debt. The pandemic has had a large negative effect on city finances in multiple ways:

- It reduced the level of financial inflows to financial institutions, as incomes and profits were impacted, and savings were drawn down. This increased the pressure on financial institutions to reduce lending and increase reserves (including buying national government bonds), which reduces the financing available to local governments. Meanwhile, local governments have had to increase spending on health at a time when tax yield is lower, requiring them to issue more bonds or seek bank lending. Although the bonds could be used to fund green/climate projects and programmes in green recovery programmes, the space for financing climate investment will likely be less (this will be further discussed below).
- COVID-19 has often reduced the revenue base of UIAs, thus reducing both off-take income from city services and tax revenues and the debt service capacity for climate investment by cities and

city implementing institutions. This is particularly the case if central governments pass a significant part of the burden of economic recovery to subnational levels of government.

- Differing perceived rates of impact of the virus on economies has lowered the credit ratings of some emerging market and developing economies (EMDE), leading to a rise in the cost of debt.
- COVID-19 curtailed economic growth and thus the potential for cost recovery from user charges for climate/environmental services. This may be partly offset, however, as many mitigation investments reduce costs in the long run.

In the context of "green recovery" from the pandemic, economic recovery and resilience strategies ought to provide immediate high-priority opportunities for climate finance. Such strategies are likely to emphasise labour intensive, critical and strategic import replacement (sustainable recovery) industries, which can also be made low carbon and resilient (Cities Alliance, 2020[12]). They should also prioritise health infrastructure and infrastructure to support the industries mentioned, and should promote other investments that will have significant co-benefits, such as pollution reduction, and that are preferably cost recoverable. As such, climate finance investments need to be formulated to include a focus on implementing these strategies, which are, in any case, a "no-regret" option and provide tangible benefits to communities.

When addressing these priority strategies, it is necessary to consider the economic and spatial context of climate finance. Intermediary cities constitute rungs in the urban hierarchy, but this characterisation is too simplistic as a basis for climate investment, and consequently for climate finance strategies. The supply chains of industry clusters based in the capital city, or large metropolitan cities, weave in and out of those cities; other clusters are based in intermediary cities or networks of small and medium-sized cities (Cities Alliance, 2019[13]). As such, their spatial circumstances and economic functions are interdependent. Different types of networks are established among economic actors in such cities. Climate finance mechanisms need to be able to address investments that will be made flexibly, enabling access to proponents across a range of sectors and in a wide variety of spatial and economic contexts.

As an indication of the range of economic circumstances encountered, Figure 5.4 shows differences in per capita GDP growth rates across intermediary and large cities. While large cities tend to be clustered around national average growth rates, intermediary cities extend in a much wider distribution, with some growing much more slowly and others much more quickly than the bulk of big cities. These rapidly growing small cities may well be those in overspill areas of megacities or in quickly growing innovative clusters. Again, the range of circumstances in intermediary cities reinforces the need for very flexible financing mechanisms that can enable access to as wide a range of cities as possible.

Figure 5.4. Differences in the GDP per capita growth rates of intermediary and large cities

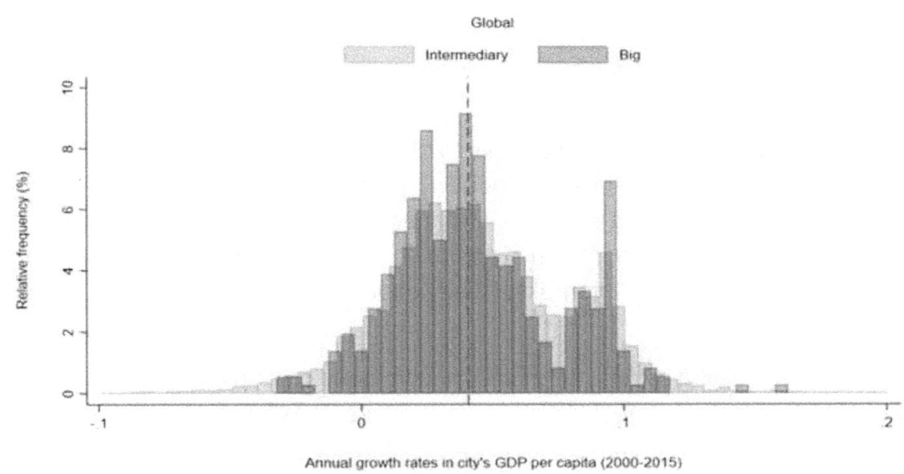

Source: Authors' computation using GHS Urban Centre Database (2019[2]).

Designing climate financing solutions becomes more complex when they span local government areas with different scales in terms of population, economic development and wealth. Yet certain large-scale, boundary-crossing investments – such as metropolitan public transportation systems (for mitigation) or restored wetland buffers against storm surges (for adaptation) – may be among the most desirable climate investments, and must not be neglected. At the level of the climate finance facility, systems of project assessment that determine financing eligibility need to reflect the broader objectives of the nation in order to be viable, and to justify potential concessional finance. Climate investments in industry clusters and infrastructure will have environmental, finance, economic and social dimensions. Green Climate Fund (GCF) investment criteria include these dimensions, which must all be considered for the investment to be viable (Green Climate Fund, 2020[14]).

Cities play a key role in implementing the adaptation and mitigation investments required under nationally determined contributions. Indeed, cities have dominant roles in national economic and climate policies, considering their dominance with respect to both the economy and GHG emissions. Thus, in the context of the NDCs, they should detail and prioritise investments in the sectors of renewable energy, energy efficiency, transport, waste and adaptation, as determined by assessments based on local GHG and climate vulnerability profiles. Important factors such as the sustainability of essential services, labour intensity, total benefits to citizens and financial sustainability should also be heavily weighted by UIAs in assessing priorities for investments. These priorities are referred to henceforward as "localised NDCs".

Given the above objectives and context, what are the likely high-priority climate investment opportunities that will also foster a green recovery? Investments with a focus on building a resilient economy should be considered to be the priority. They should encompass investments in enterprises that provide appropriate renewable energy and energy efficiency equipment, including designs appropriate to small and medium-sized enterprises (SMEs) and the informal sector. They should also focus on reinforcing the resilience of vulnerable communities and building inclusive and strong health systems. Furthermore, investment in resilient common-user infrastructure and intermodal logistics networks, hubs, facilities and systems is also very important.[4] This may include resilient and low-carbon local energy, waste and water networks, and ecosystem services investment in water/wastewater and coastal zones. Investments that should also be considered as priority are those that aim to strengthen city and intercity clusters (specifically those that build on local resource endowments) and that support cluster associations and communities of interest. Such investments should also provide support for collaborative research and development, innovation, knowledge sharing and data management focused on reducing carbon footprints and building resilience.

National, subnational and local government development strategies, budgets and intergovernmental transfers need to align so as to identify and support these priorities. Climate investments need to be seen as, and structured for, delivering the employment, infrastructure and energy required for a green recovery.

Constraints on access to climate financing in intermediary cities

Intermediary cities face many constraints on access to climate finance. The challenges can be associated with uncertainties around climate risks due to modelling limitations, the structure of the financial system, limited political will and/or the capacities of local authorities and other urban institutions. It is important that national, subnational, and local policy makers approach urban climate finance as something that all economic and sectoral policies need to internalise. They should also address shortfalls in existing financing and funding mechanisms.

Five structural shortfalls in existing climate financing mechanisms prevent effective engagement with cities. The shortfalls particularly affect intermediary cities, as they are constrained by their own limited resources and capacity (CCFLA, 2015[15]). Climate finance, whether through existing financing and funding streams or through specialist climate funds, needs to address these shortfalls. They are:

- *lack of green/climate budgeting, green taxes/fees and green procurement systems* that recognise the linkages between budgeting; appropriate revenues (taxes and fees incentivising low-carbon and resilient development); expenditure; and levels of investment vis à vis the investment needs required for localised NDCs. This dependent and/or limited revenue base also impacts cities' credit ratings, which in turn can limit financing options and consequently impact the cost of financing. Such options can also be, and often are, constrained by explicit regulation by higher levels of government. The OECD has undertaken significant work to provide a framework for tracking climate finance and maximising the impact of funding and financing flows (OECD, 2019[3]; OECD, 2022[16]; OECD, 2021[17]).
- *lack of planning and project development*. In the past, city planning processes generally did not consider climate issues, and thus provided a poor basis for funding applications. This is changing as cities develop climate action plans to address localised NDCs, but cities still need support. Similarly, city project-development systems need to be structured to foster green design solutions, which may require higher levels of co-ordination and design integration. They need to include climate finance in the design of the funding mix and the required monitoring, reporting and verification (MRV) systems in the project design. These are specialist skills that many cities may never need "in house", but that must be available if they are to access climate finance.
- *shortfalls in technical capacity and resources to access climate finance*. In many countries, assistance to negotiate with the main entry points for climate finance is needed by most cities. Local governments and other UIAs have few structural relationships with such agencies and speak a different technical language. Although local governments increasingly have environmental officers, they are generally institutionally removed from financing units. In order for financing to be accessible, applications must involve objectives couched in language that is familiar to city officials, as well as data that they are able to collect. Such information can be supplied by specialised consultants, but cities have limited consultancy budgets. More consultant inputs may be required to verify performance during implementation, and this increases costs. Finally, lead times and approval processes can be very long, which creates difficulties when officials are elected for mandates of, say, three years. In summary, it is necessary to reduce the very high transaction costs of access to climate finance for local governments and groups of local governments.
- *lack of capacity to manage the financial aspects of the project*. Once approval has been secured, understanding and managing the financial aspects of the project is very important to project success. This will often depend on capacity to manage the type of instrument used and to understand the performance metrics associated with it. Failure to achieve projected emissions reductions may involve paying back financing, while success means that cities can apply for another grant, with the same transaction costs. These potential costs are a significant deterrent to many local governments. Where finance is dependent on market pricing, cost uncertainty can deter investment decisions. Additionally, cities often also require help in putting together the underlying financing of the project, particularly public-private partnerships (PPPs).
- *lack of funding flexibility and partnerships*. Cities need to be able to access appropriate funds and to leverage/combine them for more impact. Given that most available sources of finance do not cover all aspects of project preparation and implementation, cities generally have to cobble together a combination of funding sources to develop and construct the project. This is difficult given varying objectives and access criteria. Further, cities often have limited ability to use a wider range of funding sources, such as land value capture, and when such funding is available the taxation rates may be capped. A lack of sources of funding to repay finance and to cover the unfinanced part of investments is perhaps the major constraint on up-scaled urban climate finance.

These shortfalls in access to climate finance stem from two main structural challenges: the ability of UIAs to develop, structure and implement climate projects (the "demand side" of the climate finance market), and the actual systems of financing (the "supply side" of this market). This is discussed below.

Demand-side prerequisites for climate financing in intermediary cities

Once climate investment needs are identified, it is important that UIAs be committed to following through with effective investment and have the mandate and resources to do so. In other words, the prerequisites for effective climate finance must be in place (Colenbrander et al., 2018[18]).

Governance is one of the main factors that will influence climate investment in intermediary cities. Given that mayors and other elected officials may have short-term mandates, strengthening governance to help ensure continuity of political will can have an important impact. Local enabling environments can be improved by structuring incentives for low-carbon and resilient investments, and by ensuring the efficient and transparent operation of implementing agencies. While intermediary cities may have limited powers to change governance systems, transparency can help to provide continuity and reduce perceived risk. For instance, if a given local bond issuance is approved through a public referendum, this could bolster investor confidence in the community's long-term support for servicing the debt.

Good governance provides a secure context for boosting local investment capacity.[5] It enables long-term integrated planning of green and resilient infrastructure, as well as effectiveness in the use of fiscal transfers. It also helps to build capacity to formulate and implement climate projects that are suitable for finance. Strong governance is also critical for the structuring and operation of vehicles that facilitate the participation of the private sector and institutions. However, intermediary cities may have lower levels of planning capacity than larger cities, and their lower income and the relatively small size of their projects can make them less attractive to the private sector, especially given the complexity of PPP contracts. Intermediary cities may thus not be able to fully leverage these processes.

Demand-side constraints on access to climate finance in intermediary cities

The overall lower fiscal capacity of intermediary cities can limit their access to adequate financing. They may be limited in their ability to take on debt due to the limited size of their urban economy and revenues. They may also have limited ability to raise the fees and taxes required to provide needed revenue streams and debt service capacity. Similarly, intermediary cities generally have lower land values and provide less leverage than larger cities. This limits their ability to react to and influence the commercial conditions that provide the context for private investment through instruments such as land-use controls.

Addressing these bottlenecks is critical, and the challenge increases when we consider the kind of transformational investments needed to address climate change. The main structural constraints faced by intermediary cities in terms of access to finance are outlined below.

The inflexible structure of intergovernmental transfers to intermediary cities can be a major constraint on access to climate finance. It is established that intermediary cities have greater dependence than larger cities on intergovernmental transfers – this is known despite the overall lack of disaggregated data that would allow a detailed assessment of the relative impacts of the structures of intergovernmental transfers on intermediary cities (Farvacque-Vitkovic and Kopanyi, 2014[19]). The structure of such transfers is important for intermediary cities, which can be disadvantaged and/or disincentivised by formulas based on population or by transfers being tied to specific uses or staffing levels, for example. In particular, inflexible systems tend to reduce a city's ability to undertake more innovative financing.

The limited capacity of intermediary cities to take on debt is another challenge. The ability to take on loans and/or issue bonds (green or otherwise) depends on the creditworthiness of a specific UIA. For a local government, this entails the ability to generate surplus. It thus becomes very important that: *a)* transfers are used effectively; and *b)* revenue is maximised. There are many examples of cities that do not collect all mandated taxes and fees and that do not maximise the potential revenue streams of their assets (such as markets). For instance, the specific location of infrastructure investment matters because it will lead to an increase in land value in surrounding areas. Many countries provide a legislative basis for capturing some of the value added that results from this process: this is referred to as land value capture

(UNESCAP, 2019[20]). Various countries have successfully used this concept. OECD countries use it under names such as "development levies". Colombia and Brazil[6] have used it extensively, and similar land-linked mechanisms (land pooling) have been used in China, Vietnam and Nepal (Smolka, 2013[21]). Other innovative financing methods include "green taxes", such as congestion charges, on environmental "bads" (UNESCAP, 2019[20]). However, it is often harder for intermediary cities than for large cities to put such arrangements in place, and the yield is proportionately less for them.

The structuring and operation of debt financing mechanisms can also be more difficult for intermediary cities. Debt financing at the subnational level requires sufficiently large, economically viable projects or, in the case of many intermediary cities, pooling vehicles to aggregate smaller projects. Such vehicles can be within financing institutions (see below), but can also be achieved by the use of development corporations or regional utilities.

Good financial management is important for reassuring potential investors that financing projections are based on a sound fiscal system. Movement towards compliance with the International Public Sector Accounting System (IPSAS) and International Financial Reporting System (IFRS) is desirable at both national and local levels. This is the stated policy of many countries. Yet intermediary cities have limited resources for putting the required systems in place.

Supply-side constraints on access to climate finance in intermediary cities

Intermediary cities also face supply-side barriers to mobilising large-scale private institutional and commercial (PIC) finance. These include: *a)* lack of viable investment opportunities (project development), enabling environment, etc.; *b)* lack of investor "capability", including the ability of supply-side institutions to structure systems of accessing finance that are appropriate for UIAs; and *c)* inadequate conditions for investment, including macroeconomic issues/policy (OECD, 2014[22]). Supply-side constraints have been exacerbated by the effects of the COVID-19 crisis, with revenue shortfalls arguing in favour of maximum private financing of projects.

In addition, the returns on urban climate investments need to be competitive. Indeed, even if structural barriers are addressed, there will be competition for institutional funds in the "alternative investment" category, which provide high risk-adjusted returns. Many EMDE climate investments will fall into this category. Key supply-side issues facing intermediary cities are examined below.

Lack of suitable investment opportunities

The large variations in what constitutes "suitable" investment can present a challenge for accessing climate financing. Suitable investment encompasses the concept of an acceptable risk-return profile. Institutional investments, which achieve relatively lower but steady and reliable returns, are often acceptable, and many urban investments can be characterised as being long lived, low risk and with stable returns. But the level of returns deemed adequate and the level of liquidity required will vary according to the circumstances of the investing institution. As such, developing suitable investment conduits can be a challenge for climate projects, which must meet climate objectives in addition to the general requirements of technical, financial and regulatory standards.

Credit rating is a central element of investment decisions by a financing institution. It measures the amount of risk set against the income to be derived from extending finance. A higher risk of not being repaid implies that the financing institution needs to be compensated by higher returns. The issue of risk/credit rating is central to the participation of institutions in a particular investment or investment vehicle. Yet the majority of cities, particularly intermediary cities, do not have credit ratings. Thus, government attempts to transfer inappropriate levels of the risk of project failure to the private sector and institutional financiers can be counterproductive. Such efforts can result in very high costs as the private sector and institutional financiers build the risk premium into the project or, more generally, in a failure to secure institutional finance. The definition of what is considered inappropriate risk is a big challenge. Many institutions are reluctant to take "greenfield" (construction and commissioning) risk. Others may not want to take the risk of new technologies or geographies. The OECD (2014[22]) recommends that governments use risk reduction/credit enhancement mechanisms such as public or private guarantees.

Well-resourced project development mechanisms are often needed to bridge the gap between planning and a project that is ready for financial due diligence. This is especially the case for climate projects, which will have different, and sometimes unfamiliar, technical and regulatory characteristics. The lack of long-term planning focused on reduction of emissions and resilience remains a key issue for climate investment. The OECD (2014[22]) has recommended national infrastructure plans as a means of addressing this gap.

The concept of suitability also involves the size of investment required or the volume of resources needed. To get to a scale that makes the urban infrastructure projects of intermediary cities attractive to institutional investors, these projects will require aggregation in the financing structure, either at the level of the financial instrument used or in the structure of the sponsoring entity. This has implications for project development, as standardised approaches must be used in the bidding, the contract and financial documents.

Lack of investor capability

Investors can also face critical problems on their side. First, the close attention paid by analysts to quarterly market benchmarks fosters a short-term orientation. This incentivises investors to seek quick positive returns and militates against investments that have long pre-operation periods. It also fosters a need for liquidity in investments due to the ability of pension contributors in some countries, such as Australia, to withdraw their pension proceeds at short notice (for example, to change pension providers). Second, investors lack experience with urban investment, which increases their perceived risk and thus the required return. This discourages small-scale institutional and private investors, especially national investors that would otherwise be more comfortable with financing in cities. Third, lack of appropriate financing vehicles can limit investors' capacity to provide financing – i.e. vehicles that can accommodate numbers of investors and aggregate numbers of smaller projects, and that align the interests of the managers of such vehicles with those of the institutional investors, in fee transparency and liquidity in particular. This has been a problem, for example, between private equity funds and pension funds. Fourth, regulatory barriers also constrain the mandate of investors to invest. Examples include "market to market" regulations, which incentivise institutions to avoid volatility whatever the cause; asset-class regulations that limit or ban participation in, for example, direct equity investment and unlisted funds; and credit-rating limits. These factors often impact climate investments hardest given that they are not yet fully established in the market.

Conditions for investment

The conditions that determine levels of financing of climate investments can be broken down into three categories: a) macroeconomic; b) policy; and c) demand-side capacity (discussed above).

Macroeconomic conditions can have a large influence on multiple factors that determine levels of climate investment. Macroeconomic conditions determine aggregate demand (both on the revenue side in use of services, and in the capacity to raise taxes or issue debt to fund government investment) and influence inflation, foreign exchange and interest-rate risks. The international perception of macroeconomic conditions may unfairly impact cities. Indeed, irrespective of a city's intrinsic fiscal soundness, its credit rating is generally considered to be bound by the rating of the sovereign government.

The policy and regulatory environment is rapidly evolving, particularly in terms of environmental and climate legislation and regulation. Policy consistency and transparency in areas such as standards, subsidies, incentives, carbon pricing and dispute resolution are important to investors across all infrastructure and economic development opportunities. This environment determines the size, growth potential, structure, stability/risk and profitability of markets. Policies are important at all levels, including national, state/provincial and local. The policy environment at the city level is a particular issue in view of short electoral cycles and the potential for lack of alignment between city governments and higher levels of government. Lack of alignment carries through in terms of the levels and conditions of fiscal transfers, the ability to enter into PPP contracts, lending limits and caps on fees and taxes. The policy environment also determines the quality, timing and scope of data available to investors. The cumulative effect of these issues will determine investors' perception of risk and value in the urban climate investment space.

In response to these issues, support for building climate financing capacity needs to focus on mechanisms of finance. This implies the need to develop systems of assessing enterprise proposals. Further, infrastructure-financing decisions need to ensure that the investment is the most effective possible given the country and technological context. As such the question becomes: How can urban climate financing for intermediary cities be structured to address the demand- and supply-side constraints?

Approaches to effective climate financing in intermediary cities

Approaches to effective climate financing in intermediary cities need to encompass effective action on both the demand and the supply sides. On the demand side, there is a need to assess the capacity of UIAs to plan and arrange funding for projects; on the supply side, there is a need to assess the capacity of financing institutions to respond to the needs and circumstances of UIAs. To provide context, it is important to understand the structures of financing that are applicable to urban climate finance. Figure 5.5 illustrates the flows of funds from international sources through the sources available at national levels to the sources available to the city UIAs themselves.

Figure 5.5. Flows of financing across different institutions

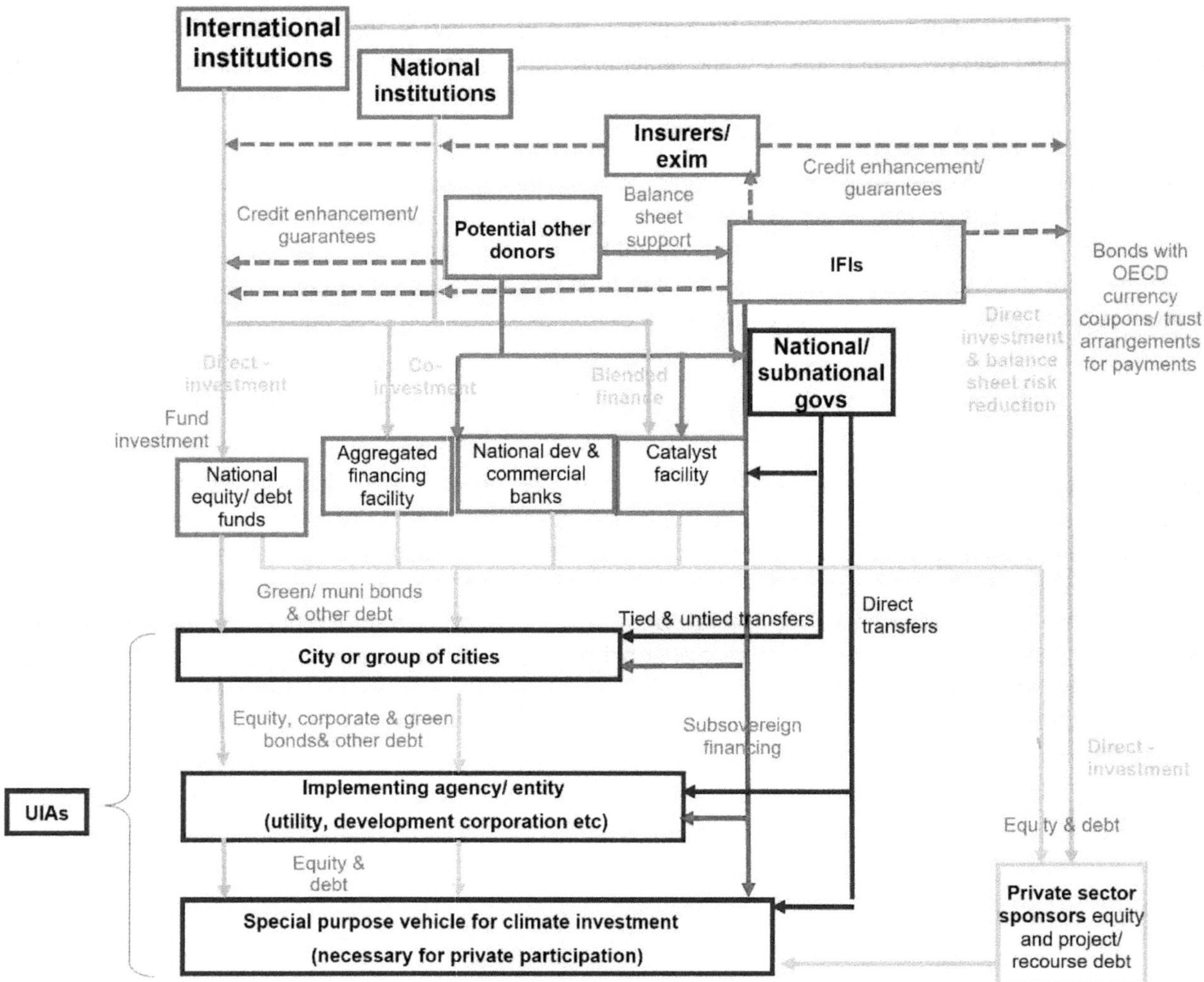

Note: Exim = export-import agencies; IFIs = international financial institutions; UIAs = urban investment agencies; RED = development assistance flows; GREEN = institutional and commercial finance flows; BLUE = national government flows; YELLOW = all other finance flows.
Source: Authors' own elaboration.

There are myriad potential sources and structures for a given investment. It is beyond the scope of this chapter to go through the advantages and disadvantages of every possible combination of financing sources, which can vary widely from city to city and country to country. However, it is possible to establish principles of structuring demand- and supply-side responses so as to maximise the potential efficiency of a climate financing process in intermediary cities. Box 5.1 outlines some of the main financing sources for climate investment across different categories.

Box 5.1. Sources of financing for climate investment at city level

Intermediary cities wishing to pursue climate investment have various options in terms of financing. Here are some of the main sources.

- **International development assistance agencies and IFIs** provide the most concessional resources at the international level (red flow lines in Figure 5.5). These sources are limited by budget constraints and the capital backing of the IFIs. This said, these programmes are increasingly shifting to focus on climate issues, so there is significant potential if UIAs can work with national governments to tap into such flows.
- **Institutions** have substantial amounts of finance available in theory (top green flows in Figure 5.5). Indeed, data from the OECD (2020[23]) for 2019 shows that pension funds held USD 32.3 trillion in assets under management, while insurers held approximately USD 33 trillion (Carter, 2020[24]) in 2020 and Sovereign Wealth Funds USD 8.8 trillion in the same year. However, tapping into even part of these funds requires addressing the critical constraints on investment identified by the OECD, as set out above.
- **Dedicated climate funds** promote urban climate investment and have dedicated programmes to this end (under IFIs above, with red flow lines in Figure 5.5). Cities can turn in particular to the Green Climate Fund, the Global Environment Facility (GDF) or Climate Investment Funds (CIF). The GCF has the larger resources and can help fund significant capital costs. But these funds require that an intermediary partner with a UIA. In the GCF's case, this may be an accredited entity, such as an IFI, or a local (direct access) entity. Arranging such partnerships is difficult for many intermediary cities.
- **The international (and national) private sector** requires the use of project structures that allow its participation – PPP structures and the like (yellow bottom box in Figure 5.5). In specific circumstances, such as the supply of transport equipment, the international private sector can mobilise lower-cost financing from export credit agencies of particular countries. Such funds, of course, tie procurement to sources from the donor country. UIAs in many intermediary cities struggle to develop projects of the scale that will attract such finance.
- **National and subnational governments** are still the dominant funders of infrastructure (more than 75% globally) (Estache, 2010[25]). But intermediary cities, for reasons outlined above, are in a weaker political and fiscal position to demand an equitable share of such finance. Even where dedicated financing institutions, such as national development banks (NDBs), are established to direct finance to cities, they are constrained by their inability to formulate "bankable projects". This caveat applies even more for private-sector financial institutions (banks, funds, etc.).
- **National private-sector entities** are familiar and often comfortable with the scale and general fiscal and regulatory context of the projects of UIAs, but their participation is often limited by government processes of project formulation and implementation. Added to this in a number of countries is reluctance on the part of citizens and politicians to see changes in government-focused procurement. This reluctance is sometimes well founded on the experience of adverse outcomes of projects involving the private sector.

Demand-side financing support structures and examples

National and local authorities and other UIAs involved in city development can take actions to better mobilise their resources for low-carbon and resilient development in intermediary cities. Strengthening the capacity of UIAs is important for building structures that address the constraints set out above. Key elements for strengthening capacity include:

- planning for mitigation of GHG emissions and climate resilience through evidence-based city climate action plans. The plans should be informed by climate vulnerability assessments and developed with the input of local communities and with the support of stakeholders across relevant investment sectors.
- use of project development entities (such as project preparation facilities) through national governments or development assistance and IFIs that can support the development of bankable projects of high climate performance. This process should assist UIAs in structuring projects so that the private sector can participate when appropriate in a manner beneficial to citizens.
- improving fiscal management, particularly in relation to maximising own-source revenue and leverage of public resources.

Best practices in planning for climate investment

Various examples can serve as reference points for effective planning for climate investment. For instance, Durban (South Africa) developed an impressive Climate Action Plan based on a rigorous analysis of the city's GHG emissions and well-modelled climate vulnerabilities. The process involved wide consultation across the agencies that would undertake the investments and the broader community. This process produced a concrete set of actions in nine thematic areas: energy, transport, waste, water and flooding, health, biodiversity, food security, sea-level rise and vulnerable communities. These actions were sufficiently detailed to provide a basis for prioritising investments in each area.

The resources for climate action plans can be provided by a range of entities. The C40 Cities Climate Leadership Group (C40), a global network of mayors taking urgent action on climate, has been supporting the development of a number of such plans. Its processes are rigorous. The C40 caters to larger cities, although some are "intermediary" in the context of their countries. Other sources of support include the Global Covenant of Mayors for Climate & Energy (GcoM), which helps cities to develop sustainable energy and climate action plans, and certain multilateral development banks (MDBs). However, these resources are very limited, and smaller intermediary cities often struggle to access them.

Best practices in project development

The need to support cities in project development is increasingly recognised. From early examples such as the Cities Development Initiative for Asia (CDIA), a variety of project development support mechanisms have been established (CDIA, n.d.[26]). They vary in countries covered, sectors covered, scale of assistance and independence from financing entities (in terms of being open to a range of possible financing sources).

At the global level, the C40 Cities Finance Facility (CFF) has provided resources for project preparation across a range of sectors (C40, 2021[27]). As an example, the process of project development for climate-positive transport projects in Mexico began with support to Mexico City (not an intermediary city). This involved a rigorous process of assessment of the type of electric vehicles the city would use for its bus system; it was determined that upgrading and expanding the existing trolleybus network was the most effective way forward. A cost-effective, locally manufactured solution was recommended and adopted. Building on this experience, the CFF then supported three Mexican intermediary cities (Guadalajara, Monterrey and Hermosillo) in relation to developing e-mobility public transport projects. The CFF also focuses on building local capacity for project development, conducting an assessment of city technical and finance skills as well as organisational options relating to implementation and financial structuring.

Other international sources provide similar support for similar projects. These organisations include the World Bank and European Investment Bank (WB/EIB) Gap Fund, supported by the German government and others (CCFGF, 2020[28]); the World Bank's Public-Private Infrastructure Advisory Facility (PPIAF)

(PPIAF, n.d.[29]); the ADB Cities Development Initiative for Asia (CDIA) (CDIA, n.d.[26]); and the technical assistance component of EBRD Green Cities, a programme of the European Bank for Reconstruction and Development (EBRD) that is co-financed by the Green Climate Fund (GCF, n.d.[30]). However, the available resources are very limited, and smaller intermediary cities struggle to access them.

At the other end of the spectrum, there are project development entities at the national scale that focus on specific sectors and/or types of project. Project development facilities have also been established within regional and national development banks, such as the Development Bank of Southern Africa, Findeter in Colombia and Banobras in Mexico. Findeter's facility is used predominantly by intermediary cities.

An example of a facility focused on specific types of projects is the Project Development and Monitoring Facility (PDMF) established by the government of the Philippines (Republic of the Philippines, n.d.[31]). The PDMF facilitates the development of well-prepared and bankable PPP projects by engaging experienced and internationally recognised project preparation and transaction support consultants. A revolving fund, the PDMF initially shoulders the cost of consulting services for PPP projects. Upon successful PPP tendering, the winning private proponent reimburses/pays the actual cost of consulting services, plus a fixed percentage cost-recovery fee. Since its creation in September 2010 with financial support from the Australian government and the ADB, the PDMF has successfully facilitated the roll-out of PPP projects. As of 2020, nine PPP projects, valued at USD 2.35 billion, had been developed and successfully tendered with PDMF support. The PDMF has also enhanced private-sector confidence. The credible pipeline of PPP projects, which are mostly PDMF supported, has encouraged both local players and international investors to participate in the PPP tendering process.

Such national facilities have a good understanding of national context and the financial and governance issues relevant to a specific project. It is important that national governments provide policy continuity and allow project development entities technical independence in order to foster their capacity and reputation for supporting viable and well-designed projects. As an example, Colombia's Findeter has significant independence and high standards of technical capacity.

Best practices in fiscal management

In terms of successful revenue maximisation, just collecting what is owed is a very important first step. For instance, Quezon City in metropolitan Manila increased property-tax collection threefold between 2005 and 2008 by computerising tax rolls, making payments easier and eliminating corrupt middlemen (Roy et al., 2020[32]). Reformulating taxes to simplify them and minimise avoidance is also important. Cities should consider their ability to levy taxes on "bads", such as the use of fossil fuels and consequent pollution, and national governments should facilitate this process. Porto Alegre (Brazil), which is internationally recognised for pioneering participatory budgeting, substantially improved tax compliance through local participatory mechanisms. Revenue yields increased substantially during a period of national fiscal reform that included major increases in intergovernmental transfers, which might have been expected to dampen local revenue efforts (UN-Habitat, 2015[33]). Property-tax reform has yielded very significant increases in own-source revenue. International support for improving urban revenue mobilisation is also available, for example from the World Bank's City Creditworthiness Initiative (World Bank, n.d.[34]).

There are also agencies that are able to engage in comprehensive planning, co-ordinate across sectoral silos and enter into long-term contracts and PPPs. They can do so by using a diverse range of financing partners and modalities, enabling them to leverage private-sector finance and oversight implementation. An example is the Pune Smart City Development Corporation in India, which includes structures for interorganisational co-ordination and co-operation fostered under the national Smart Cities programme. Participating cities need to establish a credible Special Purpose Vehicle (not the conventional use of the term, which is used for PPP financing structures) (Pune Smart City, n.d.[35]). This vehicle has the mandate to co-ordinate all necessary agencies and establish appropriate implementation vehicles for projects (including PPPs) under the Smart City programme.

Cities need to mobilise to bolster finance, both as a response to COVID impacts and in anticipation of future impacts on revenue streams from climate threats. Coastal cities suffering from seawater intrusion are likely to see property prices decline, and thus property taxes, too. Intense rainfall events that overcome drainage defences can bring entire regions to a halt. This occurred in Bangkok and its surrounding region (including intermediary cities) in 2011, when record rainfall caused severe floods, leading to 815 deaths and property damage estimated at THB 1.425 trillion (Thailand baht), or USD 46.5 billion.

Challenges in scaling up financial resources to address the costs related to the adaptation and mitigation investments of intermediary cities are particularly large in small island developing states. The remoteness of smaller settlements on islands with respect to the capital is a huge handicap. Local income sources such as tax revenues from the tourism sector need to be retained on the islands, where they can be used for viable adaptation investment in particular. Public revenues in SIDS may be affected by the COVID crisis via a variety of channels, most notably the sharp decline in global and domestic trade (as many SIDS have a high share of revenues coming from taxes on goods and services), declines in commodity and natural resource prices, and the decrease in tourism activity. To recover from the crisis, enhanced management of key sectors, including fisheries, tourism and natural resource extraction, may provide opportunities to enhance domestic revenue mobilisation in SIDS. Policies to reduce "leakages" from these sectors, especially tourism, and to support backward and forward linkages with other domestic sectors (e.g. food and agriculture, consumer goods, construction), could expand the taxable production base (OECD, 2020[36]). Special facilities are available to some least developed countries and SIDS, often at a regional level, such as the Pacific Region Infrastructure Facility (PRIF) (PRIF, n.d.[37]).

Supply-side financing structures and examples

A number of steps can be taken in efforts to establish effective financing responses to address the supply-side constraints of the finance market. One is supporting the development and sustainable implementation of bankable projects that perform well in relation to reducing emissions efficiently at scale and/or reducing vulnerabilities in a cost-effective way. This will require supporting the development of the project as well as the establishment of diverse financing structures capable of financing a variety of sectors. Another is providing support to financing facilities that are structured for a diverse range of financing contributors at fund and project levels (public/private), and that maintain flexibility with respect to the type of support (debt/equity) and type of entity supported (local government, state-owned enterprise, company and household). Providing structure to foster aggregation where investments are small, as is often the case in intermediary cities, can be particularly useful for such cities.

These interventions are common across countries, but their depth and sophistication will differ according to the human and financial capacities of the cities and relevant institutions. Because of this differentiation, a general typology of climate finance mechanisms is difficult to develop. However, the structures outlined in Table 5.1 have been, or could be, used for climate finance in intermediary cities.

Table 5.1. Typology of climate finance mechanisms

Type of institution	Type of financing	Examples
Development partners	Technical assistance by a development financing agency or NGO to bolster enabling frameworks, planning systems of project development activity	
IFI-catalysed mechanisms	IFI-catalysed facility tapping international institutional finance	IFC Managed Co-Lending Portfolio Programme (MCPP)
	IFI-catalysed blended finance facility, usually at a national development bank	Shandong Green Development Fund (SGDF)
	IFI direct lending for specific sectors	IADB cluster project (which addresses infrastructure and SMEs in the Mendoza Project in Argentina)
	IFI subsovereign lending (in theory the same mechanism could be used by international private banks)	EBRD's use of Public Service Agreements (PSAs)
National initiatives	National development bank-led initiatives (in theory, these could be led by any financial institution, including private ones)	Tamil Nadu Urban Development Fund (TNUDF) aggregation mechanism
	Tapping the private capital market	Komunminvest aggregation mechanism
	Small scale local finance	Mongolian microfinance for Cooking, Heating, and Insulation Products and Service (CHIPS)
	City green funds (numerous intermediary cities have environmental funds for use in local projects that could be leveraged for larger projects)	
Private sector	Private-sector infrastructure funds (particularly sector-specific funds such as renewable energy) and Energy Saving Company arrangements have invested/used in intermediary cities, mainly in OECD countries	

Source: Authors' own elaboration.

Of specific interest are OECD institutions and sovereign wealth funds. These institutions have huge resources, but they also have very specific requirements in relation to mobilising their funds. To move resources at scale as envisaged by the initiatives announced at the 2021 UN Climate Change Conference (COP26),[7] OECD institutions need to be able to tap into a liquid pool of products that meet the criteria and credit ratings established in their major asset allocation strategies, which are in turn based on qualifying projects or corporate investments. Key to increasing institutional investor allocation to climate-related investment is to ensure that these investments compete on a risk-return basis over different time horizons. This is because institutional investors have varying appetites for risk, investment preferences and constraints. Pension funds and insurers have to invest in accordance with the "prudent person principle", achieving required security, profitability, liquidity and quality (Kaminker, 2013[38]). In addition, in order to achieve higher allocations to low-carbon solutions, many sovereign funds would need to undertake major investments in capacity building – at the levels of board, management and staff, and across several areas. They would need capacity to engage with portfolio companies on climate-related issues; capacity to select and monitor asset managers based on their climate-related performance; and, for the stronger sovereign funds, capacity to invest directly in low-carbon infrastructure (OECD, 2020[39]).[8]

Any of the financing structures outlined in Table 5.1 can potentially be augmented with the GCF, Global Environment Facility (GEF), CIFs or development assistance finance to increase potential concessionality, given appropriate partnerships. These different mechanisms address different UIAs. A given country will almost certainly need more than one type of climate financing structure to address the range of UIAs in intermediary cities.

Where mechanisms are not specifically designed to focus on climate projects, they can be made so by applying a relevant taxonomy and changing the project-level assessment criteria to screen for quality climate-positive projects. The GCF has an assessment process that is applicable at project level. While not perfect, its investment framework does take into account both specific climate outcomes and a range of non-climate factors that are critical to ensuring that a project will actually be implemented. An example is the Shandong Green Development Fund (SGDF) project (described below).

Figure 5.6 sets out the GCF's investment criteria, which were used to assess the SGDF (GCF, n.d.[30]). After initial screening through a modified Peoples' Bank of China (PBOC) taxonomy, the impacts of the project were assessed across multiple metrics and quantified. Such assessments consider the levels of GHG reduction and adaptation benefits; the project's potential for scaling up and replication (paradigm shift); delivery of co-benefits/sustainable development (e.g. pollution reduction and employment); value added of the financing; the capacity of the proponent to implement (needs of recipient and ownership); as well as efficiency and effectiveness. The resulting performance of the project determines the level of concessionality awarded.

Figure 5.6. Global Climate Fund investment framework

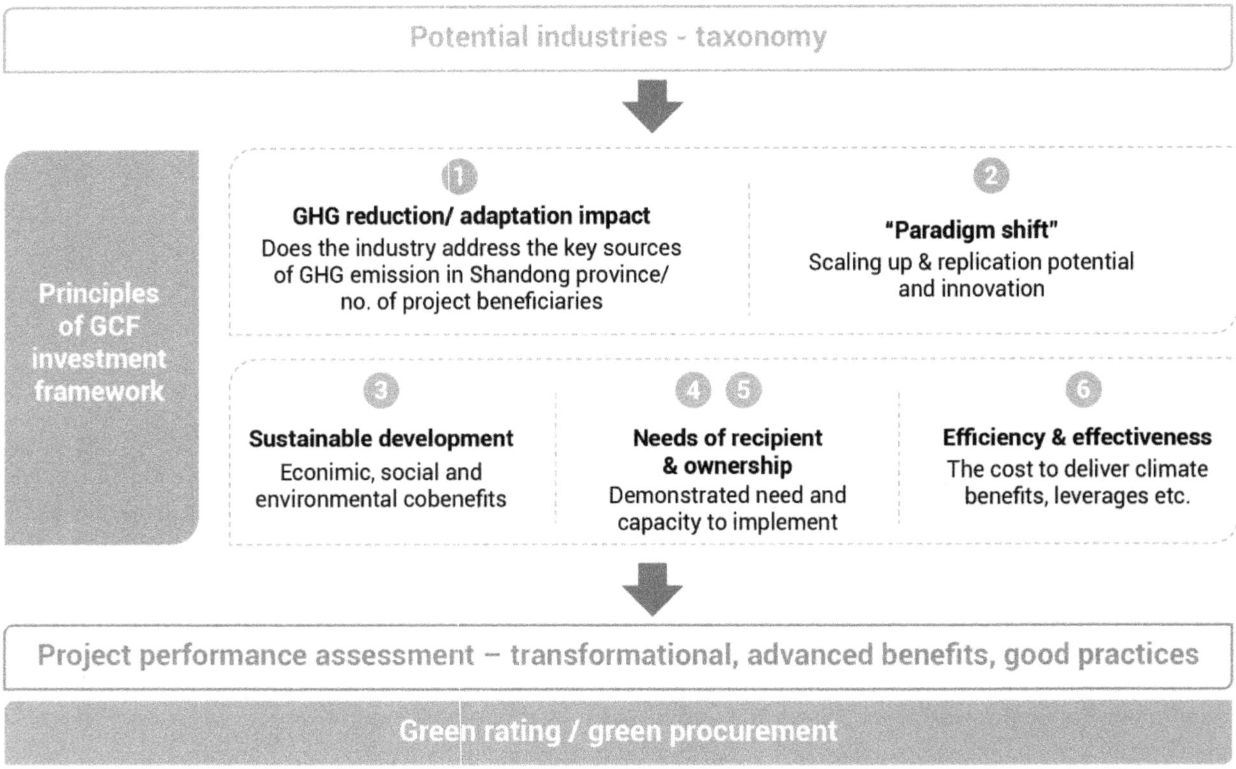

Source: Adapted based on (GCF, n.d.[30]).

Example of an IFI-catalysed blended facility

According to the Asian Development Bank (ADB) the Shandong project responds to the key challenges facing climate finance in China by using blended finance and leveraging private-sector funding (ADB, 2021[40]). As identified by China's Ministry of Finance (MOF) and the ADB, these challenges are: *a)* a lack of viable climate positive projects, particularly new technology projects; *b)* inability of the capital market to address higher-risk profiles of climate investments and to attract private, institutional and commercial (PIC) finance to such investments; and *c)* inadequate systems for defining, monitoring and evaluating climate investments. Given the scale of the problems in relation to green investment in Shandong Province, and its previous track record with IFI financing, the MOF approved Shandong as a pilot for the Green Finance Catalyst Facility (GFCF) concept in China, which led to the establishment of the SGDF. The SGDF provides finance for intermediary cities (by Chinese standards). Figure 5.7 shows the financial structure of the SGDF.

Figure 5.7. Financing structure of the SGDF

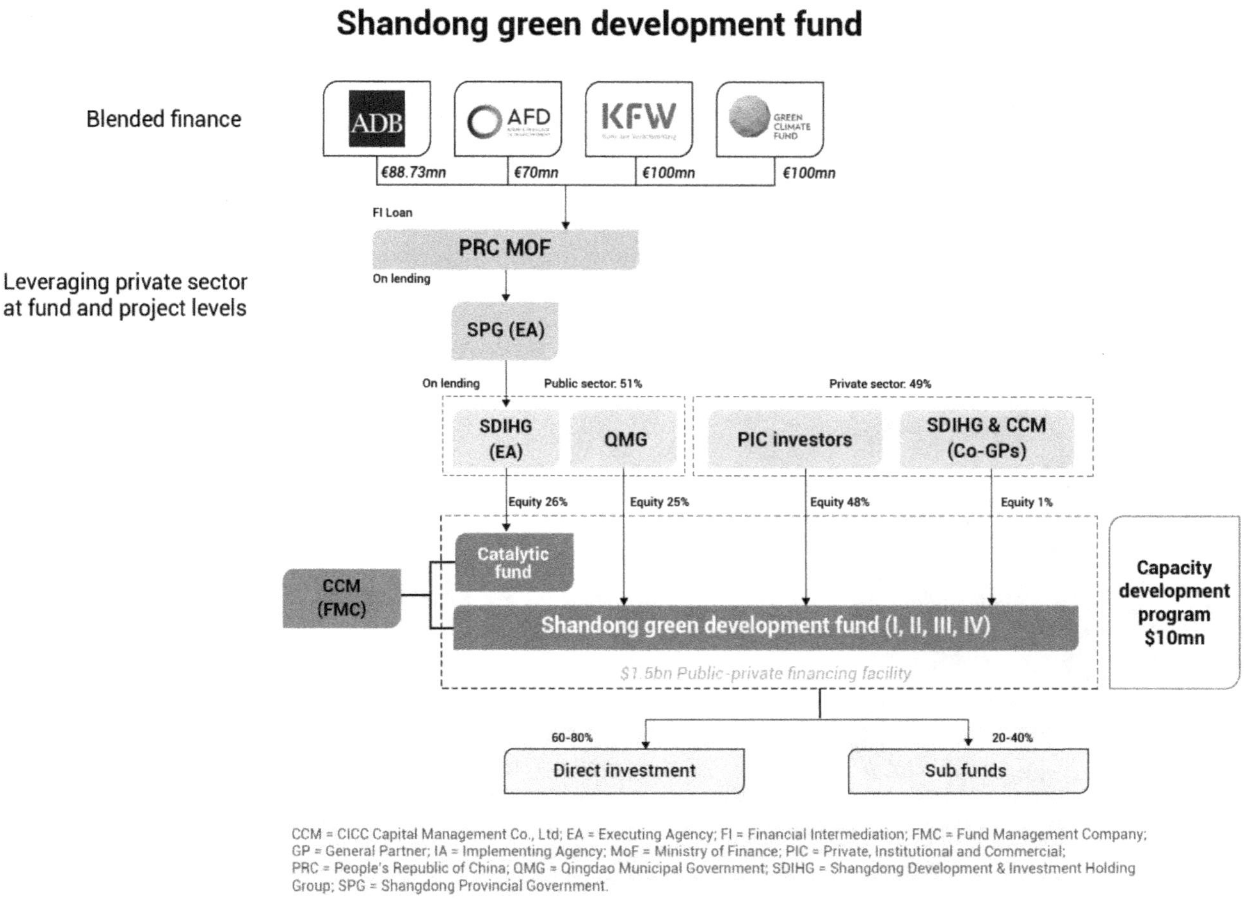

Source: Adapted based on (ADB, 2021[40]).

The GFCF concept constitutes a powerful mechanism for leveraging finance for climate investments. The basic form of the concept is to establish a green window within a credible and capable national financing institution that can act as the conduit for both international concessional and private finance flows to climate projects that are "warranted" as climate positive through a robust assessment process. Critical is the capacity to include PIC finance into the facility itself and at the project level. It is replicable in many forms: it may be based in a government entity, a national development bank or a private-sector financial institution.

Certain key characteristics need to be present for effective operation of the GFCF concept. One is the capacity to blend effectively and support a variety of financial instruments as appropriate to client needs. Project development capacity will be necessary to achieve required scale and quality, especially in small, poorer countries. The facility must also be able to design access to concessionality (enough to compensate for external benefits) for a particular project, in cognisance of: a) target market; b) local capital market; c) participating organisations (banks, development banks, pension funds, etc.); d) clients (companies, local governments, development co-operation, utilities, etc.); e) concessionality (for example, an incentive reduction in the interest rate applicable to a good-quality climate investment, as determined by standards attached to the taxonomy); this must be linked to project climate performance. The facility also needs to be able to provide effective feedback, knowledge and learning to national and provincial/state policy, and it must be open for, and structured to able to utilise, the range of sources of finance, including the need to achieve an appropriate credit rating if international institutional money is sought.

An example of direct subsovereign lending

The EBRD engages with independent borrowing entities (usually utilities), which in turn have clear contracts with local or state governments. The contracts can be in the form of public service agreements or contracts (PSAs/PSCs); local governments warrant their payment to the utility and supply any subsidy if needed (EBRD, n.d.[41]). Local governments also enter into agreements with the EBRD called municipal support agreements (MSAs). Figure 5.8 illustrates how these structures operate within the range of EBRD subsovereign instruments. The model generally applies to a utility company, such as a municipal transport operator. The operator's revenue model is "ring fenced" by a binding agreement (the PSC). The local government also agrees that it has the responsibility to ensure repayment to the EBRD (the MSC). The EBRD then lends to the operator and is repaid by them. The use of insurance helps to reduce risks.

Figure 5.8. EBRD Municipal Support Agreements

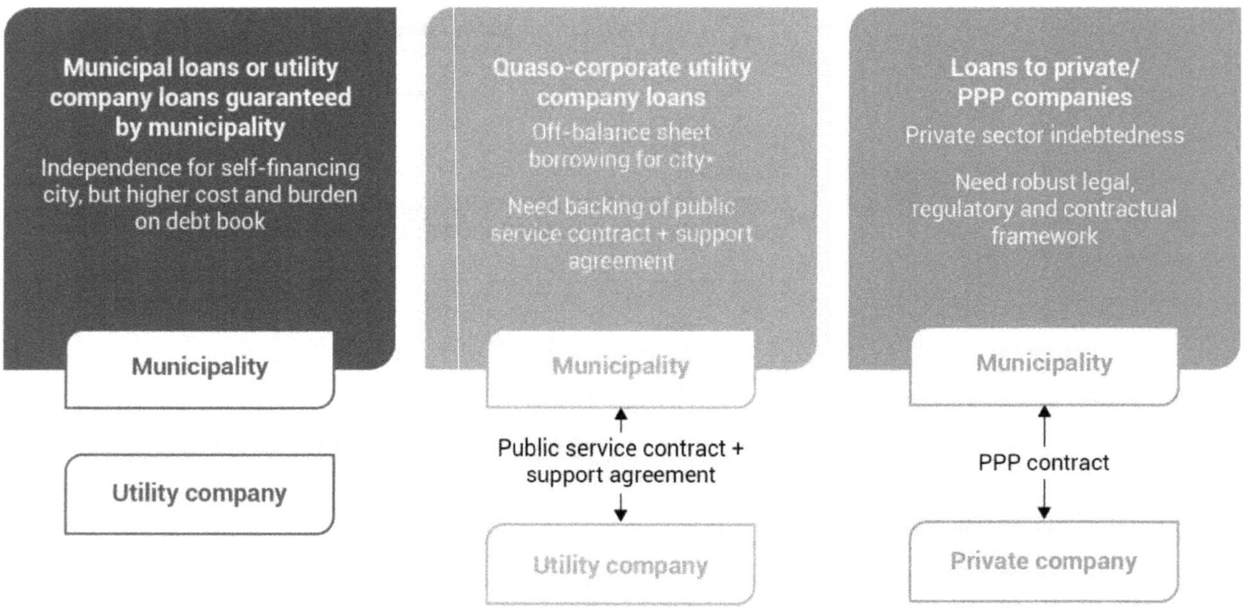

Source: Adapted based on EBRD (n.d.[41]).

Although the EBRD and the International Finance Corporation (IFC) are exceptions in that they are able to retain a significant amount of subsovereign finance in their portfolios, their investments have mainly been project by project for a particular sector. In principle, the model could be used by private international banks, but the transaction costs for such entities are high at the subsovereign level in emerging market and developing countries (EMDCs). The mechanism can be applicable directly to intermediary cities, and indeed has been used in regions such as Eastern Europe. But the principle can apply to utilities that span several local governments, such as water district agencies in the Philippines (LWUA, n.d.[42]).

An example of NDB-led financing: Aggregation structures for smaller local governments

The capacity to aggregate smaller investments has been developed in India by the Tamil Nadu Urban Development Fund (TNUDF) over many years. The TNUDF has long had a pooled lending instrument that provides loans to groups of smaller cities. Lending based on its balance sheet still predominates in its portfolio, but it has also set up a Water and Sanitation Pooled Fund (WSPF-Special Purpose Vehicle) capitalised by bond issuance taken up by Indian institutional investors. The projects were selected by 13 small and medium urban local bodies (ULBs). The WSPF has a separate management structure managed by banks. There is a debt-service reserve fund capitalised by the state government; individual ULB escrow accounts and debt-service reserve funds; a state revenue-intercept mechanism; and a United States Agency for International Development (USAID) partial credit guarantee for the bonds.

Given the success of this transaction, similarly structured bonds have been issued In Tamil Nadu and Karnataka states. In 2006, the government of India established a central government office accountable for scaling up pooled funds across the country at the state level. This office, the Pooled Finance Development Fund (PFDF) Scheme, was intended to provide credit enhancement facilities to urban local bodies based on their creditworthiness, enabling them to access market borrowing through these state-level pooled funds. Figure 5.9 shows the structure of the TNUDF.

Figure 5.9. Structure of the Tamil Nadu Urban Development Fund

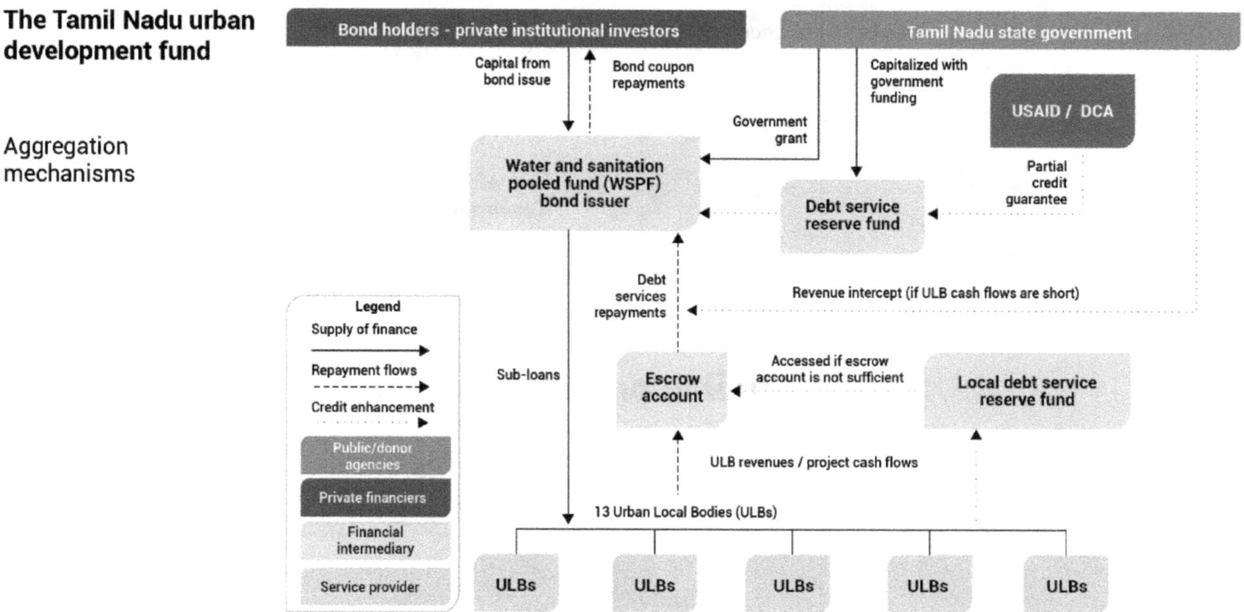

Source: Adapted based on FMDV (2021[43]).

Example of the use of local capital markets

Some cities can address the aggregation issue through issuance of general aggregation bonds or, for climate projects, green bonds, which allow a range of projects to be financed with one instrument. Generally, this course of action is more open to larger cities, such as Johannesburg. However, there is a problem in that the transaction costs for such bonds are higher than for loans. This has been solved in some countries, such as Sweden, where smaller local governments participate in a joint financing mechanism, Kommuninvest, that issues green bonds to finance their collective portfolio (Kommuninvest, n.d.[44]). This is an effective way to spread the costs of issuing green financing instruments over numerous investments from a number of local governments. Critical is the rigorous evaluation of candidate projects for their climate eligibility and strong monitoring, reporting and validation (MRV) systems that verify that the claimed performance is actually achieved, as confirmed by an independent evaluator. These systems provide the infrastructure for the issue of green bonds. Also of note is the wide range of eligible sectors. Figure 5.10 shows the key characteristics of Kommuninvest.

Figure 5.10. Characteristics of the Kommuninvest Green Bonds Framework

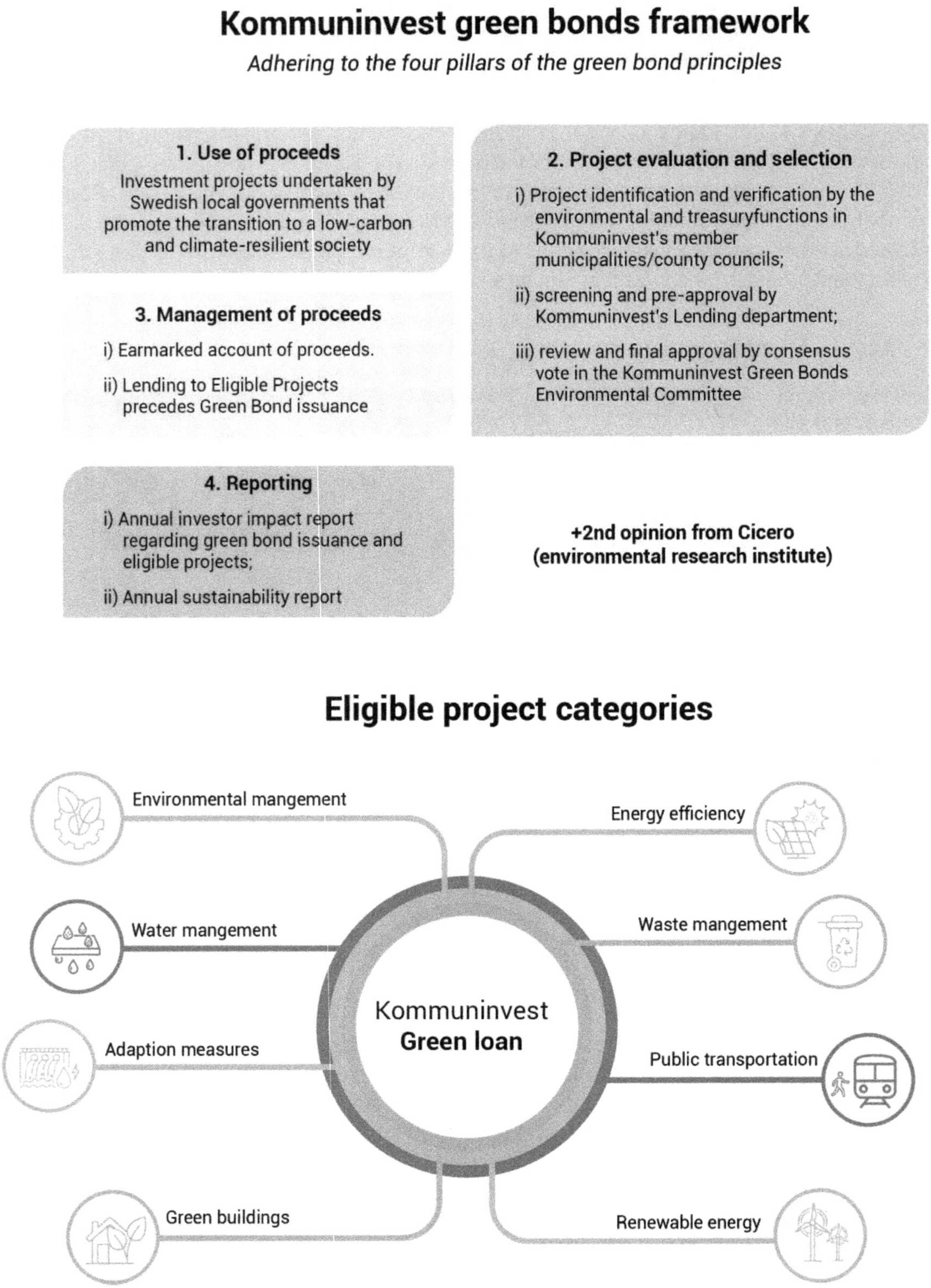

Source: Adapted based on (Kommuninvest, n.d.[45]) and (Albuquerque, 2020[46]).

An example of national private-sector financing

As private-sector financing depends on capturing a stream of revenue to make a profit, it has mainly been used on mitigation-related projects, especially those related to energy. One example is the use by Philadelphia of a power purchase agreement (PPA) to finance the conversion of the source of the city government's power to renewable energy (City of Philadelphia, 2020[47]). A private renewable energy company entered into the PPA with the city, agreeing to build 80 megawatts of installed capacity, and the city agreed to pay the power provider what it would normally pay for power. Such arrangements depend on the ability of independent producers to "wheel" power across the grid to consumers. But other arrangements are possible, such as the use of energy service companies when they commit to reduce the government's energy bill in return for a share of the savings. Such arrangements are becoming more common in EMDCs but still face some regulatory and financing constraints (Ellis, 2010[48]).

City climate funds

A city climate fund is an institution set up to finance projects that reduce emissions or improve climate resiliency. The design and operation of these funds vary by city, but common themes include a degree of independence from political decision makers in making investment decisions; specialty finance projects and terms; and investment decision criteria linked to a city's broader environmental, social or economic policy objectives. There are numerous examples of city-based climate funds (C40, 2016[49]). They vary in size, but in intermediary cities they will tend to be relatively small. Well-documented examples of city funds are generally from large OECD countries. But community development and other funds are not uncommon even in intermediary cities in EMDCs; they are usually financed from general revenue or from a specific new revenue source. Extensions of such funds, or green windows within them, can be a base for attracting other contributions from local, national and international sources. In 2020, Baguio City in the Philippines set up a green financing mechanism funded by an environmental users' fee.

Recommendations for action to facilitate access to climate finance

This chapter has been structured by consideration of the demand and supply sides of the climate finance market. This section provides recommendations for action, which will be structured as:

- demand-side actions on the part of national, subnational and local governments, and UIAs, with the aim of strengthening their capacity to finance climate projects
- supply-side actions by national and subnational governments with the aim of strengthening the enabling framework for climate financing
- actions by the international community to support the demand- and supply-side recommendations.

These actions need to produce transparent processes for defining clear city climate objectives and for detailing the programme of investments that will meet those objectives. For the required investments to be financed efficiently, they need to be structured as financing mechanisms that are appropriate to intermediary cities. Competent and effectively mandated implementing agencies need to be assigned clear responsibility for: investments in green infrastructure; enterprise capital for renewable energy (RE) and energy efficiency (EE); cluster support systems; and human capital development. These can be initially linked to COVID-19 recovery, but as recovery from the pandemic proceeds they will need increasing emphasis on the implementation of nationally determined contributions.

It is important that the demand and supply sides of the climate finance market be strengthened together. Strengthening financial institutions will be of limited use if cities do not have the fiscal space or capacity to utilise the available finance, on both sides of the market and at national and subnational/local levels. As such, interventions need to address structural issues, the enabling framework, regulatory issues, operational issues and capacity-building needs.

Extensive examples of operational instruments on the demand and supply sides of the market have been set out above. Their effectiveness depends on the strength of enabling frameworks and other capacity support structures. Figure 5.11 llustrates the process of defining the key actions at both national and sub-national levels. In this process, the enabling frameworks, the institutional structures for implementation of climate investment and the supporting capacity development systems need to be assessed.

Figure 5.11. Analysis of the demand and supply sides of climate finance

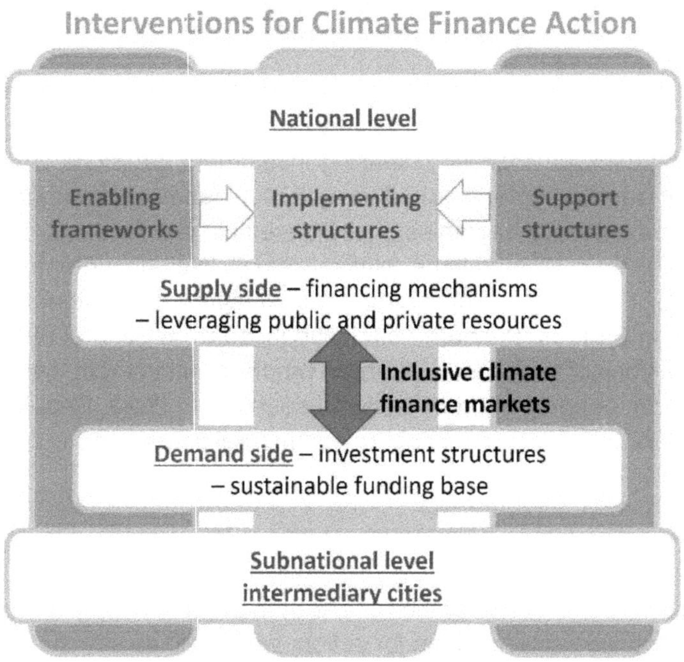

Source: Authors' own elaboration.

Priority actions for addressing demand-side constraints

For urban climate finance that is accessible to intermediary cities, national governments should promote better governance structures and effective enabling frameworks. Key actions include:

- **localising NDCs**. Processes can be designed for designating responsibilities to subnational governments for making the required investments under the NDCs and for matching these with resources.
- **establishing adequate structure and incentives for intergovernmental fiscal transfers**. In terms of required resources, transfers are likely to have a substantial role, especially for intermediary cities. These transfers need to make up for local resource shortfalls, as determined by local revenue-raising capacity versus needed investment levels. They should be structured to maximise the incentives for local revenue mobilisation and be both flexible and encouraging of innovation in using and leveraging them (Martinez-Vazquez, 2021[50]).
- **creating market incentives in NDC sectors and green government finance**. For many NDC-related investment sectors, such as energy, significant non-transparent subsidies can be present and/or regulation complicates the entry of alternative service providers. In many cases, such

subsidies are well intentioned and aim to benefit lower-income groups. However, such structures make entering the market difficult for suppliers using lower-carbon processes or more effective means of resource use/reuse. Making such subsidies available in non-distorting ways, and incentivising green procurement processes, can open additional investment pathways. Enabling the creation of flexible partnership structures for investment through the use of regional utilities and area-based development corporations (as in the Pune example), each with their own sustainable funding sources, can also open new investment pathways (for example, using PPPs). Green budgeting – the tracking and maximisation of resources deployed to efficient climate investments – needs to be strongly promoted (OECD, 2022[51]). This approach allows local governments to align expenditure and revenue-raising decisions with their green objectives; prioritise green and resilient investments; identify funding and financing gaps; and mobilise additional financial resources to bridge these gaps.

Local governments, in the above context, should:

- **establish urban climate planning and project development systems**. This may entail setting up mechanisms of planning for implementation of localised NDC investments, undertaking city climate assessments (mitigation and adaptation), and developing climate action plans (with project pipelines and budgets).
- **set up corporate structures and local area development**. Intermediary cities and networks of small and medium-sized cities should assess the most efficient spatial unit of investment for localised NDCs and design appropriate organisational structures to finance and implement required NDC investments. These actions should take into consideration interjurisdictional structures that include a number of local governments, such as a metropolitan authority, a development corporation, a regional utility, etc. As part of the structuring of such entities, consideration should be given to enabling them to provide planning and other incentives for green development.
- **promote green financial management**. Local governments and other UIAs need to maximise their own source revenue using green taxes and fees where possible. They should adopt green procurement processes, maximise the use and leverage of their assets in green investment (land, etc.) and structure to maximise the leverage of PIC finance. In addition, UIAs need to adopt and adhere to the principles of green budgeting, internationally recognised accounting standards and other means of transparent and accountable financial management.

Addressing challenges related to operational and implementation issues on the demand side of climate finance requires the following actions:

- **project development support**. Local agencies, particularly those in intermediary cities, may need support to develop projects suitable for climate finance. National support for local governments and other UIAs in establishing climate risk assessments and GHG baselines can be important, together with advice on options for project financial structuring. This support should also foster a structured process of city climate planning such as the C40 Climate Action Planning (CAP) process, which defines the investment programme that will enable the city to deliver on its fair share of NDC commitments (or Paris targets if NDCs are insufficient). In the post-COVID-19 context, these investments need further economic resilience and employment. Such support can be provided via a dedicated facility or sectoral ministries.
- **technical support**. Many UIAs may not know which technical options exist for NDC-related investments that are applicable to their particular circumstances. International sources of support for technical assessment are available, for example through the Climate Investment Funds (CIF, n.d.[52]) and multilateral development banks. Such support can be provided via a dedicated facility or sectoral ministries.

In this context, local governments should:

- **establish urban investment agencies**. These agencies need to be mandated to develop green investment programmes, aggregate projects for efficient financing, assess projects as per appraisal systems (see below) and build climate project development and structuring capacity, including through local consultants and/or local tertiary institutions, etc.
- **implement investment appraisal systems**. These systems need to be able to assess the viability of a programme of investment. They need to take into account: the scale of resources needed; the fiscal context of the UIA; the financial risk associated with the investment; the operational risk, including the availability of service; access and reliability of performance; the cost and affordability to consumers; and the complexity of proposed implementation structures relative to the UIA's technical capacity. The UIA should also be able to obtain expertise to assess the mitigation and adaptation benefits of a project, as well as its eligibility for required licences, its financial viability, other co-benefits and compliance with safeguards.

Addressing capacity gaps in access to climate finance requires multistakeholder engagement by national and local governments. Actions may include:

- **building capacity development institutions**. National governments should establish and disseminate best practices in climate technologies, green budgeting and technical and financial assessment through local government academies, professional development mechanisms and other means, ensuring that there are no barriers to the participation of intermediary city participants.
- **promoting multistakeholder involvement**. National governments should undertake dialogue with policy makers from intermediary cities and CFOS with financial institutions to build databases of city financial data and performance in NDC sector investment. They should open pathways for NDC investment by developing systems for assessing, monitoring and evaluating climate investments. This will provide data that can support investment risk assessment and project design.
- **promoting international support**. There are multiple avenues of international support for project development (CFF, Gap Fund, etc.); NDC implementation (NDC partnership, UN-Habitat, etc.); and policy development (IFIs, GEF, OECD, etc.). Special facilities are available to some LDCs and SIDS, often at a regional level (e.g. PRIF). National governments should encourage and support intermediary cities to band together and merge their potential project pipelines in order to achieve the critical mass of investment needed to justify the engagement of such agencies and facilities.

Figure 5.12 and Figure 5.13 summarise demand-side actions that can be taken at the national and subnational levels to facilitate the access of intermediary cities to climate finance.

Figure 5.12. National actions for facilitating access to climate finance

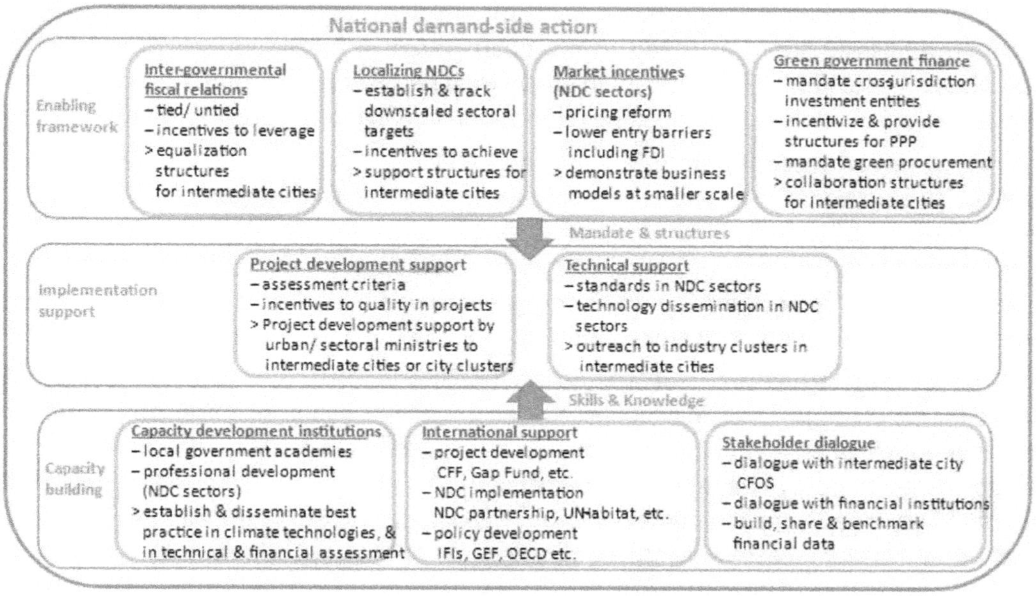

Source: Authors' own elaboration.

Figure 5.13. Subnational (city) actions for facilitating access to climate finance

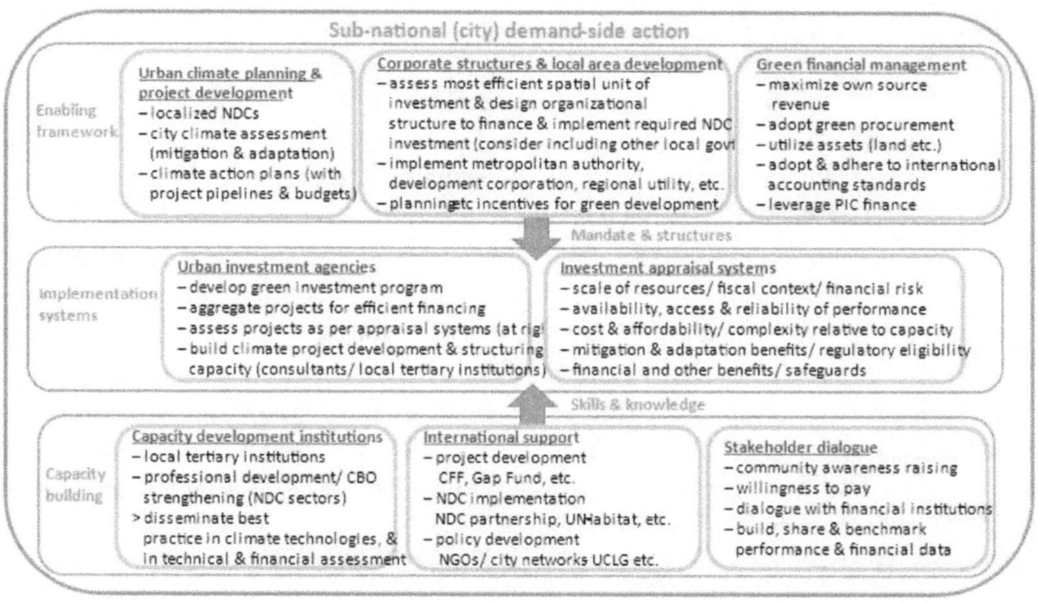

Source: Authors' own elaboration.

Priority actions for addressing supply-side constraints

On the supply side, national governments need to foster capital market institutions, which address higher risk profiles of intermediary cities and their enterprises. These are structures such as those used by TNUDF in India and Kommuninvest in Sweden. Key actions that national and local governments can take to enhance the enabling frameworks of supply-side climate financing include:

- **greening the financial system**. National governments need to put in place a regulatory and reporting framework for green instruments (green bonds, insurance, etc.) that are accessible to UIAs. They also need to create incentives to maximise the deployment of these green instruments. Climate and transition risks need to be incorporated in macro prudential regulation (to avoid stranded assets, etc.). It is important to ensure that regulations and processes do not inadvertently exclude UIAs in intermediary cities (for example with minimum revenue levels).
- **greening government finance**. Government financing needs to refocus revenue mobilisation by taxing "climate bads", such as GHG emissions, pollution and congestion, with green taxes and fees. In doing so, governments should ensure that assistance for transition is available to smaller cities, which may be more reliant than larger cities on small-scale vehicular transport. Generalised debt limits and restrictions on PPP for green investment could be revived to ensure that intermediary cities are not disadvantaged.
- **capital market regulation**. National governments can maximise potential financing for climate investments through local institutions by, for example, including NDC-sector infrastructure in permitted investments in pension funds and insurance. National governments should track NDC-sector expenditure by capital market participants. They should ensure that access to finance by intermediary cities is maintained by enabling the use of support aggregation structures, whereby a number of smaller investments can be bundled into a financing structure.

In this context local governments should:

- **identify opportunities for greening finance planning**. Subnational agencies need to be able to assess opportunities for the use of green financing instruments in the context of the investment needs of intermediary cities and their ability to undertake the funding/revenue mobilisation required for debt service and counterpart funding. Each of the instruments – green bonds, green insurance, equity, etc. – will have structural prerequisites. For example, In the case of equity, a corporate vehicle is needed. Potential green finance sources (green facilities) must be assessed in relation to the conditions they require, for example the establishment of specific MRV systems.
- **establish local climate finance instruments and incentives**. Subnational agencies will need to establish a regulatory base for new funding instruments/incentives, such as land value capture (LVC), in order to establish a funding base for UIAs. They may also need to develop a regulatory base for financing structures that support the use of aggregation instruments by financing institutions.

National governments also have a large role to play in implementing actions to address capacity gaps in the supply side of climate financing. Actions can include:

- **development of taxonomies**. Taxonomies define what is "green", and it is important that the definition be clear. The OECD has made specific recommendations on taxonomies applicable to governments (OECD, 2022[51]). To this end, it will be necessary to nominate a lead agency (Central Bank, Ministry of Finance, etc.) to co-ordinate and oversee the development and use of MRV systems. Finance ministries have a key role in facilitating the dissemination of systems to financial institutions and their clients. Special outreach systems may be required for the CFOs of intermediary cities.
- **establishing technical support for green instruments.** Finance ministries and associations of financial institutions will have a key role in fostering the dissemination of appropriate structures and the capacity to assess and structure green investments and to utilise such instruments as green infrastructure debt/equity funds and green bond systems. It is important to reiterate that support for financial institutions and their clients regarding the use of these instruments may be necessary.
- **establishing catalyst facilities**. In order to catalyse financing of NDC-linked investments, special-purpose financing facilities may be needed (such as the Shandong Green Development Fund, discussed above). This is necessary to address issues of unfamiliarity with investment types and

instruments and to leverage government finance. Such facilities can be stand alone or developed inside a public or private financial institution (typically a national development bank), and may include project development capacity, use of blended finance to leverage PIC finance and other aggregation instruments. The aim is to improve accessibility for UIAs with smaller investments (in particular, in intermediary cities).

In response, local governments should:

- **implement green financing systems.** Subnational governments (or groups of local governments) can establish local green funds and develop mechanisms such as PPPs to leverage their own resources or those of established funds. They need to prioritise lowest-cost funds for non-revenue earning projects (whether or not these funds are labelled "green" or "climate"), and to use higher-cost financing for more financially viable projects. Local funds should also consider using instruments that enable the aggregation of small projects.
- **implement green funding systems.** Subnational governments should implement new green taxes/fees, including LVC-type taxes, etc. Where structures are developed in partnership with other stakeholders or governments, taxes and fees on pollution, such as congestion charges, ensure that the mechanisms of cost sharing and co-investment are clearly established and sound.

In relation to reinforcing capacity, national and local governments should:

- **build required capacity development**. National governments can encourage capacity development institutions to establish and disseminate best practices in climate technical and financial assessment and in MRV systems focusing on investments in NDC sectors. These are institutions such as banking associations and institutions providing professional development for the staff of financial institutions.
- **facilitate international support**. International agencies can support the development of appropriate enabling environments and operational measures, including with the provision of finance. Numerous projects have been structured to include access for intermediary cities. Specifically, IFIs, the EU, GCF and GEF have supported blended finance facilities. The NDC partnership, UN-Habitat, the Green Bank Network, IFIs, GEF, development agencies such as Germany's GIZ, and the OECD have supported the development of more effective enabling environments. Development banks in some countries have support facilities such as project development assistance for intermediary cities, and sometimes for specific sectors, such as low-carbon transport.

Figure 5.14 and Figure 5.15 summarise supply-side actions that can be taken at the national and subnational levels to facilitate the access of intermediary cities to climate finance.

Figure 5.14. National actions for addressing supply-side constraints

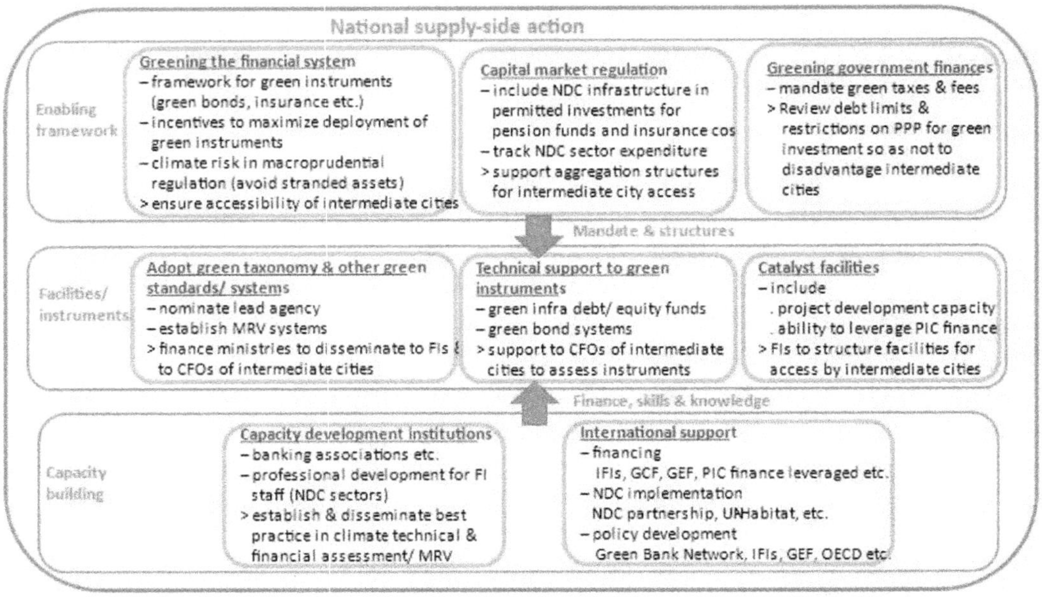

Source: Authors' own elaboration.

Figure 5.15. Subnational actions for addressing supply-side constraints

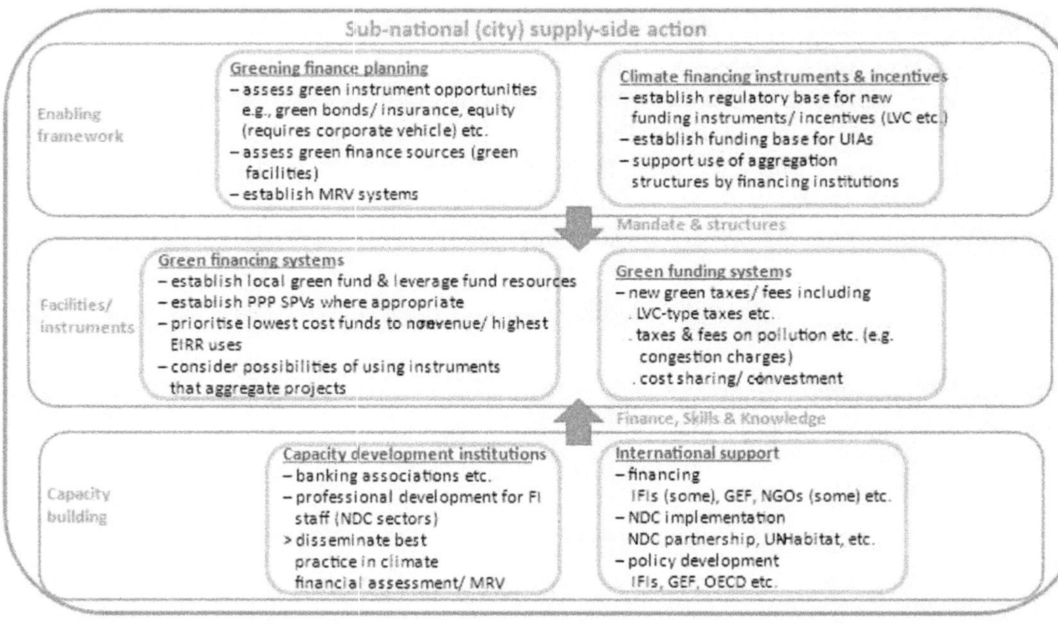

Source: Authors' own elaboration.

Conclusion

Intermediary cities in developing countries will require huge resources to meet the challenge of a warming climate. Their investment needs on the path to becoming low-carbon and resilient cities require access to climate finance, but at present they face major constraints in accessing the climate finance market. To overcome these constraints, it is important that the supply and demand sides of the climate finance market be strengthened together, as strengthening financial institutions will be of limited use if cities do not have the fiscal space or capacity to utilise the available finance.

On both sides of the market, and at national and local levels, interventions need to address structural, enabling framework and regulatory issues, operational issues and capacity-building needs. On the demand side, competent and effectively mandated implementing agencies need to be assigned clear responsibility for investments in green infrastructure, enterprise capital for renewable energy and energy efficiency, cluster support systems and human capital development. On the supply side, actions need to be taken by national and subnational governments with the aim of strengthening the enabling framework for climate financing. Measures by the international community are also needed to support these actions.

To be able to implement the scale of investment required to meet the Paris targets, all financial flows must henceforth be viewed as potentially climate finance. It is important to strengthen networks of local governments to enable them to lobby higher levels of government to ensure that the support provided for climate finance is accessible to intermediary cities. The accumulation and dissemination of best practices can be fostered through entities such as the Cities Climate Finance Leadership Alliance, while international support is needed to further comparative research and assessment of best practices globally in relation to the structures for urban climate finance for intermediary cities.

It is important to strengthen the networks of local governments to enable them to advise and lobby higher levels of government to establish relevant enabling frameworks in place and ensuring support provided is accessible to intermediary cities. National and local government associations will have a key role in this effort and international organisations should mobilise international urban networks such as UCLG and GCoM to strengthen these associations.

The accumulation and dissemination of best practice can be fostered through entities such as the Cities Climate Finance Leadership Alliance (CCFLA) and its partners. CCFLA could be resourced to further develop activities focused on the needs of intermediary cities under its action groups. In addition, international support to further globally comparative research and assessment of best practice needs to be undertaken in relation to the structures for urban climate finance for intermediary cities.

Notes

[1] In this data set, OECD defines "big" as cities with more than 1 million inhabitants. Thus some cities that are regarded in larger economies such as China and India as intermediary cities are excluded from the "intermediate" categorisation.

[2] In this document we use the words "green" and "climate" interchangeably, but it is important to note that green investments may include investments that are not climate relevant – for example, an investment that reduces a specific non-GHG pollutant may be "green" but is not a climate investment. Although most climate investments are green, in some circumstances it is possible that a climate investment could harm biodiversity and thus not be "green" in that sense. "Sustainable," an even broader concept that encompasses not only environmental but also economic and social sustainability, is also discussed when appropriate.

[3] Project implementation structures in which governments have a key role in structuring the project so that the private sector can participate – usually by providing finance, technology and management expertise – in a way that adds value to the project.

[4] Transport networks where efficient transfers of freight and people among different types of transport are facilitated by purpose-built facilities and IT solutions.

[5] Good governance, as it relates to climate finance, is the capacity and willingness to mobilise revenue efficiently and deploy that revenue in a consistent, transparent and accountable way to maximise the climate outcomes of investments.

[6] Smolka O, (2013) Implementing Value Capture in Latin America: Policies and Tools for Urban Development Martim. Lincoln Land Institute. Washington DC. https://www.lincolninst.edu/publications/policy-focus-reports/implementing-value-capture-latin-america (accessed 7 December 2021).

[7] For example, the Glasgow Finance Alliance for Net Zero.

[8] OECD (2020), The Role of Sovereign and Strategic Investment Funds in the Low-carbon Transition, Paris. https://www.oecd-ilibrary.org/sites/ddfd6a9f-en/index.html?itemId=/content/publication/ddfd6a9f-en (accessed 7 December 2021).

References

ADB (2021), *Catalyzing Climate Finance: Lessons Learned from the Shandong Green Development Fund*, Asian Development Bank, Manila, Philippines, https://doi.org/10.22617/WPS210113-2. [40]

Albuquerque, F. (2020), "Kommuninvest Issues SEK5 billion Green Bond", *NORDIC Sustainable Investment*, https://nordsip.com/2020/05/20/kommuninvest-issues-sek5-billion-green-bond/ (accessed on 19 October 2021). [46]

BPS (2020), *Gross Regional Domestic Product of Provinces in Indonesia by Industry*, Statistics Indonesia, Jakarta, https://bappeda.jatengprov.go.id/wp-content/uploads/2020/07/Produk-Domestik-Regional-Bruto-Provinsi-Provinsi-di-Indonesia-Menurut-Lapangan-Usaha-2015-2019.pdf (accessed on 18 October 2021). [9]

C40 (2021), *Developing projects to address climate change in cities*, C40 Cities Finance Facility, https://www.c40cff.org/ (accessed on 19 October 2021). [27]

C40 (2016), *C40 Cities Good Practice Guide – City Climate Funds: Sustainable Infrastructure Finance Network*, C40 Cities, New York, https://c40-production-images.s3.amazonaws.com/other_uploads/images/887_C40_Good_Practice_Guide_-_City_Climate_Funds.original.pdf (accessed on 19 October 2021). [49]

Carter, L. (2020), *Mobilizing Insurance Investment in Sustainable Infrastructure: the role of the United Nations*, United Nations Development Programme, New York, https://sdgfinance.undp.org/sites/default/files/UNDP-GPN-climate-Mobilizing_Insurance_Investment_in_Sustainable_Intrastructure%20%281%29_0.pdf (accessed on 19 October 2021). [24]

CBI (2021), *Climate Bonds Taxonomy*, Climate Bonds Initiative, https://www.climatebonds.net/standard/taxonomy (accessed on 18 October 2021). [4]

CCFGF (2020), *Turn resilient low-carbon ideas into strategies and finance ready*, City Climate Finance Gap Fund, https://www.citygapfund.org/ (accessed on 19 October 2021). [28]

CCFLA (2015), *The State of City Climate Finance 2015*, Cities Climate Finance Leadership Alliance, New York, https://sustainabledevelopment.un.org/content/documents/2201CCFLA-State-of-City-Climate-Finance-2015.pdf (accessed on 18 October 2021). [15]

CDIA (n.d.), *Cities Development Initiative for Asia*, https://cdia.asia/ (accessed on 19 October 2021). [26]

CIF (n.d.), *Clean Technologies: Transitioning to low carbon technologies is key to fighting climate change and unlocking economic opportunities*, Climate Investment Fund, https://www.climateinvestmentfunds.org/topics/clean-technologies (accessed on 19 October 2021). [52]

Cities Alliance (2020), *Secondary cities Post-COVID 19: Achieving Urban Sustainable and Regenerative Development in Emerging Economies*, Cities Alliance, Brussels, https://www.citiesalliance.org/sites/default/files/2021-03/CA_SecondaryCitiesPostCOVID-19-FinalWeb.pdf (accessed on 31 July 2021). [12]

Cities Alliance (2019), *Connecting Systems of Cities*, Cities Alliance/UNOPS, Brussels. [13]

City of Philadelphia (2020), *City and ENGIE Announce Power Purchase Agreement Staffing Plans*, Office of Sustainable, https://www.phila.gov/2020-02-06-city-and-engie-announce-power-purchase-agreement-staffing-plans/ (accessed on 19 October 2021). [47]

Colenbrander, S. et al. (2018), *Financing Low-Carbon, Climate-Resilient Cities*, Coalition for Urban Transition, London and Washington, https://www.researchgate.net/publication/323560614_Financing_Low-Carbon_Climate-Resilient_Cities (accessed on 18 October 2021). [18]

EBRD (n.d.), *Commercialising public infrastructure*, European Bank for Reconstruction and Development, https://www.ebrd.com/infrastructure/commercialising-public-infrastructure.html (accessed on 19 October 2021). [41]

Ellis, J. (2010), *Energy Service Companies (ESCOs) in Developing Countries*, International Institute for Sustainable Development, Winnipeg, https://www.iisd.org/system/files/publications/bali_2_copenhagen_escos.pdf (accessed on 19 October 2021). [48]

Estache, A. (2010), "Infrastructure Finance in Developing Countries: an overview", *EIB Papers*, Vol. 15/2, pp. 60-88, https://www.econstor.eu/bitstream/10419/45371/1/657033472.pdf (accessed on 19 October 2021). [25]

EU (2020), "Regulation (EU) 2020/852 of the European Parliament and of the Council: on the establishment of a framework to facilitate sustainable investment, and amending Regulation (EU) 2019/2088", *Official Journal of the European Union*, https://eur-lex.europa.eu/legal-content/EN/TXT/?uri=CELEX:32020R0852 (accessed on 18 October 2021). [6]

Farvacque-Vitkovic, C. and M. Kopanyi (2014), *Municipal Finances: A Handbook for Local Governments*, World Bank, Washington DC, https://openknowledge.worldbank.org/handle/10986/18725 (accessed on 18 October 2021). [19]

Florczyk, A. (2019), *GHS Urban Centre Database 2015, multitemporal and multidimensional attributes*, http://data.europa.eu/89h/53473144-b88c-44bc-b4a3-4583ed1f547e (accessed on 13 July 2021). [2]

FMDV (2021), *Aggregation Interventions to Increase Urban Climate Finance: A knowledge product for the Cities Climate Finance Leadership Alliance*, The Global Fund for Cities Development (FMDV), Paris. [43]

GCF (n.d.), *Projects & Programmes*, Green Climate Fund, https://www.greenclimate.fund/project/fp086 (accessed on 19 October 2021). [30]

GHG Protocol (2011), *Corporate Value Chain (Scope 3) Accounting and Reporting Standard*, Green House Protocol, Washington DC, https://ghgprotocol.org/standards/scope-3-standard (accessed on 18 October 2021). [11]

Green Climate Fund (2020), *Project Review*, https://www.greenclimate.fund/projects/criteria (accessed on 18 October 2021). [14]

Kaminker, C. (2013), "Institutional Investors and Green Infrastructure Investments: Selected Case Studies", *OECD Working Papers on Finance, Insurance and Private Pensions*, No. 35, OECD Publishing, Paris. [38]

Kommuninvest (n.d.), *Green Bonds*, https://kommuninvest.se/wp-content/uploads/2018/02/Green-Bonds.pdf (accessed on 19 October 2021). [45]

Kommuninvest (n.d.), *Kommuninvest*, https://kommuninvest.se/en/ (accessed on 19 October 2021). [44]

LWUA (n.d.), *What is a Water District*, Local Water Utilities Administration, Republic of the Philippines, https://lwua.gov.ph/water-districts/what-is-a-water-district/ (accessed on 19 October 2021). [42]

Martinez-Vazquez, J. (2021), *Adapting Fiscal Decentralization Design to Combat Climate Change*, World Bank, Washington DC, https://openknowledge.worldbank.org/handle/10986/35899 (accessed on 19 October 2021). [50]

Negreiros, P. et al. (2021), *The State of Cities Climate Finance - Part 1: The Landscape of Urban Climate Finance*, Climate Policy Initiative (CPI), London, https://www.climatepolicyinitiative.org/wp-content/uploads/2021/06/SCCF_PART1-FINAL-1.pdf (accessed on 18 October 2021). [1]

OECD (2022), *Aligning Regional and Local Budgets with Green Objectives: Subnational Green Budgeting Practices and Guidelines*, OECD Multi-level Governance Studies, OECD Publishing, Paris, https://doi.org/10.1787/93b4036f-en. [51]

OECD (2022), "Subnational government climate expenditure and revenue tracking in OECD and EU Countries", *OECD Regional Development Papers*, No. 32, OECD Publishing, Paris, https://doi.org/10.1787/1e8016d4-en. [16]

OECD (2021), *OECD Regional Outlook 2021: Addressing COVID-19 and Moving to Net Zero Greenhouse Gas Emissions*, OECD Publishing, Paris, https://doi.org/10.1787/17017efe-en. [17]

OECD (2020), *Pension Funds in Figures*, OECD Publishing, Paris, https://www.oecd.org/pensions/Pension-Funds-in-Figures-2020.pdf (accessed on 18 October 2021). [23]

OECD (2020), *Revenue Statistics in Asian and Pacific Economies 2020*, OECD, https://doi.org/10.1787/d47d0ae3-en. [36]

OECD (2020), *The Role of Sovereign and Strategic Investment Funds in the Low-carbon Transition*, OECD Development Policy Tools, OECD Publishing, Paris, https://doi.org/10.1787/ddfd6a9f-en. [39]

OECD (2019), "Financing climate objectives in cities and regions to deliver sustainable and inclusive growth", *OECD Environment Policy Papers*, No. 17, OECD Publishing, Paris, https://doi.org/10.1787/ee3ce00b-en. [3]

OECD (2017), *Technical note on estimates of infrastructure investment needs: Background note to the report Investing in Climate, Investing in Growth*, OECD Publishing, Paris, https://www.oecd.org/env/cc/g20-climate/Technical-note-estimates-of-infrastructure-investment-needs.pdf (accessed on 18 October 2021). [7]

OECD (2014), *Pooling of Institutional Investors Capital - Selected Case Studies in Unlisted Equity Infrastructure*, OECD Publishing, Paris, https://www.oecd.org/investment/OECD-Pooling-Institutional-Investors-Capital-Unlisted-Equity-Infrastructure.pdf (accessed on 18 October 2021). [22]

PBOC (2020), *Green Finance*, PBOC Taxonomy, https://www.hkgreenfinance.org/wp-content/uploads/2020/06/Attachment-1-Draft-for-Public-Consultation-of-Green-Bond-Endorsed-Project-Catalogue-2020-.pdf (accessed on 18 October 2021). [5]

PPIAF (n.d.), *COVID-19 and Public-Private Partnerships Practice Note*, The Public-Private Infrastructure Advisory Facility (PPIAF), World Bank, https://ppiaf.org/ (accessed on 19 October 2021). [29]

PRIF (n.d.), *Pacific Region Infrastructure Facility*. [37]

Pune Smart City (n.d.), *Pune Smart City Development Corporation LTD.*, https://punesmartcity.in/ (accessed on 19 October 2021). [35]

Republic of the Philippines (n.d.), *Public - Private Partnership Center*, https://ppp.gov.ph/view-from-the-center-4/ (accessed on 19 October 2021). [31]

Roy et al. (2020), *Property Tax Diagnostic Manual*, World Bank, Washington DC, http://hdl.handle.net/10986/34793 (accessed on 19 October 2021). [32]

Smolka, M. (2013), *Implementing Value Capture in Latin America*, Lincoln Institute of Land Policy, Cambridge. [21]

UCLG (2008), *UCLG Policy Paper on Local Finance*, United Cities and Local Governments, Barcelona, https://www.uclg.org/sites/default/files/_28fr29_uclgpolicypaperonlocalfinanceeng2.pdf (accessed on 18 October 2021). [10]

UNESCAP (2019), *The Future of Asian & Pacific Cities: Transformative pathways towards sustainable urban development*, United Nations Economic and Social Commission for Asia and the Pacific, Bangkok, https://www.unescap.org/sites/default/d8files/knowledge-products/Future%20of%20AP%20Cities%20Report%202019.pdf (accessed on 18 October 2021). [20]

UN-Habitat (2015), *The Challenge of Local Government Financing in Developing Countries*, United Nations Human Settlement Programme, Barcelona, https://unhabitat.org/sites/default/files/download-manager-files/The%20Challenge%20of%20Local%20Government%20Financing%20in%20Developing%20Countries%20_3.pdf (accessed on 19 October 2021). [33]

World Bank (2019), *Lifelines: The Resilient Infrastructure Opportunity*, World Bank, Washington DC, https://openknowledge.worldbank.org/handle/10986/31805 (accessed on 18 October 2021). [8]

World Bank (n.d.), *City Creditworthiness Initiative: A Partnership to Deliver Municipal Finance*, World Bank, https://www.worldbank.org/en/topic/urbandevelopment/brief/city-creditworthiness-initiative (accessed on 19 October 2021). [34]

www.ingramcontent.com/pod-product-compliance
Lightning Source LLC
Chambersburg PA
CBHW061206240926
51846CB00006B/1127